The lives of William Smyth Bishop of Lincoln and Sir Richard Sutton Knight, founders of Brasen Nose College; chiefly compiled from registers and other authentic evidences: with an appendix of letters and papers never before printed

Ralph Churton

Gale ECCO Print Editions

Relive history with *Eighteenth Century Collections Online*, now available in print for the independent historian and collector. This series includes the most significant English-language and foreign-language works printed in Great Britain during the eighteenth century, and is organized in seven different subject areas including literature and language; medicine, science, and technology; and religion and philosophy. The collection also includes thousands of important works from the Americas.

The eighteenth century has been called "The Age of Enlightenment." It was a period of rapid advance in print culture and publishing, in world exploration, and in the rapid growth of science and technology – all of which had a profound impact on the political and cultural landscape. At the end of the century the American Revolution, French Revolution and Industrial Revolution, perhaps three of the most significant events in modern history, set in motion developments that eventually dominated world political, economic, and social life.

In a groundbreaking effort, Gale initiated a revolution of its own: digitization of epic proportions to preserve these invaluable works in the largest online archive of its kind. Contributions from major world libraries constitute over 175,000 original printed works. Scanned images of the actual pages, rather than transcriptions, recreate the works *as they first appeared.*

Now for the first time, these high-quality digital scans of original works are available via print-on-demand, making them readily accessible to libraries, students, independent scholars, and readers of all ages.

For our initial release we have created seven robust collections to form one the world's most comprehensive catalogs of 18th century works.

Initial Gale ECCO Print Editions collections include:

History and Geography

Rich in titles on English life and social history, this collection spans the world as it was known to eighteenth-century historians and explorers. Titles include a wealth of travel accounts and diaries, histories of nations from throughout the world, and maps and charts of a world that was still being discovered. Students of the War of American Independence will find fascinating accounts from the British side of conflict.

Social Science

Delve into what it was like to live during the eighteenth century by reading the first-hand accounts of everyday people, including city dwellers and farmers, businessmen and bankers, artisans and merchants, artists and their patrons, politicians and their constituents. Original texts make the American, French, and Industrial revolutions vividly contemporary.

Medicine, Science and Technology

Medical theory and practice of the 1700s developed rapidly, as is evidenced by the extensive collection, which includes descriptions of diseases, their conditions, and treatments. Books on science and technology, agriculture, military technology, natural philosophy, even cookbooks, are all contained here.

Literature and Language

Western literary study flows out of eighteenth-century works by Alexander Pope, Daniel Defoe, Henry Fielding, Frances Burney, Denis Diderot, Johann Gottfried Herder, Johann Wolfgang von Goethe, and others. Experience the birth of the modern novel, or compare the development of language using dictionaries and grammar discourses.

Religion and Philosophy

The Age of Enlightenment profoundly enriched religious and philosophical understanding and continues to influence present-day thinking. Works collected here include masterpieces by David Hume, Immanuel Kant, and Jean-Jacques Rousseau, as well as religious sermons and moral debates on the issues of the day, such as the slave trade. The Age of Reason saw conflict between Protestantism and Catholicism transformed into one between faith and logic -- a debate that continues in the twenty-first century.

Law and Reference

This collection reveals the history of English common law and Empire law in a vastly changing world of British expansion. Dominating the legal field is the *Commentaries of the Law of England* by Sir William Blackstone, which first appeared in 1765. Reference works such as almanacs and catalogues continue to educate us by revealing the day-to-day workings of society.

Fine Arts

The eighteenth-century fascination with Greek and Roman antiquity followed the systematic excavation of the ruins at Pompeii and Herculaneum in southern Italy; and after 1750 a neoclassical style dominated all artistic fields. The titles here trace developments in mostly English-language works on painting, sculpture, architecture, music, theater, and other disciplines. Instructional works on musical instruments, catalogs of art objects, comic operas, and more are also included.

The BiblioLife Network

This project was made possible in part by the BiblioLife Network (BLN), a project aimed at addressing some of the huge challenges facing book preservationists around the world. The BLN includes libraries, library networks, archives, subject matter experts, online communities and library service providers. We believe every book ever published should be available as a high-quality print reproduction; printed on-demand anywhere in the world. This insures the ongoing accessibility of the content and helps generate sustainable revenue for the libraries and organizations that work to preserve these important materials.

The following book is in the "public domain" and represents an authentic reproduction of the text as printed by the original publisher. While we have attempted to accurately maintain the integrity of the original work, there are sometimes problems with the original work or the micro-film from which the books were digitized. This can result in minor errors in reproduction. Possible imperfections include missing and blurred pages, poor pictures, markings and other reproduction issues beyond our control. Because this work is culturally important, we have made it available as part of our commitment to protecting, preserving, and promoting the world's literature.

GUIDE TO FOLD-OUTS MAPS and OVERSIZED IMAGES

The book you are reading was digitized from microfilm captured over the past thirty to forty years. Years after the creation of the original microfilm, the book was converted to digital files and made available in an online database.

In an online database, page images do not need to conform to the size restrictions found in a printed book. When converting these images back into a printed bound book, the page sizes are standardized in ways that maintain the detail of the original. For large images, such as fold-out maps, the original page image is split into two or more pages

Guidelines used to determine how to split the page image follows:

• Some images are split vertically; large images require vertical and horizontal splits.
• For horizontal splits, the content is split left to right.
• For vertical splits, the content is split from top to bottom.
• For both vertical and horizontal splits, the image is processed from top left to bottom right.

THE
LIVES

OF

WILLIAM SMYTH BISHOP OF LINCOLN

AND

SIR RICHARD SUTTON KNIGHT,

FOUNDERS OF

BRASEN NOSE COLLEGE,

CHIEFLY COMPILED

FROM REGISTERS AND OTHER AUTHENTIC EVIDENCES

WITH

AN APPENDIX

OF

LETTERS AND PAPERS NEVER BEFORE PRINTED.

BY RALPH CHURTON, M. A.

RECTOR OF MIDDLETON CHENEY, NORTHAMPTONSHIRE,
AND LATE FELLOW OF BRASEN NOSE COLLEGE

CERTAINLY THE GREAT MULTIPLICATION OF VIRTUES UPON HU-
MAN NATURE RESTETH UPON SOCIETIES WELL ORDAINED AND
DISCIPLINED   LORD BACON.

OXFORD,

AT THE UNIVERSITY PRESS, FOR THE AUTHOR.

SOLD BY HANWELL AND PARKER, AND BY MESSRS. RIVINGTON
AND WHITE, LONDON.
MDCCC.

IMPRIMATUR,

MICH. MARLOW
Vice-Can Oxon.

Coll Di Jo Bapt
Jan 17mo 1800

TO

THE RIGHT REVEREND

WILLIAM

LORD BISHOP OF BANGOR

PRINCIPAL

AND

TO THE REVEREND THE FELLOWS

OF BRASEN NOSE COLLEGE

THIS ATTEMPT

TO ILLUSTRATE THE LIVES

OF THE VENERABLE FOUNDERS

OF THAT SOCIETY

IS

WITH SINCERE RESPECT AND GRATITUDE

INSCRIBED

PREFACE.

INQUIRIES where fuccefs is hopelefs are feldom profecuted with vigour. A notion has long and very generally prevailed, that no authentic and circumftantial account of Bifhop Smyth and Sir Richard Sutton, the munificent Founders of Brafen Nofe college, could be obtained. No monuments were raifed to their memories by their own contemporaries or their immediate fucceffors, while the tradition of events was recent, and means of information were within reach; nor was a fingle effort made to fupply the defect, till Anthony Wood and others, at the diftance of little lefs than two centuries from the time of thefe worthies, affigned them a juft place in their comprehenfive hif-

tories,

tories, and enumerated their principal preferments, benefactions, and honours. These inadequate accounts, at a later period, the curiosity of those most indebted to the liberality of Smyth and of Sutton collected and cherished with a fondness of affection, which the despair of procuring fuller information tended rather to increase than to diminish.

Thomas Smyth, a Cheshire man, fellow of Brasen Nose college at the close of the last century, and preferred by the society to the rectory of Great Billing in Northamptonshire in the year 1705, furnishes the first splendid instance of a person who endeavoured to attain a more intimate acquaintance with his illustrious namesake, who was perhaps his kinsman, than printed books were able to supply. His collections, transcribed from the college Archives, were put into my hands about twenty years ago by the Rev. John Holmes, fellow of Brasen Nose college, afterwards Rector of St Mary's, Whitechapel, and D. D. one among many whom I regret that the tardy appearance of these pages, necessarily protracted by multifarious

re-

researches concerning the times and persons reviewed, and unavoidably impeded by various calls of duty in other ways, does not enable me to gratify with what they so eagerly wished for, the sight of this sketch, however imperfect, of the lives of Bishop Smyth and Sir Richard Sutton. But if a few years sweep away the brightest ornaments of society, and rob us of our principal comfort in the death of valuable and well informed Friends, others are raised up in their stead, as well to console the survivers, as to maintain the course of the world and the designs of Providence.

Mr. Smyth's papers, if they contributed little assistance, except towards the detection of a single mistake, the report of Smyth's retreat from Oxford on account of the plague, were at the time however an encouragement to me to proceed with the subject, and the fourteen pages of extracts and references, of which they consisted, have long been multiplied into more than a thousand.

One of the first steps, which I took in

pur-

purfuit of materials, was to inquire after
Smyth's epifcopal Regifter at Lichfield; and
I had luckily infpected it before I was informed by the late Mr. Warton, that no
fuch record exifted. The miftake probably
was owing to Sir William Dugdale; who
exprefsly fays, " De tempore Joh. Hales et
Will. Smith epifcoporum—nullum extat re-
giftrum[a]." It is prefumed therefore, that in
thofe times of public diftraction, which it
was the misfortune of that juftly celebrated
antiquary to fee, as it was his happinefs to
furvive, Smyth's regifter muft have been
miffing from among the epifcopal archives;
though no memorandum to that effect appears in the Regifter, nor is there any tradition of it in the office. The volume itfelf,
with others, the firft of them commencing
in the year 1296, when Langton, a great
benefactor to the fee, was bifhop of Lichfield, remains there in perfect prefervation;
and I am much obliged to the friendly zeal
of Mr. William Mott, Deputy Regiftrar of
the diocefe, for accommodating and affifting

- Afhm Muf. MS Dugdale, E 1 p 433.

me

me at various times, when I made copious
extracts from this and the other records in
his cuftody.

The epifcopal regifters at Lincoln extend
to a date earlier, it is faid, by fome years
than any fimilar records in the kingdom,
thofe of the metropolitan church of Canterbury alone excepted. They commence in
the year 1209, in the epifcopate of Hugh
Wallis, piedeceffor to the famous bifhop
Grofthead They aie kept and continued
with exact fidelity and judgement by Mr.
John Fardell, Deputy Regiftrar of the diocefe, to whofe kindnefs I am particularly
indebted not only for free accefs to the original records, but likewife for many extracts,
and much ufeful information on points of
antiquity, communicated by letter.

Of thefe Regifters of the fee of Lincoln
there are fhort but accurate abftracts in fome
volumes of the Harleian library in the Britifh Mufeum. With the ufe of thefe volumes and others contained in that invaluable national repofitory I was liberally in-
dulged,

dulged, and commonly at fuch times (my only leifure) when the doors were not open to readers in general, through the prompt benevolence of the Rev Dr. Woide, Affiftant Librarian, the learned Editor of the Alexandrian manufcript of the Greek Teftament; and, fince the deceafe of that truly excellent man, I have experienced fimilar politenefs and owe equal thanks to the Rev. Mr Ayfcough, at prefent one of the Affiftant Librarians.

The ftore's of Oxford were nearer at hand, which, though daily ufed, are inexhauftible. Among the Archives of that Univerfity the regifter which is marked with the letter F is particularly curious   It contains a feries of letters to and from the Univerfity, many of them by our monarchs in fucceffion, and others by the principal men of the times, during the fpace of almoft a century, from the year 1422 till 1503. This ineftimable volume having formerly, as a memorandum in it fhews, been ftolen or miffing, was found at Winchefter by Dr. Abbot, afterwards archbifhop of Canterbury, and by

him

him reftored to the univerfity when he was Vice-Chancellor, in the year 1605. Large ufe has been made of this Regifter, and of others lodged with it in the Tower of the Schools, by the kind permiffion of the late and prefent Keepers of the univerfity Archives, the honourable Dr. Wenman, Fellow of All Souls' college, now deceafed, and the Rev. Dr. Landon, Provoft of Worcefter college. From the Rev. Mr. Price, Bodleian Librarian, I have conftantly received fuch advice and affiftance, as might be expected from the ready and able friend of every literary undertaking.

One defect in my materials I greatly lament. The records of the Prefidency of Wales were kept at Ludlow Caftle, in a building called Mortimer's Tower, which was repaired and fitted up for the purpofe by Sir Henry Sidney, lord Prefident, the illuftrious father of an illuftrious fon, the gallant and incomparable Sir Philip Sidney. Thefe records, when the court of the marches was diffolved by King William, were removed from Ludlow ; but to what place they were

con-

conveyed, and where they now remain, are queftions upon which I have beftowed much fruitlefs inquiry wherever any profpect of information appeared. Whenever propitious chance or fuccefsful inveftigation fhall bring to light thefe ancient documents, I am perfuaded there will be found in them, among official details and the uninterefting minutiæ of bufinefs, much that will elucidate the local peculiarities and general manners of the times, and much that will fet forth with advantage the qualities, for which Smyth is celebrated, his wifdom and addrefs, the fortitude of his mind and integrity of his adminiftration.

In the mean time it was hoped, that the want of thefe authentic memorials would be in great meafure compenfated by intelligence on the fame fubject in another quarter. The ever memorable Sir Matthew Hale bequeathed to the honourable Society of Lincoln's Inn, where he had the greateft part of his education, a collection of manufcripts, of which he thus fpeaks in his will. "They are a treafure worth having and keeping, which

I have

I have been near forty years in gathering, with very great induftry and expence. My defire is, that they be kept fafe, and all together, in remembrance of me; they were fit to be bound in leather and chained, and kept in Archives[b]." Among thefe manufcripts is a " Hiftory of the Marches of Wales collected by me, 1 vol." The hiftory of an obfcure and interefting part of our national antiquities, written by a man of confummate talents and profound learning; one of the books, of which the author himfelf, whofe virtues were tranfcendent and his modefty unparalleled, could fpeak as of a treafure fit to be preferved in Archives; fuch a book, on fuch a fubject, by fuch a man were worth traveling further than to the Indies to fee! The reader will conceive better than I can exprefs the mortification which I felt, when, upon fearching the library at Lincoln's Inn, I found that this Hiftory of the Marches, in which I anticipated fo much valuable information, this fingle volume of thofe bequeathed by the lord chief Juftice Hale, was

[b] Burnet's L of Sir M. Hale, 1682, p 195 202

not

not there, and, whatever caufe or accident might have deftroyed or intercepted it, appeared never to have reached its original deftination. Under thefe fatal difappointments of brilliant hopes the fhort account of the obfolete but once fplendid government of the marches of Wales, compiled from fuch fcattered notices as could elfewhere be procured, if it contains little that is new, will yet, I truft, ferve to point out and remove fome ancient errors.

Of the reign of Henry vii, the boundary as it may be called between light and darknefs, when the ignorance and fuperftition of rude and ferocious ages were not yet difperfed by the revival of learning and reformation of religion, the accounts which we have are faid to be lefs complete and fatisfactory than of any other period in our annals, and the defect is thought to be owing in great meafure to this, that few have fearched into thofe times with that perfeverance of inveftigation and attention to circumftances of a fubordinate nature, which perfonal hiftory requires. That the following narrative, which is limited

mited in point of time to the reign of Henry
vii and the firft years of his immediate fucceffor, will furnifh any thing of novelty likely
to intereft the general reader, I do not prefume to flatter myfelf, but in the obfcurity
of the period, and in the paucity of exifting
documents, I hope to find an apology, at
leaft for the unimportance of many anec-
dotes, if not for the general circumftantiality
of the whole. But this circumftantiality of
detail and minutenefs of anecdote, though in
a great degree infeparable from biography,
will not, I fear, meet with entire juftifi-
cation, except from thofe who can make allowance for the feelings and partialities of a
perfon, tracing the lives and actions of men
to whofe bounty he is hourly indebted;
whofe hiftory has been neglected, and of
whom little is known beyond the public
fame of their virtues and munificence. By
one who is placed in fuch a fituation every
trivial incident, relative to his great benefactors and patrons, gained perhaps by poring
over a whole volume in a difficult or eva-
nefcent hand, is feized with a portion of the
tranfport of the ancient fage, when he had

hit

hit upon the folution of a difficult problem.
It is a difcovery, a new trait, however flight,
in the character which early habits and conftant obligation have taught him to revere,
and for which every frefh acceffion of knowledge, while it more diftinctly exhibits the
worth of the object, increafes at the fame
time his efteem and affection.

But there is another point, which may demand explanation. Comprifing, in the following pages, a certain portion of the hiftory
of the univerfity of Oxford, I have fometimes
ventured to correct the honeft and laborious
Anthony Wood, and now and then others of
nearer date and higher talents, who have
treated of the fame times. The true account of this matter will, I hope, remove
from the prefent writer the charge of te-
merity, and at the fame time fecure the credit of thofe whofe miftakes are here occafionally rectified   My method was this.   I
made collections from the original regifters,
and other authentic documents firft of all,
and then proceeded to confult Wood's books
and Wood's manufcripts. Whenever we agree
there-

therefore, as in general we do, it is an evidence of his fidelity and accuracy, for such occurrences as are related in thefe memoirs after him, were feldom gathered from his volumes, though perhaps, for the convenience of the reader, reference is made to them only; but the exifting documents furnifhed both of us with the fame facts, and fuggefted to each the fame view of them. The great critic, with equal truth and candour, fays of the father of poetry, that by a fingle inftance of the fublime he more than atones for all his faults. The painful antiquary afpires not at fublimity. His praife is of another and humbler fort:

" Ornari res ipfa negat, contenta doceri."

Diligence of refearch and truth of reprefentation are his higheft boaft; and his ample information and general merits abundantly compenfate for a few errors. For myfelf, adopting the falutary advice of the poet,

——— " Laudato ingentia rura,
Exiguum colito,"

leaving to Wood, to Willis, and to Warton the praife and the profit of extenfive domains

b   mains

mains and luxuriant harvefts, I hope the favourite fpot, which it has been my endeavour
to cultivate, if it produces little fruit, will be
found to contain not many weeds.

The typographical part certainly, I have
pleafure in thinking, is very correctly executed by the fkill and attention of Mr.
Samuel Collingwood, Procurator of the Clarendon Prefs   In regard to faults of a more
ferious nature, for which the writer alone is
refponfible, I am far from having the prefumption to imagine, that my book is exempt from them.   Many miftakes I have
myfelf detected while the fheets were in the
prefs, and others, without queftion, will meet
the obfervation, and I truft obtain the pardon, of the candid Reader, who, knowing
the difficulty of the fubject, will make allowance for cafual overfights and inevitable
imperfections.   Perfpicuity and brevity have
been my ftudy, nor have I knowingly admitted a fingle digreffion, but fuch as feemed
connected with the matter in hand, or naturally refulted from it.   We have indeed
fometimes halted on our journey, and fometimes

times deviated a little from the track; but it was not αυρας θηρευων μαλακας, it was not becaufe we love to loiter; but to mark cuftoms and manners no longer familiar, to acquaint ourfelves with thofe whom we met by the way, to view the palace or the caftle adjoining the road, which common curiofity could not pafs by without admiring its beauty, or furveying its magnificence.

What is intitled a Poftfcript to the Life of bifhop Smyth, and confined, with one exception, to his kinfmen, it was once my intention to enlarge, in the form of an appendix, with an account of the friends of both the Founders, which would have led me to continue the hiftory of the college, till it was augmented, during the glorious reign of queen Elizabeth, with the twentieth and laft fellowfhip by Mrs. Joyce Frankland My perfonal feelings were gratified with the profpect of this part of the fubject, as it was my happinefs to enjoy the fellowfhip eftablifhed in Brafen Nofe college by that liberal benefactrefs to both Univerfities: and, at the fame time, the continuation of the hiftory of

the

the fociety to the period, when it attained
its full growth and complement, feemed not
unconnected with the account of its original
foundation. But my collections for thefe
fubfequent years were very fcanty and in-
complete; nor did my refidence in the country allow me to enlarge them; and the
fketch of the Founders alone was grown into
a juft volume: for thefe reafons I abandoned,
not without regret, a part of the fcheme
which pleafed the imagination, and flattered
my firft hopes. Whenever any one fhall
oblige the world with a life of Alexander
Nowell, Dean of St. Paul's, a tribute, which
his admirable learning and eminent talents,
his perfonal virtues and particular merits
with refpect to the Church of England, in
the final fettlement of which he bore fo large
a fhare, juftly demand, the hiftory of Brafen
Nofe college, of which he was fucceffively
Fellow and Principal, as he was afterwards a
diftinguifhed benefactor to the fociety, will
form, if not a neceffary part of the narrative,
at leaft a proper and graceful digreffion. I
have in my poffeffion fome of the firft ele-
ments of fuch a work, confifting of copies of

original

original letters by the Dean, a tranfcript of his life by Donald Lupton, references to large abftracts of one or two fermons, and other things; all which are freely offered to any perfon of leifure and abilities, who may be difpofed to do juftice to this neglected part of Englifh biography. It may be under-taken with evident propriety and advantage by a member of that Society, to which the Dean belonged; of which what was faid while He, its greateft ornament, was living, will, I truft, in no future age, ceafe to be true :

"Prole fua femper nobilitata domus^c."

In the mean time what is here offered to the public will not, it is hoped, with all its imperfections, be altogether ufelefs. It is a neceffary link in the chain of the Founders of our colleges, which, when the Life of Waynflete, long fince compofed by the learned Author of Travels in Afia Minor, fhall be permitted to fee the light, will con-tinue the feries from the days of Wykeham

<hr>

c See lines under the picture of Mrs Joyce Frankland in Brafen Nofe hall, printed in Woods Colleges, p 369

and

and of Chichele down to the firft years of
Sir Thomas Pope, giving perhaps the hiftory
of the Univerfity and of learning in a more
interefting form than the more prolix and
laborious details written profeffedly on the
fubject. But in thus adverting to the Lives
of William of Wykeham and Sir Thomas
Pope, which, if their refpective authors had
given to the world nothing elfe, would alone
have handed down their names to pofterity
with honour, I would willingly deprecate all
comparifon between this rough draught and
thofe pieces of finifhed excellence. Abilities
no man can command, but, without pre-
tending to rival models of perfection, which
it were no fmall praife to refemble, I hope
to efcape cenfure in endeavouring to difcharge, to the beft of my power, the debt
which public juftice and private obligation
alike impofed.

Biography is commonly efteemed the moft
pleafing and moft inftructive branch of hiftory; and when the fcene is laid in a diftant
age, the perpetual contraft between ancient
and modern manners conftitutes an additional
recom-

recommendation. The beft advantage, which the intelligent Englifh gentleman generally derives from foreign travel, is, that, while it enlarges his knowledge, refines his manners, and improves his judgement, it enables him to appreciate and difpofes him to value the peculiar bleffings of his own country; and, however he may admire Italian fkies, or Grecian ruins, or Sicilian profpects, he returns home pleafed and content, finding no place, where, upon the whole, he would rather live, than in that favoured land which gave him birth. When we travel on the page of hiftory, when we furvey remote eras, there are many luminous fpots, which detain the eye, and many of the mighty dead, founders of ftates, inventors of arts, and fathers of wifdom, with whom we fhould delight to hold converfe, and, on the contrary, in our own days there is much to lament and much to condemn, caufelefs divifions which diftract and weaken, cold neglect and culpable abufe of furrounding good: but yet when we weigh in a juft balance the fum of things, when we confider the brutality of ancient manners, the ignorance which prevailed in the feats of literature,

terature, the intolerance and fuperftition of the church, and the tyranny of the ftate, we acknowledge with juft pride and genuine fatisfaction, that there is no period in the courfe of our annals, which we could wifh to recall and to have our lot in, rather than the beneficent reign of the Patron of learning, the Guardian of liberty, the Protector of religion, and Father of his people, at the clofe of the eighteenth century.

MIDDLETON, near BANBURY,
June 10, 1800.

CONTENTS.

c   SECT.

S E C T. VII

S E C T   VIII

S E C T   IX

S E C T   X

P O S T S C R I P T.

APPENDIX.

NUM.

Wittmus Smyth
Call An Has

Epise Lincoln
Fundator

Publihed as the Act direct

THE

LIFE

OF

BISHOP SMYTH.

SECTION I.

His Birth, Education, and first Preferments.

WILLIAM SMYTH, Bishop of Lincoln, and Founder of Brasen Nose College, was the fourth[a] son of Robert[b] Smyth of Peel-house in Widdows, or, as it is now written, Widnes, in the parish of Prescot and county of Lancaster. His grandfather was Henry Smyth, esquire[c], of the adjoining township

---

[a] See Appendix, Pedigree 2   Having carefully investigated and compared these ancient documents, I have adopted from them that account which seems upon the whole most consistent and probable, submitting, at the same time, the pedigrees themselves to the Reader's better judgement.   The Bishop's undoubted kinsmen uniformly wrote their name " Smyth " this therefore I retain

[b] Ped 1

[c] Ped. 2 with A. Wood's Hist. and Antiq. of the Univ of Oxford, ed Gutch, Colleges, p 353.

of

of Cuerdley, where the ancient genealogies, varying in many other refpects, uniformly place the family, both before and after the birth of William, the principal fubject of thefe memoirs.

Sir Thomas Smyth, of Chefter and the Hough, who is alfo called Sir Thomas of Cuerdley, appears to have fprung from this family [d], though whether he was coufin-german to the Bifhop, as one account makes him [e], or nephew, as others fay [f], may be

[d] Ped 3 Thomas Smith was Sheriff of Chefter, 1496 and Major, 1511 1520 Thomas Smith fenior, Major, 1504 1515 MS Collections of Chefter by Dr Cowper, now (1799) penes Rev Hugh Cholmondeley, Fellow of Brafen Nofe See alfo Vale Royal, ut infra "Thomas Smith del Hogh prius Lancaftr married "Katharine d of Sir Andrew" (or as others fay, d of Sir William) "Brereton Chefhire Pedigrees, Brereton John Smith, a younger fon to Sir Thomas Smith of Overley [read, Cueraley] in Com Lanc (meaning the faid Sir Tho del Hogh) married Elizabeth d and h of Oldhaugh of Oldnaugh in the parifh of Wermincham ibid Ped Smith In the Brit Muf MS Harl 3526 are the arms of various Smiths blazoned "Sir Thomas Smith's of Cuerdley in Lanc" (f 2 b) are party per pale, Or and Gules, 3 fleurs de lis counterchanged creft, on a torce, a fleur de lis, Or and Gu as the field Which however are not the arms afterwards borne by the Chefhire Smiths, but the arms of the Smiths of Cuerdley, except that I have not difcovered that they affumed a creft See MS Harl 1437 f 146 b.

[e] Ped 3   [f] Ped 4.

quef

queftioned. He was the founder of a family, which flourifhed in great repute at
Hatherton and the Hough, two ancient
lordfhips in the neighbourhood of Nantwich
in Chefhire. Several of this family had the
honour of knighthood, they frequently bore
the office of Mayor of Chefter, and were
occafionally Sheriffs, both for the city and
the county[g]. At the Reftoration Thomas
Smyth of Hatherton, efquire, was created a
Baronet[h]: with remainder, for want of iffue

[g] Sir Tho Smith, Mayor, 1535 Vale Royal, B 1 p 82
In B 11 p 192 the Mayor in 1515 is Sir Thomas Smith fenior Laurence Smith, Sheriff of Chefhire, 9 Eliz ibid p 232
Sir Tho Smith, Sheriff, 42 Eliz ibid p 233 " Sir Thomas
Smith, for his great wifdome and accomplifhed fufhciency,
worthily at this time [1623] graced with the government both
of this honourable city as Maior, and of the county, as his
Majefties High Sheriff, in whofe deferved commendations I am
not worthy to fpeak, being not able to do it as I fhould " ibid
p 66 233 col 2 In the Chefhire pedigrees that of Walchett
is faid to be " ex chartis D Tho Smyth de Hatherton, Militis ' Dodfworth alfo has fome things " ex chartis Tho Smith,
Militis " Num 31 f 149

[h] Heylins Help to Hift and Sir G Mackenzie's Preced 11.
Guillim, ed 1724 p 200 2 who gives him this coat. Gules
on a chevron Or, between 3 befants, as many croffes forme
ftche, Sable Which I fuppofe was affigned him when the title was conferred, for the Smiths of Hough, which was then
more ancient feat, " bore for arms, Azure, 2 bars wavy Ermine,
on a chief Or, a demi-lion iffuing, Sable Creft, on a wreath,
an oftrich'holding a horfe-fhoe in its beak, all proper " John
Charles Brooke, efquire, Somerfet Herald, 1790. To this Gen-

tleman's

male of his body, to his brothers, Laurence and Francis, but the three dying without iſſue, the title became extinct.

The Smyths of Oldhough, in the pariſh of Warmincham, Cheſhire, another family numerous and reſpectable, alſo deduced their line from the houſe of Cuerdley[i]; and bore the ſame arms, with a creſcent for difference. William Smyth, Rouge Dragon, purſuivant of arms, 1609, one of the authors of the Vale Royal of Cheſhire, a poet as well as an antiquary was of this family[k].

t'eman s k ndneſs I owe the free communication of ſeveral pedi-grees, neatly tranſcribed from the records in the College of Arms, and accompanied with many ingenious remarks His deplo-rable death (ſee Gent Mag 1794 p 187 275) was the occa-ſion of deep regret to his friends, and a public loſs in the ſtudy of antiquities

[i] Creſh Ped Smith and ſee above, p 2 n [d] For the arms of Smith of Oldhough ſee MS Harl 1457 f 134 146 b and Vale Royal plate of arms, at the end of B 1 But MS Harl 3526 f 2 b gives the arms of John Smith of Oldhough quar-terly, the firſt and fourth, and creſt, the ſame as Sir Tho of Cuerdley (p 2 n [d]) the ſecond and third Vert, a fret Or

[k] Cheſh Ped Ger Langbain, in his account of Comic Writers, ed 1691 p 488 ſays, this Will Smith wrote two plays, " The Hector of Germany, or the Palſgrave prime Elec-tor ' and ' The Freeman s Honour, to dignify the worthy company of Taylors The latter he thinks was never printed Tne Palſgrave is in the Bodleian, ed Lond 1615 4° " as it hath been publickly acted by a company of young men of this citie ' dedicated to Sir John Swinnerton, knight, lord Mayor.

Milton s

Captain John Smyth, born in the county of Chefter, and defcended from the Smyths of Cuerdley, but whether through the family of Oldhough, or of Hatherton, is not known, was diftinguifhed by his achievements in America and in Europe He was inftrumental in fettling the province of Virginia, and fighting in Hungary under the Emperour, where with his own fword he overcame three Turks, and cut off their heads, he was authorized by Sigifmund king of Hungary to bear three Turks heads proper, their turbans Or, as an honourable augmentation of his arms[1].

Milton's nephew, Edw Phillips, in his Theatrum Poetarum, 1675, ftyles him alfo " the author of a tragedy, entitled Hieronymo" Mod P p 195 And he is probably the Will. Smyth, whofe " Cloris, or the Complaynt of the Paffion of the defpifed Sheppard," 1596, and other poems about that date, are mentioned by Mr Warton, Hift of Poet vol iii p 402 n

[1] Fuller, Worthies of Chefhire, p 179, 180 He refers to " the table over his tomb' for fome of the particulars, and alfo fays, " As Mr. Arthur Smith his kinfman and my Schoolmafter did inform me" He died in London, June 21, 1631, and was buried at St Sepulchre's in the Quire, ibid Guill.m, p 251, gives his coat thus Vert, a chevron Gules, between 3 Turks heads couped, fide-faced, proper, their turbans Or To which Edmondion (Heraldry, vol ii) adds this creft An oftrich Or, holding in his mouth a horfe-fhoe Argent, which feems to be the creft of the Smiths of Hough See p 3 n h. In the Oldhough pedigree Arthur and Jonn Smith are younger brothers of Will Smith mentioned in the preceding note

The

The Smyths likewise of Staffordshire [m], of Lincolnshire [n], and of Yorkshire [o], all respectively claimed connection with the parent stock of Cuerdley, but these I omit for the sake of brevity, and shall only add in this place, that the Egertons of Olton, and the Warburtons of Arley, in Cheshire, are both connected, by the female side, with bishop Smyth's family. Philip Egerton of Egerton, esquire, the first of the name that inherited Olton, married Johanna or Jane, daughter and at last heiress of Gilbert Smyth, the Bishop's brother, and the same Jane having also had issue by her first husband, Richard

---

[m] The Smiths of Newcastle and of Hanley, Co Staff state themselves (C 10 145 in Coll Armor) as descended from " John Smith a second brother' of Edmund Smith of Chester, father of Sir Thomas Smith, which Sir Tho it is there said, " ob 1 Jul 30 H viii " (1538) The said John and Edmund, according to Ped 4 were brothers of Bp Smyth, but John, not Edmund, is there made the ancestor of the Cheshire Smiths Edmund Smith was Sheriff of Chester, 1507 MS. Cowper, ut supra, fol 181 Vale Royal, 1 74.

[n] John Smyth of Urford, Com Linc second son of Rob Smyth of Horsington in the same county, at the visitation in 1634 stated himself great nephew to the Bp of Linc his father Robert being ' son of . Smyth in the north, about six score years ago 100 years old," and he entered his arms the same as the Bishop's, " but they were respited for proof " C 23 56 in Coll Armor J C Brooke, Somerset

[o] See Edmondson's Heraldry, vol. ii.

de

de Winnington, John Warburton, knight, matching with Elizabeth Winnington her grand daughter, the heirefs of that family, introduced the united blood of Smyth and of Winnington into the honourable houfe of Arley [p].

Thefe circumftances, fo many flourifhing branches, and refpectable connections, befpeak the eftimation and confequence of the Cuerdley family, but of what eftates they were poffeffed, or where they lay, I have not difcovered The entire loidfhip of Cuerdley is at prefent (1790) the property of Sir Richard Brooke, baronet, of Norton, Chefhire, one of whofe anceftors obtained it by grant from the Crown, A.D. 1553, as parcel of the diffolved monaftery of Joreval in Yorkfhire [q].

[p] Chefh Ped Egerton, Winnington, and Warburton, and Suppl to Collins s Peerage, p 391 John Egerton of Egerton and of Olton, knight, great grandfon of the faid Philip married Margaret, daughter of Rowland Stanley of Hooton Com Chefl. knight, by his wife Urfula, daughter of Sii Thomas Smyth aforefaid, whom we fuppofe to have been the Bifhops kinfman Ped Egerton and Stanley See alfo and correct Hift of houfe of Stanley, p 11

[q] From the information of Mr Topping of Warrington, Agent to the Norton family, and again, in anfwer to my fcruples, confirmed in the moft obliging manner, Sept 13, 1799 by Thomas Brooke, efquire, M P for the borough of Newton in Lancafhire, brother to the worthy Baronet now deceafed who

This circumstance, which has escaped the notice of our antiquaries, may account for a revolution, which seems to have happened in the family of Smyth. Being, as I presume, lessees of Cuerdley under the abbey of Joreval, they changed their situation, when the nature of their tenure was changed by the dissolution of monasteries; and, upon their removal, their history was involved and lost in the multiplicity of families of the same name in every part of the kingdom.

Cuerdley and Farnworth, in vague speech and uncertain tradition, and Polehouse (that is, Pool-house) by similar tradition, and mistake of an old manuscript[r], have each of them often been called the birth-place of Bishop Smyth. On better authority, as I conceive, I regard the mansion called Peelhouse as the real place of his nativity, where his father probably lived, while his grand-

were both educated, as their ancestors generally have been, at Brasen Nose College

[r] " In Lee s Visitation [of Oxfordshire, G 3 f 31 b in Coll Armor] the writing is such, that it may either be read Pelhouse, or Polhouse, in two other copies of the Smith pedigree, not differing materially from the other, it is spelt Pelehouse " J. C. Brooke, Somerset. Hence Wood s mistake, Colleges, p. 353 Poolhouse and Peelhouse are both in Widdows or Widnes.

father

father ftill occupied the ancient refidence in Cuerdley. As to the hiftory of the Peel-houfe, the property has changed hands fo often, that it is not eafily traced. It ftands alone, and is furrounded by a moat, which gives the place an air of antiquity and of confequence, more than the prefent ftructure, a decent farm-houfe, afpires to, and probably not even the foundations of the building old as they feem, were in their modern form and fituation, when the future ornament of the neighbourhood was born there.

Thefe minute inquiries, in an age ftudious of biographical refearch, will not, I hope, prove altogether uninterefting, efpecially to thofe, whofe gratification is chiefly fought in thefe pages, thofe, I mean, who have been educated in Bifhop Smyth's College, or are actual partakers of his bounty Individuals, like ftates, often rife to eminence from fmall beginnings, by fteps which their contemporaries fcarcely obferve, and neglect to record. Times of curiofity fucceed, when the biographer or hiftorian is eager to inveftigate the origin of inftitutions and the progrefs of arts, to develope the habits or haunts of genius, and trace the paths endeared by virtue and wifdom Diftant hints are then brought

toge-

together, fcattered notices are collected and compared, and every relic and fragment, faved from the wreck of time, is carefully ' piled up, in memory or monument to ages "

The exact period of Smyth's birth is not known.   He is faid to have been born about the middle of the fifteenth century ; but if, as has been fuppofed, he was an undergraduate in Oxford fo late as the year 1478, the meridian of that century was probably paft fome time before he appeared.

The Oxford Hiftorian informs us, " He was trained up in grammar learning in his own country '," but in what feminary, or under whofe care he was inftructed, it were, I fear, vain to inquire.   The whole province, it is probable, did not in thofe days afford a fingle inftitution, that could properly be called a Grammar School.   What Smyth himfelf afterwards endowed was, as far as we know, the firft eftablifhment of this fort in the county   Amidft the general darknefs the lamp of fcience glimmered faintly in the convent   and here, in the penury of ufeful

A Wood, Colleges p 353

knowledge,

knowledge, the fcholar received his fcanty
pittance from the hands of thofe who had
little to beftow, but what they had they
imparted freely and without reward.

There was, however, another mode of education in ufe. A certain number of youths
were received in the houfes of the bifhops
and nobility[u], where they were inftructed in
learning, and occafionally filled up the retinue of the mafter, nor, in an age of honeft
fimplicity, was it deemed a difparagement,
but regaided as an honour, by the knight or
the efquire, to be the page of a pielate, or
wear the livery of a lord. In this domeftic
inftitution if there was probably lefs of fcholaftic fcience, than was to be found within

[t] Of fchools in religious houfes, fee Tanners Not Mon
ed Nafmith, pref p xx Athen Oxon i p 114 642 Wartons Hift of Poet ii p 444

[u] Pace, one of the reftorers of letters in England, a friend
of Erafmus, imbibed the rudiments of learning in the palace
of Langton bifhop of Winchefter Sir Thomas More was
educated as a page with Cardinal Morton, archbifhop of Canterbury, about 1490, who was fo ftruck with his genius, that
he would often fay at dinner, " This child here waiting at table is fo very ingenious, that he will one day prove an extraordinary man Mr Warton, in his Hift of Poet ii 427 n
who gives other inftances Of the like practice in noblemens
families, fee a later inftance in Gent Mag 1797, p 564

the

the walls of a cloifter, the defect was compenfated by fuperior advantages Practical
knowledge was affociated with the ftudy of
books, the pupil, as he grew up, became
acquainted with men, his manners were po-
lifhed, and he was prepared for bufinefs.

No connection of Smyth with any monaftery is known. His talent for bufinefs, tried
in a variety of active fituations, argues rather
a different fort of difcipline, which perhaps
we fhall not err in fuppofing him to have
received in the houfhold of that illuftrious
nobleman, Thomas the firft Earl of Derby.
Knowfley, one of the ancient feats of the
family, is in the parifh where Smyth was
born. The great and good Lord Derby, who
was beheaded by the rebels in 1651, fays,
" the beft, if not all the good families in
Lancafhire, had formerly dwelt in his houfe[x]."
A perfon of the name of Hugh Smyth, who
held certain offices by patent from the crown,
was a fervant to Lord Strange, fon of the firft
Earl[y]. The Countefs of Richmond, fecond
wife of the firft Earl of Derby, retained Mau-

---

[x] Peck, Defid Curiof p 435
[y] Act of Refumption, 1 H vii Rolls of Parl. vol vi
p 365.

rice Weſtbury, an Oxford man, for the expreſs purpoſe of inſtructing "certayn yonge
gentilmen at her findyng[z]." She was an
early patron of Smyth, and it is probable he
was firſt known to her as a promiſing eleve
of the Stanley family, educated with the ſons
of her huſband, the youngeſt of whom,
James, was deſtined for the church, in which
he attained rapidly various preferments, and
was at laſt made biſhop of Ely[a].

[z] See her Letter to the Univerſity of Oxford, requeſting
Weſtbury's abſence might be diſpenſed with on that account
Dat "Windeſor, 12 Jan "probably 1492–3 Reg F Ep 458
Wood's Annals, 1 p 655

[a] He was conſtituted Dean of St Martin's the Great by patent 1 H vii 1485, and an act of parliament, that ſame
year, ordered the patent to be in force from the date of it,
againſt the excluded Dean, Stillington, biſhop of Bath, charged
with treaſonable practices Rolls Parl vol vi p 292 He
was preſented by the Earl of Derby to Winwick, Lanc on the
reſignation of Robert Clyffe, penult Feb 1492–3 Reg Lichf
xiii f 157 b Had a diſpenſation from the Pope to ſtudy in
the Univerſity, notwithſtanding he was poſſeſſed of a benefice
with cure of ſouls, 16 Kal Jul 1492 ibid f 160 b Permiſſion to be admitted Dr of canon law by two Doctors in
that faculty, June 18, 1506 Reg Acad Oxon G f 19 b,
and that the archbiſhop of Canterbury (Warham) and (Fitzjames) biſhop of London ſhould put on him " pileum pro gra-
du Doctoratus, being then biſhop of Ely ibid t 51 b The
Earl, his father, one of whoſe brothers had been educated at
Oxford, had a ſon there, probably this James, in 1485, as appears by a letter to him Reg F Ep 327 The ſaid James,
who was archdeacon of Cheſter, then of Richmond, Warden

of

The time of Smyth's removal to Oxford is
not known nor has it been difcovered with
certainty of what college or fociety there he
was a member Wood fays, he fettled in
Oriel or Lincoln college, or fucceffively in
both . in the former, he fuppofes, becaufe
feveral of his name and kindred were of that
fociety foon after, if not in his own time ,
and in the other, becaufe among their Burfars' accompts he finds one Mr. William
Smyth to have been a commoner there, before, and in the year, 1478, being the fame,
without all doubt, with this perfon that we
now fpeak of [a].

I have not met with any thing, which directly confirms or confutes this account in
either of its parts , but as it is pretty certain, that Smyth did not obtain a fellowfhip

of Manchefter, &c ' built the fair houfe of the bifhops of Ely
at Somerfham, Hunts MS Dodfworth, 153 f 152 James
Stanley was alfo admitted Rector of Warrington by proxy,
Sept 7 1476 Reg Lichf xii f 110 b If this was, as I
apprehend, the fame perfon, tren, what fome of the preceding
circes is probable, is certain, that he was not, as has been
fuppofed the man whofe tuition Erafmus declined in 1496 ,
or that young man whoever he might be, was not born in
1476 See b   i d 18 whofe conjecture Jortin
adopts, I of Er fm i p 6

b Coll reg of fter a and Athen Oxon i 650

in Oriel, or in Lincoln, I fee no reafon why
he fhould remove from one college to the
other. It is true, as Wood obferves, that
he was a benefactor to both thofe colleges;
but as bifhop of Lincoln he was Vifitor of
both, and that fingle confideration was fufficient to call forth his liberality, folicitous as
he was to encourage and reward the ftudy of
letters, wherever it was found, but efpecially
in his own Univerfity.

With refpect to Oriel college, had he ever
been a member of that fociety, circumftances
occurred, when it would naturally have been
mentioned. There are two letters from the
Provoft and Fellows of that college addreffed
to him [c], in the higheft ftrain of gratitude for
favours received and honour conferred, but
not a hint is dropped of what they muft have
known, and would hardly have fuppreffed,
that the college, to which he now was a diftinguifhed benefactor, was proud to enroll
him alfo among her fons

On the whole, if he ftudied in either of
thefe colleges, which after all is not clear, it

[c] Coll Oriel, Reg Decan p 64 68. There will be occafion to fpeak of thefe letters again

pro-

probably was in Lincoln, where Wood finds William Smyth a commoner in 1478[d].

How long he refided in the Univerfity, and to what degrees he was admitted, we have not been able to difcover; there being no regular regifter of thefe matters prior to the beginning of the fixteenth century. It appears from his inftitution to the Rectory of Chefhunt in Hertfordfhire, June 14, 1492, that he was then Bachelor of Law[e], in which faculty they whofe views were directed to the church, as well as others, often proceeded. Smyth's friend, the friend alfo of Erafmus, Warham archbifhop of Canterbury, was a doctor both of civil and canon law[f].

But here occurs another point, which requires inveftigation For Wood pofitively affirms, "Sure I am, that he with divers other

---

[d] MS Wood 28 (8490) i 127 A perfon of the name of Smyth was Fellow of Linc in 1487 Vide Calcul huj is Coll Num 2 p 9, &c But I fuppofe this was "Rob Smyth, S T P who was Fellow, as Wood (ibid) fays, "3 H vii In a volume of extracts from the old account books, p 67, 68. it appears by references to B vol 1 Calc 3 (which is now loft) that "R Smyth was Burfar in 1477, 1478

[e] Newcourt, Repert 1 p 821

[f] Jortin s Eraim 1 p 41 n

fcholars

ſcholars of Oxford, being fearful of a peſtilence raging in Oxford in their time, receded
to Cambridge; where he became Fellow,
and afterwards Maſter, of Pembroke Hall[g]."
Browne Willis corrects this in part, by informing us, that he became Fellow, but not
Maſter, of Pembroke Hall[h]. And here the
matter reſts, our authors in general having
been content to admit what is ſo confidently
aſſerted by thoſe who do not uſually aſſert
without good ground. If the whole is a
miſtake, it will be neceſſary to prove it ſo by
deciſive evidence.

In the beginning of the laſt century Biſhop

---

[g] Colleges, p. 353 Athen Oxon i 651 Wood ſays (ibid
and Annals, ii p 7 ad ann 1514) Ep 494 [r 484] in
Reg F was " writt to the ſaid Biſhop" Smyth, but there is
no internal mark, nor collateral circumſtance, which deter-
mines it to be addreſſed to him It is the incorporation of
ſome biſhop (" colendiſſime antiſtes," " piiſſime preſul," &c)
formerly of Oxford, who had obtained a Doctor's degree, as it
ſeems, in ſome other, probably a foreign, Univerſity " noſtros
quanquam alienis gignaſiis evectos, atque ſummos gradus con-
ſecutos " No date, but probably towards the end of 1497 In
the preceding year, 1496, three Oxford men were promoted to
biſhoprics, Dean biſhop of Bangor, Arundel of Lichfield, and
Sever of Carliſle, and one of theſe moſt likely is the perſon
complimented, rather than Smyth, who had been dignified
with the mitre five years before
[h] Cath iii p 59

Wien.

Wren, who had himself been Fellow of
Pembroke Hall, collected with great diligence a History of the Masters and Fellows
of that society. He says, William Smith
was chosen Fellow in 1486, and that his
name occurs occasionally in the transactions
of his own college, or those of the University, till the year 1500; when he was presented by his society to the rectory of Overton Watervile, in the county of Huntingdon,
which he held till his decease in 1532[i]. He
was born in Yorkshire, and was instituted
to Overton by Smyth bishop of Lincoln[k], a
native of Lancashire, who has so often been
supposed to have been the same person

Still however he might " recede to Cambridge," and become a member of this college, though not upon the foundation. Let
this too be examined

When Archbishop Grindal was translated
from York to Canterbury, the Master and
Fellows of Pembroke Hall, of which the

· Historia de Custod et Soc Aulæ Pembr MS Harl·
7929 ç p 541 See also Add to Lel Coll vol ı p 405
ᵏ Will Sm in M A instit 26 Nov 1500 MS Harl 6957
p 59 He was Inceptor in Arts 5 Jul 1490 Cantab Academiæ
Regist Beta f 27 and occurs in 1500 or 1501 ib f 150

Arch-

Archbifhop had been fucceffively Scholar, Fellow, and Mafter, wrote to congratulate him on the occafion. In their letter, dated 1576, they diftinctly mention five bifhops, fome of them prior to the days of Smyth, who had been educated in their college, but not a word is faid of any bifhop of Lincoln[1]. No fuch perfon therefore was then known to have been member of that fociety.

In 1496 the Univerfity of Cambridge, by a decree of their Senate, gave leave, that certain perfons, members of Oxford, fhould be incorporated among them, whenever they fhould come thither, whether in term or vacation[m]. The firft of thefe was " the Bifhop of Rochefter," (Thomas Savage) The fecond is " the Bifhop of Lincoln;" to which fee Smyth had been tranflated the preceding year The lift is clofed by Warham, then Mafter of the Rolls, afterwards Lord Chancellor and Archbifhop of Canterbury How

[1] Strype's Grindal, App 107
[m] Reg Beta, ut fupra, f 99 Ibid f 227 anno 1505, vel 1506, is this article 'It R [i e recept] pro incorporatione Doct Smyth 20 D ' Who this was is uncertain, but as he is fimply called Dr Smyth, it probably was not the Bifhop of Lincoln Compare Parker de Antiq Brit p 455 ed Drake; and MS Parker cvii ad fin

many,

many, or which, of thefe eminent perfons availed themfelves of the privilege fo honourably conferred, we have not difcovered; but without doubt none of them were, and of courfe Smyth was not, antecedently a member of that Univerfity: and, upon the whole, the report of his removing to Cambridge, fo often related by grave hiftorians of both Univerfities, is totally deftitute of foundation; the miftake having originated in his being confounded with the perfon before mentioned, Fellow of Pembroke Hall, who was contemporary with him, and had both his names.

Oxford therefore, as far as appears, was the only Univerfity, in which he ftudied, and it is no unreafonable demand upon candour to allow, that he cultivated what was then the beft literature of the place in the beft manner. The Greek language was at this time fcarcely underftood by any one in the kingdom, and about twenty years afterwards, when Grocyn, Linacre, and others, who had ftudied in Italy, attempted to introduce it, the knowledge of it was profcribed, and *Græculus ifte* was fynonymous with a heretic. Hiftory, poetry, and what are ftyled the Belles Lettres, were unknown

or

or difregarded. Grammar, fcholaftic logic, and fcholaftic theology, a fuperficial acquaintance with fome of the later claffics, and a portion of civil and canon law, conftituted the entire but fcanty fund of a fcholar in the latter part of the fifteenth century With this learning therefore, which alone was in repute, we may fuppofe it was the ambition of the young academic to ftore his mind: but to thefe frivolous fciences and barren fpeculations the fuperior tafte or good fortune of Smyth led him to join the more liberal ftudy of the Roman authors of the pureft age; for his latinity, though not faultlefs, poffeffes however a degree of accuracy, fulnefs, and ftrength, which was not then common[n], and could only be acquired by careful infpection of the beft models

But the veffel is not freighted to remain in the port, but to traverfe the ocean. We muft accompany the Oxonian into active life, carrying with him from the general empo-

[n] "Such of our countrymen as wrote in Latin at this period [about 1480] and were entirely educated at home without any connections with Italy, wrote a ftyle not more claffical than that of the Monkifh Latin annalifts, who flourifhed two or three centuries before" Mr Warton, Hift of Poet ii 421

n x

rium,

rium, the Univerſity of ſtudy°, as it was called, qualities and attainments calculated alike to grace mediocrity, or dignify elevation

When Henry vii, after the memorable battle of Boſworth, aſcended the throne, his firſt care was to ſecure the crown, which he had wreſted from an uſurper, by repaying the kindneſs of thoſe who had eſpouſed his cauſe, and forwarded his pretenſions The ſucceſs of the deciſive battle was in great meaſure owing to the courage and addreſs of Thomas lord Stanley, who, in reward of his ſervices, was created Earl of Derby; and was alſo, with his ſon Lord Strange, called to the privy Council°, and received, perſonally and in his family, many other marks of royal regard and munificence.

While the favours of the Court flowed in this channel, Smyth was brought forward, and promoted. The firſt appointment, as far as appears, which he enjoyed from the Crown, was a place in Chancery. The King,

° " The Vniuerſite of the ſtudy of Oxenford " Reg F Ep 182 Ubi vigebat ſtudium generale, as Pope Innocent expreſſed himſelf, 1492 Reg I ichf xiii f 160 b.

ᴾ Pol Verg p 566

by

by patent dated Sept 20, 1 Henry vii, 1485, granted to William Smyth the office of Clerk of the Hanaper for life; with an annual ftipend of 40l. and an additional allowance of eighteen pence a day, whenever he or his deputy fhould be employed, in the bufinefs of his poft, to attend upon the Lord Chancellor, or the Keeper of the great Seal[q]. It is obfervable, that this falary, whether it was in compliment to Smyth, or whatever might be the reafon, is more than double the fum affigned to the office by a fubfequent patent of this reign, and even more ample than was allotted to it a full century afterwards, when the value of money bore a much lefs proportion to the nominal amount[r].

There is a letter from the Univerfity of Oxford to the Clerk of the Hanaper, which,

[q] MS More, 507 f 21 b [in Biblioth publ Cantab Ii 5 31]

[r] Pat 27 Jan 20 H vii to Simon Stalworth off cler Hanaperii cum feodo 20 librar Rolls Chapel Mi Oldfworth was Clerk temp Jac 1 with a falary of 36l. 13s 6d MS Afhm 821 f. 6 b Stalworth, who was Mafter of St Johns Hofpital, Banbury, before 1483, was at this time Subdean of Lincoln, and died before 12 Nov 1511 MS Harl 6953 p 13 25 He was Clerk of the Hanaper only one year, being fucceeded 21 H vii by George Kirkham, (Rolls, ut fupra,) who was of the privy Council. Dockets of Court of Requefts, p 41

while

while it leaves no room to doubt, that he, who is the object of our present inquiries, was really the person then invested with the office, is connected with some particulars curious in themselves, which have not been accurately stated by historians. The letter in question is also perhaps the earliest extant addressed to Smyth.

Upon the suppression of Lambert Simnel's rebellion, Stillington, bishop of Bath, before suspected [s], and now accused of treason, fled to Oxford for shelter. The King by letter required him to be surrendered. The University, in excuse for not complying with his Majesty's demand, pleaded the fear of incurring the censures of the Church, if they attempted any violence against an ecclesiastic; as also their oath to maintain their own statutes and privileges, by which they were forbidden to give up a member of their body to any extraneous jurisdiction. Several letters passed on the occasion [t]. At last the

---

[s] See above, p 13 n a

[t] Reg F Epp 329 (from Shene, Mar 7) 342 (no date) 343 347 (Mon of Chertsey, 22 and 27 March) 348 (Mon. of Bury, April 9) are all by the King to the University respecting this business Wood assigns them to the year 1487. (See his Annals, 1 643—645) And though it is certain the

chro-

prudence of Henry contrived matters fo as to accommodate the oppofite claims of prerogative and privilege. An order was iffued, that the Bifhop fhould be delivered up to an academic officer and an officer of the crown, to Edmund Hampden, Steward of the Univerfity, and James Parker, Efquire of the King's body[u]; which was accordingly done.

In the courfe of this bufinefs his Majefty, in one of his letters[x], dropped an intimation, that the franchifes of the Univerfity, not having been confirmed by him, depended upon his royal grace and pleafure. This naturally awakened the fears of the Univerfity, and they fpared no endeavours to make intereft at court for obtaining the neceffary ratification. The letter to Smyth was one of thofe written by the Univerfity at this juncture: in which they tell him, that, after much deliberation upon the critical fituation of their affairs, they had come to a refolution to apply to their friends, and to Him in par-

chronological order is not always ftrictly obferved in this Regifter, yet they do appear, by collateral dates, to belong to the end of 1487 and the beginning of 1488

[u] Ibid Ep 347

[x] Ep 342 the " auctorite of your faide privileges as it is not by vs confirmed hangeth at our pleafure and grace "

ticular,

ticular, as one of whom they had ever entertained the greateſt hopes, who, having always
been ſteadily devoted to their intereſt, might
now by his authority eſſentially ſerve them[y].

In conſequence of this and ſimilar appli-
cations, the privileges of the Univerſity received the royal confirmation by Inſpeximus on the firſt of March, 2 Henry vii[z],
(1486-7.) and were again recogniſed in a
patent of the ſeventh year of that reign[a],
and finally ratified by an act of the legiſla-
ture, ſigned by the King, and enrolled in
parliament[b].

[y] F Ep 369 App Num 1

[z] Archi Bodl A 90 And yet ſee what his Majeſty ſaid,
apparently a year after the date of this Inſpeximus, p 25 n x
Wood, by not mentioning the Inſpeximus, eſcapes the difficulty which I cannot ſolve

[a] Rolls Chapel But I ſuſpect a miſtake in the extract for
a patent 17 Hen vii (hereafter to be mentioned) Sir Reginald
Bray being called Steward of the Univerſity in both, and it
is not known that he was Steward before 9 H vii

[b] So I underſtand the following entry in the Comp Burſſ
of Magdalen college, 11-12 H vii from Mich 1495 to
Mich 1496 " Clerico Parliam pro regiſtratione ſignata per
D Regem vocat B lia de proviſo pro omnibus Coll Oxon
vi S vii ſed ad onus Coll B M Magd xx D However
nothing of this appears in the Journals, nor in the Statutes at
large The privileges of both Univerſities were confirmed by
13 Elizabeth, c 29

The

The letter to Smyth is without date; but it was accompanied by one of the third of May to Mr. Robert Sherborn, defiring him to deliver the attendant "royal refcript" (probably the Infpeximus, ready for the feals) to the Clerk of the Hanaper, and to ufe his perfonal intereft with him on the occafion; being perfuaded, that "he would readily grant whatever Sherborn fhould requeft[c]." This fuppofes Smyth to have had a great efteem for Sherborn; of which, from another quarter, there is more direct proof. For when he was bifhop of Lincoln, the firft dignity in his cathedral which he had to beftow, the archdeaconry of Buckingham, he conferred on Mr. Robert Sherborn[d], reward-

---

[c] F Ep 368 " Cui hoc regium fcriptum per te afferri cupimus " And it is exprefsly faid, that this " regium fcriptum," which Dr Fitzjames had procured, had for its object the confirmation of their privileges Epp 365 384 are alfo to Sherborn In the latter they feem to fpeak as if the privileges were already confirmed by the King, but they were apprehenfive of difficulties on the part of Archbifhop Morton, (who was then Lord Chancellor) and they requeft Sherborn to remove any impreffions which his Grace might have received to their difadvantage Thefe letters have no date of the year, but all three feem to have been written in 1488, or 1489

[d] 13 Feb 1495-6 on the death of John Bourchier MS. Harley, 6954 p 154 The faid J Bourchier was alfo archdeacon of Canterbury, and a brother or kinfman of Archbifhop

ing the worth, with which he had been long acquainted. Sherborn, who was Fellow of New College, and a liberal benefactor to the society, was about this time, 1495, Mafter of St. Crofs, and in 1499 Dean of St. Paul's*. In 1505 he was confecrated Bifhop of St. David's; when he was fucceeded in the arch-deaconry of Buckingham by Charles Bothe[f], afterwards Bifhop of Hereford, in the maf-terfhip of St. Crofs by John Claymond, the firft Prefident of Corpus Chrifti college, and at St Paul's by the ever memorable Dean Colet. In 1508 he was tranflated to Chi-chefter, where he died in 1536, at the age of 86; and was buried in the fouth tranfept of the cathedral, which he had adorned with a complete feries of the bifhops of the fee, which remained there till they were demo-

bifhop Bourcher Somners Ant of Cantero by Batteley, P 1 p 161

[e] A Wood, Colleges, p 184 Athen Ox 1 p 12 671

[f] S May, 1505 MS Harl 6953 p 22 Correct A Wood, ut fupra, who fays he was archdeacon of Huntingdon The fimple fact, whether a bull of plurality, granted to Sherborn to hold the archdeaconry of Bucks with the hofpital of St Crofs had or had not fuffered a rafure, occupied the court of Rome above half a year Reg Linc Smyth, f 200—221 He had alfo the prebend of Langford manor, Lincoln MS Harl. ibid

lifhed

lifhed by Waller's foldiers in 1642, while their commanders robbed the church of its plate and veftments[g].

While Smyth was Clerk of the Hanaper, he was engaged in another bufinefs; but whether he was affociated with the illuftrious perfons that are named with him, on account of his office, or from motives of perfonal regard and efteem, does not appear. The matter was this.

Henry Norbridge and Thomas Kyngeftone, of Guildford, Surrey, were defirous to found a chantry in the parifh-church of the Holy Trinity in that town. For this purpofe, as lands or rents for the maintenance of the chaplain were to pafs into mortmain, it was neceffary to procure a licence from the Crown. In confideration therefore of forty marks paid into the Hanaper, no fmall fum in thofe times, a writ of privy Seal was granted, in which, for the more ample honour and effect, thefe names are joined with the founders: Elizabeth confort of Henry vii, Mar-

[g] Mercur Ruft P ii p 139, 140 The grant of a park by Bp Sherborn, 25 H viii is mentioned in Gent Mag 1797 p 929

garet

garet countess of Richmond his mother, Thomas Bourghier[h] and Reginald Bray, knights, Mr. William Smyth, clerk, and John Clopton, rector of the church, whose consent was neceſſary. Permiſſion is given to endow the chantry with ten marks a year; the perſons named, or any one of them, is authorized to frame rules for the charity, and the officiating prieſt, as cuſtomary, is to pray for the King and the Founders during life, and for their ſouls after death[i].

It is needleſs at preſent to cenſure theſe ſuperſtitious practices, which it was part of the glory of the Reformation to extirpate; but the principle of charity, which inſpired them, it is impoſſible not to applaud. The generoſity of Norbridge, the principal founder of the chantry in queſtion, demands higher praiſe. It was not the benefaction of one, who gave to the church what he could no

[h] Tho Bourchier, knight, is mentioned in a writ of ſupplies, " Pro ſagittariis providendis,' both for Surrey and Herts, A D 1488 Rymer, vol xii p 355 He was probably the fifth ſon of Henry Bourchier, earl of Eſſex, and nephew of Thomas Bourchier, archbiſhop of Canterbury Dugd Baron ii 130 col 1. Sir R Bray, the friend of Smyth and ornament of the court of H vii, will often be mentioned in the enſuing pages

[i] Rymer xii. p 284 The date is Feb 6 1 H vii (1485-6)

longer retain or enjoy. It was the deliberate
act of mature and married life, the founder
himfelf faw the plan duly executed, and,
having furvived near thirty years to fuperintend his own pious inftitution[k], was interred
in the Lady chapel adjoining the church on
the fouth, at the fouth-eaft corner of which
chapel Norbridge chantry ftood. The epitaph of the founder was at the head of Archbifhop Abbot's monument, who was a native of Guildford, and a great benefactor to
the town. But of all thefe, the church having been rebuilt in 1740, no veftige remains.
A building at the upper end of the high
ftreet, now converted into an alms-houfe for
a cripple, is fhewn as the fuppofed refidence
of the chantry prieft[l].

[k] As appears by his epitaph, preferved by Aubrey, Surrey
vol iii p 292   See alfo the Guildford Guide, p 15.

[l] Some of thefe particulars I learnt (June 4, 1787) from
the Sexton, a fenfible man, aged 82, who remembered the old
church perfectly well   Sir Richard Guilford had a patent to
build it in 1499 MS Parker, CLXX p 111   He fhone with
great luftre, both as a warrior and ftatefman, in this reign,
defending Henry's crown, which he had been inftrumental in
procuring, by his wifdom in council and valour in the field
He was appointed Mafter of the Ordnance, 1 H vii (MS
More, 507 f 9 31 b Cotton MS Cleopatra, C iii f 3 9
b 380) and privy Counfellor, Pol Verg p 566   He was
Comptroller of the Houfhold in 1495, Rolls Parl vi p 461
being then member of the Houfe of Commons, ib 478 b
ubi

It was probably not long after Smyth was made Clerk of the Hanaper, that he received another mark of royal munificence in the deanery of St. Stephen's, Weftminfter. This collegiate church, begun by King Stephen in honour of the protomartyr of his own name, was built anew by Edward III; and enjoyed from his fplendid generofity ample eftates and privileges, which fucceeding monarchs enlarged. As it ftood within the precincts of the palace, the deanery, which was in the gift of the Crown, was ufually beftowed on a favourite chaplain, whom the King wifhed to have near his royal prefence. The time of Smyth's appointment to this dignity has been fearched for with fruitlefs induftry, both in the original regifter[m] of this free Chapel, and in other ancient records[n]. We only know, that it muft have been fubfequent to July 28, 1480; for at that time Henry Sharpe

ubi plura, 444. 472 b 510. Created a Knight Bannerett, with his friend Sir R Bray, at the battle on Blackheath, 1497 Cotton MS. Claudius, C iii f 30 His relict Johanna had an annuity of 20l granted by Henry viii for fervices in that and the preceding reign, Nov 3 6 H viii. 1514 Rymer, xiii p 470.

[m] Cotton Lib. Fauftina, B viii

[n] Patents in the Tower, and at the Rolls, archiepifcopal Regifters at Lambeth, &c

occurs

occurs as Dean°. When Henry vii returned
from his progrefs into the north, in the year
1486, the Chapter of St. Stephen's received
him upon his landing at Weftminfter bridge,
and conducted him to the palace with folemn proceffion[p]. And at the coronation of
the Queen, November 25, 1487, on the fecond day of the celebrity, the Royal Pair, attended by the Earl of Derby and other nobles, heard mafs in St. Stephen's chapel[q].

By the ftatute for diffolving chapels and
chantries, 1 Edward vi, 1547, this collegiate
foundation came into the King's hands[r], and
he thereupon configned the chapel to the
purpofe which it ftill ferves as the Commons'
Houfe of Parliament. Its ancient fplendor
as well as modern ufe deferved that the
beauty of its perifhable walls fhould be refcued from oblivion, and the tafk has been
executed, under the aufpices of the Society
of Antiquaries, in a magnificent fet of en-
gravings, plans of the building, and fpecimens of the architecture ; accompanied with
a fhort hiftory of the foundation by the pen

° Fauftina, ut fupra, f 37 b
[p] Lel Coll ed 1770 vol iv Add p 202
[q] Ibid p 230
[r] Stowes Surv by Strype, B vi p 54

D   of

of Mr. Topham'. A lift of the Deans, corrected and enlarged, which did not form a
part of the ingenious Author's defign, may
be feen in the appendix' to thefe memoirs of
Smyth ; who, while he was Dean, and refided, as he informs us, in Canon Row", was
alfo a privy Counfellor, though we have not
learnt when he was firft called to that right
honourable board

We have already feen Smyth's name affociated with that of Margaret countefs of
Richmond. He was foon after employed as
her agent, in an article of bufinefs, now
chiefly memorable as a mark of her efteem
and confidence. She appointed him her
proxy to receive for her the advowfon of
Swinfhead in Lincolnfhire from Thomas
Weft, knight, lord La Warre, ftyling him
in the patent, 10 March, 7 Henry vii, 1491-2,
" Our beloved in Chrift, William Smyth,
clerk, Dean of the royal chapel of St. Stephen's, Weftminfter'." In 1493 fhe prefent-

---

' London, 1795 See Brit Crit vol viii p 457—460.

' Num iii

" Dat in domo folite refidentie noftre ly Chanone rowe,
londone, xii Jan. 1492 Lichf. Reg vol xiii f 138. Corrupted into " Channel Row " Newcourt Repert i 746 Pennant's London, p 91

' Madox, Formul Num. DCXXIII. p 352. The manor and
ad-

ed Hugh Oldham, perhaps through Smyth's intereſt, to this rectory[y], and a few years afterwards beſtowed the advowſon, together with the rectory of Cheſhunt in Hertford-ſhire, upon the abbey of Weſtminſter[z]: on which occaſion Swinſhead was erected into a vicarage, the rectory being appropriated to the abbat and convent of Weſtminſter; which may be noted as one of the laſt inſtances of this ſpecies of ſacrilege, whereby parochial churches were robbed to enrich monaſteries.

About the ſame time that the Counteſs employed Smyth in the purchaſe of Swinſ-head, ſhe preſented him to the rectory of Cheſhunt, to which he was inſtituted, June

advowſon of Swinſhead had been in the noble family of La Warre from 16 Edw iii, or earlier, according to Dugdale, Baron ii 16 But Johanna de Bohun, counteſs of Hereford, preſented to " Swyneſhede" in 1405 and 1408 MS Harl. 6952 p 108

[y] Inſtituted Feb. 3, 1493 MS Harl 7048 p 304 Upon his reſignation John Marſhall, M A was preſented by the convent of Weſtminſter to the newly erected vicarage, Sept. 9, 1500 MS. Harl 6953 p 27

[z] A D 1499 Reg Linc f 19—36 There was a penſion of 5s from Swinſhead to the Dean and Chapter of Lincoln, but it was withheld upon the diſſolution of religious houſes MS Parker, cviii 47 p 225 Of the origin and progreſs of vicarages ſee Pegge's L of Groſſeteſte, App. Num vii

14,

14, 1492[a]. This valuable rectory, the advowson of which had been in the earls of
Chester and Richmond, and in the Crown,
had long been a finecure The rector for
the time was patron of the endowed vicarage; but there was no vacancy during Smyth's
incumbency, for he soon quitted this for
higher preferment, and was succeeded by
Oldham, before mentioned, on the presentation of the same munificent pationess,
whose right in both instances was recognised
and secured by the Crown[b] Oldham was
instituted 4 July, 1494[c], and he was the
last rector, as it was appropriated shortly afterwards to the convent of Westminster, and
passed upon the suppression of monasteries
into lay hands. Of Cheshunt another circumstance ought to be remembered. For as

---

[a] Newcourt, Repert i p 821 He succeeded Oliver Dyn-
ran, or Denham who was presented by Edw iv 30 Apr
1461 Of Cheshunt see also Fullers Worthies of Hertfordshire,
v 29 his Church Hist B vi p 317 § 3 and Knight's I
of Colet, p 85 n In MS More, 715 is a Rental of " Chel-
erannte "

[b] Pat 9 Nov 5 H vii Rolls' Chapel For free access to
this national Repository I am indebted, through the favour
of his Honour Sir Richard Pepper Arden, Master of the Rolls,
to the obliging attention of John Kipling, esquire, Clerk of
the Rolls' Chapel

[c] Newcourt, as above

in this age it was one of the earlieſt preferments of Smyth and of Oldham, two ſuc-
ceſſive rectors, who both became biſhops;
ſo at a later period it gave to the church a
ſtill greater man, being the firſt curacy of
Archbiſhop Tillotſon[d]

There is ſtill one particular matter of truſt,
in which, about this time, Smyth was concerned for the ſame illuſtrious Counteſs. She
had obtained letters patent from Edward iv
to enable her to enfeoff ſeveral manors and
eſtates, lying in the counties of Somerſet and
Devon, for the performance of her laſt will.
The licence was renewed at her deſire, when
her ſon was on the throne, and, after other
intermediate grants, an eſtate in fee was
made of the premiſes, 7 Henry vii, to Fox
biſhop of Exeter, Elias Dawbeney knight,
William Smyth dean of St. Stephen's, and
others By virtue of this grant the feoffees
were ſeiſed of the eſtates, when the Counteſs
made her will, 6 June, 1508; wherein ſhe
directs, that her executors ſhall have the free
and entire receipt and diſpoſal of the ſaid
eſtates, and the profits therefrom accruing,
for the purpoſes there ſpecified[e].

[d] Birch's Life of Tillotſon, p 24
[e] Royal Wills, London 1780 p 383

It

It has commonly been said, that Smyth was Archdeacon of Surrey; and Le Neve places him in this dignity next after John Patten or Waynflete, brother to the venerable Founder of St Mary Magdalen college, Oxford. But Rymer, the authority alleged, does not mention it, and the whole appears to be a mistake. John Waynflete was collated to the archdeaconry of Surrey by William of Waynflete, as soon almost as he became bishop of Winchester, namely in 1447-8[f]; and he held this with other preferment till his death, which happened in 1481[s]. He was succeeded by Leonel Wyde-

---

[f] Jan 5, 1447. Reg Waynflete, P i f 2 Both the volumes of Waynflete's Register were examined throughout with the greatest care, for the purpose of this undertaking, in 1799, by Mr John Ridding, Registrar of the diocese of Winchester The late Mr Warton, prompt to encourage and assist antiquarian literature, which he loved so well and adorned so highly, had with unsolicited kindness searched the same records for me before Fresh doubts were the occasion of fresh inquiries, for the forwarding of which to One so able to answer them as the intelligent and liberal Registrar, the Rev Dr Huntingford, Warden of Winchester College, will accept my best thanks

[s] Rev Dr Chandler, in his Life of W Waynflete—a work, which it is much to be regretted, that he withholds from the public In the mean time I am indebted to my learned and valuable Friend for the following authorities in proof of what is said above Two acquittances remain. One " Johannis de Giglis" [I suppose bishop of Worcester in 1497] " facta Fundaton pro 5l. 13s. id exequuton fratris sui Johannis Waynflete

vile, fon of Richard earl Rivers, and brother
to the Queen; who, being a rifing man, did
not retain the archdeaconry long. He read
the Theological Lecture of Edward iv at
Oxford in 1481, in the prefence of the King
and Bifhop Waynflete, being at that time
Dean of Exeter, and Chancellor of the Univerfity[h]. Having the following year been
made bifhop of Salifbury, he was fucceeded
in the archdeaconry of Surrey by Oliver Denham, or Dynham[i], already mentioned, brother to the lord Treafurer, John baron Dynham; and he died poffeffed of this preferment in the year 1500[k]: fo that there is evi-

flete Archidiac 1481 " Cartæ regis &c. n 6 Index (of Deeds
&c in the Tower at Magdalen College) The other is dated
May 19, 20 Edw iv. [q ' 21] for 20l received for dilapida-
tions and all repairs whatfoever, by Lionel Wydevyle, his fuc-
ceffcr as Archdeacon of Surrey

[h] Wood's Fafti, p 63 ad ann 1479—1483 Annals, i
p 637

[i] Ult Mart 1482 Dominus contulit archid Surr Mro
Olivere Denham vacant per liberam refign Mri Leonelli
Wydevile ult archid ibidem Reg Waynflete, P ii f 88.
Mr Ridding See and correct Le Neve by inferting Wyde-
vile inftead of Smyth

[k] He is ftyled archdeacon of Surrey in his will, which is dated 22 April, 1500, and was proved 30 May following Prerog
Office, Moone, ix f. 67 b He orders his body to be buried
before the image of St Swithin " in ecclefia mea de Farnyf-
ham,' and appoints his brother, John lord Dynham, one of his
executors and refiduary legatee He was of Oxford, B. A. 1458

Reg

dently no period, when Smyth could have been archdeacon of Surrey.

He is also reported to have had the Prepo-fiture of Wells, to which a prebend was an-nexed, one of the numerous preferments en-joyed by William of Wykeham in the pre-ceding century[1]. But fince no fuch name, as I am informed[m], can be difcovered among thofe who are known to have occupied this poft, I judge it to be a miftake, which re-quires no further notice; and we may fol-low the Dean of St. Stephen's in the un-doubted courfe of his promotion and ho-nours.

Reg A2 f 111 b 112 b Rector of Chefhunt, 1461 (fee above, p 36 n a) Prebendary of Lichfield, 10 Oct 1467 Willis, Catu 11 476 and fucceeded Hugh Oldham in a better ftall there, 21 Mar 1499 ibid 430 Lord Dynham was made Treafurer 1 H vii Pat 14 July, 1486. Dugd. Chron Ser He had, with Sir R Bray and others, the grant of a prebend in St Stephen's, 26 Apr 8 H vii, 1493 Rolls' Chapel He died a few months after his brother the archdeacon, and was buried in the church of the Grey Friars, London, Jan 30, 1500–1501 Stowe s Ann ed Howes, 1631 p 482 See alfo Hen viith's Will, publifhed by Mr Aftle, 1775, p 22

[1] Lowth s Wykeham, 1758 p 28 33, 34

[m] By my worthy and much efteemed Friend, Dr Arnold, Advocate in Doctors Commons, who kindly procured the ne-ceffary fearch to be made in the records at Wells

SECT. II.

Bishop of Lichfield.

WE have furveyed, as far as we can at prefent trace them, the firft fteps of Smyth's advancement. We muft now view him in a higher fphere, to which the kindnefs of his Sovereign, having had trial of his abilities, took an early opportunity to raife him.

The fee of Lichfield and Coventry, or, as it was then more ufually ftyled, Coventry and Lichfield, became vacant by the death of John Hales, December 30, 1490[a], and on the 30th of March following, the King by writ of privy Seal, dated from Canterbury,

---

[a] Godwin de Præfulibus, ed Richardfon, p 322. Hales appears to have been a contributor towards the building of St Mary's church in Oxford Ep 401 in Reg F is addreffed to him on that occafion, and Ep 417 to his executors, requefting the payment of his promifed benefaction of 20l.

com-

committed the cuftody of the temporalties
to William Smyth, by the ftyle of " Our beloved and faithful Counfellor, Dean of our
free Chapel within our Palace at Weftminfter[b]." How foon he was elected in form
does not appear, except that it was before
the 10th of July, 1492[c]; and confequently
before the bull of provifion came over, which
was not iffued at Rome till October 1, in
that year[d]. The time and place of his confecration are uncertain. The Archbifhop's
difpenfation, for the facred rite to be performed out of the church of Canterbury, was
procured December 30, 1492[e], and it has
been faid, he was confecrated on the fecond
of April following. But this is a miftake.
For he gave inftitution, which implies that
he had plenary poffeffion of all his rights,
fpiritual and temporal, on the fifteenth of

[b] Roils, Pat 6 H vii Rymer, xii 439

[c] See a grant of lands of that date (7 H vii) to Will Smyth
elect of Cov and Lichf Univ Arch S E Prefs, K 2 9

[d] Reg. Morton, f 15 b. Free permiffion to confult thefe
records was obligingly granted by the Rev Dr Lort, late Librarian at Lambeth , to whom I was introduced by my honoured Tutor, the Rev Houftonne Radcliffe, D D then domeftic Chaplain to his Grace the Archbifhop of Canterbury,
now Prebendary of Canterbury and Vicar of Gillingham in
Kent.

[e] Hift Lichf. in Angl Sacr. 1 454 Godwin, p 323 n 1.

March,

March, 1492-3[f]. His regifter, which ftyles
him in the cuftomary form of the times,
" William by the grace of God Bifhop of
Coventry and Lichfield[g]," commences February 11, in the fame year. And, earlier ftill,
the reftitution of the temporalties, the laft of
all the preliminaries neceffary to full and final poffeffion, was granted by writ of privy
Seal, dated at Weftminfter, 29 January,
8 Henry vii, 1492-3[h], and writs in the ufual
form were directed to the Chamberlain of
Chefter and the Efcheators of the crown in
the feveral counties, wherein the property of
the fee lay[i].

Again, if we look further back, the inftrument which conftitutes John More and Thomas Reynalde his vicars general, runs in the
name of " William Smyth bifhop of Coventry and Lichfield Elect and confirmed[k]." It

[f] Reg Lichf vol xiii f 140
[g] Ibid f 139
[h] Rolls, Pat 8 H vii Rymer, xii 514
[i] Rymer, ibid.
[k] Reg Lichf f. 138 Willis (Cath ii 442) makes More
(who was Dr in canon law) prebendary of Flixton, Lichfield,
Feb 28, 1492; but his appointment to be vicar general the
preceding month indicates, that he had a ftall there before
that time T. Reynalde, LL B was prebendary of Pipe parva, May 21, 1471 (ibid 457) of Oloughton Decani, Jan 27,
1471 (468) of Bobenhull, Apr 17, 1473 (428) of Cur-
borough,

is dated 12 January, 1492, and fealed with
the feal[1] of the deanery of St Stephen's,
which he ftill held.   As yet therefore he was
not confecrated, and confequently his confecration muft have taken place between the
twelfth and the twenty-ninth of January,
1492-3.   He was probably confecrated in his
own chapel of St. Stephen's, as Courtney, bifhop of Exeter, one of his predeceffors in the
deanery, had been not many years before[m].

It appears by this account, that the fee
was vacant full two years, before Smyth was
invefted with all the epifcopal powers   To
what caufe this was owing is uncertain.   If
we were fure, that he was an undergraduate
in Oxford in 1478, he might not yet have
attained the epifcopal age   But this is very

oorough, Sept 1, 1475 (432) and of Wellington, Dec 4,
1488 (473) of which he died poffeffed, about 1497, when he
was fucceeded by Adam Grafton, LL B whom Smyth had
collated to a prebend of St Chads, Salop, Jan 26, 1494
Reg L chf f 155 b
    [1] For the feal, which has, I believe, never been engraved,
fee the mifcellaneous plate   It is from an impreffion, the only
one known, in the Archives of Brafen Nofe college, Drawer 3,
Box infcribed " Cold Norton ' The impreffion is unfortunately
mutilated, but the moft material parts remain, exhibiting, as
I prefume, tne protomartyr St Stephen, and a group of figures
praying to him
    [m] Godwin, p 414.

                                              doubt-

doubtful. The more probable ground of delay was fome difficulty in procuring the bull of provifion from Rome; for it was not the policy of that court to afford quick difpatch, in their beft humour, and when there was no averfion to the bufinefs in hand. In the mean time, that the want of epifcopal fuperintendence might be lefs fenfibly felt, Archbifhop Morton vifited the diocefe in the firft year of the vacancy[n], and, towards the clofe of the fecond year, holy orders were adminiftered two fucceffive days (the number of candidates being too large to be difpatched in one) by a fuffragan bifhop, duly commiffioned[o], with the privity and advice per-

---

[n] Parker Ant Brit in Vita Morton

[o] Ric Epifc Olonenfis [fub archiep Patracenfi in Græcia] Reg Lichf f 136 b The pious and learned Dean Colet was ordained deacon in 1497 by John Epifc Olonenfis Knight's Colet, p 22 n p The account of Suffragan Bifhops in England, and Bifhops in partibus infidelium, by Lewis, Pegge, &c. Biblioth Topogr No xxviii Nichols, 1785, mentions no fuffragans of Lichfield or of Lincoln during Smyth's time to the lifts therefore, which are there given, thefe additions may be made Lichfield, 1494, 1495 Thomas (Fort) Achadenfis Epifc [Achonry, in Ireland] Reg Lich f 178–189 b Lincoln, the faid Thomas Achadenfis (of whom more hereafter) 1495–1504 During which period he ordains at Oxford, Banbury, Stamford, Sleaford, Lincoln, Leicefter, Lidington, Northampton, and Buckden Thomas Rathlurens [fub Archiep Armach] ordains at Buckden in 1496, deputed by the Vicar general

Auguftin

haps of the Bishop elect. As soon as the custody of the temporalties was given to Smyth
by the Crown, (which were not often, as in
this case, committed to the destined Bishop
himself,) the patronage of the see, by virtue
of that grant, became vested in him, and, in
consequence, the person whom he made
choice of for the first dignity which he had
to bestow, was Sampson Alyne, Chancellor
of Hereford, whom he presented to the prebend of Dornford in the cathedral of Lichfield, November 24, 1492[p]; and two years
afterwards he gave him the mastership of St.
John's Hospital in that city[q].

Augustin Lidensis [of Lydda in Palestine] 1501–1511, at Bigglefwade, Bedford, Buckden, Lidington, Lincoln, Bishop's Woburn, Wycombe, Thame, Oxford, and Banbury John Maionen-
sis [sub archiep Nazaren] 1506–1513 at Buckden, Lincoln,
and Lidington Hence it appears, that, in the larger dioceses, there
was often more than one suffragan at the same time, and I believe
the same suffragan often was commissioned by several bishops to
exercise his functions in their respective dioceses, or in certain
districts of them Of the curious and learned dissertation on
this subject above mentioned see some corrections in Gent
Mag. 1791, p 1088 from a copy of the late John Loveday's,
esquire, L in the notes being his initial He died universally
and deeply regretted, May 16, 1789

[p] Per honorabilem virum M W Smyth Cov et Lichf
elect says the register, vol. xiii f 135 b. Willis, Cath. ii
435 543.

[q] June 3, 1494 Reg Lichf. f 145 b He died the same
year.

The care of his diocefe, from the moment he ftood in the important relation of a fpiritual father to it, feems to have engaged his whole attention ; and though his confecration was in the depth of winter, he repaired to his charge with all convenient fpeed. Of his firft arrival at Lichfield, and of his inthronization, I find no memorial. On the thirteenth of February he was in London[r]; and on the twenty-eighth of the fame month at Colefhill[s] in Warwickfhire. In the interval probably he had, either in perfon or by proxy, taken poffeffion of his cathedral, and received the cuftomary homage of the chapter ; for he was now employed in bufinefs of higher moment than matters of ceremony and parade. It was the Ember week in Lent ; and on Saturday (at that time, for no very obvious reafon, the ufual day of ordination[t])

year, before September 21 ib f 146 He was Bachelor of Canon law

[r] Reg Lichf f 157

[s] Ibid f 143.

[t] " Die fabbati in vigilia Pafche," " die fabbati in vigilia S. Trinitatis," &c I have noted in Smyths Lichfield and Lincoln regifters above an hundred ordinations, by him and his fuffragans, uniformly on Saturday , with the exception only of a few inftances, where the regifters or my extracts do not fix the day Sabbatum, the known appellation of the *laft* day of the week (Hor Sat 1 1 ix 69 Juv vi 158 Perf v 184)

not

he admitted, in the conventual church of
Tutbury in Staffordſhire, no leſs a number
than two hundred and three candidates to
the different orders of Acolytes, Subdeacons,
Deacons, and Prieſts[u]. He held a public ordination, at the two enſuing cuſtomary ſea-
ſons, in the cathedral at Lichfield[x], when
the numbers were nearly as great as before.
We may hence form ſome idea of the vaſt
body of eccleſiaſtics in thoſe days, when a
ſingle dioceſe, not larger in extent, nor more

not as modern ſectariſts affectedly call the *firſt* or Lord's day
" ſabbath day," was retained or adopted by the early Chriſ-
tians The Roman names of the other days were continued, I
preſume, as being much more commodious than the Jewiſh
circumlocution, " The Third day of the week," " The Fourth,
&c " And it has been remarked as a very curious circumſtance, that not only our anceſtors in the weſt of Europe, but
the nations in the extremity of the eaſt, denominated the days
by the names of the ſame pagan divinities, and in the ſame
order, as the Romans did See in Brit Crit vol iii p 158
iv 414 ix. 234 As to the more direct object of this note,
doubtleſs the validity of a ſacred ordinance does not depend on
the circumſtance of the day, upon which it is adminiſtered,
but yet it is a ſingular trait in the character of the times, that
banquets, dances, interludes, and diſguiſings, the pompous en-
tertainments then in vogue were commonly given (as at Prince
Arthur's marriage, Add in Lel Coll v 352, &c MS Tanner, 85 p 142—145) on the appropriate day of Chriſtian
worſhip, while the ſolemn act of ordaining paſtors was performed on a week day

[u] Reg Lichf i 17.   [x] Ibid f 172 b. 174

popu-

populous, nor more plentifully fprinkled with
religious houfes, than feveral others, required
an annual recruit of many hundreds.

Having admitted proper minifters into the
Church, his next attention was directed to
thofe, who already filled the facred offices;
from whofe lips, efpecially when the art of
printing was yet in its infancy, and the Scriptures were locked up in an unknown tongue,
the people at large were to receive what they
knew of the word of life. He firft vifited
the Regular and Monaftic clergy, which
was a meafure fuggefted partly by refpect,
and partly by policy. It was a juft compliment to thefe privileged bodies, that he waited upon them before he attended the parochial clergy, and at the fame time he was
ftudious to preferve his jurifdiction over them.
The bifhops were the ordinary vifitors of all
the religious houfes within their diocefe, but
the monks, affluent, ftubborn, and defigning,
were perpetually on the watch for any opportunity or pretence of exempting themfelves from epifcopal controul. They often
refifted the bifhops in the exercife of their
authority; and often appealed to the Pope
againft their decrees and injunctions[y]

[y] Of this long fubfifting controverfy, and of the oppofite

Aware of thefe difputes, and anxious for the injured peace of the Church, Smyth fet himfelf without delay to vifit the monaf-teries. He began in March, and, in the courfe of the year, vifited moft of the confi-derable convents and principal towns in his diocefe. In the intervals of his progrefs he refided fometimes at his palace in Lichfield, and fometimes at the epifcopal feats of Beau-defert and Pipe, nor does it appear, that, during the fpace of twelve months after his advancement, he ever went beyond the boun-daries of his diocefe.

His favourite refidence feems to have been Beaudefert, a charming fpot, as the name in-timates, in the neighbourhood of Lichfield. The caftle hill there, Plot fays, commands a view of nine counties[z]. But the profpect, three centuries ago, if equally pleafing, was probably lefs extenfive, as the country then abounded in wood, and the large adjacent plain of Cank-wood, on which fcarcely a tree is to be feen, was a perfect foreft, one of the

decrees and ineffectual attempts of popes and councils to com-pofe it, fee a curious account in Stillingfleet's Idolatry of the Church of Rome, 2d ed. 1671. p 352, &c.

[z] Staff ch 11 § 14

bifhop's

bifhop's manors, given to the fee by Edward the firft for a free chace[a], which was fuperintended by an officer ftyled the Rider of Cank-wood[b].

He refided much at Pipe alfo, another epifcopal manor near Lichfield[c], but feldom occupied by the bifhops, and therefore not noticed in the common accounts of this fee. About the time when a valuation of all ecclefiaftical benefices throughout England was made by order of pope Nicolas, William Booth, bifhop of Lichfield, by letter dated June 15, 1448, acquainted his Holinefs, that

[a] May 28, 18 Edw 1 (1290) Dugd Mon iii 236 "Bofcos de alto Canoko," of which the boundaries are defcribed It appears by the grant to have belonged to the bifhops of Lichfield before, but the King's itinerant juftices had feized it for his Majefty's ufe I remember to have feen fomewhere in Dugd Mon a royal grant 7 H iii of 12 hinds from the foreft of Cank

[b] Concedimus duos bigatus feu quadrigatus lignorum focalium de nemore noftro vulgariter appellato ly Cankwode—quos officiarius nofter—ly Ryder of Cankwode—deliberabit Reg. Lichf f 169 b William Smyth was made Ranger of the feven " heyes" within the foreft of Cank 22 H vii 2; Nov (1506) and Ranger of the foreft of Cank, 4 June, 22 H vii. (1507) Patents in the Rolls

[c] Rob de Pipe tenet magnam Pipe per fervicium quarte partis unius feodi militis, &c Extent manerior Epifcopi Lichf 26 Ed v MS. Afhm. 864 f 10 b

the

the caftles and palaces, attached to his bi-
fhopric, were more in number than were
neceffary for ufe, or convenient to repair out
of the revenues of the fee, and requefted
the direction of the foveicign pontif on the
occafion   The pope in confequence iffued a
bull, dated September 1, 1450, in which he
decrees, that the palace in Coventry, the palace in Lichfield, the caftle and manor of
Ecclefhal, the manor of Heywode, the manor of Beaudefeit, and the manfion in the
Strand near London, are fufficient for the
bifhops of Coventry and Lichfield, and that
they fhall not be obliged to build, repair, or
fuftain any other[d]

In this curious pontifical refcript Pipe is
not mentioned, and of the manfions which
are fpecified there are fome which do not
appear to have been occupied by Smyth,
during the few years of his continuance in
the fee   Moft of them, together with many
other ample eftates, the donations of ancient
piety, were alienated in the reigns of Edward vi, and Elizabeth : and in lieu of them
a few meagre impropriations were given to
the fee   Beaudefert was granted by the

[d] Reg Lichf x f 53 b —55

Crown

Crown to an anceftor of the Earl of Ux-
bridge, and ftill continues in that noble family The palace in Lichfield, at the north-
eaft angle of the clofe, was fpacious and
fplendid. Bifhop Langton, who built it, commanded the great hall, an hundred feet long
and fifty-fix broad[e], to be painted with the coronation, marriages, wars, and funeral of his
patron, Edward the firft which fumptuous
decorations of this ftately room were probably frefh and unimpaired in Smyth's time ,
fince many of the figures, " very lively pour-
trayed, with their banners of arms bravely
before them," and writing defcriptive of the
fubjects reprefented, were remaining fo late
as the time of Erdefwicke's furvey, 1603[f].
Eccleshal, which when Domefday was tak-
en was in the bifhop's tenure, and had been
held by St Chad in the feventh century, is
judged to have been part of the original endowment of the fee[g].

As to the London refidence of the bifhops

[e] See the Ichnography of this palace in MS Tanner, 217
f 54 and fketches of its ruins, ibid f 66

[f] Erdefwicke s Staff 1723 p 101 Gough's Topogr 1768
p 485 Warton s Hift of Poet ii 216

[g] Pegge's Hift and Antiq of Eccleshal, Biblioth Topogr.
Num. xxi Plot s Staff x § 83

of Lichfield, ftyled in Smyth's regifter, " his houfe without the Bars of the New Temple, London," it was commonly called " Chefter Place[h];" and under that title was affured by act of parliament, 31 Henry viii, to Edward earl of Hertford, to whom the King had made a grant of it, having wrefted it from the fee without any compenfation[i]. The earl, who was created Duke of Somerfet, 1 Edward vi, (1546,) built a magnificent houfe on the fite, and when the popular tide began to turn againft this favourite of fortune, among other things which aggravated the general odium, it is remarked by a grave author, that " many well difpofed minds conceived a very hard opinion of him for caufing a church near Strand Bridge and two bifhops' houfes to be pulled down, to make a feat for his new building, called Somerfet Houfe[k]." Yet what Fuller, with his ufual quaintnefs, obferves of this houfe, perhaps may deferve mentioning. that it is " fo

[h] Chefter Place without Temple Barre Rot Parl MS Harl 22 f 208 b.

[i] So Spelman, Reliq p 212 and after him Strype, in Stowes Survey, b iv p 105 But in the Cotton Library, Vefpafian, E xvi 2 there is a note, which fays, " the Bifhop had in recompens the parfonage of Hanberry Com Staff "

[k] Dugd Baron ii 363

tena-

tenacious of the name" of this celebrated but
unfortunate Duke, " though he was not full
five years poffeffed of it, that it would not
change a dutchy for a kingdom, when folemnly proclaimed by king James, Denmark
Houfe, from the King of Denmark's lodging
therein, and his fifter queen Anne her repairing thereof[1]." The name ftill furvives;
and if a building, the moft beautiful perhaps
and the moft ample, that ever was dedicated
by a wealthy nation to the elegant arts and
civil police, carried on without intermiffion
during a moft expenfive war, when Europe
and America were leagued againft Britain,
if thefe circumftances can give immortality
to human operations, and fecure a place in
the page of faithful hiftory, Somerfet Houfe
will be known by the lateft ages, to the honour of a patriotic Monarch, and a brave, generous, and loyal people

This fhort account of the fate or fame of
thefe houfes, the feats of bifhop Smyth's occafional refidence, if not a neceffary part of
our hiftory, will appear, I hope, a pardonable
digreffion. We muft now turn our attention

[1] Church Hift b vii p 410 with 407 and b v p 357
xi 119

E 4   to

to other matters, and view the Bifhop in a
civil department, Prefident of the Prince's
Council within the Marches of Wales. As
this was an office of great honour and confequence, and the notices refpecting it, in our
moft approved hiftorians, are full of miftakes,
I fhall, on this firft occafion of mentioning it,
bring into one connected view the beft account of it, which I have been able to collect

SECT III.

Prefident of Wales

———

OUR writers are unanimous in fixing Smyth's appointment to the Prefidency of Wales in the feventeenth year of Henry vii, which commences Auguft 22, 1501; but we have indubitable evidence, that he prefided in the Prince's Council in the Marches of Wales, " fome years" before that time[a]. The fact therefore, with its introductory fteps, probably was as follows.

From the moment that Henry vii came to the crown, his liege fubjects and kinfmen, the Welfh, peculiarly engaged his royal attention, and, the better to fecure the peace

[a] Cujus [fc illuftriflimi Principis Arthuri] Confiliariorum Prefidentis officium—regebat, prout nonnullis retroactis annis laudabiliter rexerat. 10 Jun 1500 Act Capit Linc F f 167.

and

and welfare of the principality, various grants
and commiffions were iffued in the firft year
of his reign. Sir William Stanley, brother
to the Earl of Derby, was made Juftice of
North Wales[b], and Jafper, duke of Bedford,
of South Wales[c], who alfo, with others, had
a commiffion to hear and determine caufes in
Wales and the marches thereof[d]. At the
fame time Sir Richard Pole, coufin german
to Henry vii, and father of the celebrated
cardinal Pole, was appointed Conftable of
Hardlogh caftle and Sheriff of the county of
Merioneth for life[e], and in 1491 he was

[b] Pat 2 Feb 1 H vii (1485-6) Cotton Lib Cleopatra,
C iii f 370 b The ufual fee was 50l but as a mark of favour to Sir W Stanley, who turned the fortune of the day, and
put Richards crown on the head of Richmond in Bofworth
field, the office was granted to him for life with a fee of 133l
8s 8d Perc, Lagerbies Cambria Triumphans, ed 1661.
p 339 He was not however fuffered to enjoy it long, as he
was beheaded in a fit of jealoufy about Perkin Warbeck, on
Tower-hill Feb 16 1494-5 See his trial, MS More, 703
[Ee 3 1]

[c] Pat 13 Dec 1 H vii Cleopatra, ut fupra

[d] Pat 28 Feb 1 H vii ibid f 380 He had alfo a commiffion, March 11, (fame year) to appoint commiffioners to inquire concerning treafon and mifdemeanors " in diverf comit
infra regnum Anglie ibid and was, with the Earl of Pembroke, conftituted Lieutenant of Ireland fame dates ibid

[e] Pat 26 Feb 1 H vii (1485-6) MS More, 507 [Ii 5
31]

fent into the principality and the marches of
Wales with offers of the King's grace and
pardon to all perfons guilty or fufpected of
treafon[f]. The next year prince Arthur, who
had been created Prince of Wales and Earl
of Chefter, was made Guardian of the kingdom, during his father's abfence in the wars
in France[g]. Shortly afterwards he was included in a commiffion of the peace for the
county of Warwick, with archbifhop Morton, Smyth bifhop of Lichfield, and others[h];

31] f 32 Hardleigh Caftle in the county of Merioneth, on
the bay of Cardigan Sir John Dodridge fays, the Conftable's
fee was 50l Hift of Princip of Wales, &c 1630, p 71
which however he thinks was for both offices of Conftable and
Captain, the feparate fee of the former being 26l 13s 4d ib
p 58

[f] Pat 21 June, 6 H vii 1491 Rolls' Chapel

[g] Pat 8 H vii 1492 Rymer xii p 487 T rege ap Do-
vorr, 2 Oct The Prince was now fix years and twice as many
days old, for he was born at Winchefter "on St Euftas day
[Sept 20] 1486, 2 H vii," and chriftened the Sunday following The Earl of Derby was one of the godfathers, and gave
a rich falt of gold covered MS Harl 7048 p 504 from
Julius xii Add to Lel Coll iv p 204, &c Mr Warton
(Hift of Poet ii 422 n a) mentions fome elegant Latin
verfes by one John Opicius, our countryman as it feems, "De
regis Hen Sept in Galliam progreffu MS Cotton, Vefpafian, B iv They begin,

"Bella canant alii Trojae, proftrataque dicant"

[h] Pat 10 Feb 8 H vii 1492–3 MS Dugd O f 266 b
This patent was renewed, 10 Apr. 9 H vii 1494 and again,

and was then, 20 March, 1492-3, conftituted his Majefty's Juftice in the counties of Salop, Hereford, and Gloucefter, and the marches of Wales adjoining, to inquire of all liberties, privileges, and franchifes, poffeffed or claimed by any perfon, which were to be feized into the Kings hands , and of all efcapes and felons , and thefe inquifitions, taken from time to time, were to be certified into chancery[1]. The fame commiffion alfo gave him power to fubftitute proper perfons under him, for the better and more effectual execution of the delegated truft By virtue of this charter, a council, it is prefumed, was appointed for the Prince, in which, whoever were his co-adjutors, bifhop Smyth prefided , but the patents of office, if extant, have eluded inquiry.

It was in confequence probably of reports made by thofe who acted under this commiffion, that foon afterwards, October 14, 11 Henry vii, 1495, an act of refumption was paffed, to make void divers leafes, granted for lives or a term of years, under the

10 H vii ib.a f 267, 267 b. Smyth was in London, 11 and 13 Feb 1492-3 Reg Lichf f 157

Dodridge, ut fupra, p 28, &c

feals

feals aforetime ufed within the principality; but which, to the Prince's detriment, were held at a lefs rent, than they might reafonably be fet for[k] This act of refumption, it is moft likely, Smyth was affifting in carrying into effect, when he affigned as a reafon for appointing a vicar general, February 1, 1495-6, that "he was obliged to be abfent from his diocefe fome time in" the fervice "of the Prince of Wales[l]" As to the act itfelf, which in better days would hardly have been carried, it was foftened in its rigour, and rendered more palatable, partly by allowing the former tenants the firft option of renewal, and partly by exceptions and provifions to fecure the right of many favoured individuals.

Another circumftance, connected with the Prince's court, under this its firft eftablifh-

[k] Parl Rolls, vol vi p 465 MS Harl 22 f 120

[l] Reg Linc f 2 b I have fupplied the word "fervice," a word or words to that effect being omitted in the Regifter, both in this and a fimilar commiffion, 10 Jan 1499–1500 Ibid f 118 In another inftrument, "In *obfequus* fereniff' Principis, occurs, (MS Harl 6953 p 75) which is probably the word wanted above We find Smyth at Bewdley, 27 April, 1494 (Reg Lichf f 157 b) and it appears that he refided principally there and at Ludlow, during the remainder of that and the following year

ment,

ment, muſt not be omitted.   In 1498, Thomas Smith of Cheſter, merchant, ſervant of
Arthur prince of Wales, intending at the
approaching vintage in Bourdeaux to provide
a large ſtock of wine of Gaſcony for the uſe
of his royal Highneſs, had leave given him,
by writ of privy Seal, to import a hundred
pipes to the city of Cheſter for that purpoſe[m].
There can be little doubt, this merchant was
the Thomas Smyth above mentioned[n] as a
kinſman of the lord Preſident, whom he
afterwards conſtituted one of his executors,
ſtyling him expreſsly, Thomas Smyth, merchant of Cheſter.   The Prince himſelf perhaps was the bearer of this royal grant, for
he viſited Cheſter a fortnight afterwards (Auguſt 14,) and was ſumptuouſly entertained at
the city's experce.   Juſts were exhibited;
and the play or myſtery of the Aſſumption
was acted before him at the Abbey gate
When he had kept his court here a full
month, he took his leave of the city with
great affection and reſpect, September 19,

---

[m] Brit. Muſ. Donation MS 4618 p 31   T Rege ap
Weſtm 27 Jul 13 H vii   It was ordered by a late ſtatute
(4 H vii c 10) that " no Gaſcoin or Guion wine ſhould be
brought into this realm, but by Engliſh ſhips, and Engliſh
maſters   A ſimilar injunction was made 1 H vii c 9.
   [n] P 2

having

having conferred on the Mayor, Richard
Goodman, merchant, the rank of Esquire[o].

When this provincial government had stood
the trial of some years, it is natural to conclude, that it was found to be in some re-
spects capable of improvement. The powers
therefore of the former commission were re-
modeled and renewed. From the date of
this second appointment, 17 Henry vii, and
not before, the historians assign the Prince
a regular council, which was composed, as
they observe, of men of wisdom and experience, that the Heir apparent of the
throne might from his youth be acquainted
with good government[p]. The whole number was ten; six of them knights, Sir Henry
Vernon, Sir Richard Crofts, Sir David Phi-
lips, Sir William Udall, Sir Thomas Engle-
field, Sir Peter Newton, with the forenamed
Sir Richard Pole at their head, in quality of
chief Chamberlain, John Wilson and Henry
Marian, gentlemen, and Smyth, at this time
bishop of Lincoln, lord President Charles
Bothe, afterwards bishop of Hereford, was
Chaplain to the council, or, as Godwin calls
him, Chancellor of the marches[q].

[o] Chester Coll. Dr Cowper, p 182.
[p] Pol Verg. p 610.   [q] Godwin, p 493.

Smyth

Smyth is commonly ftyled the firft Prefident of Wales, which is not ftrictly true.
He is the firft, whofe name is found in the
records, and had the honour of filling the
office, when it firft received a regular form
and permanent eftablifhment, but others, in
preceding reigns, had occafionally been entrufted with fimilar powers.

It was the policy of the Conqueror to
place fome of his Norman nobles on the
confines of Wales to awe or to fubdue " a
nation proud in arms';" and, for their accommodation, eftates in other parts were
granted on condition of providing foldiers,
one or more, to ferve in the marches⁵. Each
of thefe barons marchers (as they were called)
had a kind of palatine or fovereign jurifdiction
in his territory: the vaffals were amenable
to the baron, the baron to the King Henry
the firft, in the ninth year of his reign, fent

˗ Milton, Comus, 50.

ˢ Gent Mag 1797 p 826. Thefe lordfhips marchers were
taken away by ftatute 27 H viii and made fhire ground,
being annexed to counties of England or Wales Lord Bacon
on the Jurifd of the Marches, Works, Lond 1765 4to vol ii
p 477 The word marches, he obferves, " fignifieth no more
but limits, or confines, or borders," whence " was derived at
the firft marchio, a marquis, which was comes limitaneus "

Richard

Richard de Beaumis, bifhop of London, to be Lieutenant or Prefident of the marches; and he continued a long while at Shrewf-bury[t]. In 18 Edward iv John Alcock, bi-fhop of Worcefter, a predeceffor of Smyth's in the deanery of St. Stephen's, was his pre-deceffor alfo as Prefident of the Prince's council in the marches, and he, with An-tony earl Rivers, uncle and governour to the Prince, made at Shrewfbury certain ordi-nances for the welfare and tranquillity of that town[u].

Thefe were the occafional and preparatory fteps to this government, when Henry vii gave the inftitution fhape and ftability, and appointed the council already mentioned; though the nature and extent of the powers with which he invefted them do not feem precifely afcertained by thofe who have writ-ten on the fubject. For the ordinary admi-

[t] MS More, 390 f 115 " as appeareth in Cronicle of the Princes of Wales," the MS fays

[u] Ibid " as appeareth by Records of the towne hall of Sa-lope—10 Apr 18 Edw iv " This " firft Council of the Marches, it is conceived, began in or about 17 Edw iv Do-dridge, p 38 But Earl Rivers, the Queen's brother, was ap-pointed Governour to the Prince 13 Edw iv, and had been, to-gether with the faid John Alcock, of the Prince's council from July 8, 11 Edw iv ibid p 24, 25

F   niftration

niſtration of the laws, courts of aſſize, and
gaol delivery, were holden, as formerly, at
Caernarvon for north Wales, and at Caermar-
then for ſouth Wales, and ſometimes in the
ſeveral counties, by the juſtices of the two
provinces reſpectively. With theſe matters,
and in this form, it does not appear that the
Preſident and council of the marches inter-
fered, except in ſuch cauſes as were ſpecially
aſſigned to them by the King's Majeſty. In
general they appear rather to have proceeded
in a ſummary way, as a council, to repreſs
riots and miſdemeanors by examination, fine,
and impriſonment, without a formal trial.

Perhaps queen Elizabeth and the incomparable ſtateſmen of her court, aided by the
experience of more than half a century, in
ſome reſpects improved upon Henry's ſyſ-
tem, but the outline, without queſtion, was
the ſame in both : and from her inſtructions
to the Earl of Pembroke*, lord Preſident,
with other collateral information, ſomewhat
may be added to the common accounts of
this local government.

* Cotton MS Titus, b viii p 1—44. dat 1586 Compare
lord Bridgewater's commiſſion, temp Car 1 Rymer xix p 449
—465

A mace

A mace of majefty was borne before the
Prefident by a ferjeant at arms [y], as before
the lord Chancellor, and the Speaker of the
Houfe of Commons. Three of the council,
the Prefident or Vice-Prefident being neceffarily one, conftituted a Quorum for ordinary
bufinefs ; but four were to fit at every council in term time. The feffions in Hilary and
Michaelmas terms were holden at Ludlow ;
but at other times, as well in term as vacation, at any place within the principality
or marches, where they thought proper. Errors in pleas perfonal, complaints of perjury,
of falfe imprifonment, and of unjuft poffeffion were heard and rediefied by the Prefident and council [z] ; and the precepts and
warrants, which they iffued, were current
through the whole principality [a]. They were
included in every commiffion of peace for
Wales, and the lord lieutenants of counties,
the fheriffs, the efcheators of the crown, and
other officers were appointed with their advice [b] In litigations concerning property,
which lay in the principality or the marches,

[y] Guillim's Heraldry, 1724 p 287
[z] 26 H viii. c. 4 c 6. §. 2. 34 & 35 H viii. c 26 §.
102 113
[a] 34 & 35 H viii c. 26. § 62, 63. 124.
[b] Ibid § 54, 55. 61 66.

the

the caufe was remitted by the courts in Weftminfter to the Prince's council[c], unlefs the
plaintiff were neceffarily attendant upon his
Majefty's court; in which cafe the defendant
might be fummoned to anfwer in town; but
not otherwife[d]. When a jury was impanneled,
it confifted, as in England, of twelve men;
and it was wifely ordered, that, in the
marches, fix of them fhould be Welfh, and
fix Englifh[e].

The Prefident adminiftered an oath of office to the other members of the council[f],
and he with the aid of the court thus
formed, affifted by their fubordinate officers
and furnifhed with a feal of office[g], had the

---

[c] Dockets of Council, p 52 64 7 H viii &c
[d] Ibid p 115, 116 3 & 4 Phil. & Mar
[e] Dugd Orig Jurid p 64
[f] Cotton MS ut fupra, p 44 Rymer, ut fupra, p 463
[g] See an engraving of one temp Car ii in Gent Mag
1796 p 185 "A fpecial feal, named the feal of the marches,'
was abolifhed, and " the broad feal ordered inftead, 4 H vii.
c 14 But this regarded folely, as the act expreffes, grants to
be made by the King of any parcel of the earldom of March,
which earldom was then in the crown, and did not conftitute
part of the eftates of the Prince of Wales, till it was granted,
or a principal part of it called the lordfhip of Wigmore, to
the Prince, to be held of the King during his pleafure, at the
annual rent of 200l by patent, Nov 5, 9 H vii (1493) Do-
dridge, p 30. Compare p 16 A clerk of the Signet was one of
the

management of the eftates, rents, and fines, appendant to the princıpality. From the revenues thus accruıng to the Prınce's fervıce the lord Prefident was allowed twenty pounds a week, for a table for hımfelf and the councıl, wıth the addıtıon of a hundred marks for other expences[h]. The ftıpend of the Chaplain, who was to be a Mafter of Arts at leaft, was fifty pounds, and board for hımfelf and fervants.

Such, as far as appears, was the plan and conftıtutıon of the court of the marches: whıch was ıntended, as lord Bacon obferves, to brıdle and controul the prıncıpalıty; to make a better equalıty of commerce and ıntercourfe between Wales and England, and to furnıfh a convenıent dıgnıty and ftate for the manfıon and refıdence of the King's eld-

---

the officers of the prefident and councıl ıbıd p 54   Rıchard Smyth and Margery hıs wıfe, tenants by patent under the feal of the earldom of March, were faved ın the aɛt of refumption, 1 H vıı Rolls Parl vı p 374

[h] Cotton MS ut fupra, p 24   In Haward (Charges of Engl and Wales, p 17) and Peck (Defid Cur ıı 52) the ftıpend ıs only 1040l and fo MS. Afhm 821 f 8 b temp Jac 1 when lord Every was prefident   Whıch yet ıs more oy 40l than the prefident of the north had   Dodrıdge however (p 76) makes "the allowance of the dyet of the Councell of the Marches 1106l 13s 4d '

eft

eft Son[1]. Some few matters connected with this provincial government, while Smyth was the prime agent and mover in it, will be mentioned as they occur in the courfe of our narrative. At prefent it is only neceffary to add, that the lord Prefidents and council, the guardians of peace, were the patrons alfo of genius and of literature. The court of the accomplifhed prince Arthur was graced with a conftellation of learned men[k], and when the Mufes awoke from the long flumber of the dark ages, Ludlow caftle, with its romantic views and enchanting fcenery, became one of their favourite haunts, and the prefidency was " married to immortal verfe." Milton in his Comus adorned it with " a crown of deathlefs praife[1]," and Butler, Steward of Ludlow and Secretary to the Earl of Carbery, lord Prefident, the celebrated patron of the excellent Jeremy Taylor, wrote his inimitable Hudibras within its walls.

[1] Jurifd of the Marches, as above, p 479

[k] Linacre, Bernard Andree, &c

[1] Comus, ver 973   Mr Warton, in his admirable edition of the Comus and leffer poems of Milton, defcribes Ludlow caftle with the congenial feelings and tafte of a true poet See p 112 of the firft ed or 123 of the fecond edition See alfo, for fome lords Prefidents, ibid and on verfe 34, and likewife his L of Sir T Pope, p 245 with 191 218 fecond edit.

SECT.

SECT IV.

Founder of St. John's Hospital, Lichfield.

———

THOUGH Smyth was thus engaged in the affairs of the Prince of Wales, and, in virtue of his high office, refided for the moft part at Ludlow, or at Bewdley, where a ftately manfion had been built for the Prince's accommodation[a], yet he did not forget or neglect his diocefe. To fupply his abfence on this occafion he deputed Vicars general[b] to give inftitution to benefices, and

[a] " There is a fair manour place weft of Bewdley in a goodly park well wooded, on the knappe of an hill that the towne ftandeth on, called Tikenhill, fomewhat new, and in a manner totally erected by king Henry vii for prince Arthur " Lel Itin vol iv p ii f 183 b It is vefted in the Crown, and is leafed out, together with the manor of Bewdley, to Sir Edward Winnington, baronet Nafh's Worc vol ii p 277 The old palace has been taken down ibid Add and Corr p 30 A handfome modern houfe, built on the fpot, appears in the back ground of the view of Bewdley ibid 274

[b] Two of thefe, Reynalde and More, have been mentioned above, fect ii p 43 Richard Salter, D of Canon Law, is another, who often acts for him in the fame capacity He had

the

appointed a fuffragan bifhop, Thomas Fort[c],
Prior of Stone, in whom he feems to have
repofed great confidence, to adminifter holy
orders, to confecrate churches, and to perform
other epifcopal acts.   Not fatisfied with this,

the prebend of Hanfacre in Lichfield, May 30, 1489 Willis,
Cath ii 449 which he quitted for the Chancellorfhip, May 1,
1501 (407) and that for the Precentorfhip, Feb 14, 1504
(405) in which and the following year he occurs as Principal
of New Inn hall   Woods Colleges, p 678 He was alfo Rector of Stanlake, Oxfordfhire, and adorned the chancel with a
window, 1503 There is a letter to him, about 1490, requefting his aid towards the building of St Mary's church in Oxford, and that he would folicit the affiftance of the Bifhop of
Lichfield (Hales) on the fame occafion   Reg F Ep 399 He
died 1519, and was buried in the cathedral at Lichfield.

[c] Reg Lichf f 139 This Thomas Fort, already mentioned,
fect ii p 45 note o and of whom we fhall hear again, had been
Canon of the Priory of St Mary and St Petroc at Bodmin, in
Cornwall (fee Ware de Præful Hib Dublin, 1665 p 278)
and was confirmed by Bp Smyth Prior of Stone, 26 Aug
1493, on condition of paying a penfion, at the Bifhops appointment, to Robert Wife, the late Prior ibid f 143 b And
the fame day the Bifhop affigned to Robert Wife, late Prior of
Burton, (the fame perfon, I fuppofe,) a penfion of 23l 6s 8d
out of the manor of Stalington belonging to Burton, with
fourteen loaves and fourteen flagons of beer, weekly, from the
convent, fixteen loads of wood, and two loads of coals, called
" ly feecole ," and the entire new building, lately erected by
the faid Wyfe, within the precincts of the Priory ib 144 b
Thomas Maiot was confirmed Abbat of Burton the fame day
ib 144   Fort was inftituted to the rectory of Egmond in
Shropfhire, 1 Feb 1493–4, on the prefentation of the Monaftery of St Peter, Salop ib 155 b

he

he alfo made frequent returns from the frontiers of his diocefe, where the Prince's court generally was kept, into the central parts of the diftrict committed to his care.

One circumftance redounding to his honour fhould be mentioned. He feems to have been particularly careful in examining into the qualifications of thofe, who came to him for inftitution to benefices. During the fhort time that he was bifhop of Lichfield, there are two inftances of perfons, whom he rejected on fuch occafion for infufficiency; and he accordingly collated proper perfons in their ftead It is obfervable, that, in both cafes, the clerks rejected were prefented by monafteries, which gives room to fufpect, that when thofe fhrewd corporations had once fecured to themfelves the profits of a parifh, they were not very folicitous to fulfil the invariable condition, on which appropriations were granted, that a fufficient and able paftor fhould be found for the performance of parochial duties; but that, on the contrary, if the pious vigilance of the diocefan prevented not, fuch churches as were appendant to religious houfes were in danger of being filled with clerks lefs competent than fuch as belonged

longed to other patrons among the laity or
clergy[d].

If thefe circumftances indicated inattention in the Religious to their external con-
cerns, another matter, now to be noticed,
fhewed them culpably negligent within their
own walls St. John's Hofpital in Lichfield
had been fuffered to grow fo ruinous, that

[d] Thefe illiterate clerks were prefented, one by the monaftery
of Repindon or Repton, co Derby, 1494, the other by Beau-
chief, in the fame county, 1495 Reg Lichf f 153, 153 b
Mr Warton, fpeaking of the illiteracy of the inferior clergy,
but at an earlier period than that now before us, fays, the moft
extraordinary anecdote of incompetency which he had feen was
in the cafe of a perfon prefented (as thefe were) by a monaftery, Merton priory in Surrey, to the parifh of Sherfield in
Hampfhire, 1448 The rector, previoufly to his inftitution,
" takes an oath before the bifhop, that on account of his infufficiency n letters, and default of knowledge in the fuperin-
terdence of fouls, he will learn Latin for the two following
years, and at the end of the firft year, he will fubmit himfelf
to be examined by the bifhop, concerning his progrefs in
grammar, and that, if on a fecond examination he fhould be
found deficient, he will refign the benefice " Reg Waynfl f 7
Mr Warton gives other inftances of clerical ignorance and
enormities, and then adds a reflection, which I cannot refift the
pleafure of tranfcribing " From thefe horrid pictures let us
turn our eyes, and learn to fet a juft value on that pure religion, and thofe improved habits of life and manners, which
we at prefent enjoy Hift of Poet ii 428 n z

the

the Bifhop refolved to rebuild and re-endow it on another plan.

The early hiftory of this College, Priory, or Hofpital, is involved in much obfcurity. Bifhop Godwin, in Tanner[e], fays, He had read that Roger, bifhop of Lichfield, was the original founder; and Tanner rather choofes to afcribe it to one of the Rogers (Wefeham or Molend) in the time of Henry iii, than to Roger Clinton in the reign of Stephen. The earlieft notice of it, which has been found in the Lichfield regifters, is during the epifcopate of Northbrough, (1322——1360;) when many Religious were ordained upon titles from this houfe. It was then a Priory of Friars, and fo ill conducted, that the Bifhop found it neceffary, more than once, to interpofe his vifitatorial authority, and the rules which he eftablifhed, and the care which he fhewed on thefe occafions, had they been known to the learned biographer of the Englifh Prelates, might have exempted the memory of Northbrough from the farcafm, with which he concludes his account of him. that, during a long epifcopate, he could difcover nothing which he had done

---

[e] Notit Monaft. ed Nafmith, Staffordfh. xvii. 4

well,

well, unlefs it might be faid to be well that
he died[f].

But whatever might have been done in
this houfe by the vigilance of Northbrough
or his fucceffors, reformation was become
more neceffary than ever, when Smyth came
to the fee   The buildings were dilapidated,
divine offices were omitted, no alms were
beftowed. The good Bifhop therefore, amidft
the variety of important matters which engaged his time and attention, feems to have
formed an early refolution of eftablifhing the
hofpital on fuch a footing, that it might be
lefs likely to fall into abufe or neglect. For
monaftic inftitutions he appears to have entertained no very great affection, and perhaps, with fome others, he had fagacity to
difcover, from the general and incurable and
increafing depravity of the Religious, that
the whole fyftem was haftening to its overthrow[g]. He thereiore determined to appro-

---

[f] Godwin, p 320   For the foregoing particulars, and alfo
for a lift of the Mafters of this Hofpital, contained in the Appendix, Num. iv   I am indebted, through my friend Mr Mott,
Deputy Regiftrar of Lichfield, to the obliging communication
of the Rev Theophilus Buckeridge, the prefent Mafter, who
had taken pains to collect materials for a Hiftory of the Hofpital.

[g] Bale informs us (f 246 b) that he forefaw this approach-

priate his renovated hofpital chiefly to the
benefit of thofe, of whom, whatever revo-

ing event, but the immediate caufes, which produced it, had
then begun to operate Pierce Ploughman, almoft two centuries before, had predicted the fame overthrow in terms fo remarkable, that the cautious Mr Warton fufpected the paffage
to be a forgery, till he found it in manufcripts older than the
year 1400.

    " And *ther fhall come a King*, and confeffe you religious,
    And bete you as the bible telleth, for breking of your rule.—
    And then fhall the abot of Abingdon, and all his iffue for ever,
    Have a knocke of a King, and incurable the wound"

Hift of Poet 1 282 note o where more is quoted, as alfo in
the inftructive Hiftory of Selborne, Hants, by my late ingenious and excellent Friend, the Rev Gilbert White, p 381
But there is a more extraordinary inftance of " old experience
attaining, as Milton fays, to fomething like prophetic ftrain,"
and, as it is on a kindred fubject, and not generally known, the
curious reader will not be difpleafed to have it laid before him.
It is a prediction of the fuppreffion of the Jefuits, by George
Browne, the firft Proteftant archbifhop of Dublin, in a fermon
preached in Chrift Church, Dublin, A D 1551 " There are
a new Fraternity of late fprung up, who call themfelves Jefuits, which will deceive many, who are much after the Scribes
and Pharifees manner amongft the Jews They fhall ftrive to
abolifh the truth, and fhall come very near to do it, for thefe
forts will turn themfelves into feveral forms; with the heathen,
an heathenift, with atheifts, an atheift, with the Jews, a
Jew, and with the reformers, a reformade, purpofely to know
your intentions, your minds, your hearts, and your incli-
nations, and thereby bring you at laft to be like the fool, that
faid in his heart, There was no God Thefe fhall fpread over
the whole world, fhall be admitted into the council of princes,
and they never the wifer, charming of them, yea, making
your princes reveal their hearts, and the fecrets therein unto
               them,

lution might take place in civil focieties or monaftic forms, it was the intention of Heaven, that there never fhould want a fucceffion, while the world endures.

With thefe pious views, and a mind thus capacious, he laid his defign, and began to execute it. The firft ftep towards this was to rebuild the hofpital; which accordingly was accomplifhed before the third year of his confecration expired. In the mean time he was framing and digefting a code of ftatutes for the regulation of the fociety, deriving

them, and yet they not perceive it which will happen from falling from the law of God, by neglect of fulfilling of the law of God, and by winking at their fins Yet in the end, God, to juftify his law, fhall fuddenly cut off this fociety, even by the hands of thofe who have moft fuccour'd them, and made ufe of them, fo that at the end they fhall become odious to all nations · they fhall be worfe than Jews, having no refting-place upon the earth, and then fhall a Jew have more favour than a Jefuit " The Phenix, or a Revival of fcarce and valuable Pieces, &c London, 1707, 8vo vol 1 p 136 For an account of the faid G Browne, fee ibid p 120, &c Hofpinian dates the commencement of the Jefuits from the year 1540 See his Hift Jefuit l i c 1 Tigur 1670 The prophetic bifhop Browne did not forefee, that this pernicious " Society," after they had been " fuddenly" fuppreffed " *by the hands of thofe who had moft fuccour'd them,*" would be fuffered in a *Proteftant country*, in the face of day, and in defiance of law, to reeftablifh themfelves in a College on the high road to the Univerfity of Cambridge ! and in the diocefe of London ! !

probably

probably fome hints from the former rules of the houfe, but the greater part of the ordinances are manifeftly original, adapted to the altered and enlarged plan of the inftitution.

The ftatutes, twenty-nine in number, which he caufed to be inferted in the public regifter of the fee [h], it is not neceffary to detail, but the preamble to them, as it fhews the defign of the Founder, may be properly introduced here. It ftates, that Whereas the mercy of our Lord and Saviour Jefus Chrift, in virtue of his redemption, to remedy the fall from primeval dignity, had inftituted facraments, maffes, prayers, alms, and other works of piety, which might redound to the glory of God, of the Virgin Mary, and of all faints; He therefore, mindful to advance to the utmoft of his power thefe works of piety, and efpecially, under divine Providence, defirous to reform and reftore fuch inftitutions, as the devotion of thofe now deceafed had ordained, but which had long been neglected, to the decreafe of divine worfhip, the detriment of

[h] Reg Smyth, f 148–151 b   There is a tranfcript of thefe Statutes, but with fome omiffions, in MS Afhm 855 f 150, &c.

the

the poor, and the great hazard of many fouls,
and finally wifhing, as far as it was given
him from on high, to accomplifh thefe purpofes of piety and reformation in the Hofpital of St. John Baptift, without the Bars of
the city of Lichfield, proceeds to make the
following ordinances and ftatutes, invoking
firft of all the grace of the Holy Spirit.

The foundation confifts of a Mafter, or
Warden, a Prieft, to be appointed by the bifhop of the diocefe; and, under him, a
Mafter of Grammar, or a perfon profoundly
fkilled in that art; with an ufher', to affift

' " Honeftus vir in fcientia grammaticali fatis peritus, qui
—officium gerat *Hoftiar*, fcholarefque—diligenter doceat '
Stat vi   Hence, I fuppofe, the French *Huiffier*, and our word
Ufher; which formerly bore a nearer refemblance to the
French, if the orthography of the Court was the ftandard of
the times   For his Majefty, Henry vii, fpeaking of " Maifter
Henry Erle," M.A of Oxford, calls him " *Huiffhere* off the gra-
mer fcole withyne owre college of Etone." Letter to the Univerfity of Oxford, dat Wincheftre, 17 Oct (probably 1487)
Reg F Ep. 334. The truth is, till fome time after the Reformation, there was no uniform or confiftent mode of orthography, but writers differed from each other, and from themfelves, in every page and almoft in every line   I have before
me " The honourable pedigree of the *Knightleys*" [of Fawfley,
Northamptonfhire] in which that fhort name has at leaft
36 varieties   This however extends from the conqueft to the
year 1696

him

him in inftructing in grammar, gratis, all
fcholars whatfoever, but efpecially fuch as,
by the indigence of their parents and friends,
are deprived of opportunity of learning and
improvement. There is alfo a Chaplain, to
celebrate divine offices daily in the chapel;
and thirteen Almfmen, bachelors or wi-
dowers.

The Schoolmafter's ftipend is Ten pounds
(the cuftomary and fufficient allowance in
thofe times[k]) the Ufher's Five, the Chaplain's Eight marks, that of the Almfmen a
penny a day. They are all to be appointed
by the Mafter of the hofpital, excepting one
almfman to be nominated by the Prebendary
of Freford. They are to pray for the Founder,
for Henry vii, Elizabeth his Queen, Prince
Arthur, the lady Margaret the King's mother,
Reginald Bray, knight, and his confort Catharine The prayer prefcribed on the occafion, altered from the Miffal, is fo excellent,
that it deferves to be known:

" O God, who by the grace of the Holy

---

[k] The original endowment, as I have been informed, of the
Head Mafter in the ample feminaries at Winchefter, at Eton,
and at Wainfleet, is no more than 10l

Spirit,

Spirit, the Comforter, poureſt the gifts of charity into the hearts of the faithful, Grant to thy ſervant William the biſhop our Founder, and grant to thy ſervants and to thy handmaids, for whom we implore thy clemency, Health of mind and of body, that they may love Thee with all their ſtrength, and with all joyfulneſs perform ſuch things as pleaſe Thee, through Chriſt our Lord   Amen ”

The Founder, “ humbly and devoutly intreating, and in the bowels of Jeſus Chriſt ſolemnly injoining,” the Maſter and others concerned, to obſerve and enforce theſe his ordinances, affixed his ſeal to them at Lichfield, November 3, 1495, in the third year of his conſecration.

While the ſtatutes were receiving his laſt hand, he was concerting meaſures for the endowment of the hoſpital ; that it might be adequate to the maintenance of the enlarged ſociety.   For this purpoſe, in addition to the former revenues of the houſe, whatever they were, he united and appropriated to it the hoſpital of Denhall in Cheſhire, and the chapel of Freford near Lichfield.   The latter was the free gift of George Dawne, prebendary of Freford in Lichfield cathedral, who,

who, in right of his prebend, was patron of
the chapel, and, in return for this donation,
the prebendary of Freford, for the time being,
has the privilege of nominating one of the
almfmen. In regard to Denhall, all our
hiftorians fay, it was given to this hofpital by
Henry vii, but on what ground they affert
this does not appear. His Majefty's royal
licence was probably obtained for the union,
as the Crown thereby loft a contingent intereft in the nomination to the hofpital:
which would lapfe to the King, if the intermediate patrons neglected to prefent. But
the mere relinquifhing of fuch a claim could
not reafonably intitle the benefaction a royal
donation; nor is there any expreffion or intimation of the fort in the act of union,
which is recorded at large in the epifcopal
regifter. It is fimply ftated, that the hofpital belonged to the bifhop's patronage, and
was His gift, without any mention of royal
munificence. The bufinefs was tranfacted in
the Confiftory Court, in Lichfield cathedral;
and, after three days of examining witneffes,
and receiving depofitions, was concluded on
Tuefday, January 8, 1495-6[l], and confirmed by the Chapter the next day[m].

---

[l] Lichf Reg f 165—169   [m] Ibid 169 b.

When

When the Bishop thus provided for the general support and perpetuity of the hospital, he, by another benefaction of the same date, though in itself less important, contributed to the convenience and comfort of the individual members. This was a grant of wood for fuel, from the forest of Cank; two loads to each of the sixteen members of the hospital, (the Master, amply endowed otherwise, not being included,) to be delivered by the Rider of Cank wood[n]· and, if on this occasion it is worth mentioning, perhaps the chimnies, which the paupers as well as others enjoy in this hospital, were some of the first erected in private houses in England Before this period fires were made on a hearth in the centre[o] of the apartment, or hall, over

[n] Reg Lichf f 169 b See above, sect ii p 51 note b

[o] This may serve to explain some popular or proverbial expressions as, "Round about our coal fire, &c Plot mentions a whimsical custom of driving a goose round the fire in the hall at Hilton, Staffordshire, every new year's day Staff ch x § 65 A chimney, as Mr Warton observes, (Hist Poet i 432 note n) was a sufficient circumstance to distinguish and denominate one of the academical hospitia Thus in Oxford we had Chimney-hall, Aula cum Camino Bryan Twyne Miscell ad calc Apol pro Antiq Acad Oxon fignat Hhh 2 p 2 In 2 On the subject of chimnies see also a well informed writer in Gent Mag 1 87 p 111 It is said there are at present no chimnies in Bengal ibid 1797 p 31. b

which

which a cupola, fenced with shelving weather boards to exclude the rain, gave a vent for the smoke. The halls of some of our nobility and gentry, in their venerable country mansions, retained this custom about fifty years ago, when the festal log as well as festal cheer, during the Christmas holidays, exhilarated the social circle of friends and neighbours The Universities of Oxford and Cambridge, not prone to innovate even in trifles, have preserved the ancient practice to the present day[p] in many of their common refectories or halls, though there too the central fire of charcoal is now gradually giving way to the more modern inventions of a stove or a grate.

But to return to our hospital, respecting which one or two particulars must still be mentioned. The chapel, built of stone, is neat, lofty, and well lighted. It was fitted up with pews, at the expence of the corporation of Lichfield, in the year 1619[q], hav-

---

[p] This was written about ten years ago I am informed there is a fire in the centre of Lincoln's Inn Hall during the sittings 1799

[q] On one of the pews, in black letter " These seates weare made & erected at the propar costes & chardges of the Incorporation of this Cittie, 1619 William Hawkes & Thomas

Thacker

ing originally had benches only, of which
fome maffy ones remain: and this was, in
times of popery, the invariable mode of accommodation in churches.——For it was neceffary the feats fhould be moveable, that
they might give room occafionally for the folemn proceffions and fplendid ceremonies of
that religion of pomp and parade.

The Mafter's houfe, adjoining the chapel,
is large and commodious. The poor men
have each of them a feparate room, a plot of
garden, and other advantages. The fchool,
for which as well as for divine offices the
chapel was deftined, was the earlieft provincial eftablifhment of the kind, next to the
foundations at Winchefter, at Eton, and
Wainfleet: but how many men of genius or
of learning fprung from the infant feminary
has not with any certainty been difcovered.
Robert Whittington[r] of Lichfield, an emi-

Thacker bayliffes" There is a view of the Chapel, with part
of the Alms-houfes and maffy chimnies of the Hofpital, in
Shaw's Staff vol. i pl. xxxi p 322, contributed by the Rev
Mr Buckeridge, the prefent Mafter

[r] When he had been a fcholar of rhetoric 14 years, and an
informer of boys 12, he was admitted to the degree of Bachelor in Rhetoric in 1513, allowed to have his hood lined with
filk, and was crowned with laurel at the act that year .Reg

St. John's Hospital Lichfield 1495

nent grammarian, author of many noted
works, probably received part of his education
at this school, or was for a time master of it.
Richard Walker, a provident man, as the
Lichfield historian calls him, was chosen
from this school by Rowland Lee, bishop of
Lichfield and president of Wales, to be steward of his houshold. He afterwards ordained
him, and collated him to a rectory in Wir-
hal, Cheshire, and, as a final proof of confidential esteem, made him executor of his
will[s]. In later days Smyth's school has commonly been held with the adjacent seminary
of Edward vi · since which time bishop
Smalridge and bishop Newton, lord chief
Justice Willes and lord chief Baron Parker,
Addison and Johnson, are some of the illustrious persons, who, in the splendor of their
names, have reflected honour on Lichfield
school.

These institutions, the fruits of Smyth's
beneficence in the diocese of which he had
been such a short time bishop, we have exhibited perhaps with unnecessary minutenefs

G 173 b 187 187 b Bale, f 215 b 232 b Wood's Annals, ii 721. Athenæ, i 24

s Chron Lichf in Angl Saci vol i p 456

of

of detail. But it is certainly curious and important to know what meafures were devifed, what fteps purfued, and by what felected inftruments in the hands of Providence, gradually to diffufe knowledge, and prepare the way for better learning, and a more pure form of religion To furvey the revolutions of life and manners, which have taken place on the theatre of the world, without an eye to that Power, who fuperintends the whole, and bids every movement accomplifh his will, is to embark on the ocean without a rudder to guide, or a compafs to direct " Religion," it has been remarked, " without policy is too fimple to be fafe, as policy without religion is too fubtle to be good˙ " In hiftory, as in life, they fhould go hand in hand.

MS Afhmole, 783 p 93.

SECT V

Tranflated to Lincoln.

—————

SMYTH had been bifhop of Lichfield little more than two years, when, by the favour of his Sovereign, he was tranflated to Lincoln. Ruffell, his predeceffor in the fee, died at the epifcopal feat of Netilham near Lincoln, December 30, 1494[a], and the eighteenth of May following was appointed by the chapter for the election of a fucceffor. The bull of Smyth's tranflation, from pope Alexander vi, bears date November 6, 1495[b]. It is directed to the bifhops of Hereford and London, (Edmund Audley, and Richard Hill,) injoining them, or one of them, to receive from him the cuftomary oath of fubmiffion to the Holy See. This was accompanied with three other bulls of the fame date, one addreffed to the clergy of the diocefe, another

———

[a] MS Harl 6953 p 17 And fee the beginning of fect. vi in thefe papers

[b] Reg Linc Smyth, f 1 8 Id Novembr

to the laity, and the third to the tenants of
the fee, requiring obedience to the new bifhop[c]. The fpiritualties of the fee were
granted by archbifhop Morton on the laft
day of January, 1495-6[d], and the temporalties were reftored by the Crown on the
fixth of February following[e]. When he arrived at his new cathedral, he was met by
the Chapter, according to the cuftom of that
church, in folemn proceffion, but the time
of this firft vifit does not appear. For being
perfonally engaged in the fervice of the King
and the Prince of Wales, he appointed James
Whytftons, Doctor of canon law, Commiffary
general during his abfence[f], and alfo iffued
letters to the feveral archdeacons, authorizing
them to prove wills, and adminifter other

[c] Reg Linc f 1 2 MS Harl 6953 p 65

[d] Reg Morton, t 117

[e] Rymer xii p 578

[f] In Hofp noftro ap vetus Templum Lond 1 Feb 1495-6
Reg Linc f 2 b A like commiffion and for the fame reafon
to him and Car Bothe 10 Jan 499-1500 ibid f 118 James
Whitftons was collated to the prebend of Welton Brynkhall,
June 18, 1496 MS Harl 6954 p 155 He refigned the
prebend of Gretton in 1498 ibid 6953 p 18 and was collated to the prebend of Banbury, July 23, 1498 ib 6954
p 155. to which, upon his death, Matthew Smyth was collated Dec 2, 1512 ib 6953 p 26 See and correct Willis,
Cath iii p 141 187. who calls him Whifton

eccle-

ecclefiaftical matters, in their refpective dif-
tricts, till he fhould fee good to recal the
powers thus conferred[g].

The fee of Lincoln, which is ftill the
largeft in extent of jurifdiction, reaching from
the Thames to the Humber, was in many
refpects, when Smyth was tranflated to it,
one of the moft fplendid in the kingdom In
the Minfter, which juftly ranks among the
moft beautiful and magnificent of our ca-
thedrals, were ftalls for feventy dignitaries,
according to the fecond order of our Lord's
difciples, a number furpaffing that of any
other cathedral in England. Of all thefe dignities, the deanery and fix refidentiaries excepted, the bifhop was patron; and his
eftates and revenues were ample in proportion to the magnitude of his diocefe. For
he had near forty manors, and ten palaces.
Four of thefe, befides the palace in Lincoln,
and Lincoln Place in Southampton buildings,
London, were frequently honoured with the
prefence of bifhop Smyth; Lidington in Rutland, Buckden in Huntingdonfhire, Woburn,
Bucks, and Banbury Caftle, Oxfordfhire. He
chofe, without doubt, thefe places for his re-

g 6 Feb 1495–6 London Reg Linc f 3

fidence,

fidence, becaufe, by their advantageous fituation, he was beft enabled to fuperintend the
feveral parts of his immenfe diocefe The
manors of Lidington, Buckden, and Woburn
were part of the barony of the fee.

Lidington belonged to the bifhops of Lincoln at the time of the conqueft. When it
was taken from the fee, it was granted by
the Crown, firft to Gregory lord Cromwell
(2 Edward vi,) for life, and then in rever-
fion (5 Edward vi,) to William Cecyl, afterwards lord Burghley   His fon, Thomas lord
Burghley, about the year 1602, converted
part of the palace into a hofpital for a warden, twelve poor men (now fifteen,) and
two nurfes, by the name of Jefus Hofpital
In the hall, full fifty feet long by twenty
broad, to which you afcend by a flight of
ftone fteps, bifhop Smyth's motto, 𝕯𝕺𝕸𝕵-
𝕹𝖀𝕾 𝕰𝖃𝕷𝕿𝕬𝕮𝕵𝕺 𝕸𝕰𝕬, is ftill to be feen
in large golden letters, infcribed bendwife in
almoft every divifion of the four Gothic windows. Moft of the panes likewife are adorned
with a fmall rofe, part of his arms, and his
arms remain in the fourth or uppermoft window[h]. They are alfo exhibited, neatly cut in

---

[h] See and correct Wright's Rutland, p 81, where thefe
                                                    arms

ftone, on a fmall octagon watch tower, at one corner of the orchard, facing the ftreet; which was, no doubt, erected in his time.

Edward Watfon, efquire, an anceftor of the noble family of Rockingham, was Secretary or Auditor at Lidington to bifhop Smyth, and to his fucceffors, Atwater and Longland, a circumftance which was deemed fo honourable, that it was celebrated on his tomb in Englifh profe and Latin verfe[1] He married Emma, daughter and coheir of Antony Smith, efquire, whom fome writers regard as

arms are called Bp Ruffell's, but Ruffell's coat was Az 2 chevronels, between 3 rofes Or Willis, Cath iii p 58 or perhaps Az 2 chevronels Or, betw 3 rofes *Arg* as they appear in the eaft window and in one of the windows of the fouth aile of St Martins church, Stamford They are alfo on one of the pillars there, as are bifhop Smyths on the fouth fide of the middle pillar of the north aile (Aug 26, 1790) It is probable both thefe bifhops were benefactors to this church Ruffell's arms are on the north fide of the weft door of St. Mary's church, Oxford, to which he was a benefactor See Woods Annals, ii p 785 It muft be noted however, that in this Lidington window the chevron is Argent, diapered, and the field Sable, and fo Mr Nichols gives them, Leic vol iii p 310, whereas in other places univerfally the chevron in Smyth's arms is Sable, the field Argent There is a view of this Hofpital in Gent Mag 1796 p 457

[1] See the epitaphs in Wright, ut fupra The Englifh is gone, the Latin remains on the graveftone, July 24, 1798

a broa brother of bifhop Smyth[k]; an opinion for which I can find no other foundation, than what has occafioned many other miftakes, the accidental identity of names.

Of Buckden, which had the good fortune to efcape the general fpoliation of ecclefiaftical property, we have little to add to the common accounts. In the year 1501, Smyth's friend and patronefs, the excellent countefs of Richmond, graced this manoi with her prefence great part of the fummer[l], accommodated, as it feems, with the epifcopal palace. The Bifhop conftituted Richard Smyth, one of his retinue and probably a relation, keeper of the park at Buckden, by a patent, dated May 17, 1504[m], a fpecies of grant, which about this time was growing into ufe. Such appointments had aforetime been held without a written inftrument of conveyance, dependent merely on the will of the donor; but it was found to be the beft provifion for the equitable difcharge of an office of truft, that the tenure fhould be for

[k] See Edmondfon s Genealogies, and Collins's Peerage.

[l] Reg F Epp 504 509

[m] Reg Linc f 56 confirmed by the Chapter, 12 June f. 56 b.

life;

life; and a proper deed was hereupon made out to fecure the right[n].

The manor of Woburn near High Wycombe, which had belonged to earl Harold, was beftowed by the Conqueror on Remigius, the firft bifhop of Lincoln[o], who granted it to his kinfman Walter Deincourt, and this family, who were allied to the Conqueror, enjoyed it, as leflees under the church of Lincoln, upwards of three centuries, till Henry the fixth's time, whence the town was called Bifhop's Woburn, and Woburn Deincourt[p].

[n] Upon occafion of a fuit pending in the courts at Weftminfter, 1788, between the archbifhop of Canterbury and others, to try the validity of reverfionary grants, Mr Topham having carefully examined all the archiepifcopal records, fome of which go back as far as the year 600, it was ftated in evidence, that no grant whatfoever of the important office of Regiftrar of the Prerogative Court could be found prior to the year 1502 However in the Lichfield regifters there are two grants for life, one of the Apparitorfhip, 1450, the other of the Clerkfhip of the Spiritual Court, 1451 But the donor feems to apologize for it as a novelty Reg x f 8 Smyth granted the Regiftrarfhip to Thomas Godfalve for life, in confequence of his having difcharged the office well, durante beneplacito, Sept 6, 1493 Reg xiii f 161 At the trial above mentioned it was determined, that all grants of fuch offices muft be grants in poffeffion

[o] Dugd Mon iii p 259 268, 269 Of Remigius fee Willis's Cath and Nichols s Leic vol i on Domefday

[p] Browne Willis's Collect MS Tanner fol No 10 It

was

The latter name (corrupted into Deins court)
is still attached to a large old house near the
church-yard on the west, in which, I suppose, the family lived. The church was appropriated, June 18, 1334, to the bishop's
table[q], a specification peculiar, but not without example, the design of which was, that
if the temporalties were seized by the Crown,
as sometimes happened in time of war, the
revenues arising from Tithes, which it was
deemed sacrilegious to divert to secular purposes, might afford a temporary subsistence
The bishop's palace, in this delightful vale,
was at Woburn Green, a small distance east
of the church and the village Upon the site
is a handsome modern mansion, which Mr
Dupre lately purchased of the family of the

---

was hoped, that one of the " two portraitures of bishops,"
there mentioned, might prove to be Smyth; but inquiring
(2 Oct 1788) of Dr Cleobury, the Vicar, who remembered
these relics, and hoped to preserve them, I heard with regret,
that they were destroyed and gone Of the Deincourts see
Gough s Sep Mon vol ii p 78 Weevers Fun Mon p 651
Gent Mag 1789 p 314 Peck Defid Cur p 320 from
Dugd Bar i 386, 387 and Sprott Chron ed Oxon 1719
p 16 a grant to Rad de Dencourt, by Hen i Dugd Mon
iii 266 Evident conc Maner de Wouburn episcopi, MS
Harl 6952 p 210 See also Langley's Hundr of Desborough,
&c London, 1797 4to

[q] Lib de Chart pension Linc f 10.

Berties,

Berties, into whofe hands it had paffed from the family of the earl of Wharton.

At what time the bifhops of Lincoln obtained property in Banbury is not known. In the reign of Stephen, Alexander, then bifhop of this fee, built a ftately caftle here[r] on the banks of the Cherwell; which was a place of fuch fize and ftrength, that, in the grand rebellion, it contained a regiment of eight hundred foot, and a troop of horfe, and, when garrifoned for the King, nobly fuftained a fiege of full thirteen weeks, when it was relieved by colonel Gage and the gallant earl of Northampton[s]. About the year 1160 Henry II granted to Robert de Chefney, fucceffor to the forenamed Alexander, a free market in his town of Banbury every Thurfday[t], as at prefent. In the fame century three fucceffive popes confirmed to the bifhops of Lincoln their poffeffions in Banbury, Cropredy, and elfewhere[u]. On the

[r] Camden, ed Gough, i 286 297

[s] Clarendon, ii 544, 545 ed 8vo

[t] Cotton Lib Vefpafian, E xvi f 14 b Dugd Mon iii p 267

[u] Vefpafian, ut fupra, f 20 23 25 The earlieft is anno 1125 Baneberia, Croperia, Oxinafortdfira, are fome of the names. The fecond of thefe is written ' Cropri," June 20,

fifth of February, 1500-1, a privy council
was holden here^, at which probably bishop
Smyth assisted   Richard Emson, knight, and
Thomas Emson, esquire, held under him the
offices of Constable and Steward of the hundred of the castle and town of Banbury, for
their joint lives^, Robert Cutts was constituted
Bailiff of the town and Warder of the castle^.

1370, when "Philip de Pighesle (Litchley, Northamptonshire) was instituted to the vicarage MS Harl 6952 p 4

^ 16 H vii Dockets from Court of Requests, p 26

^ Act Capit Linc t 145 b 14 Mar 23 H vii confirmed
by Chapter, 28 May, 1508 I suppose this Richard Emson,
knight, was the famous ' Judex ficalis," as P Vergil styles
him, p 613, 615 who, with his colleague Dudley, was beheaded by H viii ibid 620 He often occurs in the affairs of
Smyth and Sir R Bray He was born at Towcester, in Northamptonshire Athen Oxon 1 p 7 was a member of the
House of Commons 1495 Rolls Parl vol vi p 458 b one
of the Assessors of the Vice Chancellors court, when Bray was
Steward of the University of Oxford, 17 H vii 1501 Donat
MS Brit Mus 4618 p 267 He and Bray joint keepers
of Fitbury park Northamptonshire Pat 12 Mar 9 H vii
1493-4 Rolls And guardians of the estates of Francis Chey-
r , a minor Pat 14 Mar 18 H vii 1502-3 ibid He and
William Cope were two of the executors of Bray, 4 Aug
1503 Prerog Off vol bla nyr, xxvi

^ 10 Apr 1509 Act Capit Linc f 49 b Of Robert
Cutts I find no other mention Sir John Cutte or Cutts was
one of Brays executors (ubi supra) and MS Harl 6953
p 62 and in Trin term, 1504, with his wife Elizabeth,
suffered a recovery for the manor of Bolington, given by Bray,
&c to Westm Abbey Morants Essex, vol ii p 618 He
also

and William Cope, efquire, leffee of the manor of Hardwick and the river[a], all by grants in writing.

We have paufed for a moment to furvey thefe feats of ancient fame and magnificence, as there will be frequent occafion to mention them in the enfuing pages. We now

alfo joined in the recovery of an eftate at St John's Bedwardyn, Com Worc for the bifhop of Lincoln, Trin term, 1501 Anc Charters, Br t Muf 43 I 6 Strype mentions a Sir John Cutts Life of Sir T Smith, p 3

[a] 22 Jun 11 H vii (1496) MS Harl 6954 p 155 An augmentation of the vicarage of Banbury, ib 6952 p 214 William Cope was Cofferer to H vii died 7 Apr 1513 and was buried at Banbury Athen Oxon i 79, 80 He was the father of Antony Cope, educated in Oriel college, who publifhed " Godly Meditations on 20 Pfalms, and a Hift of Annibal and Scipio Tanner, Biblioth Bale, f 233 b He was buried at Hanwell, 1551 Leland fays, " Mr Cope hath an old manor place called Hardwick, a mile north of Banbury, and another pleafant and gallant houfe at Hanwell, two miles weft of Banbury " Itin vol iv 163 The gatehoufe at Hanwell ftill remains This branch of the Copes terminated in the two daughters of the late Sir Charles Cope, baronet, one married to a brother of the Duke of Gordon, and the other, Arabella Diana, to the late Duke of Dorfet Gent Mag 1799 p 630 The Rev Sir Richard Cope, bart. of Bramfhill in Hampfhire, reprefentative of the Copes of Balfcot near Banbury, another branch of the fame family, is poffeffed of confiderable eftates in the neighbourhood Hardwick was fold by her Grace the Duchefs dowager of Dorfet this prefent year, 1799.

pro-

proceed with our more immediate bufinefs, the narrative of facts

Epiftolary correfpondence, when pofts were not eftablifhed, was a matter of rare occurrence, it happens however, that one of the firft tranfactions, which has been difcovered, between Smyth and the Chapter of Lincoln, is rendered memorable by an Englifh letter written on the occafion, the only one in that language known to remain of his inditing John Mordaunt, "a fpecial lover and friend" of the Bifhop's, had recovered certain lands from St. John's Hofpital in Bedford, upon the plea, that the conditions and purpofes, for which the eftate had been given, were not performed[b]   However, that the charitable inftitution might fuftain no lofs, he had made over to the Mafter of the hofpital lands of equal value . but which were to him, I prefume, lefs eligible, than thofe which he had recovered   The Mafter had releafed to him the forfeited eftate ; which the Bifhop, as ordinary, and the Mayor and Corporation of Bedford, patrons of the hofpital, had confirmed, under their proper feals.   The object

[b] By a Ceffavit action   See Blackftone, vol iii 232 4to edit.

of

of the letter therefore is to requeſt the Chap- .
ter, that they would alſo ratify the ſame;
and, being a matter of convenience only, not
of profit, that it might be done without fee,
and with all convenient diſpatch, as the
Maſter of the hoſpital, Henry Ruding, was
" very aged and ſickly," and in caſe he died
before the buſineſs was completed, the whole
muſt commence anew[c]   In conſequence of
this application, which was in March, (1496-7)
the recovered eſtate was confirmed by the
Chapter the ſame month.   Smyth's letter
on the occaſion may be ſeen in the appendix[d]; but of the perſons mentioned in it, eſpecially of Mordaunt, who was the anceſtor
of a diſtinguiſhed benefactor of Braſen Noſe,
ſome account here may not be unaccept-
able.

Henry Ruding, I take it, was brother to
John Ruding, archdeacon of Bedford, 1460;
who, dying archdeacon of Lincoln, 1481,

[c] The recovery was at Weſtm 10 H vii The letter is dated
" 20 March,' (no year) The confirmation of the Chapter
(perhaps antedated) 14 Mar 12 H vii (1496-7) The releaſe and confirmation by Ruding and the Corporation of Bedford, 16 July Act Capit Linc 1501 1507 f 1 and f
1 b

[d] App Num v

gave to that cathedral a rich cope of red velvet[c]: his motto was, All may God amend[f]
Of John Mordaunt, defcended from Ofbert
le Mordaunt, a Norman knight who came
over with the Conqueror, we hear firft in
the fecond year of Henry vii, when he was
one of the commanders at the battle of
Stoke[g] The following year he was chofen
Speaker of the Houfe of Commons[h] He
was Serjeant at law, November 16, 10 Henry vii, when a fplendid feaft was given by
the new Serjeants at Ely Houfe, which was
honoured with the prefence of the King and
Queen, and the fame month he was conftituted King's Serjeant[i] He was Juftice of

[c] Dugd Mon iii 279 2 He was executor and refiduary
legatee of John Quych, Rector of Clopton, buried in St Fridefwides, at Oxford See his Will, dat Oxon, 26 Jul 1461
proved 8 Oct following Reg Aaa f 188 Ruding rebuilt
the Chancels of Buckingham and Bigglefwade, having been
Prebendary of both, and is buried at Bigglefwade He had various other ftal's, together or fucceffively, in Lincoln See Wil-
l s s Cath and Hift Buck p 57 and fee a pedigree of the
Rudings in Gent Mag 1796 p 217

[f] Gough s Sep Mon vol ii p 274 where fee an engraving of the brafs on his tomb, his epitaph, &c

[g] Pol Verg p 574.

[h] Rolls of Parl vol vi p 386

[i] Dugd Orig Jurid p 127 Chron Jurid and MS
Dugd O f 267 b

Chefter

Chefter 15 Henry vii[k], one of the Knights of the fword at the creation of Henry prince of Wales, February 18, 19 Henry vii[l], and feoffee the fame year in an indenture between the King and the monaftery of Sion[m]. He died in 1504[n]. His fon John was fummoned to parliament as Baron Mordaunt, 24 Henry viii, and was one of the brilliant retinue, that attended the King at his interview that year with Francis the firft[o]. He died in 1562 His fon, alfo named John, the fecond baron, was created Knight of the Bath at the coronation of Anne Bolein, on Whitfunday, May 31, 1533[p]. In the time of queen Mary he was joined with Sir Thomas Pope and others in a famous commiffion for the fuppreffion of heretics[q], which

[k] MS Dodfworth, (4173) 31 f 144

[l] Cotton Lib Claudius, C iii f 64 b

[m] Rolls of Parl vol vi p 527 fee alfo p 536

[n] Collins s Peerage See alfo Hen viith's Will, p 25 and correct Dugd Bar vol ii 311

[o] Dugd. ibid. Donat. MS Brit Muf 4620. p 605 4621. p 31

[p] Cotton Lib Claudius, C iii f 119

[q] Wartons L of Sir T Pope, 2d edit p 52 There is a pedigree of this noble family in MS Dodfworth, 81 p 56. See alfo Dugd Orig Jurid p 221 224 333 MS Tanner, 183 p 71 MS Claudius, ut fupra, f 228 b Donat MS. 4620 p 402 4622 p 466 673 Weever, Fun Mon p 656.

however

however feems not to have been rigoroufly
executed. There is an original portrait of
him in the hall of Brafen Nofe college,
which breathes nothing of the malignity of
the perfecuting Bonner, but rather the plea-
fantry of Sir Thomas More. The date of it
is 1564, when he was 56 years of age By
his will in 1571, he gave to the college,
founded by the Friend of his Grandfather,
the manor of Tiptofts and other lands in
Effex, for the maintenance of three fcholars
to be nominated for ever by his heirs.

Few parliaments were holden during the
reign of Henry vii , and it does not appear
that Smyth was fummoned to any of them.
Such omiffions were, in thefe days, not uncommon , but as he was known to be effec-
tually promoting the King's fervice in the
principality and the marches of Wales, he
was, for that reafon probably, not called to
affift in the national council. In the bufinefs however of raifing fupplies, as that
matter was then tranfacted his concurrence,
though not his prefence, was neceffary. Accordingly the Convocation, which fat in London from January 23, till March 11, 1496-7,
having granted the King a fubfidy of 40,000l
for the province of Canterbury, a writ from
the

the Crown and a letter from the Archbifhop were directed to the Bifhop of Lincoln, for levying the proportion due from his diocefe'.

Smyth appears to have vifited fome parts of his diocefe in the firft year of his tranflation', and here, as in his former fee, the monafteries engaged his peculiar attention. One of thefe, Ofeney Abbey near Oxford, was found to be in fuch a ftate, with refpect to its revenues, buildings, and difcipline, that he judged it neceffary to fufpend the abbat from his office, till the debts fhould be difcharged, and good order reftored. To accomplifh thefe falutary purpofes, having vifited the monaftery in perfon, he tranfmitted from Banbury, February 10, 1498-9, certain injunctions, twenty three in number, to be obferved by the Abbat, the Prior, and the Canons of the houfe.

He begins, where reformation always fhould begin, with the duties of religion, command-

---

' Letter from Thomas Savage Bp of London, reciting one from Abp Morton Reg Linc f 180 Hen &c Willielmo Linc &c T meipfo ap. Weftm 15 Mar 12 H vii (1496-7.) ib 183 b.

' Mr Fardell, from the Reg

ing

ing them, by their ſtrict and devout obedience to God, to ſet before the world and
each other a pattern of virtue This foundation being laid, he proceeds to impoſe ſuch
regulations as he judged expedient, for the
better management of their temporal affairs.
committing the whole to John Audley, bachelor of canon law and to Richard Colum-
bine and John Walton, canons of the convent[t].

The interference of the viſitor, at this
juncture, appears to have been not more neceſſary, than wiſely conducted. The Abbat
himſelf, moſt in fault, as firſt in ſtation, was
ſuſpended with his own expreſs conſent, and
the reſtrictions in general were received with
the approving gratitude of the whole ſociety.
The ſequeſtration, which appears to have
continued for the ſpace of four years[u], hav-

---

[t] Reg Linc f 52–54 b MS Harl 6953 p 66 Perhaps
an imperfect extract of the ſhort notice reſpecting this viſitation in the Harl MS "ubi abbas Robertus ſuſpenſus fuit ab
adminiſtratione durante beneplacito domini Epiſcopi, occaſioned a ridiculous miſtake of Browne Willis "Robert Oſeney
was hanged 1498, as Bp Tanner noted" Principals of Rel
H prefixed to Not Mon And, as one blunder often leads to
another, he goes on to ſay, "I ſuppoſe on ſiding with the York
party againſt Hen vii

- There are many entries in the Regiſters of the Chancellor s

ing retrieved the finances of the abbey; and
the rules prescribed having leffened what
they could not remove, moral delinquency;
the convent fubfifted under the fpirit of this
reform, till the church was erected into a cathedral, 1541, in which Robert King, then

cellor's court, which throw a light on the ftate of the monaftery at this period The Abbat of Rewley and the Abbat of
Ofeney (the latter by John Grampond, prior of the houfe,) were
mutually bound to keep the peace, 26 and 27 July, 1498
Reg α f 2 b This was previous to the fufpenfion of the
Abbat Mr Audley appears as commiffioner for Ofeney, under
the authority of the bifhop of Lincoln, 10 Mar 1499–1500
ib 32 And John Walton, canon of Ofeney, acts in the fame
capacity, and by the fame authority, 19 Feb 1502-3 ib 193
As yet therefore the fequeftration continued, but it was fuper-
feded, I prefume, and the Abbat reftored, in the courfe of this
year For a proctor in the court was appointed for him, 3 Oct
(1503) with his exprefs approbation, (ut idem Abbas afferuit,
18 Oct) ib f 54 And the court foon afterwards ordered feveral payments to be made to the Abbat, without mentioning
the commiffioners namely, 24 Nov f 54 b (fee alfo 22 Nov
ib) 4 Dec f 56 b There is however fome uncertainty in
the affair, as William Barton, fenefhal of Ofeney (and confequently a canon) in the name of the Abbat and monaftery appointed Bryan Higdon their proctor, 30 Mar 1502 ib f 125
b which was while we fuppofe the fequeftration to have been
in force The Abbat alfo made a demand by one of the canons,
his officer, 28 Oct 1502 ib 159 b but this was, I prefume,
the canon allowed him for his chaplain, by the articles of fufpenfion, in his allotted refidence at Medley See alfo of this
abbey, ib f 58 66 b 234 b Reg 7 f 59, 60. 80 Reg
Aaa f 263

abbat,

abbat, (but not the fame Robert, who was
fufpended[x],) fat as the firft and only bifhop;
for, five years afterwards, the epifcopal chair
was .tranflated to the church of St. Fridefwide, by the ftyle of the Cathedral Church
of Chrift in the city of Oxford, of which the
faid King was bifhop till his death in 1557.

A charter of privileges was granted by the
King in 1499 to the city of Lincoln[y], where
his Majefty had twice, in the beginning of
his reign, held his royal court During his
northern progrefs in the year 1486, he celebrated the feaft of Eafter at Lincoln with
great magnificence[z]; and in June 1487, after
the battle at Stoke, he again kept his court
there three days; at which time folemn proceffions were made for the recent victory[a].
In the matter of the charter the good offices
of the Bifhop were ready, no doubt, to forward the inclination of the Sovereign towards
this his ancient and loyal city.

[x] John Barton intervened, who was abbat in 1531 Woods
Annals, i p 52 and he, wtn others, figned certain articles
about religion in 1536 Burnets Reform vol 1 Add p 315

[y] Pat. 8 Jul 14 H vii Rolls Chapel

[z] Lel Coll iv Add p 185 &c

[a] Stowe's Ann p 471

About

About this period Smyth feems to have made his firft purchafe of landed property. The eftate lay in St. John's Bedwardyn, near the city of Worcefter; for which Walter Rufford and Alianora his wife fuffering a fine and recovery, acknowledged the bifhop's right in the eftate, and releafed it to him and Sir Reginald Bray, Sir John Shaw, Hugh Oldham, and others, in fee, for the bifhop and his heirs for ever[b]. St John's Bedwardyn is diftinguifhed as the birth-place of Sir Reginald Bray[c], but whether Smyth procured this eftate for him, or alienated it to him, or difpofed of it to others, is uncertain; as no further notice of it whatfoever has been difcovered, either in the hiftory of the county, or in the life of Smyth or of Bray.

In the year 1500 the plague raged with

[b] 16 H vii ap Weftm (1501) 40 marks were paid for the recovery Anc Chart in Brit Muf 43 I 6 Mr Ayfcough s MS Catalogue, who very kindly obliged me with a copy of the original deed

[c] Nafh's Worc vol ii p 309 Among the incumbents of St John's Bedwardyn is "Will Smith, capellanus, 27 Feb 1471. But as he feems to have continued rector till 1513, "Thomas Ellys, capellanus, 8 Dec. 1513," being the next, I do not fuppofe this was bifhop Smyth, or any of his kinfmen. The Convent of Worcefter were patrons of the church Nafh, ibid p 312.

great

great violence in many parts of the kingdom.
The University of Oxford was almoſt depo-
pulated by death and flight.   In London
alone, as we are told by a contemporary writer, the number of deaths amounted to thirty
thouſand; and ſo great was the panic, that
the King and Queen, after ſeveral removals
from place to place, fled from the face of the
evil to Calais[d]   A moment of ſuch diſmay,
aggravated by the recollection of the devaſ-
tation lately made by that extraordinary malady, the ſweating ſickneſs, could not but
awaken the attention of the pious and confi-
derate biſhop Smyth; and, as became a
Chriſtian paſtor, he had recourſe to the aids
and comforts of religion; the beſt ſupport in
every affliction, but eſpecially ſeaſonable when
the kingdom languiſhed under a calamity,
which ſeems always to have been regarded as
an evil peculiarly of God s ſending   Anxious
therefore, amid the general conſternation, to
-" invite" thoſe whom Providence had committed to his care, " to implore the mercy of
Chriſt our Saviour," he iſſued orders throughout his dioceſe, that, in all conventual and
parochial churches, ſolemn proceſſions ſhould
be made every Wedneſday and Friday, with

---

[d] Pol Verg p 609 and Stowe s Ann. p 481

litanies

litanies and prayers, and, the more to encourage such acts of piety, he granted an Indulgence of forty days to all that with true contrition repented and confessed their sins, as often as they made these processions[e]. Whatever there might be of superstition in this episcopal precept, or in the execution of it, we charitably hope it was pardoned in an age of ignorance The general principle was undoubtedly good, and the motive laudable, the people were humbled, and the plague was stayed

In this same year he began to put mat-

[e] Reg Linc f 119 b dat Lidington, Oct 1, 1500 No bishop was permitted to grant an Indulgence for a longer time than 40 days (Gibson Cod Tit xxi cap 1) The trade was too profitable for the bishops of Rome to part with it, they themselves granted Indulgences for as long a time as they pleased, in this world and in the next, an historical fact, which in the present day, when popish seminaries and monasteries of the worst sort are starting up among us, ought not to be forgotten See many curious instances of Indulgences in Weever Fun Mon p 119 160–167 Burnet's Reform vol ii Collect of Rec p 150–152 Stillingfl on the Idolatry of the Ch of R p 421–433 2d edit Bishop Fisher, in his famous Funeral Sermon of Margaret, countess of Richmond, makes " Indulgences and pardons graunted by divers Popes, one distinct argument, among others, for " grete lyklyhode and almoost certayn conjecture,—that the soule of this noble woman, —in that houre of departynge,—was borne up into the country above, with the blessyd aungells ad finem

ters in train for an act, the recital of which
occupies a large fpace in the records of
the diocefe; and the fpectacle itfelf muft
doubtlefs have been very fplendid and ftriking. This was the folemn vifitation of his
cathedral at Lincoln, which he gave notice
that he intended to hold on the morrow of
the great feftival of Corpus Chrifti. In the
mean time the Chapter had much confultation, in what manner they might receive
their fpiritual father with greateft propriety
and refpect. Public proceffion was the higheft mark of honour, but no order or precedent of their church could be found for receiving their bifhop in this way, except (as
they had already received Smyth) when he
firft came to the fee, or when he returned
from abroad. However, confidering the favourable regard, which he was known to en-
tertain, as well towards his cathedral, as the
individual members of it, confidering alfo
the large fums of money, which he had generoufly expended, and purpofed to expend,
for the reparation of the church, it was at
laft, on thefe grounds, unanimoufly refolved,
that they fhould receive him with folemn
proceffion, attired in their richeft habits.

The refult of their deliberations was communicated

municated to the Bifhop by a fpecial meffenger; who had it alfo in charge to learn
his Lordfhip's pleafure on the occafion, and
to adjuft other neceffary preliminaries. The
day arrived, the Chapter affembled, and fat
in anxious expectation of their vifitor, when
his commiffary and chancellor, Charles Bothe,
LL.D treafurer of Lincoln, came, and informed them, that the Bifhop, greatly againft
his wifhes, was prevented from vifiting his
cathedral at that time. When he had proceeded a day's journey on his way to Lincoln, he was overtaken at Lichfield by an exprefs from the King, which obliged him to
return to Bewdley, in order to direct certain
arduous affairs of the Prince of Wales, who
was then at Bewdley, where he had for fome
time kept his court. Bothe added, that the
Bifhop, defirous that his intention fhould not
entirely be fruftrated, had given him in command to begin the vifitation; and then to
adjourn the bufinefs, till he could attend in
perfon.

The Chapter, in reply, acknowledged
themfelves under the greateft obligations to
the Bifhop, and lamented his abfence extremely; but fince it was neither pleafing to
them, nor, as appeared by the muniments,

I   agree-

agreeable to the cuſtom of their church, for
a biſhop of that ſee to commence the viſitation of the cathedral by deputy; and ſince,
in the preſent inſtance, the precept required
their appearance before the Biſhop himſelf,
without any mention of his commiſſary;
they therefore moſt earneſtly intreated the
chancellor to forbear any further interference.
With this requeſt, after ſome conference and
inſpection of the alleged records, he complied, carrying with him from the Chapter
a written and circumſtantial account of the
whole tranſaction, and engaging to explain
the matter alſo in perſon to the Biſhop, that
they might ſuffer no loſs or alienation of his
paternal regardᶠ.

ᶠ Act Capit Linc F f 167, 168   Charles Bothe, ſo often
and confidentially employed by biſhop Smyth, was of Pembroke hall, Cambridge   He was collated by Smyth to the
treaſurerſhip of Lichfield with a prebend annexed, Nov 18,
1495, on the reſignation of John Bothe, who was alſo Maſter
of Denhall hoſpital in Cheſhire Reg Lichf f 154   Afterwards Smyth gave him, in the cathedral of Lincoln, the prebend of Clifton, Apr 6, 1501 the prebend of Farendon, Aug
31, 1504 and the archdeaconry of Bucks, May 8, 1505 MS
Harl. 6953 p 19 21, 22   In 1516 he was made biſhop of
Hereford   He died 5 May, 1535, and was buried in his cathedral near the north-door, in a tomb built in his life-time
Athen. Oxon 1 654, 655   Among the plate belonging to
Lincoln cathedral, 1536, was "one chalice, ſilver and gilt,
and a paten, of the gift of the lord Charles Boothe, biſhop of

The bufinefs thus interrupted was poftponed till the following fpring; when the

Hereford' Dugd Mon iii 272 And in the original Inventory of the plate of Brafen Nofe college, is a " Cuppe with a cover of filver and gylt, ex dono dni Herford Epifcopi," of which I prefume Bothe was the donor Plate Book, p i John Bothe above mentioned refigned Denhall before Jan 2, 1495-6. Reg Lichf f 165 and he (or a perfon of both his names) LL B was inftituted to " Thorntone upone the more," in Chefhire, Feb 15, 1494-5, void by the death of Richard Rothe, on the prefentation of William Bothe, efquire ibid f. 158 and ordained in 1495 on the title of that benefice ibid f 185. In the Chefhire pedigree of Bouth is " Will Bouth Miles, dominus de Dunham, 14 H vii " (1498) who is probably the faid William, patron of Thornton, and, on the whole, it is likely that all thefe Bothes were of that family; which, on this fuppofition, appears to have given to the church of England two bifhops and two archbifhops Godwin (p 693) calls William Boothe, archbifhop of York in 1452, a native of Chefhire, and makes Laurence Boothe, tranflated from Durham to the fame fee in 1476, brother to the faid William by half blood The Chefhire pedigree of Bouth ftyles Laurence Bouth archbifhop of York, and gives him a half brother named William Of the extraction of John Boothe, bifhop of Exeter in 1466, Godwin is filent, but in the Bouth pedigree " Johannes epifcopus de Exceftre' is the nephew of the forenamed Laurence and William. The Bouths of Twemlow, Chefhire, whofe eftate and name were bequeathed to the Rev Charles Everard, the late Rector of Middleton Cheney, by his maternal uncle, Thomas Booth, efquire, (Gent Mag 1793 p 325 123. 221) were a younger branch of the Bouths of Dunham and in 1618 John Bouth of Twemlow wrote the " genealogy' now alleged, from whofe " laborious collections' the Chefhire Pedigrees, fo often quoted in thefe papers, were " carefully tranfcribed by Jof Higgs of Utkinton [in that county] 1685 "

vifi-

vifitation was conducted with the utmoft folemnity On Monday, March 29, at nine in
the morning, mafs for the day and other canonical fervice being ended, the Bifhop came
through the great gates of his palace, adjoining the clofe, to the weft door of the cathedral. The bells in the weft tower an-
nounced his approach, and the Dean and
Canons, with the whole choir, in their proper habits and hoods, awaited his arrival,
ranged in proceffional order, in the nave of
the cathedral, with the crofs, and torches,
and incenfe, carried before them. A ftool
covered with filk was fet on the uppermoft
ftep, without the great weft door, where, as
his lordfhip kneeled before the ftool, and
devoutly adored the crucifix[g], the dean and
canons honourably received him The dean
and chancellor cenfed him. Then the dean,
on his knee, delivered to him holy water,
which the Bifhop fprinkled, and kiffed the
crofs, which the dean prefented This done,
the dean on the Bifhop's right hand and the
chancellor on his left, preceded by the canons and others, conducted him in ftately

[g] Placed, I fuppofe, upon the ftool The crucifix was a
portable crofs, with an image of our Saviour crucified upon it
See H ith s Will, p 33

pro-

proceffion, along the nave and centre of the choir, to the high altar, the choir at the fame time chanting refponfes to the Holy Trinity. When the refponfes were finifhed, the dean pronounced the cuftomary prayers over the Bifhop devoutly kneeling before the high altar. Then the Bifhop, having made a magnificent offering to the image of the Virgin Mary, placed on the centre of the altar, put on his pontifical robes, a rochet, amice, and black cope[h]. Thus arrayed, he repaired to the chapter houfe, attended by the dean and canons, with a vaft concourfe both of laity and clergy. When he had taken his feat, and the reft were feated and filent, Ed-

---

[h] " The Rochet, Surplice, and Albe are made in the fame form, except that the Rochet and Albe have clofe fleeves, the Surplice wide and open fleeves, and the Albe reaches down to the feet, whereas the other two are fhort, being tucked up a little, and tied round All three are commonly laced " The Amice, a kind of mantle covering the fhoulders and tied with two fillets acrofs the breaft, is defcribed as the firft or undermoft of the facred veftments The Cope was a fort of long cloak, firft ufed to cover the body in rain, and hence called Pluviale It was thrown over the fhoulders, and clafped on the breaft The venerable Wiclif's Cope, of purple velvet, embroidered with angels, is fhewn at Lutterworth, where his pulpit and arm chair alfo are preferved.—The firft part of this note I owe to my ever dear Friend, the late Dr Townfon, who heard with patience many parts of thefe memoirs in their firft and rudeft form many years ago

ward

ward Powel, B D of the Univerſity of Oxford, delivered a Latin ſermon, in a very elegant ſtyle, on the appoſite text, "Go and
ſee whether it be well with thy brethren."
Gen. xxxvii. 14. Vulgate.

After the ſermon was ended, and Indulgence of forty days granted by the Biſhop to
all preſent, thoſe not concerned in the viſitation were ordered to withdraw, when the
buſineſs, which had been uſhered in with ſo
much ſacred pomp, commenced in form,
and was continued, with ſome adjournments,
a full fortnight, from March 29, till the
twelfth of April. From the detail of particulars, which in this long period came under
the Biſhop's inveſtigation, it may be proper
to ſelect ſuch names and circumſtances, as
tend to illuſtrate the character of the viſitor,
or throw light on the hiſtory of the times.

Among thoſe who appeared on this occaſion, not perſonally, but by their proxies, was
William Smyth, archdeacon of Northampton[1], in whoſe behalf it was alleged, that he

[1] He was collated to the archdeaconry of Northampton
about a year before, Jan 4, 1499–1500 MS Harl 6953
p 19 and inſtalled by proxy, 1 Feb being perhaps then abroad
MS Harl. 6954 p 155

was

was abfent with the Bifhop's leave, profecut-ing his ftudies in foreign parts. He was a nephew of the Bifhop's[k]; and the caufe of his abfence is the more memorable, as it is probable he was one, perhaps the only one known at prefent, of thofe alluded to in the Bifhop's epitaph; where it is faid, that he " maintained many of the clergy," no doubt in purfuit of literature, " both at home and abroad[l]."

John Walles, refidentiary and prebendary of Farendon, another abfentee, had for fome time been attending his Majefty's pleafure at court; where he had bufinefs to tranfact for the benefit of the cathedral, but of what fort we are not informed He had been guardian of the fpiritualties, fede vacante, upon the death of Ruffell, 1494[m]. His refidence was difpenfed with by Smyth, on certain condi-tions, May 9, 1500, he being then chaplain in ordinary to his Majefty, and a privy coun-fellor[n]. He was prefent, with Sir Reginald Bray, Hugh Oldham, and others, when John

---

[k] See Append Ped 2

[l] —————————— Amator
 Cleri, nam multos cis mare tranfque aluit

[m] MS. Harl 6953 p 17   [n] Ibid 6954 p 156

Iflip,

Iſlip, abbat of Weſtminſter, on the part of the King, laid the firſt ſtone of Henry viith's chapel, January 24, 1502-3[o] He died before Auguſt 31, 1504; when he was ſucceeded in the prebend of Farendon by Charles Bothe[p], ſo often named in theſe papers.

Henry Hornby, D D. prebendary of Naſſington, dean of the chapel and ſecretary to Margaret counteſs of Richmond, was engaged with important buſineſs of that illuſtrious princeſs. He appears to have poſſeſſed much of her confidence, for ſhe appointed him, by the ſtyle of " our Chancellor," one of her executors; and intruſted to him and biſhop Fox the reviſal of her will[q]. Smyth gave him the prebend, which he enjoyed at Lincoln[r], and had alſo preferred him to the Deanery of St. Chad's, Salop, in his former diocese He was a Lincolnſhire man, educated at Cambridge, and Maſter of Peterhouſe in that Univerſity He wrote and addreſſed to the counteſs of Richmond, " The

---

[o] Dart s Weſtm Abbey, vol 1 p 32 Stowe's Ann p 484

[p] MS Harl 6953 p 21

[q] Royal Wills, p 366 388.

[r] Willis Cath 11 225 Collated to St Chad's, Feb. 2, 1493-4 Reg Lichf f 155 b He reſigned Normanton in the archdeaconry of Derby, before Jan 7 1495-6 ibid f 154 b

Hiſtory

Hiſtory of the Name of Jeſus," and " The Hiſtory of the Viſitation of Mary " As executor to the Counteſs he was an active co-adjutor to biſhop Fiſher, another of her executors, in completing her deſign of founding St. John's college, Cambridge, and when the ſaid Biſhop had conſecrated the chapel, he and Dr. Hornby made their ſolemn entrance, July 29, 1516, conſtituted the firſt Maſter, and appointed the firſt Fellows. He died February 12, 1517[s].

George Fitzhugh, the dean ſo often mentioned, was ſtrongly intrenched in papal reſcripts. He exhibited an " apoſtolical diſpenſation," that is, a papal bull, to hold any benefice or dignity, inferior to a biſhopric, when he was not more than ſixteen years old[t]. He had letters from the pope's col-

[s] See Baker's Pref to Fun Serm of Margaret Counteſs of Richmond, p xxviii—l and Tanner's Biblioth Pits, p 688 and Knights Eraſm p 145

[t] " A man had tnought there had not been ſo much corruption in the Romiſh church, as to admit children to church livings, (for which men are hardly ſufficient[1]) but that Sir Antnony St Leiger [Lieutenant of Ireland, temp H viii] was forced to make this law, *That no children ſhould be admitted to benefices* We had not known this ſin, had not the law ſaid, *You ſtall rot inveſt any under ſixteen years of age in benefices* " Lloyds Worthies, vol 1 p 102 Alexander, ſon of James iv king

lector to be ordained prieft, when he was only three and twenty   He had papal letters for a plurality of benefices, papal letters to unite the rectory of Byngham in Yorkfhire to the canonry of Whitingdon in the cathedral of York, and papal letters to unite for his life Kirby Ravenfworth to Bedall in Yorkfhire.   He was the fourth fon of Henry lord Fitzhugh, a name firft appropriated to the family in the reign of Edward III; but their anceftors were poffeffed of feveral fair lordfhips in Yorkfhire, in the time of the Conqueror[u].   This younger fon of the fifth baron was, in 1479, prefented by Alice lady dowager Fitzhugh to the rectory of Wyntyngham or Wintringham[x], for which probably, fince his eldeft brother was then but juft of age[y], the difpenfation above mentioned was procured.   In addition to the benefices and dignities already enumerated, he held, with the deanery of Lincoln, the pre-

king of Scotland, was archbifhop of St Andrews before he was twenty years of age   Erafmus, who was tutor to him abroad about 1506, celebrates his accomplifhments and laments his death   He was flain with his father at the battle of Flodden field, 1513   See Knight's Erafm p 96 101 350

[u] Dugd Bar 1 405

[x] Inftit 15 Mar 1478-9   MS. Harl 7048 p. 330.

[y] Dugdale, ut fupra

bend

bend of Cropredy in that cathedral[z], and was at the same time Master of Pembroke hall in the University of Cambridge[a]. Thus honourable by birth, conspicuous in station, and overflowing with preferment, he had, according to the style of the higher ecclesiastics in those times, a numerous train of retainers and domestics, who are charged with various acts of irregularity and misdemeanor. They broke the windows of the cathedral, and damaged the stone work and the roof, with their arrows and cross-bows[b]: in which

[z] He was installed in the deanery and prebend, 3 May, 1486 MS Harl 6954 p 153 He gave a cope of white damask to the Cathedral Dugd Mon iii 281 to which also lady Alice Fitzhugh gave a " Corporafs with a cafe " ib 274 and a " Chefable of black velvet," richly ornamented ib 284 2

[a] MS Harl 6953 p 59 As prebendary of Cropredy he prefented Roger Lupton, B of Can L to the vicarage of Cropredy, 17 Aug 1487 MS Harl 7048 p 295 to which he was inducted, 24 Aug ibid 6954 p 153 The faid Roger Lupton, fifty-eighth Fellow of Eton, was elected the fixth Provoft, 27 Feb 1503 and confirmed by bishop Smyth, 4 March following and continued Provoft in 1534 (Rymer, xiv p 505) MS Catal of Prov and Fell of Eton, by Ant Allen, efq in Eton college He was collated to the Preb of Keyfter, on the death of John Conftable, 17 Aug 1528, being then D D MS Harl 6953 p 92

[b] Arcubus et baliftis Reg f 143 b Two years after this the parliament, which allowed the free importation of Bowftaves (19 H vii c 2) enacted, that no one fhould fhoot in the crofs-bow, without the King's licence, except he were a

Lord,

acts of wantonnefs however they were not
the only offenders, but were joined by other
fervants belonging to the chapter One enor-
mity, ftill more opprobrious, is laid to the
account of one of the dean's fervants. In his
retinue was a ' gentleman" of the name of
Wigmerpole, a married man, who had a
chamber contiguous to one of the chantries ,
to which the chaplains often reforted, and
played at dice and cards till it was paft mid-
night .

<hr />

fend er had 200 marks a year in land c 4 which prohibition was confirmed 25 3 H iii c 13 6 H viii c 15
12 H vii c 7 25 H vii c 17

— " Maurotiers ludebant ad alias, taxillos, et cardos fupra me-
dia noctem are the words of the fchedule, exhibited to the
Vifitor In Vol vi of the Archæologia, Num xvi—xviii are
ingenious differtations on Cards, by the Hon Daines Barrington Mr bower, and Mr Gough It feems to be agreed, that
the are a Spanifh invention and were difcovered rather more
than a certain before this time But the paffage before us
fhews them to are been in vogue in England at the period,
when they are thought to have been but little known here , one
conjecture upon it being that they were introduced by the
princefs Catharine of Spain, who did not arrive in England
till autumn in the feventh year, 1501 They are prohibited in
the ftatutes of Brazen Nofe college, but permitted at Chriftmas
by Sir Richard Sutton in his revifed edition of the Bifhop's ftatutes Nemo de collegii ad taxillos, aleas, chartas, aut
pilam ludet —Permittimus tamen quod tempore Natalis Domini chartas feu alium ludum honeftum—publice in aula exercere valeant cap xxiii Of ' taxilli" in thefe paffages I do
not

When the Dean, confcious of fuch mif-
rule, under his eye and in his own houfhold,
was interrogated on the ftate of morals and
difcipline, he anfwered, He hoped all was
well. The Vifitor, it is probable, in a long
private conference, which he had with him
and the refidentiaries, gave both him and
them to underftand, that there was need of
reform.

When thefe points of moral and religious
confideration had been inveftigated, other
matters of inferior moment were not neglected The revenues appropriated to the repairs of the cathedral were infufficient for
the purpofe. In order therefore to apply an
adequate remedy, when the extent of the
deficiency fhould be known, the clerk of
the works and the receiver of the rents were

not know the diftinct meaning, and therefore have not tranflated it An ingenious friend conjectures it is tables (that is,
he thinks, backgammon) partly becaufe he finds " aleæ, taxilli,
chartæ," and " dice, tables, cards,' generally mentioned together Of cards fee alfo Gent Mag 178- p 78; Brit
Crit 1 p 353 Mr Warton thinks the Arabians were the inventors of cards Hift Poet ii 316 note e fee alfo ib iii
p 312 note c Ames Typogr p 1628 Cards are alfo prohibited in the ftatutes of Magdalen college, given in 1479 See
Johnfton s Kings Vifitatorial Power afferted, Lond 1688, 4to
P 337.

ordered

ordered to produce proper ſtatements; which
were examined by the viſitor in perſon It
appeared, that large ſums of money, beſtowed
by the liberality of the Biſhop himſelf, and
by others at his ſolicitation, had been carefully laid out, but ſtill much remained to
be done.   It was therefore judged neceſſary
to procure contributions for the purpoſe, for
the full and final accompliſhment whereof,
he determined, with the approbation of the
chapter, to ſummon, upon a future day, the
archdeacons and others that were now ab-
ſent.   With this reſolution, perceiving nothing further that demanded reformation, he
cloſed the buſineſs, and diſmiſſed the chapter
and others in peace[d].

Such was the care and attention mani-
feſted by the Biſhop on this occaſion.   Nor
did he, when his perſonal viſitation was
ended, ſuffer the ſubject to eſcape from his
thoughts, contenting himſelf with having
recommended what the moment ſuggeſted.
On the contrary, revolving the matter in his
mind, he reduced the particulars into form,
and tranſmitted from his caſtle at Banbury,

[d] Reg Linc f 140—147 b See alſo an abſtract of the
viſitation in MS Harl. 6953 p. 68, &c

before

before the month expired, a commiffion to the dean and chapter, requiring them to correct, within the fpace of three months, and to certify him of it before the feaft of Affumption (Auguft 15) fuch matters as he had found to ftand in need of reform, a fchedule whereof was fent at the fame time[e]. This fchedule does not now appear, but the lofs is compenfated by another memorial, of a fimilar nature and fubfequent date. For the good Bifhop, whofe folicitude for the honour of religion and his church did not ceafe, while aught appeared capable of reform or improvement, had another interview and confultation with his chapter, on Saturday, October 7, 1503. On this occafion, with a view as well to correct what was paft, as to eftablifh good government in future, certain articles, eighteen in number, were propofed and agreed to, which, when put into form upon paper, were fubfcribed by the Bifhop, and by the dean and chapter; who engaged ftrictly to obferve and enforce the falutary regulations, of which they caufed a fair tranfcript to be preferved in their regifter[f]. Of thefe rules and injunctions fuch

---

[e] Reg Linc f 105 b dat 20 Apr 1501
[f] Act. Capit Linc 1501—1507 f 71—73

as

as regard the receipt and expenditure of money, the obfervance of the ftatutes, and the
interior police of the chapter, matters ufeful
and prudent in their day, may at prefent be
omitted, but one or two articles of an hiftorical nature fall within our province

Smyth's predeceffor Ruffell had bequeathed
money to endow a chantry and obit for himfelf, and an obit for Thomas Fitzwilliam[g],
but though the legacy had been received, the
purpofe of the teftator had not hitherto been
fully executed   It is now therefore refolved,
that lands fhall be purchafed for the maintenance of the chantry; wherein the Bifhop
promifes his advice and affiftance.

Another of his predeceffors, bifhop Alnwick, who adorned the cathedral with its
beautiful fouth porch, had caufed a tripartite
inventory to be kept of the jewels, plate, and
reftments, belonging to the church   He com-

---

[g] This Tho Fitzwilliam, efquire, was of Mablethorpe,
Com Linc and was buried in Linc Minfter, near the furtheft
pillar from the choir eaftward on the fouth fide, where (as
Mr Fardell informs me) upon a marble lying near the pillar,
is the portraiture in brafs of a man armed, and his wife, and
ten children   He died 9 April, 1479   Margaret his wife,
20 June, 1463. See the epitaph in Willis s Cath. iii p 15.

mands

mands the revival of this laudable cuftom, with exprefs reference to the author of the plan; whofe memory he appears to have held in great veneration; and, as a proof of it, he gave direction in his will, that his body fhould be interred clofe to the grave of this pious prelate, in the fpirit of the prophet, who faid to his fons, "When I am dead, then bury me in the fepulchre wherein the man of God is buried, lay my bones befide his bones." 1 Kings xiii. 31

While he thus laboured to eftablifh good order in his cathedral, he was not inattentive to his diocefe at large. He gave ample inftructions and powers to Henry Apjohn, his commiffary for the archdeaconries of Lincoln and Stow, to inquire into fuch matters, as he had found upon his vifitation required correction. At the head of thefe, as a matter of prime confequence, ftands the cafe of non-refidence, about which the commiffary is injoined to make ftrict inquiry, and to give annual and circumftantial information on the fubject to the bifhop, or his chancellor. The ftate of chancels and parfonages is next recommended to his care; and in regard to fuch moral delinquencies as ufually fell under ecclefiaftical cognizance, where he fhould

K   judge

judge it proper to impofe or accept from the offending party a pecuniary fine, he is ordered to convert the money fo received to pious ufes, efpecially to the repairs of the cathedral at Lincoln. He is to record his proceedings in the general execution of this truft, and to lay the accounts before the Bifhop at a time appointed, and likewife to keep exact regifters of wills and other matters, and to deliver them up every third year, to be preferved in the archives of the church. Laftly, to pafs over feveral minute articles of ecclefiaftical jurifdiction, the Bifhop, jealous as it feems of papal encroachments, ftrictly commands him to admit no difpenfations granted by the collector of the fovereign pontif, unlefs he himfelf, as ordinary, fhall previoufly have been fatisfied as to the original bull[h].

---

[h] Reg Linc f 121   Apjohn's appointment as commiffary is dated Feb 6, 1495-6 ibid f 3 where he is ftyled B of Canon law, and Precentor of Lincoln   Smyth collated him to the prebend of Langford ecclefia, June 27, 1501   MS Harl 6953 p 19 and, on his deceafe, gave the precentorfhip to Richard Cowland, prebendary of Lowth, Aug 17, 1504 ibid p 21 whom he had collated to Stanton Harcourt, Oxfordfhire, Apr 24, 1498, in confequence of a difpute between the convent of Reading and Sir Robert Harcourt, knight, about the right of prefentation ibid p 41

One

One specimen, and perhaps only one, of the Bishop's manner in his parochial visitations is still extant; and it is a singular monument of his industry and discretion. It is the visitation of Leicestershire in 1510[1], a period later by some years, than what is now before us; but, from its connection with our present subject, it may not improperly be brought forward here. The record exhibits a very striking picture of the depravity of those times; which, if contrasted at length with any period since the days of Edward vi, would authorize us to conclude, that, greatly as every good imparted to man is impeded in its effects by the perverseness of the receiver, yet that invaluable blessing, the Reformation of religion, never has been destitute of sensible influence of the best kind: it has enlightened the understanding, and meliorated the heart, and lessened the empire of immorality and vice.

But the visitor himself, rather than the

---

[1] "Visitation Book of Leicestershire, 1510." f 38—57 in Archiv Dom Episc Linc apud Buckden For the inspection and use of these Records I with pleasure acknowledge myself indebted to the obliging permission of a learned and intelligent Successor of bishop Smyth, the present Bishop of Lincoln. 1799

persons

perfons vifited, is the object of our refearch
Of his exact age at this time we are uncertain, but this is manifeft, that his patience
to hear and examine grievances, and his ability and zeal to redrefs them, appear in all
their vigour.   In his progrefs, during feveral
fucceffive days, he received, at Bofworth,
Melton Mowbray, and other places, the minute and often intricate accounts of the various circumjacent parifhes, from the information of the clergy, the church wardens,
and others; and while the facred functions
of religion, and the morals as well of laity as
clergy, pafs in review, neither the revenues
of the churches, nor their repair and decent
cleanlinefs, are overlooked or neglected.   In
fome cafes fuitable remedies, whether of advice or reprehenfion, are adminiftered on the
occafion; for others a further hearing is appointed; and it muft be obferved to his honour, that the acts of penance and humi-
liation, impofed by him on offenders, are free
from thofe odious and offenfive, not to fay
indecent, circumftances, which too often
marked the ecclefiaftical cenfures of thofe
days[k].

[k] See an injunction dat 1516, in the fame archives, Book,
F E f 6 that a perfon " induta fola camifia, nuda caput, pe-
ces, et tibias, fhould walk, with a torch in her hand, once
through

It were to be wifhed, that the wifdom and moderation, with which the Bifhop proceeded in punifhing crimes and reforming moral conduct, had appeared with equal advantage, when matters of opinion and points of religious doctrine were the fubject of his cognizance. But perfection is not the attribute of man · and we learn with lefs furprife than regret, that Smyth did not efcape the common fault of condemning heretics to the prifon or the ftake.

The doctrines of Wiclif had, from the firft, found many ftrenuous and able advocates in the Univerfity of Oxford; and fo great was the alarm, fpread among the friends and fathers of the church, that Lincoln college, in which Smyth is thought to have been educated, was founded for the avowed purpofe of counteracting and extirpating the growing mifchief[1]. The friends however of dawning truth, both in the Univerfity and the country, if more fecret, were not lefs numerous, nor lefs determined. They read the

through the public market, and three times at church. Strange blindnefs[1] to imagine this could promote piety, either in the fufferer or fpectators.

[1] Wood, Colleges, p 234

Scrip-

Scriptures in Wiclif's tranflation, oppofed the invocation of faints, and denied the corporal prefence in the euchariſt.

It does not appear that Smyth, in whofe time the number of thefe heretics (as they were called) was very confiderable, took an active part in fearching for and convening them; but when they were accufed before him, he was fufficiently rigorous in enforcing the laws to their conviction and punifhment His predeceffor Ruffell, haraffed and fatigued, as he feelingly complains, with the multitude of heretics at Oxford in the year 1491, having met with the book of the venerable doctor Thomas Waldenſis[m], a Carmelite friar, who wrote early in that century againft the

[m] Thomas Netter, commonly called Waldenſis, from Walden in Effex, where he was born, was Provincial of his order, ne flourifhed about the year 1410, and died in 1430 His work intitled " Doctrinale Antiquitatum fidei Ecclefiæ Catholicæ,' in 3 tomes, was printed at Paris, 1532 The third tome, " De Sacramentalibus, was the part abridged by Ruffell See Cave, Hift Lit vol ii App p 112. Oxon 1743 I take this opportunity of mentioning, that the Notes and Additions fubjoined to the fecond volume of this valuable edition of a capital work are moft certainly not by archbifhop Tenifon, to whom they are afcribed in the preface, &c of this fecond volume, but by the celebrated antiquary, Henry Wharton, chaplain to archbifhop Sancroft. See Gent. Mag 1791 p 698

Wic-

Wiclevifts, he refolved to make extracts from the bulky volume for the more fpeedy and effectual refutation of the "infane dogmas, with which, he fays, fo many of his countrymen were infected" Having framed his compendium with great care, by a written injunction under his own hand he ordered it to be preferved in the Regiftry of the fee, for the benefit of his fucceffors in their examinations of " heretical depravity ;" pronouncing an anathema at the fame time againft any one, who fhould obliterate the title, expreffive of the defign of the performance and the name of the compiler[n].

This choice manual, the touchftone of error, which was completed at Woburn on the feaft of the Epiphany, 1491-2, perhaps Smyth had in his hands in the fame palace of Woburn, at once to ftimulate his zeal and

---

[n] " Philofophi in his ipfis libris, quos fcribunt de contemnenda gloria, fua nomina infcribunt " Tufc Quæft 1 xv and fo, alas ! do the advocates of perfecution, fulfilling our Lords Prophecy, John xvi 2 The original copy of this memorable work of bifhop Ruffell's, with his autograph, is ftill extant in the Library of Univerfity college, L 17 The curious note of the author is given at length by Tanner in his Bibliotheca, v Ruffil, Johannes.

affift

affift his inquiries, in 1506, when Thomas
Chafe of Amerfham, in which town and
neighbourhood the heretics abounded, was
brought before him The Bifhop examined
and rebuked him, not without afperity, in
regard to the controverted points, but the
culprit being inflexible, neither intimidated
by menaces to difavow his opinions, nor induced by argument to alter them, he was
committed to the Bifhop's prifon called Lit-
tle-eafe Here the Bifhop's chaplains daily
vifited him, in hopes to convert him, but
their attempts in this way meeting with no
better fuccefs, than his lordfhip's endeavours
had before, they at laft " moft cruelly ftran-
gled and preft him to death; and caufed it
to be bruted abroad, that he had hanged
himfelf;" which the nature of his confinement, our hiftorian fays, rendered impoffible
" For the prifon was fuch, that a man could
not ftand upright" in it, " nor lie at eafe,"
as thofe who knew it alleged.   In the prefent age of greater humanity, the name itfelf, together with the practice, of fuch clofe
cuftody, is become obfolete, but in the middle of the laft century it was ftill fo familiar,
that the word was ufed as an obvious meta-
phor for reftraint in general, and Mr. Mede,

perhaps

perhaps with greater force than elegance of expreſſion, ſpeaks of " putting a prophecy in *Little-eaſe°*."

In the ſame year, and at the ſame town of Amerſham, in Stanley cloſe, William Tylſworth was burnt for hereſy, when his daughter, Joan Clerk, was compelled to ſet fire to her father, and her huſband, John Clerk, was one among many, who at the ſame time bore a faggot, and did penance[p].

Fox has recorded a few inſtances beſides, of ſimilar perſecution under biſhop Smyth. I have ſelected thoſe, which are peculiarly marked with circumſtances of ſeverity. As the martyrologiſt gathered theſe accounts from oral information[q], at the diſtance of

---

° Works, p 752 Ep xii See alſo Mercur Ruſt ed 1685 p 107 137 Gent Mag 1783, p 920

P Fox's Martyrs, ed 1596 p 710, 711 See alſo Wood's Annals, ii p 4

q He often cites Regiſters, but not for theſe inſtances The martyrologiſt's veracity has ſometimes been needleſsly called in queſtion, becauſe the Records which he quotes are at preſent ſeldom to be found Mr Fardell, as accurate as he is communicative in his intelligence, ſays he is " fully perſuaded Bp Longland kept a regiſter of the examination of heretics, to which Fox refers, though it is not now at Lincoln ' Bonner had a famous commiſſion from queer Mary to ſearch all Re-

giſters,

threefcore years from the events, it is reafonable to fuppofe, that the minute circumftances might not be reported very correctly;
and, certainly, that the colouring of the
whole was not foftened, by thofe who were
friends to the fufferers and to their caufe.
But if all that is related was literally done.
this at leaft the character of Smyth induces
us to believe, that, although the fentence
might be his, the ftudied barbarity, which
difgraced the execution, was the refult of
bafer minds, without his fuggeftion or concurrence[r] It was not his nature to add in-
fult to mifery, nor to degrade the dignity of
juftice by the littlenefs of malice and rancour
of revenge. Inftances of perfecution, like as
inftances of murder, may be found in individuals of every religious creed or denomination, but Popery, ever true to itfelf and
ever the fame, *juftifies* to this day the fhock-
ing *principle* of thefe inhuman deeds[s]. It is

grifters, and to take out of them every thing inimical or difre-
putable to popery burnets Ref 1 351 Records, 301

[r] The fentence of the court on thefe occafions was executed
by the Sneriff who " by 2 H iv c 15 was bound *ex officio*, if
required by the bifrop, to commit the unhappy victim to the
flames, without waiting for the confent of the crown. Blackftone, B iv c iv Ayliffes Parerg p 292

[s] " The *Hiftory of the Variations of the Proteftant Churches*, by
Bolluet,

the praife of Smyth, that, profeffing this religion in an age of bigotry and blindnefs, he
was lefs intolerant than many of his contemporaries. Fox himfelf, whofe zeal againft
popery would not fuffer him to be more
tender than the truth compelled him to be,
even to the Founder of the college where he

Boffuet, is in every Roman Catholic's hands, it is efteemed de-
cifive, and very few Papifts will appeal from it's authority
Yet hear this eloquent and *merciful* Prelate, in a familiar and
popular work addreffed to all perfons ' As to the exercife and
ufe of the power of the fword in matters of religion and of
confcience—it is a point not to be called in queftion—THE
RIGHT *of it is certain*. There is no illufion more dangerous
than to confider TOLERATION as a mark and character of *the
true* church' I will give the words in the original 'L exercice
de la puiffance du glaive dans les matieres de la religion et de
la confcience—Chofe, qui ne peut etre revoquée en doute —LE
DROIT *eft certain* il n y a point d illufion plus dangereufe que
de donner LA SOUFFRANCE pour un caractere de *la vraie* Eglife '
Boff Hift des Variations, &c l 10 p 51 ed Paris, 1740
12mo ' See p 33 of a very elegant ' Letter to the Lord Marquis of Buckingham,' on the fubject of the Emigrant French
Priefts, and on the fpirit and principles of the Church of Rome,
by a Layman Lordon, 1796, 8vo Mr Berington having
honeftly " owned, that his church has perfecuted," and " that
intolerance is the profeffed doctrine of her decrees," this frank
confeffion of the truth " gave offence to many perfons of his
communion ,' and he fays, in his " retractation," I know not
whether with ferioufnefs of conviction, or with folemn irony,
" That my church ever *perfecuted*, I fhould not have conceded ,
and fhould have gloried in the *intolerance* of her profeffions "
Gent Mag 1799 p 654 1023

received

received part of his education[t], says however of Smyth, that " although he was somewhat eger and sharpe against the poore simple flocke of Christes seruants;—yet was he nothing so bloudy and cruell, as was Longland, which afterward succeeded in that Dioces. For so I finde of him, that in the time of the great abiuration,—diuers he sent quietly home, without punishment and pennance: bidding them go home, and liue as good christian men should doe[u]." I shall only observe further on this unpleasing topic, that it may be said of Smyth, as it has on the like occasion been remarked of St Augustin, that " he seems to have been severe by religion, and gentle by temper; which shews how important and necessary it is to have reasonable principles, without which the best-natured man is capable of doing the most ill-natured actions[x]."

---

[t] Fox was first of Brasen Nose college, then a Demy of Magdalen

[u] Fox, ut supra, p 750

[x] Jortins Six Dissert Diss ii p 30

SECT. VI

Chancellor of the University of Oxford

IN the preceding section we anticipated some few ecclesiastical occurrences on account of their connection with the subject then in hand. For a similar reason we have deferred till now one or two circumstances relating to the University of Oxford, the rest follow in order, and these academical matters, with some others of a miscellaneous nature, will lead us to the foundation of Brasen Nose college and the end of our inquiries.

In 1494, Ruffell, bishop of Lincoln, the first perpetual Chancellor of Oxford, perceiving himself grow infirm, was desirous to resign the office, which he had filled with great credit for ten years. He expressed his wishes to that effect, more than once, by letter to the King, and waited for his royal approbation, before he actually vacated the post. In the mean time the King being at Woodstock,

ftock, and underftanding that the Univerfity
were taking meafures for the election of a
new Chancellor, wrote to them to forbear
all proceedings on the occafion, till Ruffell
fhould have refigned in form , and till they
knew, as they fhould in a fhort time, his further pleafure[a]. The Univerfity expreffed their
thanks for this gracious condefcenfion to their
affairs, on the part of his Majefty; and he
was pleafed to fay, he would fpeedily recommend fome " fubftantial, wife, and virtuous
perfon to be their Chancellor[b]."

Whether Ruffell actually refigned, or not,
is uncertain[c], but upon his deceafe, which
happened about the end of December[d], his
Majefty fulfilled his promife of recommen-

[a] Reg Γ f 176 Ep 462 Wodftoke, 9 Oct Ep 463 is
the anfwer of tha ths, 13 Oct

[b] Ibid Ep 464 At our Caftell of Wirdefore, 17 Oct

[c] Ibid Ep 466 is to Sir R. Bray, Steward of the Unive-
fity, with thanks for the donat on of 40 marks towards
building St Mary s church, and defiring him to procure the
Chancellor s refignation, faid to be in the King's hands The
date is 6 Id Dec

[d] His will, dated 30 Dec 1494, was proved Jan 12 Ri-
hardfon s notes in Godwin See alfo the following note here,
and correct Tanner, Biblioth v Ruffel, Joh who fays he died
Jan 30 MS Harl 6953 p 17 fays, " debet effe 30 Dec ut
patet ex inftitutionibus "

dation,

dation, in thefe words : " To thentente—
yow fhulde haue fuch an honorable actyff
and difcrete perfon to be your hede and go-
uernor, as myght bothe ouerfe [overfee] yow,
promote your caufes vnto vs, and defende
yow in your ryghts and priveleges; We re-
commende vnto yow the ryght reuerende fa-
dres in Gode, our full trufty and ryght wel-
belouyde the byfhoppis of Cheftyr and Ro-
cheftyr, for yow to chefe, fithens [fince]
they both be of yow and browght vpp
amonge yow, the oon of them to be your
Chaunceler[e]."

The firft of the two prelates, thus approved
and recommended, was Smyth, at this time
bifhop of Chefter, that is (for the titles were
ufed indifcriminately) of Lichfield and Coventry. The other was Thomas Savage, afterwards tranflated to London, and thence to
York, whom Godwin, by miftake, as appears from this letter, calls a Cambridge
man[f] The letter was brought to Oxford by

[e] F Ep 469 From the Tower of London, 11 Jan He
mentions their late Chancellor, " now deceffyde '

[f] He was incorporated at Cambridge, being then bifhop of
Rochefter, A D 1496, at the fame time that Smyth, " Doctor
Fitzjames," and other Oxford men were Reg Cantab Beta,
f 99 See and correct A Wood, Annals, 1 651 who fays Dr
Fitzjames

Edward Willoughby, the King's chaplain,
January 17, at the very moment when the
University, having waited as long as the ftatutes permitted, were finging mafs, on having unanimoufly chofen cardinal Morton,
archbifhop of Canterbury, for their Chancellor. Of this they informed his Majefty,
with all fubmiffion, hoping he would be gra-
cioufly pleafed with the choice they had
made ; and the two bifhops, as Wood fays[e],
feconding the requeft, all parties were, or appeared to be, well pleafed.

The next occurrence, which connects Smyth
with the Univerfity, a matter of no great moment in itfelf, is rendered interefting by the
number of exalted perfonages, who took a
part in it. The place of fuperior Bedel in
Arts being vacant, in the year 1500, the
prince of Wales, and the bifhop of Lincoln,
Prefident of his council, folicited the appointment for Thomas Pantry. The Queen and
the countefs of Richmond alfo wrote in fa-

Fitzjames was one of the two propofed by the King But he
was not made Bp of Rochefter till 1497, and was appointed
one of the delegates to tender the oath to the new Chancellor,
by the title merely of Dr Fitzjames, his Majefty s Almoner
Ep 472 F f 177 b Feb 9 1494-5
   [e] Annals, ut fupra

                                        your

vour of the fame candidate; who was accordingly elected, October 12, 1500[h]. The perſon, ſo honourably recommended and choſen, was living and poſſeſſed of his office in 1522, when another royal letter was written in his favour. Henry viii, being engaged in a war with France[i], had directed a commiſſion to the Mayor of Oxford, to ſearch for Frenchmen and Scots, and to ſeize their goods for his Majeſty's uſe. By virtue of this warrant Pantry was arreſted, on ſuſpicion of being a Frenchman. Henry therefore wrote to the Mayor to releaſe his bail, and defiſt from all proceedings againſt him; as he was one of his liege ſubjects, had refided in England more than forty years, and was born within his Majeſty's dominions, in the town of Calais[k].

Smyth was in Oxford twice during the

---

[h] Œ f 84 b A later hand ſays the letters are in F but it is a miſtake The writer meant, I preſume, certain letters relating to an election of the following year, which will be noticed preſently

[i] Wood's Annals, ii p 22

[k] To Tho Shelton, Mayor of Oxford "Yeven under owre ſignett, at Byſshoppeſhatfeld, 25 Nov 14 H viii Reg F F Bodl Arch A 166 f 58 " Thomas Shelton, Bruer," occurs in 1510 Reg T. f 118

I   ſummer

fummer of 1500, Auguſt 4[1], and September
26[n]. At the time of this fecond viſit the
chancellorſhip had been vacant ten days by
the death of archbiſhop Morton[n], and it was
fuffered to remain void, whatever might be
the reaſon, feveral weeks. At length however,
when the buſineſs of election was brought on
in form, the biſhop of Lincoln was, in the opinion of the Univerſity, " as well by heavenly
infpiration, as by human judgement, unanimouſly chofen." In their letter, announcing
this, November 5, they intreat him to accept
the office, the higheſt honour they had to
beſtow; which they conferred, not only as a
mark of gratitude for daily favours received
at his hands, but from regard to thofe talents, which fo eminently fitted him for the

[1] Mr Fardell, from the Regiſters

[n] Reg Linc f 123

[n] He died Sept 15 Godwin, p 131 note h He was of
Baliol college Athen Oxon i 642 See a view of his effigies
and of the beautiful crypt, which he built for his fepulture, in
Drakes Parker, p 448 and in Mr Goughs Sep Mon vol ii
where is a large account of him, p 342—344 In Reg F is
a letter of thanks (Ep 389) to him from the Univerſity of
Oxford, about 1490 another (Ep 451) about 1492 Epp
468 471 474 to him on his being elected Chancellor of the
Univerſity, 1494–5 Epp 470 473 from him on that occafion

truſt,

truft, his extraordinary prudence and many other virtues[o].

Smyth's anfwer was delayed beyond his wifhes, by " inceffant employment in defending the caufe of innocence" (in his own courts probably, for he was now in his diocefe[p],) and by ferious deliberation on the weight and difficulty of the charge. When he found leifure to write, he expreffed himfelf fully fenfible of the diftinguifhed honour they had fhewn him by unanimoufly electing him, the moft unworthy among the venerable bifhops of the realm, to prefide over the academic body, a ftation which demanded abilities lefs unequal to the truft. However, in obedience to his Majefty's command, and at the requeft of many illuftrious perfons, he would not oppofe their wifhes; but thankfully accept the office, and ufe his beft endeavours, with God's affiftance, to accomplifh whatever might advance the peace and credit and welfare of the Univerfity.

But as the letter contains advice as well as

[o] F Ep 495 See it in the App No vi

[p] At Lidington, 6 10 15. and 21 November Reg f 70 120. b

thanks,

thanks, that we may be able to judge whether the counfel fuggefted was prudent and feafonable, it will be neceffary to view the ftate of the Univerfity at that time. And this account, if it prove as diftinct and yet as concife as we wifh, will not merely be of ufe in this part of our fubject, but will help us alfo to form a proper eftimate of Smyth's fubfequent benefactions to this feat of literature. We fhall fee, in the circumftances of the Univerfity at that period, whether, being already abundantly endowed and profperous, what was beftowed upon it was the idle facrifice of oftentatious folly, or whether, on the contrary, in thefe interefting days, when tafte and learning were beginning to revive, the generous aid of the wife and good was loudly called for, to render this ancient feminary lefs inadequate to the important tafk of educating half a nation's youth.

In the firft part of the reign of Henry vii the plague vifited Oxford, in the fpace of fifteen years, no lefs than fix times[q], and in the year 1500, when Smyth was elected Chancellor, the calamity was aggravated by

---

[q] 1485, 1486. 1489 1493 1499, 1500 A Wood, Annals

the

the ravages of an inundation and high price of corn. It is needlefs to inquire here, whether what our ancient regifters call the plague was the fame difeafe, which is now underftood by the term. It was fome malignant and contagious diforder, increafed probably by crowded and unwholefome modes of living, and fuch was the devaftation and alarm occafioned by the repeated attacks of the malady, that out of fifty five halls, then in Oxford, thirty two only were thinly inhabited[r]. Many public edifices, particularly the Divinity fchool, the Law fchool, and St. Mary's church, had been recently built, at a great expence, which had nearly exhaufted the finances of the Univerfity and the refources of her friends

Poverty and calamity did not produce internal peace. There were frequent and bloody affrays, many between the gownfmen and the citizens (who were commonly the aggreffors,) jealous each of their refpective privileges; and not a few among the academics themfelves They formed themfelves into parties according to the faculties, in which they ftudied, and the jurifts, probably

[r] Wood's Annals, ad ann 1503

the

the moſt numerous, were the moſt formidable. But the grand diviſion, which ran
through the place, was between the natives
of the northern and ſouthern counties, and
buſineſs in its nature the moſt remote from
hoſtility could not be tranſacted without an
eye to the line of demarcation, the banks of
the Trent. When the Divinity ſchool was
building, two Maſters of Arts, one from each
diſtrict, were appointed to ſuperintend the
work[s]. The ſame mode was obſerved in
electing the Proctors, which, though a neceſſary meaſure to prevent diſputes, ſerved
however to perpetuate the difference

When the Univerſity was thus divided by
faction, waſted by peſtilence, and depreſſed
by poverty, in addition to the common im-
pediments which then obſtructed the paths
of ſcience, it will eaſily be imagined, that the
ſtate of literature, in all its branches, was
truly deplorable. The inſtitutions of Waynflete had produced ſome men of real learning, but the general body was little improved. Grocyn, Latymer, Colet, and Linacre, had acquired in the ſchools of Italy the
knowledge of the Greek language; which

[s] Reg. Aaa. f. 245. A. D. 1467

they

they endeavoured to eftablifh and propagate
in their own Univerfity. but few were at
the pains to learn what a great majority
loaded with contempt, and even branded as
herefy Ptolemy's aftronomy, Ariftotle's lo-
gical and metaphyfical works, in miferable
tranflations and with more miferable com-
ments, fomething of natural philofophy (Ariftotle's probably,) ethics[t], the two firft books
of Euclid[u], and, in the fiift years, fomewhat
of grammar and rhetoric, feem to have
formed the beft part of what was ftudied
preparatory to the firft and fecond degree in
arts.

They were permitted to anticipate the regular time of degrees, upon paying certain
variable pecuniary fees, which, for the high-
ei degrees, weic often very confiderable: for

[t] Reg Aa f 24 b 35 60 b 69 76 b 78 This is a
regifter of degrees and other matters, from 1449 till 1463
Volume G (to be quoted prefently) is a regifter of degrees,
with other notes interfperfed, from 1505 till 1516, both in-
clufive The account of the intermediate time, during which
no fuch regifters are extant, is derived partly from comparing
thefe two periods, and partly from general obfervations, or in-
cidental notices, in other records It is of courfe lefs certain,
but probably not much wide of the truth.

[u] Reg Aa f 23 b. 79 b

L 4   the

the doctorate in theology twenty pounds
was no uncommon sum[x]. Liveries, knives[y],
gloves, and cloth for gowns to the Regents[z],
had been some of the ordinary perquisites,
and when, in the room of these, it was common to substitute a literary exercise, some
part of Cicero[a], or a book of Sallust[b], to be
read to the undergraduates, a copy of Latin
verses[c], or a comedy[d], with a fine of a few

[x] Aa f 35 et alibi

[y] Ibid f 77 117

[z] Ibid f 113 b

[a] Reg G f 70 b 124 b

[b] Ibid. f. 145 b 162 163 b.

[c] Ibid f 72 134 143 145 b 173 b 183 b An hundred verses was commonly the stipulated number, and the
praise of the University the usual theme, which once likewise
(f 145 b) was the subject of the comedy demanded But 50
verses were accepted from a Master in Grammar (f 72) in
1508, and an epigram to be affixed to the gates of St Mary's
church from another licensed to teach in 1513 f 183 b

[d] Ibid f 143 145 b Mr Warton, whose name will be
ever dear to the Antiquary, the Scholar, and the Poet, was, I
believe, perfectly well informed, when he observed, that " it
was not uncommon to call any short poem, not serious or tra-
gic, a comedy " Hist. Poet i 234 But—" aliquando bonus
dormitat Homerus " this same incomparable writer is wrong
in all his dates (unless it be Skelton s, which does not occur in
our registers) when he speaks of degrees in Grammar, which
included rhetoric and versification vol ii 129, 130 Edward
Watson was not graduated in grammar " about the reign of
Edward iv" (i 234) nor " John Watson [read, Edward] about
the year 1470" (ii 129,) but on the eighteenth of March
1511–12. G. f 143 b the " conception" spoken of having been

obtained

shillings, to repair the convocation house[e], to glaze a window[f], repair a dial[g], or mend a

obtained on the eleventh of that month ibid f 143 Another, who by the reference, "f 162," should be Richard Smyth, petitioned for leave to teach, May 12, 1512 f 145 b. and he was ordered, 17 January following, to proceed to his degree before Easter f 162 The date of Maurice Byrchynshaw's grace (as we term it) is Dec 8, 1511 f 134 he was admitted to his degree afterwards, Feb 6, on condition, that he should not read to his auditors Pamphilus, nor Ovid s Art of Love f 139 John Bulman is June 3, 1511 f 124 b but the circumstance that " a crown of laurel was publicly placed on his head by the hands of the Chancellour of the Univerfity" (which Wood also mentions, Annals, vol ii p ii p 721) has escaped me. Robert Whittington (see above, sect iv p 86) April 15, 1513 f 173 b permitted to wear a silk hood, July 3, and crowned with laurel next day f 187 187 b Nor is it true that he " affords the last instance of these rhetorical degrees at Oxford," for Thomas More occurs June 13, 1513 f 183 b. John Ball in 1514 f 232 and Thomas Thomson, June 13, 1514 f 233 It is some excuse for a mind intent upon objects great and various, that the dates in this Register do not form a part of each distinct entry, but must be collected (as they generally may with certainty) by tracing them back Possibly too Wood's Annals (ubi supra) then in manuscript, contributed to these mistakes, but certain it is, that all these stipulated compositions, symptoms of growing taste and attention to learning of a better cast, belong to a period later by 30 years, than that to which most of them are assigned by the Historian of English Poetry See above, p 151 note t

[e] G f 3 b et alibi saepe

[f] Ibid f 102 b

[g] Ibid f 125 185 b It was at last decreed, that it should be repaired at the expence of the Univerfity f. 201 b

bedel's

bedel's ftaff[h]; thefe alterations indicate fome improvement in the tafte for literature, but are no proofs of the affluence of the place

In this abject ftate of the Univerfity there were fome, among the great men of the nation, who had thoughts of reducing it ftill lower by retrenching its privileges; and others, we are informed, went fo far as to talk of fuppreffing it entirely[i].   But her fons, who filled the moft honourable offices of ftate, were fuccefsful advocates for the place of their education   The rancour and animofity, which fo frequently difturbed academic repofe, they confidered as originating in the turbulent fpirit of the times; which public diftractions had kindled, and which had not yet perfectly fubfided in any part of the kingdom.   It occurred alfo, that the inftitutions of the place, fanctioned by ages, had even in the prefent day produced many men, who were the ornaments of their country, and that here were depofited the feeds of learning, which time and culture

---

[h] Ibid f 4. b 27 &c   I have noted only one livery in this Regifter, zones or fafhes for the Regents, to be given by a perfon incorporated from Cambridge, A D 1512 f 147 b

[i] So archbifhop Warham fays, in a letter to the Univerfity, fpeaking of the reign of Henry vii Reg. F F Ep 110

might

might bring to perfection. Thefe confider-
ations, reafonable in themfelves and preffed
with affection, fruftrated the defigns of thofe,
who were hoftile to the Univerfity, and
kings and other auguft perfonages came forward as her friends and benefactors, guaranteed her rights, and confirmed and enlarged
her privileges.

In procuring fome of thefe advantages, as
we have already feen, Smyth was inftrumental, and he probably exerted himfelf
with fimilar fuccefs in other inftances. When
the Univerfity therefore, fecure in their chartered immunities, put themfelves under his
care, by electing him their Chancellor, he
applied his thoughts to improve the difcipline
and habits of the place, as the beft means to
infure the perpetuity of the eftablifhment.
On this he infifts in the letter before mentioned, and with much earneftnefs defires the
learned body themfelves to lend their affiftance, and give effect to his endeavours "In
every ftate," he obferves, "men whofe object
is felf intereft are apt to difregard the general
welfare. He therefore hopes, that none of
them will look merely to perfonal emolument and honours, but rather ftudy to promote the public good. To this end he intreats

treats them to encourage and lead on the youth that were among them, both by word and by example, to the attainment of learning and the practice of virtue " He concludes with informing them, that he had appointed for his Commiffary the reverend William Atwater, D. D. who was ftrongly recommended to him for his merits and diligence; and he requefts them to give him their countenance and fupport in the difcharge of his office[k].

Candour will believe, that this letter of the Chancellor was not totally without effect; and it was perhaps not the lefs likely to make impreffion, as it did not enlarge on the reigning vices, but tacitly alluded to them in the remedies fuggefted, peaceable demeanor, the cultivation of literature, and a common folicitude for the common good.

When the Bifhop had fignified his acceptance of the chancellorfhip, the Univerfity addreffed him a fecond time in terms of unbounded refpect and gratitude. They applaud their good fortune in having obtained for their governour and patron a magnificent

[k] F Ep 496 See App No vii

Prelate,

Prelate, who could not fail to adminifter their affairs in the beft manner. They declare themfelves convinced, that they were born for each other, He to ferve their academic polity, and They to advance his honour; who had, through them, received into his protection fuch a renowned Seminary; where if virtue and ingenuous arts had ever flourifhed, they would now appear with additional luftre, under the aufpices of a Prelate, crowned with every virtue, the friend and patron of good learning.

Having difpatched the complimentary part of their letter, they proceed to the bufinefs of it, which was to defire him to take the cuftomary oath of office, which they had delegated Mr John Reed, chaplain to the prince of Wales, and Mr. John Dunham, bachelors in divinity, to receive in their name[l]. Smyth's predeceffor, archbifhop Morton, declined this oath, alleging it was unneceffary, as he had already more than once fworn obedience to the Univerfity, upon admiffion to different academical degrees; and on this plea he was at laft excufed[m]. As no-

[l] F Ep 497   See Append No viii
[m] Ibid Ep 472—474

thing

thing of this fort is recorded of Smyth, I fuppofe he did not hefitate to renew the obligation And it was partly, no doubt, in
compliment for this fervice, that he collated
both the perfons, deputed on the occafion, to
ftalls in his cathedral[n]. Reed was afterwards
fuccceffively Warden of Wykeham's two colleges, and Mafter of St. Crofs near Winchefter[o]. Dunham was Fellow of Lincoln
college, to which alfo he was a benefactor,
and Rector of Barnack, near Stamford, in
Northamptonfhire.

The Proctors this year, 1500, were Edward Darby, Fellow of Lincoln college, and
Thomas Claydon, of New College. What
preferment the latter obtained, I know not.
Darby was foon afterwards collated by the
Chancellor to the prebend of Dunham in his
cathedral[p], and he gave him, within the year,

---

[n] Reed to Preb Crackpole, 4 Apr 1503 MS Harl 6953
p 20 Willis, Cath 1 173 Dunham to Preb 60 Sol 1507
to Bedford Major, 15 Sept 1509 Willis, Cath 11 238 143
Willis and A. Wood (Colleges, p 240) call him Denham ,
but it is the fame name See Reg U 1 164 168 b 176 b
177 b where one and the fame perfon is called Richard Dun-
cam, Denham, and Dynham

[o] Wood, Colleges, p 188 202

[p] M 20, 1503 MS Harl 6953 p 20 On the refignation

the rectory of Winwick in Northamptonfhire[q]. After this he preferred him fucceffively to two better prebends, and to the
archdeaconry of Stow[r] in Lincolnfhire.   In
gratitude for this repeated kindnefs, Darby,
who gave three fellowfhips to his own college[s], endowed one alfo in the college found-

nation of John Conftable, who was afterwards dean of Lincoln

[q] Ibid p 32. Jan 24 1503–4 Edm is a miftake for Edw.
See the collation of his fucceflor Crofton, ibid

[r] Preb Lidington, Dec 16 1506 Willis, Cath ii 211
Preb Ketton and archd of Stow, Dec 14 1507 MS Harl
ut fupra, p 22 collated to both on the death of William
Smyth, one of the Bifhop's nephews See Pid 2 He had alfo,
for a few months in 1528, the prebend of Spaldwick , in which
he fucceeded, and was fucceeded by, the famous Dr London,
Warden of New College MS Harl 6953 p 92

[s] 26 Henry viii (1534) Wood, Colleges, p 239 His benefaction to Brafen Nofe, four years afterwards, (1538) was
120l the ufual fum, as Mr Baker obferves, for founding a fellowfhip in thefe times, when 6l per ann was enough to maintain a Fellow Pref to Fun Serm of Countefs of Richmond,
p xlv Darby died Jan 9, 1542–3, and was buried in the
Chanteis aile of the cathedral at Lincoln His anniverfary
was obferved in Brafen Nofe the following year Rot Burff
Peck has preferved his epitaph, which was on a verge of brafs,
furrounding his marble grave-ftone Hic jacet humatum corpus venerabilis viri Edvardi Darby A M archidiaconi de
Stowe, olimque canonici refidentiarii in ecclefia B Marie Virginis, Lincolnie , et prebendarii prebende de Ketton in eadem
Qui obiit ix° die Januarii, an dom [m° cccc° xlii°] animabus omnium Chrifti fidelium defunctorum propitietur Deus,
Amen

ed by Smyth; extending his beneficence to the diſtricts with which he was moſt connected, the archdeaconry of Stow, the counties of Leiceſter, Northampton, and Oxford, and the dioceſe of Lincoln at large.

The Commiſſary at this time, as we have ſeen, was Dr. William Atwater, who had filled the office before, and was continued in it afterwards. The Biſhop promoted him to the chancellorſhip of Lincoln, July 5, 1506[t], and likewiſe to the prebend of Lidington, October 30, 1512[u]. He was Fellow of Magdalen college; and in 1514 was made biſhop of Lincoln.

Amen   Anno regni Henrici viii[t] D G Anglie, Francie, et Hibernie regis, fidei defenſoris, et in terra ecclefie Anglicane et Hibernie ſupremi capitis [xxxiv°] Defid Cur vol ii. p 297 4to ed 1779

[t] Willis, Cath iii 91

[u] MS Harl 6953 p 26   See more of him among the Oxford biſhops, Athen Ox i 658   He gave certain veſtments to the Cathedral of Lincoln Dugd Mon iii p 283 b 291 b 296 b and iſſued a decree, that all feaſts of Dedication (or Wakes) ſhould be celebrated annually throughout his dioceſe on the third of October Dat 7 Dec 1519 MS Harl 6953 p. 84. William Horman addreſſed to him a work, which he called " Vulgaria, concluding his dedication with this emphatic wiſh . " Vale, pater ornatiſſime, et Matuſclemmum feliciter vinas ævum " Pynſon, 1519 Winkin de Worde, 1530 Ames's Typogr by Herbert, p 181 265 Atnen Oxon i 35

Sir

Sir Reginald Bray was appointed Steward of the Univerſity in the beginning of June, 1494[x], but the office, in theſe days, ſeems to have been conſidered as expiring with the death or ceſſion of the Chancellor. Smyth therefore, when he became Chancellor, nominated his friend anew to the important and honourable truſt, and in that capacity preſented him to the King for his royal approbation Henry, in his letters patent to the ſaid Steward, knight of his body, recogniſing the franchiſes of the Univerſity as including, beſides other matters, the right of hearing the criminal cauſes of ſcholars and other privileged perſons, accepts the nomination; and allows him and his twelve aſſeſſors (named in the patent) or any two of them, to proceed in the common form againſt offenders[y].

Smyth had not long been in poſſeſſion of his office, when he was conſulted in a matter,

---

[x] F f 175 b Ep 460 dat. 4 Jun (1494) deſiring him to " accept the offyce" Ep 461 to Dr Mayow, to uſe his intereſt with him for that purpoſe Ep 466 8 Dec thanks to him for accepting the ſtewardſhip

[y] T R ap Weſtm 4 Jan 17 H vii (1501-2) Donation MS Brit Muſ 4618 p 267 N 37

wherein

wherein the privileges of the Univerſity were thought to be concerned, but the buſineſs was otherwiſe of no great moment, nor is it certain how it ended.   Mr. Robert Crake of Lincoln college had drowned himſelf; and it was diſputed to whom the forfeited chattels of the felo de ſe belonged.   The Chancellor, grounding himſelf upon the ſtatutes, thought the effects were to be diſtrained, and diſpoſed of at his pleaſure in pious uſes; in which opinion the Univerſity concurred with him. But the King, being apprized of the affair, ordered Dr. Bankes, Rector of Lincoln college, and Commiſſary of the Univerſity, to deliver up the ſaid chattels to his royal Almoner, or elſe to appear within ſix days at court, to ſhew cauſe for detaining them[z].

In this dilemma the Univerſity judged it beſt to depoſit the effects in ſafe hands[a], and to

<hr/>

[z] Reg F Epp 500 503 both dated, 4 Id Julias, (1501) A deodand on a like occaſion was claimed, and, I apprehend, received by tne Univerſity n 1676 Wartons L of Bathurſt, p 91, 92 Tne King granted to Chriſtopher Urſewyke, his almoner, " bona et catalla felon in augment. elemoſine   Pat 1 H vii 24 Nov (1485) Cotton Lib Cleopatra, C iii f 379 b

[a] 14 Jul 150¹ Reg D f 96 b Dr Banke or Bankes in his will (which was proved, 11 Aug 1503 ibid f 207 b— 210 b) bequeathed to the Curite of Kirkby Monachorum " Bibliam

write to his Majefty's late almoner, Fitzjames bifhop of Rochefter, who had been Warden of Merton college, and to Dr. Mayow, Prefident of Magdalen college, the prefent almoner. They afk the bifhop's advice, and engage to follow it[b], but in their letter to Mayow they defire him to do what fhould feem moft equitable[c]: which in effect, as they were aware that he thought the merits of the cafe were againft them, was a tacit relinquifhment of their claim; fince they rely on his forbearance, rather than his juftice.

This fame year, 1501, the commencement of an important century, was diftinguifhed by a vifit of the Prince to the Univerfity; but the memorials concerning it are more fcanty than might be wifhed. The defect however may in fome meafure be fupplied by the particulars of two former vifits of the fame illuftrious Prince, which appear entirely to have efcaped the notice of the laborious Antony Wood: infomuch that the year of thefe memorable occurrences (one or both of them) is one of the very few, which are totally

---

" Bibliam unam emptam de M[ro] Crake " It feems, Crake fold his Bible, and then drowned himfelf

[b] Reg F Ep 500   [c] Ibid Ep 503

omitted in his Annals   The year alluded to
was 1496, 11, 12 Henry vii; when prince
Arthur was twice received and entertained
in Magdalen college. A pursuivant at arms
rode exprefs for the prefident[d], to whofe
lodgings the royal gueft was conducted. the
nobles of his court were accommodated in
the fellows' apartments[e]. Rufhes were provided for the Prince's bed-chamber[f]. He

[d] " Vni purfevant equitant pro domino Prefid " Comp
Burff coll B. M Magd ab anno 11 H vii Mich ad Mich
12 H vii (1495, 1496) The particular time of thefe vifits is
not mentioned, the expence of each is entered in this Computus, but it feems by one item as if the firft vifit was in the
preceding year . " pro carbonibus confumpt primo adventu
Principis anno fuperiori vii D

[e] Veyfey, afterwards Bp of Exeter, was one of thofe, whofe
rooms were thus occupied

[f] " It is the maner in every place of worfhyp at this daye
[Eafter funday] to do the fyre out of the hall and the blacke
wynter brondes,—and there the fyre was fhall be gayly arayed
with fayre floures, and ftrewed with grene ryffhes all aboute '
Feftival, f 36 printed temp H vii See Amess Typogr
p 43 124 136 146 287 et alibi faepe Wartons Hift Poet
i p 14 note h Erafmus, in a letter to Francis the phyfician
in 1515, gives a picture of the domeftic economy of our anceftors, which is lefs to the honour of Englifh cleanlinefs
' The floors, he fays, are commonly of clay, ftrewed with
ryffes, under which lies unmolefted an ancient collection of
beer, greafe, fragments, bones, fpittle, excrements of dogs and
cats and every thing that is nafty " See Jortin's Erafm i
p 76

was treated with a brace of Jack, and a brace of tench[g]. and both his Highneſs and the courtiers in his train received preſents of gloves, and were refreſhed with red wine, with claret, and ſack. In the ſame year veniſon in great abundance, ſome of it probably on the occaſion of theſe viſits, was ſent in by lord Broke[h], and by various other perſons.

[g] " Pro duobus dentricibus et tincis emptis et datis D Principi cum fuerat in coll viii S viii D ' Du Cange ſays, Dentrix means a Pike, and a Canary bird the former, without doubt, is here intended In the ſame Comp we have " pro dentrice (iii S) duobus caponibus (ii S iiii D) et fragis (viii D) datis D Dawbeny Camerario Regis " " pro dentrice et lagena vini dat Doct Fytzjamys The other word, as it ſtands in the MS (" tinc " and in the paper duplicate, " et ii tinc ") foiled me, as it had done others a century ago but the ſuperior ſagacity of my friend Mr Gough made it out at once, and he refers, in illuſtration, to Warhams bill of fare, where in the firſt courſe were " Pike in Latmer ſauce," and in the ſecond, " Tinches for ſhed ' Sec Somner's Canterb by Batteley, P ii App Numb x b Dentrix occurs often in the Magd Compp. the Port meadow Jack are reputed excellent Tinca has been found in this Computus only, that fiſh being more rare about Oxford, for as honeſt Walton informs me, " The Tench, the phyſician of fiſhes, is obſerved to love ponds better than rivers, and pits better than either " Compl Angler, c xi

[h] Sir Robert Willoughby, lord Broke (from whom, through heireſſes of Willoughby and of Greville, the preſent worthy nobleman, lord Willoughby de Broke, is deſcended) was Steward of his Majeſtys houſhold, and in that capacity was ſent to provide for the princeſs Catharine of Spain on her landing at Plymouth in 1501 Lel Coll v Add p 352 MS Tan-

ner,

The Venetian ambaſſadors, lord Dawbeny
the king's Chamberlain, Dr. Harward the Vice-
Chancellor, Dr. Fitzjames, and others, appear
to have been entertained in the courſe of this
year at Magdalen college, but whether it
was while the Prince's court was there is
doubtful. One item in the account muſt
not be forgotten. A perſon was " rewarded
for bringing ˙ to the college " two animals,
called mermoſetts " Whether theſe were
intended to furniſh paſtime for the Heir apparent of the kingdom, now barely ten years
old, or provided for the gratification of learned
academics, is not clear from the audit, nor
have I learnt, from ſimilar inſtances elſewhere, in what repute the wit and waggery
of the monkey were held by our anceſtors in
the days of the Henries, but it is certain that

ner, 85 p 121 He was one of the gueſts at Warham s magnificent inthron zat on teaſt, and ſat at the archbiſhop s board,
on his left hand Somner, ut ſupra, P ii p 60

" Pro diverſ ferculis aat Doct Harward occupanti officium cancellar˙ ˙ Comp ut ſupra He ſeems to have been
of Magdalen college, and is perhaps the William Herward,
who being B A was nominated by Waynflete one of the fellows of the hall which he endowed in 1448 Wood s Colleges,
p 308 Wood has him not among the Commiſſaries of the
Univerſity, but as Cancellarius natus (the ſenior divine reſi-
dent) in 1500, on the death of cardinal Morton Hiſt &c
Faſt., p 69

a kin-

a kindred animal of graver afpect long had
afforded, and long continued to afford, recreation to the ripeft years and moft exalted
perfonages. So late as the year 1554, when
queen Mary vifited the princefs Elizabeth at
Hatfield houfe in Hertfordfhire, where fhe
refided under the cuftody of Sir Thomas
Pope, they were entertained with a grand
exhibition of bear-baiting, " with which their
highneffes were right well content[k] "

But we muft confine ourfelves to the time
of the predeceffors of Elizabeth. The bifhop
of Lincoln, one of prince Arthur's council,
was probably in his fuite when he made thefe
vifits to the Univerfity of Oxford in 1496;
but it is more certain, that he attended his
Highnefs when he came thither the third
time, in the year 1501 On this occafion,
as before, the Prince was lodged in Magdalen
college, where likewife he was entertained
in a manner fuitable to the dignity of the
place and his growing years for Wood fays,

---

[k] Warton, Hift Poet ii p 391 In the fame curious and
interefting Hiftory we are informed, that in the accompt roll
of Bicefter priory, for the year 1431, there is a charge of
" iiiiD " given " cuidam *Urfario*,' and that at Winchefter college, in 1472, prefents were made to the King's minftrels, and
to two *Bearwards* of the Duke of Clarence vol 1 p 90, 91

" he

" he was kindly received there with speeches;
and afterwards visiting other colleges, was
received with the same ceremony[1]."

Of all this I find no memorial, the record
for the year in the Magdalen archives being
unfortunately lost[m].   What I have met with
on the subject is nothing more than a pro-
clamation by the authority of the Chancellor,
fixing the assize of beer for the season of the
Prince's being in Oxford   This however is
sufficient to ascertain the fact, and to shew
the time of the visit   It is dated September
25 ; and by the tenor of it prepares us to
expect a visit of some continuance[n], and as

---

[1] Annals, 1501 16, 17 H vii

[m] There is commonly a draught on paper, as well as the
authentic Computus on parchment, but for the year 1501
there remains only a part of the paper abstract, which furnishes
no particulars respecting the Prince s visit   The Rev Dr
Routh, President of Magdalen college, and many of the fellows
of this ample seminary have frequently afforded me most kind
assistance in searching the very curious and copious Archives of
their society, a favour which I acknowledge with much pleasure and with sincere thanks.

[n] 25 Sept [1501] proclamatio—By the auctorite of my
Lord Chaunceler that the Bruers of Oxford takyng on theym
to serve wel and sufficiently my Lord Prince for the season
beyng here, and tne Vniversite and the town, to selle every
quart [r quarter] of tnem best ale to Inholders and typplers for
2S under the Syste, as long as hit shalbe thought resonable
and

the Prince was at Eynſham, near Oxford, on the fourth° and fifth° of the enſuing month, it is not improbable, that, during the intermediate time, he had kept his court in the Univerſity.

But if our records afford little information reſpecting this royal viſit, there is one tranſaction, connected with it in time, if not otherwiſe, which makes a conſpicuous figure in the regiſters of the day The reader probably, though prepared in part by what has already occurred, will be ſurpriſed, when he is told, that this was in itſelf an affair neither of greater nor leſs magnitude, than the election of the ſuperior Bedel in divinity. Were ſuch a place now to be diſpoſed of, notwithſtanding the facility of modern intercourſe, " our very neighbours," as Socrates ſaid of the birth of Alcibiades, " would ſcarcely be the wiſer for it°." But we ſhould

---

and expedient to my Lord Chaunceler As to 16 peny ale, 12 peny ale, and other, after the olde cuſtom ☾ f 103 What the aſſize of ale was at this time, I am not informed In 1513 it was ordered, that ale ſhould be ſold at "2 S a quarter when the beſt malt (braſium) was at 5 S a quarter, when below that, at 20 D " ℈ f 213 and ibid f 212 the price of ale was 20 D a quarter

° ☾ f 108   ° F. Ep 508

° Plat Alcib. 1 § 17

form

form a very erroneous notion of the fafhion
and habits of the period in queftion, if we
fuppofed the higheft honour, which the Univerfity has to beftow, likely at prefent to intereft the world, as much as the conferring
of a bedel's ftaff did three centuries ago.

It does not appear when the place became
vacant[r], but on the twelfth of Auguft, 1501,
the Prince of Wales, with the concurrence
of the bifhop of Lincoln, Prefident of his
council, and Chancellor of the Univerfity,
(whofe wifhes he hoped they would not
greatly oppofe,) wrote from Bewdley, requefting that his trufty fervant, John Stanley, might be elected to the office; and he
was pleafed to affure them, that he would fo
remember the favour, that they fhould have
reafon to think their readinefs to oblige had
been well employed[s].

The Univerfity, in their reply, inform his

---

[r] Henry Michgood, who made the vacancy, was living
7 Oct 1500 Œ f 84. and dead before 29 Sept 1501 ib f
107 b

[s] F Ep 507 The curious reader will probably wifh to fee
fome of the letters of thefe illuftrious perfonages, which have
never appeared in print This therefore and two others are
given in the Appendix, Num ix xi, xii

High-

Highnefs, whom they ftyle "the luminary of learning and afylum of fcholars," that the plague had fo wafted and difperfed the ftudents, that there were fcarcely any left to conduct the neceffary bufinefs of the place. They therefore were not able to comply with his wifhes, and, befides, it was vacation, during which, it feems, as the ftatutes then ftood, there could be no election[1].

There is a letter of the fame date, Auguft 18, to the Chancellor, which, no doubt, has reference to the fame bufinefs, but unfortunately the letter from the Chancellor, to which it is an anfwer, does not appear. The affembly of Regents fignify to his lordfhip, that perfuaded as they were before of his boundlefs affection towards them, his letter however had not been in vain. By fhewing his unceafing attention to whatever might redound to their honour or advantage, it fhewed that he performed the part of a good magiftrate, and was moft worthy of the poft which he held. In return they promife to be careful to follow his wife counfel, to do nothing precipitately, nor enter upon any

[1] F Ep. 501. 15 Kal Sept.

election

election without confulting him   And fo
they bid him farewell in the Lord[a].

The next folicitation, but in behalf of
another candidate, was from the Countefs of
Richmond   She, fpecially tendering the credit and advancement of divinity, recommended Richard Wotton to the favour of
the Univerfity, being credibly informed by
Fitzjames bifhop of Rochefter, and certain
others, " verray loueis of the faid faculte,"
that he was an extremely proper perfon for
the office[x]

On the twenty eighth of September the
Queen, then " at my Lordys manor of Rychemount," by her royal letters defired and
prayed the Univerfity, that John Greton,
fervant to Dr. Mayow, privy Counfellor and
Almoner to his Majefty, might be preferred
to the vacant place, before any other[y]. And
four days after this his Majefty, from the
fame favourite refidence, recommended the
fame candidate, almoft in the fame words[z].

[a] F Ep 502 App Num x
[x] F Ep 509 App Num xi
[y] Ibid Ep 506 App Num xii
[z] Ibid Ep 505

The

The anfwers to thefe letters, if the Uni-verfity, as we may prefume, did anfwer them, are not recorded.

The Prince of Wales having in the mean time, as above related, honoured the Uni-verfity with a perfonal vifit[a], repaired to the neighbouring monaftery of Eynfham, of which Miles Salley, bifhop of Landaff, was abbat[b]; and from thence he enforced his former re-commendation, chiefly on this ground, that it was the firft requeft, which he had ever made to the Univerfity, for any fervant of his[c].

When perfonages fo auguft, the Mother of the king upon the throne, the King him-felf, and the Prince of Wales, with the in-ferior but illuftrious auxiliaries of each, pa-tronifing three diftinct candidates, conde-

[a] See p 167

[b] Smyth injoined him, 25 Nov tnis year, to produce within eight days his difpenfation, if ne had one, for holding the bi-fhopric together with the monaftery, which he exhibited ac-cordingly to Bothe, the Vicar general, 1 Dec Reg Linc f 124 b See of him Athen Ox 1 655

[c] F Ep 508 5 October Thomas Pantry therefore, whom he had before recommended, was not his fervant See above, p 114

fcended

fcended to canvafs for an academical office,
it may well be fuppofed the Univerfity found
themfelves in no fmall difficulty how to proceed.   They wifhed to oblige the Chancellor, to whom they were much devoted,
and whofe application, in conjunction with
the Prince, was the firft in point of time,
but when their great benefactrefs, the Countefs of Richmond, intreated them to favour a
different perfon, they were at laft carried almoft unanimoufly to efpoufe her candidate.
So they inform her, in a letter, dated October 16; in which alfo they extol the learning, mildnefs, and virtue of Wotton, the
new bedel.   But it was rumoured, that the
Chancellor was much difpleafed with them
for what they had done, and if his good
will, which before they enjoyed, fhould now
be turned into ferious antipathy, the burden,
which they had brought upon them, was
more than their fhoulders were able to bear.
They therefore implore the Countefs, who
could fo eafily affuage anger and mollify re-
fentment, to interpofe her good offices with
the Bifhop in their behalf [d].

However they did not confide their caufe

[d] I Ep 510

folely

folely even to fuch a powerful advocate ; but
apologized for themfelves in a very fubmiffive
letter to the Chancellor.   No one, they fay,
was ever fo uniformly fortunate, as not to
find it neceffary, in certain conjunctures, to
yield both to times, and to men.   Cicero,
with his confummate eloquence and wifdom,
Pompey, with all his humanity and prowefs,
and Cæfar himfelf, unparalleled in his exploits, his genius, and valour, were yet not
able, in every inftance, to achieve their purpofes, nor to ferve their neareft friends.   Of
this they had now an example before their
eyes, when, by a great majority of votes,
they were driven from their hopes and intention of complying with his wifhes.   Nor
would this appear matter of furprife, when it
was confidered, that the king's Mother, to
whofe kindnefs and munificence they were
fo much indebted, preffed and intreated them
to prefer a different candidate.   They therefore earneftly befeech him to continue, as he
had begun, to be their moft kind patron,
promifing, that they would, at another time,
with the applaufe of all good men, punctually perform whatever he fhould command[e]

[e] F Ep 512 App Num xiii

Wotton,

Wotton, who was chosen in preference to candidates so powerfully recommended, appears to have been inferior bedel of divinity some years prior to this election He was present and bore the more honourable staff in that faculty, March 6, 1507-8, when a decree was made, that the superior bedels should pay annually to the inferior the sum of forty shillings for their commons[f]. His name occurs on other occasions; and he enjoyed the office many years.

This was not the first instance in the present reign of a royal, but unsuccessful, canvass for a subordinate academical office The King. ten years before, recommended Edward Mortimer, servant of the same Dr. Mayow, then chaplain in ordinary, to be yeoman bedel in divinity[g], and his Majesty, as far as appears, had then no royal or noble competitor in his suit, yet John Johnson,

---

[f] G f Ric Wotton bedel about 1498 F f 181 Ep 490 Inferior B of Divinity, 4 Oct 1501 D f 108 Superior B of Divinity, 1 Feb 1501-2 ib f 122 150 164. 5 Oct 1513 H f 200 b and in 1529 Woods Ann ii l 57

[g] F Fp 447 6 Feb probably 1491 Edw Mortimer seems to have been a bedel 14 Jul 1501 D f 96 b His name then occurs in the Comp Bursi of Magdalen college

Wood

Wood fays[h], carried it by an unanimous election. It fhould therefore be noted 'to Henry's honour, that repeated difappoint- ment did not alienate or abate his princely and paternal regard for his Univerfity. Very foon afterwards, while Smyth was ftill Chan- cellor, he had it in contemplation to beftow on the Univerfity fome permanent mark of his royal grace and approbation He was pleafed to tranfmit a letter on the fubject by Fox, bifhop of Winchefter', probably (for the letter itfelf does not appear) in order to confult the Univerfity, in what manner his intended bounty might be beft applied. They acknowledged, with exuberant grati- tude, his Majefty's goodnefs[k]; and defired Fox alfo perfonally to fignify their juft fenfe and unanimous acceptance of the royal fa- vour. At the fame time they wrote to Warham, now bifhop of London, and Fitz- james bifhop of Rochefter, to act for them, referring the whole matter to their judge- ment and difcretion[l].

---

[h] Annals, 1491 John Johnfon occurs in 1500 Œ f 31 Superior B of Law, 5 Nov 1502 ib 166 and Superior B of Arts in 1507 G f 54

' See F Ep 525 Mar 20 (1502–3) to the Bp of Win- chefter

[k] F Ep 522 xiii kal Apr (Mar 20)

[l] Epp 523 524 Ep 526 is alfo on the fame occafion, to

Geoffry

Wood thinks this promifed donation, whatever it might be, never took effect[m], which perhaps is true. The intention itfelf, which from the date and object of it is connected with our fubject, fufficiently evinces, that there was no diminution of kindnefs in the royal breaft towards Oxford, in confequence of the election before mentioned. Of this indeed, it fo happens, we have additional proof in the benefaction of ten pounds a year, for an annual mafs at the Univerfity church, which his Majefty beftowed the enfuing year[n].

But we muft return to Smyth, who, when he was in Oxford in the Prince's fuite, or about that time, endeavoured to prevail on Dr. John Roper, Fellow of Magdalen college, to accept the Lady Margaret's pro-

Geoffry Simeon, Dean of the Chapel, and Dr Mayow, Almoner to his Majefty

[n] Annals, under the year 1508. It was probably the projected exhibition for three fcholars to ftudy at Oxford " in the fcience of Divinity." See Hen viith's Will, p. 13. 60 This accords with the words of the Univerfity, who in their letter to the King, Ep. 522 ftyle it " Divinum mentis veftræ inftitutum."

[n] Indent 16 Jul 19 H vii. at the end of Henry viith's Will, p 67 Wood, Fafti, under the year 1504.

feſſorſhip

fefforfhip of divinity. The Countefs inftituted a divinity Lecture in Oxford in the year
1497; and paid the reader an annual ftipend
out of her privy purfe°. The Univerfity
wifhed Edmund Wylford, Fellow and afterwards Provoft of Oriel, to undertake the of-
ficeᴾ; but he withftood their united intreaties,
till the more powerful perfuafion or command of archbifhop Morton, the Chancellor,
at their defire, prevailed upon him. It yet
remained to endow the lecturefhip with a
permanent income; and when this bufinefs
was in readinefs, a new charter was obtained
from the Crown. But a new lecturer was
alfo to be fought for, probably becaufe Wylford had refigned, or wifhed to decline profe-
cuting any longer the honourable but weighty
tafk.

On this occafion the eyes of the Univerfity
were fixed upon Roper. He had read
Waynflete's theological lecture in his own
college with univerfal applaufe fome years;
and when he was fummoned to attend the
courts in Weftminfter, upon fome bufinefs
pending there, the Univerfity lamented this

° Wood, Annals, 1 p 654. 11. p 826, &c.
ᴾ F Ep 486

N 2   his

his temporary abſence, and addreſſed a letter
to the archbiſhop of Canterbury, lord Chancellor, to expedite his return[q]. Perhaps he
was then thought of as a ſucceſſor to Wylford, but when it was propoſed, and preſſed
upon him, it was found, that, with abilities
and learning ſuperior to his predeceſſor, his
diffidence was not leſs, and he ſubmitted
only to the earneſt intreaty of Smyth, in
conjunction with the ſolicitations of the academic body at large[r]   When his conſent
was obtained, the Univerſity, in a letter
abounding with expreſſions of gratitude to
their benefactreſs, and with high encomiums
of Roper, informed the Counteſs of their
choice[s]; and he was in conſequence nominated Reader of this lecture in the charter of
foundation, dated on the nativity of the Virgin Mary (Sept. 8.) 18 Henry vii, 1502.
He filled the office with repute, but for how
many years is not known   He was Principal
of Saliſbury Hall[t], one of thoſe upon the ſite

[q] Гp 189 probably in 1498

[r] Ep 499

[s] Ibid See alſo Ep 521 dat March 20 (1502-3) which
was carried to the Counteſs by Roper

In 1502 Cf 153 b When Saliſbury was let to the
founders of Braſen Note, Roper became Principal of St.
George's Hall in St Mary's pariſh, 1509—1512 Reg Af
109

of which Brafen Nofe college was foon after founded , was occafionally Commiffary of the Univerfity[u], and finally one of the firft Canons of Chrift Church[x].

Smyth continued Chancellor almoft two years after Wotton's election, which was

109 119 149 169 He was one of the Lent preachers, 1511 1514 ibid f 263, 264 and one among others employed by the Univerfity to write againft Luther, 1521 , but on this un-promifing fubject he was thought to be furpaffed by Edward Powell, of Oriel college, (Reg FF f 45, 46) who has been mentioned before fee p 118 of fect v Smyth appointed him (Powell) arbitrator in a difpute between Edm Ayleard and St Fridefwides, in 1502 Œ f 150—151 b gave him the Prebend called Centum folidorum, Jul 26, 1503 MS Harl. 6953 p 20 and Carlton Thurlby about two years afterwards, Willis Cath iii p 166 with 160 His contract for a new roof for the congregation houfe, his benefaction, the fum 30l May 15, 1507, may be feen in Reg ¶ f 18 He occurs as Commiffary June 8, 1508 ibid f 60 b Bp Audley gave him a canonry at Salifbury After he had long enjoyed thefe and other honours, he offended Henry in the matter of the divorce and by denying his fupremacy, who thereupon committed him to prifon, and burnt him in Smithfield, A D 1540 Woods Annals, ii p 19 Athen Oxon i 53 Pits, p 729 His work againft Luther in 3 books was printed by Pynfon in 1523 Ames's Typogr p 273

[u] Commiffary, Feb 1503-4 Œ f 64 b Aug 1505 ibid. f 223 Mar 1505-6 ibid f 234 June &c 1508 ¶ f 61 69 Aug 1509 ibid f 96 98 June &c 1511 ibid f 144 Vice Commiffary in 1516 Reg G f 290

[x] Wood, Colleges, p 428 Athen Oxon i 34

fuppofed

fuppofed to difpleafe him. The exact time
or occafion of his refignation is not known.
On the fixth of Auguft, 1503, he was ftill
in office[v], and he had vacated before the
eleventh of that month, when Fitzjames, fo
often mentioned, bifhop of Rochefter, being
then in Oxford, became Cancellarius natus[z],
and in November following, but not without
much previous difpute and difturbance[a], Dr.
Mayow, Prefident of Magdalen, who bore a
large fhare in the affairs of the Univerfity in
thefe times, was elected Chancellor[b].

[v] See Œ f 207 where the Commiffary Atwater (for it is
his hand fee ib f 149, &c) tranfacts bufinefs as ufual

[z] Ibid f 207 b Upon a vacancy of the chancellorfhip,
the fenior Divine then refident in the Univerfity was called
Cancellarius Natus, and under that title exercifed the office of
Chancellor till a new Chancellor was elected Wood's Fafti,
ed Gutch, p 3

[a] Wood, Annals and Fafti, under the year 1502

[b] Richard Mayhue, Maiewe, Mayeo, &c was King's chaplain about 1491 Reg F Ep 447 collated by Smyth to the
Archdeaconry of Oxford, 29 Jan 1496 MS Harl 6954
p 155 Reg F Ep 461 472 Admitted ad eundem at Cambridge in 1500, being then Almoner Reg Cantab Beta,
f 145 Privy Counfellor about 1501 F Epp 503 505, 506
He was often Commiffary of the Univerfity, was elected
Chancellor before 2 Dec 1503 Œ f 56 refigned May 28,
1505, being then Bp of Hereford, and archbifhop Warham
was chofen in his room the fame day Reg G f 18 See alfo
of him, F Epp 384 514 526 Œ f 37 b 96 b &c

SECT.

SECT VII.

Affairs of his Diocese, and of the Presidency of Wales—attends the marriage and funeral of prince Arthur—Executor to Sir Reginald Bray—Verses addressed to him —assists in a Decree respecting the Merchants of the Staple.

———

SMYTH had occasionally availed himself of the assistance of Fort, his former suffragan[a],

---

[a] See above, p 45 note o and p 72 note c to which add, Bp Fleetwood, in queen Anne's reign, thought " Seacoal had not been in common use 150 years, at least not in London ' Chron Preciof p 118 The preceding grant shews it was brought up the Trent and used in Staffordshire, by its distinctive name of seacoal, 60 years or more before the reign of Elizabeth, to which the former date carries us. Mr Pegge, the late venerable Rector of Whittington, in an ingenious paper on this subject, observes from Bp Watson (Chem. Effays, ii p 364) " we have good reason to believe that the Newcastle coalpits were wrought in the time of the Romans ; for coal cinders have been found at the bottom of the foundation of a city built by the Romans in that country " Gent. Mag. 1789. p 705. See also ibid. p 1098

from

from the time of his translation to Lincoln.
But the amplitude of his diocese and increas-
ing cares made him wish for the permanent
" aid of persons, adorned with science, and
recommended by virtue." He therefore gave
a commission to Fort, in 1501, to consecrate
altars and perform other subordinate offices
of episcopacy, within the counties of Lincoln,
Leicester, Huntingdon, and Rutland[b], which
were most distant from his usual residence,
as President of Wales, and at the same time
most convenient for the suffragan to superin-
tend. For he was now Prior of Huntingdon, and Abbat of Bourn in Lincolnshire,
having recently been collated to the latter by
Smyth[c].

[b] Dat in Castro de Banbury, 21 Apr Reg Linc f 125 b.

[c] 21 Jan 1500-1 by lapse Reg Linc MS Harl 6953
p 2~ He was instituted to Willesforth, 3 June, 1501 on the
death of Robert Bacon MS Harl ib p 28 The manor of
Willesford in Lincolnshire (I suppose with the advowson appendant) was granted to William abbat de Brune [i e Bourn]
in Com Linc Pat 12 Mar 1 II vii (1485-6) Cotton Lib
Cleopatra C iii f 380 The word *Bourn*, among other things,
is said to signify a *spring*, and, no doubt, the " well-head," at
this place, determined the site and the name of this market
town, for it is indeed " Fons etiam rivo dare nomen idoneus,'
sending forth a stream, which in the space of a mile turns
three overshot mills Yet it does not, like the far-famed fountain of St Winefrid at Holywell in Flintshire, burst out at the
foot of surrounding hills, but in a perfect plain, there being no
                                                    ground

In this same year, 1501, he was engaged
in defending the privileges of his fee against
the military order of Knights Hofpitalars,
commonly ftyled Knights of St. John of Jerufalem, afterwards Knights of Rhodes, and
then of Malta, who were charged with
having trenched in certain points on his epifcopal jurifdiction In order that the matters
in difpute might be fettled, if poffible, in an
amicable manner, a conference was appointed,
by confent of the parties, which was held in
St Paul's cathedral, on the third of December.
The commiffioners were, on the part of the
Bifhop, Charles Bothe, his Vicar general, and
others; and, on the part of the Religious,
Thomas Newport[d], knight, treafurer and prefident of the order (the priorfhip being vacant[e])

ground within the diftance of two or three miles, that is apparently at all above the level of the well-head

[d] The right worfhipful brother Sir Thomas Newport, Com-
mander of the Commandery of Dalby and Rothley, was called
to the fervice of the fraternity, by the lieutenant Mafter and
convent of the order, by their bull under lead, dat Rhodes,
Sept 2, 1503 His brother Robert allo was a knight of the
order See more in Nichols's Leic vol iii p 246

[e] Thomas Docwra was prior 1502—1523 Gent Mag.
1798 p 765 1788 p 854 John Wefton and John Kendall
both occur as priors of the order, 1 H vii Rolls Parl vi
p 313 482

Nicholas

Nicholas Weſt[f] LL. D. conſervator of their privileges, and others

At this interview it was firſt of all objected, that the Hoſpitalars pretended to have juriſdiction in Dalby parva, Rethorby, and Rotheley, within the archdeaconry of Leiceſter, and in other places   It was anſwered in behalf of the Religious, that they were privileged by authority of the apoſtolic fee; and that all their " cuſtomary tenants[g]" were of the juriſdiction of the Hoſpitalars , ſo that the correction of manners and proof of wills belonged to them.   They were aſked, who were to be eſteemed their " cuſtomary tenants."   The preſident replied, they were ſuch as held of the Hoſpitalars by copy, or indenture, or at will , who are commonly called " Hoole tenaunts of Saint John's "   It was further objected, that Chaplains keeping Preceptories are accuſtomed to abſolve excommunicated perſons, and to grant certificates thereupon.   They anſwered, that their

[f] This Nicholas Weſt, born at Putney, educated at Eton, and at Kings College, Cambridge, a man of great experience in the civil and canon law, and Doctor of both, was Archdeacon of Derby, in 1486, Dean of Windſor, 1510, and Biſhop of Ely, 1515. Willis, Cath 1 421 Athen. Ox 1 653

[g] " Ipſorum more tenentes "

privi-

privileges did not extend to this, nor was it
their intention, that the chaplains fhould ab-
folve any perfons excommunicated, unlefs in
the article of death, and that only in regard
to confcience, but not to courts of law. It
was moreover objected, that the chaplains
were wont in the faid preceptories to fo-
lemnize clandeftine marriages, without publication of banns, and within the prohibited
degrees. They anfwered, it was not their
intention, that fuch things fhould be done,
and they defired, that, if any thing of the
fort fhould happen, information might be
given to the confervator of their privileges,
that the offender might be punifhed   It was
objected alfo, that fome of their commiffaries
claimed the privilege of granting the probate
of wills of perfons dying in houfes, on which
a Crofs was erected[h]. They replied, that the
proving of wills, unlefs of their tenants as
before defcribed, did not belong to them.
Finally the prefident and confervator requefted, that a time and place might be

---

[h] " Ubi habetur fignum crucis fupra domos " The knowing and accurate Dugdale mentions this cuftom, obferved by
the tenants of the Hofpitalars " for the better fruition of their
privileges " And he refers for it to " Rot Fin 1 H vi m 4 '
Hift Warw p 683 where fee a print of a Knight Hofpi-
talar They wore a black mantle with a white crofs

affigned

affigned them to exhibit the privileges and
immunities, on which their claims were
founded. The Vicar general faid he would
confult the bifhop thereupon, and that afterwards, with confent of both parties, fuch
time and place fhould be appointed[1].

This curious memoir throws fome light on
a point not perfectly underftood, what thefe
Preceptories were. It is known, that the
name originally denoted houfes of fome defcription belonging not to the Hofpitalars,
but to the Knights Templars And it has
been well explained, how, upon the fuppreffion of the Templars, when their eftates
were given by act of parliament to the Hofpitalars, the name furvived, and paffed with
the property, and fo, by degrees, not only
thefe houfes, but others which had originally
been vefted in the order, and as fuch properly
ftyled Commanderies, were often called Preceptories[k]. It has been further faid, and the
document before us corroborates the opinion,
that they were manors or chief meffuages,
fubordinate to the principal houfe of the order in London. But they appear not to have

[1] Reg Linc f 124.
[k] See Whites Selborne p 352 n m

been,

been, or not always, as has been fuppofed, in
the hands of one of the Knights, who were
all laymen; but fometimes in the cuftody
and fuperintendence of Chaplains[1]; which is
the more material to be noted, as the number of clergy, belonging to the whole body,
is faid to have been very inconfiderable.

Whether the charters of their privileges
were afterwards exhibited, agreeably to their
requeft, or whether any other fteps were
taken towards a final termination of the difpute, does not appear. It is not improbable,
each party acquiefced in the requifitions made
by the other; and was fatisfied with the con-
ceffions granted in return

Before the Pope's fupremacy was extermi-

[1] In MS Parker, CLXX 71 is a letter of P Alexander vi
to the Prior and Preceptors of St Johns in England, permit-
ting them to vifit churches for the fake of collecting alms
dat 17 Dec 1498 See and correct Nafmith s catalogue Radulphus Le Feen gave to the fraternity of St John's, " et nominatim fratri Roberto fil Ric hermitorium de Yevelia' [q.
Eveley, in Com Derb] on condition that the faid Robert
fhould poffefs it for life, and be " Procurator' there , and that
the brothers fhould receive the body of the donor " ad habitum
religionis corum," whenever he pleafed, in health or in ficknefs
the date, as is probable, temp H ii MS Dodfworth, 110
f 113 It is called Precepturia de Yevelia

nated

nated by Henry viii, and the reigning Sovereign declared Head of the church as well
as of the ftate, the ecclefiaftics and their officers, and in procefs of time all who could
read, were allowed, when convicted capitally
in a fecular court, to claim the Benefit of
Clergy, in arreft of judgement Hereupon
they were difcharged from the King's courts,
and delivered over to the ordinary, to be
dealt with according to the ecclefiaftical canons. The bifhop or his commiffary received
the clerk, with a copy of his indictment and
conviction, which were not however admitted in the fpiritual court as proofs of
guilt, but a new canonical trial was inftituted. This was held before the bifhop, or
his deputy, affifted with a jury of twelve
clerks. Here, firft the party himfelf was required to make oath of his innocence. Next,
twelve compurgators were to fwear, they believed he fpoke truth, then witneffes were
examined upon oath, but in behalf of the prifoner only, and laftly the jury brought in
their verdict upon oath; which, as might be
expected in fuch a ftrange procefs, ufually
acquitted the prifoner, otherwife, if a clerk,
he was degraded, or put to penance[m].

<hr/>

[m] Blackftone, vol iv p 358—362 ed. 4to

For

For the purpofes of this mockery of juftice, the genuine offspring of papal domination, the bifhops, in their refpective diocefes, were furnifhed with prifons in the nature of dungeons; of which the bifhop of Lincoln had two or more, one at Banbury, and one at Newark[n] The religious houfes alfo were fometimes required by the ordinary to provide a temporary cuftody for clerks convict; but this appears to have been a matter of favour, rather than of duty, on the part of the monafteries For when a commiffion to this effect was directed by the Vicar general, January 8, 1500, to the abbat of Peterborough, he replied, that it was a thing totally unprecedented, what had not been feen or heard, that fuch a commiffion was made to any of his predeceffors. Nertheleffe, fays he, doyng my Lord a pleafure, if it will pleafe yow to entyr in your faid commiffion, that I fhalbe alowed for my cofts,—I will accepte and gladly receive your commiffion[o] " A fimilar commiffion was iffued, fome years afterwards,

---

[n] The caftle at Newark was built by Alexander Bp of Lincoln, temp H 1 See a fhort account of it, with a view of its ftately ruins, in Gent Mag 1798 p 17 See alfo Dugd Mon iii p 263 265 b 266 Of the caftle at Banbury fee above, p 97 of fect v

[o] Reg Linc f 87 87 b

to the abbat of Ramfey, with the like confent on the part of the abbat[p].

It is fome fatisfaction, to whatever caufe it may have been owing, that we find very few inftances of this perverfion of juftice under the forms of law, while Smyth prefided in a diocefe, which extended over fo many counties. A perfon convicted of horfe ftealing, who was imprifoned in the bifhop's caftle at Newark, was cleared before the Commiffary Apjohn, April 6, 1501, in Beckingham church, the place affigned for his purgation, on his own oath and that of twelve honeft men who could read, no one appearing to give evidence againft him[q]. A commiffion

[p] Ibid f 87 March 9 1512

[q] Reg L nc f 60 ' juramento 12 poneftorum literatorum ' I fuppofe from its being mentioned that ' no contradictor appeared the man if had a right to produce evidence, if he pleafed. The horfe that had been ftolen was " coloris albi, but probably not the fame as Virgil's ' color deterrimus albis (Georg 3 82) as the value, ' 14 fhillings, was the price of a good horfe at that time. Ammon is prebendary of St Ste- phen's Weftminfter) in 1513 made Erafmus a prefent of a horfe, of which he fays, ' Sed quando video te equo egere, albo equo (tis quanti hoc olim fuerit) a me donaberis, ex Juverna ultima advecto. Accipe qualemcunque tibi nunquam impu- tandum. To which Erafmus anfwers, ' Perplacet equus can- dore infignis, at magis animi tui candore commendatus. Jor- tins Erafm 1 p 47 Erafm Epp 145 147 ed Lugd

alfo

alfo was made out, about the fame time, to try certain cleiks convict, detained in the caftle at Banbury, who had robbed Paul Bombyn, a London merchant, in Bradfton field near Enftone, of the fum of two hundred pounds, but the iffue of their purgation does not appear[r].

It has been faid above[s], that the Prince of Wales made a vifit to Oxford, attended by Smyth chancellor of the Univerfity and others, towards the end of September, 1501. On the fixth of November following, having joined his royal Father the preceding day, he met the princefs Catharine of Spain at Dogmersfield, near Odiham in Hampfhire, whence, after the firft falutations, they went by different routes, the Prince to the Wardrobe in Black Friars, the Princefs to the archbifhop's palace at Lambeth[t]. When preparations were made in the city, under the direction of Fox bifhop of Winchefter[u], for the folemn

---

[r] Reg Linc f 70 I find only one commiffion befides thefe, dated 7 Jan 1499–1500 ib f 60 b

[s] See p 167 of lect vi

[t] Lel Coll v Add p 352, &c MS Tanner, 85 p 119—162 Stowe's Ann p 482

[u] Wood, Colleges, p 386 Warton's Hift Poet ii p 202 203 both quoting Bacon's Henry vii Mi Warton on other

authority

entrance of the Princefs, agreeably to her dignity and to " the old and famous appetites of the Englifh people in welcoming acceptable ftrangers`," fhe came riding from Lambeth, Friday November 12, through the borough of Southwark, to London bridge; where fhe was received with a coftly pageant of St. Catharine, St. Urfula, and a train of virgins.   In her proceffion through the city to London Houfe other fuperb pageants were difplayed, and the great conduit in Cheap ran with Gafcoin wine, and was furnifhed with mufic.   The marriage ceremony, on Sunday the fourteenth of November, was performed with great folemnity in St. Paul's

---

authority remarks, that the perfonages in thefe pageants " fuftained a fort of action, at leaft of dialogue ," and that " the Lady was compared to Hefperus, the Prince to Arcturus " Erafmus had anticipated and perhaps fuggefted this allufion, in the verfes which he prefented to prince Henry about 1497, where Britannia thus fpeaks of Arthur

> " Hic meus Arcturus, qui nominis omine felix,
>   Virtute reddet, quem refert vocabulo
> Afpice quod fpecimen generofæ frontis in illo eft,
>   Ut lucet oculis vividus mentis vigor
> Præcoqua nec tardam expectat fapientia pubem,
>   Prævertit annos indoles ardens fuos
> Talis Iefides, illique fimillima proles,
>   Hic quum timendas diffecat puer feras, &c "
>   Knight's Erafm p. 69. & App Num vii p xxiii

` MS Tanner, ut fupra, p. 127.

cathe-

cathedral by the archbifhop of Canterbury, affifted by nineteen bifhops[y]. The youthful Prince and his Bride were arrayed in white fattin ; and the fplendor and magnificence of the nobility and courtiers, vying with each other on this joyous occafion, was beyond all example Chains of gold were worn of the value of a thoufand or fourteen hundred pounds. The Duke of Buckingham had a gown of needle work, fet on cloth of tiffue, and furred with fables, which was valued at 1500l. But Sir Nicolas Vaux, afterwards lord Vaux of Harendon in Northamptonfhire, eclipfed all the company in his robe of purple velvet, richly furred, and plated with gold fo thick and maffy, that the gold alone was valued at 1000l. The dowry of the Princefs was guaranteed to her by the bifhop of Lincoln, in conjunction with the two archbifhops, the bifhop of Winchefter, the Duke of York, Sir Reginald Bray, and others, witneffes to the deed of fettlement[z]. In honour of the nuptials jufts and turnaments were exhibited feveral days in the large void fpace before Weftminfter hall, with fumptuous banquets and difguifings and interludes within

[y] Stowe, ut fupra Parker, Antiq Brit p 307
[z] Rymer, xii p 780

the

the hall; and the celebrity concluded with a numerous creation of knights of the Bath, and of the Sword[a].

From these scenes of gaiety and spectacles of triumph the Prince hastened again to his province in the marches; but he did not live to verify the hopes and expectations, which as well the nation in general, as those near his person, had largely entertained from the contemplation of his early virtues.   He died, universally regretted, in Ludlow Castle, the second day of April, 1502   The funeral was conducted with much mournful pomp; and the bishop of Lincoln bore a principal part in the sacred offices attending it.   The corpse was inveloped in cerements, and lay in state in the Castle, during the space of three weeks.   Then, on St. George's day in the afternoon, it was removed in solemn procession to the parish church.   The Earl of Surrey, as principal mourner, followed next to the corpse; and after him a large train of noblemen and others; among whom were many of the principal citizens of Chester, who had come thus far to attend the

[a] Cotton MS Claudius, C in f 50, &c

obseьоſequies of their beloved Prince[b]. His banner was borne before the corpſe by Sir Griffith ap Rice[c], who was preceded by biſhops, abbats, and others. When the corpſe was conveyed into the choir, the dirge began; and the biſhops of Lincoln, Saliſbury, and Cheſter, read the three leſſons. On the morrow the biſhop of Lincoln ſung the maſs of requiem. Doctor Edenham, almoner and confeſſor to the Prince, " ſaid a noble ſermon, and took to his antyteme, Bleſſed are the dead, who die in the Lord."

On St. Mark's day the proceſſion moved from Ludlow to Bewdley; and, obſerves my author, " it was the fouleſt cold windye and rainey daye, and the worſt waye, that I have ſeen." The corpſe was placed in the choir of the chapel; and dirge and maſs of requiem were performed, and every church where it reſted was decorated with eſcutcheons. When they came to Worceſter, the order of Friars cenſed the corpſe at the town's end; and at the city gate the bailiffs

---

[b] Dr Cowper's Cheſter Coll p 183 " From an old MS." the Collector ſays

[c] I ſuppoſe " Sir Gryffith ap Sir Res Thomas," who was one of the Knights of the Bath at the Prince's marriage Cotton Lib Claudius, C. iii. f. 50

and

and corporation met them   At the entrance
óf the church-yard, the bifhop of Worcefter
having now joined the train, the four bifhops
in rich copes cenfed the corpfe; which was
then borne under a canopy through the
choir, to a herfe illuminated with eighteen
lights, and fumptuoufly garnifhed with arms.
At dirge were nine leffons, after the cuftom
of that church.   The firft five were read by
abbats, the fixth by the prior of Worcefter,
the reft by the bifhops, the bifhop of Lincoln
reading the ninth.   That night there was a
goodly watch of Lords, and Knights, and
many others.

In the morning at eight the facred rites
were refumed; when the third mafs, of
requiem, was fung by the bifhop of Lincoln.
Cuftomary offerings were made at the mafs,
" but to have feen the weepinge when the
offeringe was done, he had a hard heart that
wept not." The fermon by "a noble doctor"
followed.   After this all the prelates cenfed
the corpfe, and then " with weeping and
fore lamentation it was laid in the grave,"
at the fouth end of the high altar, where
were all the divine fervices. " The orifons
were faid by the bifhop of Lincoln, alfo fore
weeping. He fett the croffe over the cheft,
                                        and

and caſt holye water and earth thereon."
The comptroller of the Prince's houſehold,
his ſteward, and others brake their ſtaves of
office, and caſt them into the grave. And
" thus, concludes my author, God have
mercye on good Prince Arthur's ſoule[d]."

Of this Prince both contemporary and
ſubſequent writers ſpeak in terms of the
warmeſt applauſe and admiration. His parts,
his learning, and accompliſhments far ſur-
paſſed what could be expected from his
youth, his rank, and the age. But He, who
from the conflict of human paſſions often
produces great and unexpected good, had

---

[d] Add to Lel. Coll v 373—381 See alſo Sandford's Ge-
neal p 445, &c where the Prince's epitaph is given, with an
engraving of the ſouth ſide of his tomb, the north ſide is engraved in Thomas's View of Worc Cath p 38 The pome-
granates introduced among the badges on this beautiful tomb
were in compliment to the princeſs Catharine of Spain, which
from this match became a faſhionable ornament on ſilver plate,
and decoration in architecture Warton's L of Sir T Pope,
2d edit p. 129 n Mr Gough informs us, that in the Wardrobe account of H vii there is this charge " 18 H vii June
18—for the burial of my lorde prince 566l 16s " Sep Mon
vol ii p. cciii where alſo is another item—" for burying Sir
Ric Pole, 40l " There is a portrait of prince Arthur behind
the Levee Room at St James's Pennant's London, p 109
and in St Bartholomew's Hoſpital ibid 179.

pur-

purpofes to accomplifh by the turbulence and impetuofity of Henry, the younger brother, which the mild virtues and fuavity of Arthur would never have attempted.

Upon the Prince's death all his titles and powers reverted to the Crown, but Smyth continued Prefident as well after as before the Duke of York was created Prince of Wales, and held the office till his death. In one of the ftate apartments of the Caftle at Ludlow the arms of prince Arthur were " excellently wrought," in a fuperb efcutcheon of ftone; and there was an empalement of St. Andrew's crofs, with prince Arthur's arms, painted in one of the windows of the hall. His arms, two red lions and two golden lions, were alfo in another chamber, with the arms of North Wales, and South Wales. And in the chapel, which was " moft trim and coftly," the arms of Smyth and other lords Prefidents were " gallantly and cunningly fet out⁵ "

---

⁵ Churchyard's Worthines of Wales, p 79—83 London, 1776, from the ed of 1587 The names of fourteen lord Prefidents, " as they are written in the Chappell at Ludlowe," are given in MS More quoted above, fect iii p 65 They begin with Beaumis Bp of London, and end with Sir Henry Sydney The names and arms of eighteen, from bifhop Alcock to William

In the reign of Henry viii many whole-
fome regulations were framed refpecting
Wales. Certain barbarous cuftoms and peculiar tenures were abolifhed[f]. The eftates
of the lords marchers were made fhire
ground, and annexed to the adjacent counties
of England and Wales Four new counties
were erected; and the whole principality,
thus commodioufly diftributed, when Lee
bifhop of Lichfield was lord Prefident and
partly by his procurement, was united and
incorporated with England, to enjoy the
fame privileges and to be fubject to the fame
laws[g]. If this act of confolidation, amidft
much good, contained fome evil, and, by

liam lord Compton, earl of Northampton, may be feen in Davies Heraldry MS late Dr Cowpers, now penes Rev Hugh
Cholmondeley, p 79

[f] 27 H viii c 7 Perfons paffing through forefts in Wales
and the marches without a token were fined by the walkers of
the foreft; and if they were found at the diftance of 24 feet
from the highway, they forfeited all the money found upon
them, and a joint of their hand or a fine inftead Stray cattle
alfo were feized in the forefts For other ftatutes of this reign
refpecting Wales, fee 26 H viii c 4 c 6 c 11 28 H viii
c 3 c 6 31 H viii c 11

[g] 27 H viii c 26 Donation MS Brit Muf 4900 f 23
fays bifhop Lee was famous for two things, for marrying
H viii to Anne Bolein, mother to Q Elizabeth, and for procuring this union of Wales with England.

not

not mentioning the court of the marches,
fufpended its jurifdiction, or leffened its controul, the inconvenience being felt was not
fuffered to remain, for, in a revifion of the
ftatute a few years afterwards, the Prefident
and council were eftablifhed with full power
and authority as before[h]. James the firft
projected a change of lefs magnitude, to feparate the four fhires marches from the government of Wales, but the earl of Salifbury, lord Treafurer, grounding himfelf on
hiftory and the laws of the land, laid before
his Majefty fuch weighty reafons againft the
meafure, that the defign was given up. He
concluded with an obfervation, which deferves to be maturely weighed by all who
meditate innovations of any fort· " I conclude, he fays, with this, that Subftructiones
antiquæ nec facile deftruuntur, nec folæ
ruunt[i] "

However as peculiarity of manners, under
the operation of uniform laws, gradually wore
away, and as the Englifh language came to
be underftood in the principality, and a more
eafy accefs and intercourfe was opened be-

[h] 34 & 35 H viii c 26 fect 4
[i] Cotton MS Titus, B iii 1 p 47, &c

tween

tween the two countries, fome of the chief reafons for inftituting and maintaining this local jurifdiction no longer fubfifted, and the principality court was diffolved by king William[k]. but Ludlow caftle and its appendages ftill continue part of the royal domains, of which the earl of Powis is the prefent leffee[l].

Sir Reginald Bray has frequently been mentioned in the foregoing pages. He was an early and conftant friend of Smyth, and at the fame time a man of fuch exalted wifdom and refplendent piety, that fome further account of him, now we are arrived at the period when we muft record his death, feems to be a neceffary part of thefe memoirs. He had been Receiver general to Sir Henry Stafford, fecond hufband of the Countefs of Richmond[m], and he was put in truft for her dowry on her marriage to Thomas earl of Derby[n]. This noble earl and Bray were two

[k] 1 Will & Mary, c 27

[l] Leafe June 30, 1772, for 31 years old rent 28l 2s to be paid to the Governour of Ludlow Caftle Report of Comm of Crown Lands, 1787 p 64

[m] Ballard's Memoirs, 4to ed p 11 He bequeathed to Bray his " grifeld courfer "

[n] Rolls of Parl vol vi p 311. Her dower in lands was to
the

of the auguſt Council, with which Henry on
his acceſſion adorned and fortified his throne[o],
and they were alſo the attendants and part-
ners of his ſocial hours; eſpecially at Chriſt-
mas and other feſtivals, which it was Henry's
cuſtom to keep with great magnificence[p].
When Smyth was biſhop elect of Coventry
and Lichfield, the manor of Harleford, and
other lands between Henley and Marlow,
purchaſed of Sir Richard Pole, were conveyed to him and others; for the uſe, I preſume, (though it is not ſo expreſſed) of Sir
Reginald Bray[q]   For the biſhop and Bray
levied a fine and recovery for the eſtates[r],

the value of " ſic Marcs " and he had made over to the Earl
eſtates to the value of " ſic Mircs   One of the eſtates conveyed to the Earl was the manor of " Mycull billinge" in
Northamptonſhire, the advowſon of which is now in Braſen
Noſe college

[o] Pol Verg p 506

[p] Lei Coll ſi Add p 254—255 255

[q] 10 Jul - H vii 1492 Univ Arch S L Preſ K 2 9
where are various deeds and conveyances (K 2 8—18) of
theſe eſtates which were finally ſettled on the Univerſity by
patent 17 June, 11 Car 1 for the maintenance of three Fellows in Exeter, Jeſus, and Pembroke colleges, who are to be
natives of Guernſey or Jerſey ibid Long Box, 18

[r] Exemplif 7 Jul 4 H vii of a fine Tern Hil 11 H vii
(1495–6) by Sir R Poole to the Bp of Lichfield &c K 2
13 ut ſupra

which

which were finally releafed and fettled on Bray's nephew, Sir Edmund Bray, by William Smyth, archdeacon of Lincoln, the bifhop's coufin and heir (as he ftyles himfelf) and others, in the year 1522[s]. The next prefentation to St John's Hofpital, Salop, was granted by the Crown to the bifhop of Lichfield and Bray, in conjunction with King, bifhop of Exeter, and Robert Foreft, clerk, for whom perhaps the preferment was defigned[t]. A patent of free warren was alfo made to the bifhop of Lincoln and Bray, with others, for Cotefbroke in Northamptonfhire, at prefent the feat of Sir William Langham, baronet; which Bray had purchafed of John Markham, of Sidbroke in Lincolnfhire, for the fum of 4000 pounds[u] Bray availed himfelf of Smyth's name and affiftance in deeds of conveyance as well as of purchafe, particularly in the fale of the manor of "Mariborn," with lands in " Tybourne, Lillefton, Weft-

[s] Ibid K 2 18 Nov 27 14 H viii

[t] Pat 8 Aug 10 H vii (1494) Rolls' Chapel

[u] Pat 31 Oct 16 H vii (1500) Will Linc Epifc Reg Bray &c ibd and fee in Bridges Northampt i p 554 an account of the purchafe, and two fines levied, one 14 H vii for the ufe of the Bifhop and others, and another 16 H vii as it feems for the Bifhop alone

borne,

borne, Charyng, and Eye," in Middlefex[x].
The price was 400 marks; the purchafer
was Thomas Hobfon, gentleman, whofe widow Johan married John Blenerhayfet, by
which name her right in the manor of Ty-
borne and its appendages, together with the
right of Richard Hobfon, fon and heir of her
former hufband, was fecured by an act of
parliament, 4 Henry viii, made in favour of
Thomas earl of Surrey[y]. Bray was born, as
has been faid[z], in the county of Worcefter;
but defcended from a family, which had
flourifhed in Northamptonfhire from the
time of the conqueft He prefented Thomas
Cawce, fteward of the bifhop of Lincoln's
houfhold, to the rectory of Hinton[a] in that

[x] Madox, Formul No ccclii 21 Jun 14 H vii (1499)
Henry Colet, Knight, probably the father of the incomparably
learned Dean of St Paul's, is joined with Bray and Smyth in
this deed See the fale, 8 June, fame year, ibid No cccclviii.

[y] Rolls prefixed to Journ of Lords, f ix Thomas Blen-
drehaffet, Gent was attainted with the Earl of Lincoln and
others, after the battle of Stoke, 1487 Rolls Parl vi p 397.
The will of "Thomas Blenerhaffet, Miles," is in the Prerog
Off proved about 1530 Mr Warton calls one of the writers
in the Mirrour of Magiftrates, ed 1610, Thomas Blener Haf-
fet. Hift Poet iii 270

[z] P 109 of fect v

[a] MS Harl 6953. p 29 And fee Gent Mag 1788.
p 1051.

county, in 1496-7; the manor of Stene and
of Hinton having been recently conveyed
to him in perpetuity by the Crown[b]. He
received from that fountain of honour innu-
merable patents, marks of favour or grants of
emolument; which, as they did not corrupt,
served only to display, the integrity of the fe-
nator[c] and the statesman. He censured with
freedom and firmness the faults of the court[d],

---

p 1051 Cawce was Principal of Staple Hall in 1499 ꭸ f
23 39 39 b 101 109 b which he resigned, Oct 29, 1501
ibid f 111 b and became Principal of great St Edmund
Hall, Nov 10 ibid f 112 b See More, f 191 192 b He
is a party with Smyth, by the title of Senescallus hospitii,
Sept 1, 1510 Yate, p 64 and was collated by him to the
prebend called Centum Solidorum, Jul 13, 1511, being then
B D MS Harl ut supra, p 25

[b] Pat 27 Aug 11 H vii (1495) Rolls' Chapel Stene is
now (1800) the property of the right honourable earl Spencer,
and Hinton the property of William Ralph Cartwright,
esquire, of Aynho, M P for the county of Northampton, a
permanent benefactor to Brasen Nose college, his ancestors,
besides many occasional donations, having established in the
society two scholarships, to which the heir of the family no-
minates

[c] He was in the House of Commons with Sir Richard
Guildford 11 H vii 1495 Rolls of Parl vi p 458 b and
they two, with others, were constituted feoffees of certain royal
manors, when the King was going to the wars in France,
20 Feb 7 H vii 1491-2 ibid p 444 472 b

[d] "R Braius, vere pater patriæ, homo severus, ac ita recti
amator, ut si quid interdum peccatum esset, illud acriter in
Henrico reprehenderet Pol Verg p 612 who styles him and

arch-

where his counfel carried fo great fway, that,
had he not died before Henry, the acts of ra-
pacity and oppreffion, with which that monarch's later annals are difgraced, if not entirely prevented, would no doubt have been
lefs numerous, and lefs flagrant.

This unblemifhed courtier, knight of the
Garter and high Treafurer of England, departed this life Auguft 5, 1503[c]. His will,
which bears date the preceding day, is witneffed by "M Fraunces the phifition," who was
fhortly afterwards phyfician to cardinal Wolfey, and honoured with the friendfhip and
correfpondence of Erafmus[f]. "Mr Lenacres
the phifition" is another witnefs, who was
alfo a friend of the fame great foreigner,
Italian preceptor to prince Arthur and his
Confort, phyfician to Henry vii, and one of
the reftorers of learning in England[g]. The

---

archbifhop Morton " regiæ potentiæ moderatores   The Univerfity of Oxford in 1502 thus addreffed Bray " Quoniam—
apud metuendiffimum Principem noftrum tantum tibi liceat
quantum libet (libet autem nichil quod non liceat) &c F Ep
516.

[c] Stowe's Ann p 484

[f] Jortin s Eraf'n vol 1 75 150 11 341

[g] Linacre had been fellow of All Souls college   He tranflated Proclus s Sphere, and dedicated it to his royal pupil, informing his Highnefs in the dedication that if he wifhed to
be

executors are " Maifter William Smyth, bifhop of Lincoln, maifter Hugh Oldom,
clerk ," and feven laymen, moft of them
counfellors learned in the law, whofe names
often occur in the tranfactions of Bray and
of Smyth[h]. To each of his executors he bequeathed the fum of twenty pounds, and
ten marks annually to thofe who fhould adminifter, until fuch time as the intent and
directions of his will were fully accomplifhed.

be acquainted with the original Greek, there were now to be
found among his countrymen thofe who could affift him in the
attainment of that language, " in qua omnis humanitatis mo-
numenta funt condita ' The act which incorporates the College of phyficians, of which he was firft Prefident, calls him
phyfician to the King 14 & 15 H viii c 5 (where Frances
alfo is mentioned) Having been ordained, he had about 1520
the valuable living of Wigan in Lancafhire He was alfo prebendary of St Stephen's, Weftminfter See Athen Oxon
i 19 Tanner Biblioth Knight s Colet, p 215

[h] Richard Emfon, John Cutte, John Shaa [Shaw,] knights,
Humphry Connyngefby, ferjeant at law, William Coope, Simon Dygby, and Nicholas Compton See the Will, Prerog.
Off Blamyr, xxvi proved, Nov 23, 1503 Moft of thefe perfons occur elfewhere in thefe papers, or are otherwife not unknown Sir John Shaw is probably the fame " John Shaa,
who petitioned parliament, i H vii, 1485, for the eftates of
" Sir Edmund Shaa, knight, late Mayor,' as fecond in entail,
in defect of heirs male of Hugh Shaa, fon of the faid Sir Edmund, to whom they were firft bequeathed Rolls Parl vi
p 488 Sir Edmund Shaw was lord Mayor in 1482, and Sir
John Shaw in 1501 Heylin's Help to Hift.

P Dying

Dying without iffue, he devifed moft of his
eftates to his nephew, Edmund Bray, but
his eleemofynary legacies were large and numerous.   He bequeathed fixty fhillings to
every houfe of friars throughout England, for
a trental[1] of maffes, and to the friars at
Guildford, where his mother Johanna was
buried. two hundred pounds. to pray for his
foul. and for the fouls of his father and mother   He alfo gave inftructions for his executors to finifh St George's Chapel, Windfor,
which he had begun in his lifetime, and to
convey certain lands to the Dean and Chapter of that royal foundation for charitable
purpofes   He was interred there in the chapel erected by him, which ftill bears his
name. in the fouth aile of that beautiful fabric to which, living and dying. he was fo
great a benefactor[k].

---

[i] " Trentals were called Trentals, from Tryntalus, and in
Englifh a Morth's Mind, becaufe the fervice lafted a month, or
30 days, in wnich they faid fo many maffes " Fleetwood, Chron
Preciof p 133

[k] In making a vault for the excellent Dr Waterland in
1742, in Bray's chapel, " a leaden coffin of ancient form was
found, fuppofed to be Sir R Bray's By order of the dean it
was directly arched over ' Gough's Sepulchr Mon vol ii
p LXV See his Life in the new ed of Biogr. Brit A writer
in Gent Mag 1799 p 394 941 calls him, I know not on
what authority, the architect of Henry the feventh's chapel, and

                                                                    feems

It has been obferved, that popular ftates have feldom or never been known to pardon offenders; but that Mercy is the attribute of Monarchy[l]. A year had not paffed from the time of Sir Reginald Bray's death, when a pardon was granted by the King to the bifhop of Lincoln and the other executors[m], which however is not to be regarded as affording any ground for fufpicion of fraud or negle&, either in Smyth and Oldham, who did not adminifter, or in the others, who did adminifter to the will. Men in high ftation, or in any public truft, were very folicitous formerly to obtain this mark of their Sovereign's approbation, as a fecurity againft the malice of thofe enemies, which the management of great and extenfive affairs, with whatever integrity and caution they may be conducted, is fure to create, and on the part of the Crown, if no pofitive delinquency or mal-adminiftration appeared, fuch favours were readily difpenfed. A few years after-

feems to think (ib 942) he faw it completed, whereas he died within feven months after he had affifted in laying the firft ftone Stowe's Ann p 484 Dart's Weftm Abbey, i 32 The fame writer refers for a portrait of Bray, whole length, to Carter's Antient Sculpture, vol ii

[l] Fuller's Good Thoughts in worfe Times, Perfon Medit. xii

[m] Pat 19 H vii 22 Jul (1504) Rolls Chapel.

wards

wards the Bishop asked and obtained another pardon, in a case which gave frequent occasion for royal clemency, an escape from prison[n]. The name of the fugitive was Hugh Johns; but the nature of his offence, or from what prison he had escaped, is not specified. He was a " yoman" of Collyweston near Stamford in Northamptonshire, one of the manors of the Countess of Richmond, where she had recently finished and enlarged a palace for her residence[o] Smyth granted a dispensation to Gerard son and heir of the Earl of Kildare to be married to Elizabeth Zouche of the Countess s houshold in her domestic chapel at Collyweston, with single publication of banns[p]: as he had before given a general permission to the Countess herself to have masses

---

[n] Don MS Brit Mus 4618 p 829 N 88 Teste R ap Westm 4 Feb 22 H vii (1506-7)

[o] Bridges Northampt ii p 433

[p] Reg Linc f 126 dat 26 Jul 1503 on the ninth of the same month he granted a similar dispensation to Elianora Zouene, also of the Countess s houshold, to be married to John Melton of the diocese of York, without fixing any place for the celebration of the marriage ib An act passed for John Zouene lord Zouche and Seymour, 11 H vii (private act 21) in which a patent to Sir R Bray of June 28, 7 H vii was saved Rolls Parl vi p 484 An act for the earl of Kildare in the same parliament priv act 17 Of Zouche see also Gent Mag 1799 p 1013 1104

and

and other divine offices celebrated in any of her chapels within his diocefe, where fhe fhould happen to refide[q]. On her death the lordfhip of Collywefton devolved to the Crown, and was fettled as a jointure on queen Anne Bolein[r].

In 1503 Warham was tranflated from the fee of London to Canterbury; on which oc-cafion King, bifhop of Bath and Wells, and the bifhop of Lincoln, were commiffioned by the pope to adminifter the cuftomary oath of office[s]. Shortly afterwards his Holinefs, at the archbifhop's requeft, fent over the Pall, and along with it a commiffion to the fame two bifhops to inveft the archbifhop with it, and to receive from him the ufual oath of allegiance to the fee of Rome[t]. The facred veftment was delivered to the arch-bifhop, February 2, in his chapel at Lam-

[q] Reg Linc f 116

[r] 27 H viii priv act 23 I have added on this occafion thefe few particulars refpecting this ancient royal domain, as they appear to have efcaped the induftrious and accurate county hiftorian John Durrant of Collewefton had reftitution to all his lands and tenements, 1 Ric iii priv act 15

[s] 1 Dec 1503 MS Harl 7048 n 11 p 439, 440

[t] 1 Jan 1503-4 ibid 440 Edw. Scott cler. had been fent to requeft the pall

beth,

beth[u], with great folemnity, in a prefcribed form of words: "For the honour of Almighty God, and the bleffed Virgin Mary, and the bleffed Apoftles Peter and Paul, and of our lord Pope Julius the fecond, and alfo of the Church of Canterbury committed to you, we deliver the Pall taken from the body of St. Peter[x], that is, the plenitude of the pontifical office; that you may ufe it within your church on certain days, expreffed in the privileges granted thereto by the apoftolical fee." Then followed the oath of fubmiffion to the pope; whereof one claufe was a ftipulation to vifit, in perfon or by proxy, " the threfhold of the Apoftles," every year, if the court of Rome was on this fide of the Alps, and every fecond year, if it was beyond.

[u] Anglia Sacr i 124   Colliers Eccl Hift i 701

[x] It was laid on the ftatue of St. Peter, and remained there all right—to imbibe virtue from what connoiffeurs regard as a ftatue of Jupiter metamorphofed   It was made of wool, about the breadth of three fingers, with two labels hanging down before and behind, and was worn by archbifhops about the neck, over their other ornaments   Allen, archbifhop of Dublin, 1528, wrote an Epiftle concerning the active and paffive fignification of the Pall   Athen Oxon i 35   See more in Guilim s Hera dry p 286   Mafons Vind of the Ch of Engl by Lindiay, Lond 1728, folio, p 94 205 who tells us, from Fox (Acts and Mon i 223) the price of it amounted by degrees to 27,000 florins.

The

The certification to his Holiness, of the performance of these ceremonies, is dated the sixth of February, and the final act of inthronization, with the attendant feast, on Sunday the ninth of March, was performed in a style of grandeur answerable to the solemnity of these initiatory forms.

The Duke of Buckingham, distinguished by the brilliancy of his dress at the marriage of prince Arthur[3], was lord high Steward to the archbishop, as lessee of one of the archiepiscopal manors, and he came to Canterbury the day before, attended with a hundred and forty horse, to view the palace, and see that nothing was wanting to the magnificence of the approaching solemnity. Next day at dinner, the Archbishop having been previously inthroned, the Duke rode into the great hall, bare-headed, in a scarlet robe, with a white staff in his hand, followed by two heralds, and the chief Sewer bringing in the first course of the entertainment. While the table was served, he alighted, and made

---

[3] See p 195 of this section His fee, as Steward at this feast, was 7 robes of scarlet, 30 gallons of wine, 50lb of wax, &c Somners Canterbury by Batteley, P ii App p 20 Num x a

his

his obeyfance to the Archbifhop fitting alone
at the middle of the high board , and then
retired into a feparate apartment to dine   In
the hall the King fitting in his parliament,
the embattled towers of Oxford, the Chancellor of the Univerfity and Doctors in their
proper habits, prefenting Warham, then lord
Chancellor, to the King, were exhibited in
confectionary, with appropriate fpeeches affigned to the refpective perfonages.   The
choiceft viands and dainties of every fort, to
the number of 1385 meffes, fix pipes of red
wine and four of claret, with a profufion of
other liquors, were provided for this fumptuous inthronization feaft[z], the laft of the
kind · and it is but juftice to fay of Warham
who gave it, that while he complied with
the pompous fafhion of the times, as his
public ftation and high honours feemed to
demand, he poffeffed in himfelf a foul that
was far fuperior to this ufelefs parade.   He
was eminently learned, and truly modeft,
generous, and benevolent ; plain and fimple
in his own habits, as he was dignified and
fplendid when the formalities of ftate re-

---

[z] See Somner, as above P ii p fo Lel Coll vi Add
p 16 Parker De Antiq in vita Warham Godwin, p 155
Woods Annals, i 661 .

quired

quired it. Notwithftanding he was archbifhop of Canterbury almoft thirty years, and
lord Chancellor half as long, yet, like fome
of his worthy fucceffors in the fee, at his
death he fcarcely left behind him fufficient
to defray the expence of his funeral.

Smyth feems to have ordained this celebrated Archbifhop[a], and it is certain, that he
was one of his early patrons, having collated
him, April, 28, 1496, to the archdeaconry
of Huntingdon[b]. The court of Rome therefore, in delegating Smyth on this occafion to
adminifter fome of the introductory ceremonies of the primacy, fhewed their ufual addrefs in recommending their favours by the
manner of beftowing them and by the perfons employed in conferring them   Warham
was fucceeded in the fee of London by the
fame perfon, who had lately fucceeded him
as Mafter of the Rolls, William Barons or
Barnes[c]; at whofe confecration by the new

---

[a] Sept 21, 1493, among the fecular fubdeacons ordained by
Smyth at Lichfield, is Will Warram, by letters dimiffory from
the Bp of Hereford, upon a title given him by the monaftery
of Byldwas, Co Salop Reg Lichf f 174

[b] On the refignation of Chriftopher Urfewyke MS Harl
6953 p 18 who was collated to it by Smyth, Mar 5, 1495
ib·d 6954 p 155

[c] Will Barons Mafter of the Rolls, Pat 17 H vii 1 Feb
1501−2

archbifhop, November 24, 1504, the bifhop of
Lincoln affifted; as we are informed by a
very curious contemporary record[d].   Of this
Barnes, who died within twelve months after
he was made bifhop, very little is known;
but he is probably the fame " Barnys," who,
having been of Oxford, and having after that
ftudied long abroad, was, on his return, honoured by the Univerfity with the degree of

---

1501-2 Dugd Chron Ser ' Dr Barnes Mafter of the Rolls"
was prefent, when the firft ftone was laid of Henry the feventh s cnapel, Jan 24, 1502-3 Dart's Weftm Abbey, vol 1
32. His name is Barons in the Prerog Office, and in Stowe s
Ann p 484, fpeaking of the fame ceremony of laying the
firft ftone of the faid chapel

[d] " Summo Incomprehenfibili Invifibili eterno uni et
trino deo Chrifufereque virgini Marie toti quoque celorum
exercitui [*O turpem notam temporum iftorum !*] fit laus honor atque victoria quorum ope et adiutorio prefens confcriptus eft
l bellus Sumptibus et expenfis Reverendiffimi domini Chrifto-
phori Vrfwyke Windefore Decani arte vero et ingenio Petri
Megnen monoculi, theutonis nacione Brabantini," &c anno
1505 [! 1504] 20 H vii Nov 28 " Confecratus quoque
erat eodem menfe die xvi ii Re erendiffimus dominus Dominus
Will Barons London Epifc per Cantuar Archiep ac Norui-
cenf et Lincolienf Epifcopos " Ad fin d Ieronimi in Epp
Canon &c MS 8° vellum, in the extremely choice and valuable Library of Michael Wodhull, efquire, at Thenford in
Northamptonfhire, from which, through the very friendly ci-
vility of the intelligent Proprietor I have derived great and
frequent affiftance in preparing thefe papers for the prefs.

Doctor

Doctor of the civil law by Diploma[e], when Smyth was Chancellor.

In the expiring age of barbarifm, when Smyth lived, there were few writers within his diocefe, whofe works are known to us Father Richard, a Benedictine monk of Bardney near Lincoln, wrote the life of the famous bifhop Grofthead or Groffetefte, in hexameter and pentameter verfe; which he addreffed in the fame fpecies of verfe to bifhop Smyth. The dedication, confifting of fixteen lines, is a favourable fpecimen of the author's verfification and ftyle, but it conveys little hiftorical information: unlefs perhaps the following inference from a fingle line may feem juft. A dedicator does not tell what his patron would not like to hear; and few care to be reminded of the evening of life before it is begun When the poet therefore expreffes a wifh, that his lordfhip's " old age may be happy[f]," we may con-

---

[e] F Ep 498 Ad Doctor Barnys, offering him " eam fedem Oxoniæ,—quam —Juftinianæ legis maximi proffeffores cum fumma gloria hic gentium confcenderunt " No date, but probably 1500–1

[f] See the lines, App No xiv Henry Valefius threw away in a rage a letter written to him by the younger Gronovius, becaufe, in concluding, he had civilly wifhed him " a long and happy

clude, I think, he had already, that is in
1503, entered upon that period; and though
nothing hinders but he might be then above,
he was scarcely under, threescore. If this is
admitted, he must have been at Oxford long
before the date affigned by Wood, 1478,
and was more probably, as Brian Twyne
conjectured, the William Smyth who proceeded bachelor of arts in 1453, but from
what college does not appear[s].

Of this Richard of Bardney it must further
be obferved, that when he ftyles his patron
" the brilliant gem of the clergy, the lamp
of his flock," and pays him, as might be expected, other high compliments, this contemporary teftimony to his merit was not the
adulation of vague panegyric, nor the mere
echo of public fame, but, in part at leaft,
the refult of the writer's perfonal knowledge
and obfervation, as Smyth had vifited the

happy old age," when he was already in his feventieth year
See Jortin s Erafm i p 28

[s] 3 Nov (1453) Suppl dominus Will Smyth capellanus
et fcolaris facultatis artium quatenus 4 anni—una magna vi
catio cum mult s parvis point fibi ftare pro forma &c Reg
Aa f 77 Twynes conjecture is in his Collect vol xxii
p 213.

monaftery

monaftery of Bardney a few years before[h].
Richard, who had ftudied at Oxford among
the Benedictines, and was bachelor of divinity[i], wrote alfo, in the fame kind of
metre, " the martyrdom of St. Hugh[k]," the
Lincoln boy, who was crucified by the Jews,
and canonized by the church for his fuffer-
ings. The deed was perpetrated, Richard
fays, on the firft of Auguft, 1255; and fince
the King's Commiffion for trial of the fact,
and his Warrant to fell the goods of the
Jews executed for it, have been produced[l],
I fuppofe it was not, like many things alleged againft this wonderful outcaft people, a
legendary tale, the invention of calumny

In this fame year a patent was granted to
the bifhop of Lincoln, with others, to be-

[h] 18 Oct 1500 Reg Smith, f 116 b

[i] Athen Oxon i. 5 and Tanner, Bibl'oth. See alfo Dr
Pegges L of Groffetefte, p 2 301 &c

[k] MS Harl 6974 prope fin ex Otho, C xvi

[l] See them in Tovey s Angl Jud. p 137 where alfo,
p 143 is the fhrine, as it is thought, of this infant faint
Mr Warton, Hift of Poet ii p 108 fays " the martyrdom
of faint Hugh, a child murthered in 1206 by a Jew at Lincoln,
was reduced into French verfe" " about the fame time,' 1210
But there muft be a miftake in the dates The two warrants
above mentioned are dated, the firft Mar 27 40 H iii (1256)
and the other in the fame year

ftow

ftow certain manors and advowfons, in Suf-
fex, Berkfhire, and Effex, on the Abbey of
Weftminfter[m], but either it fo happened,
that only a fmall part of this intended benefaction was actually given, or elfe the circumftance has efcaped the refearches of thofe
who have inveftigated the hiftory and en-
dowments of this opulent abbey.

The court of Star Chamber, which had
long fubfifted under the fanction of the common law, was regulated, and its authority in
certain cafes confirmed, by act of parliament
in the third year of Henry vii[n]. By this ftatute, in order to give effect to their proceedings, the prefence of a fpiritual lord was
made neceffary[o], in aid of the lord Chan-

[m] Pat 20 Jul 18 H vii Rolls Chapel The eftates are
" Maner de Bradwater al Brodewater—nuper Will Rad-
mylde Milits, in com Suff ac advocat ecclef de Bradwater,
et Cantariam in eadem—Cantar de Knyll ac maner de Pi-
nenham cum advocat ecclef ejufdem in Com Berks—et maner de Pinchpole &c in Effex The laft only occurs in Tanner, Middl xii

[n] 3 H vii c 1

[o] This was what lord Bacon efteemed wifdom in queen Elizabeth, to have counfellors " fome of every fort,—one bifhop
at the leaft,—one or more fkilled in the laws,' &c Advice to
Sir Geo Villiers, afterwards D of Buckingham, Works,
Lond 1765 4to vol ii p 268.

cellor

cellor and certain other great officers of ftate.
Accordingly we find the bifhop of Lincoln
affifting in a decree of this court, November
26, 1504, in a matter between the Merchants Adventurers and the Merchants of the
Staple. The merchants " hawntyng Tharche-
dukeys Cuntreys" complained, that the merchants of the Staple had infringed the peculiar privileges of their company. In anfwer
to this, the Mayor of the Staple, producing
copies of their charters, of which he affirmed
the originals remained in the town of Calais,
infifted, that the Merchants Adventurers had
no jurifdiction over the Merchants of the
Staple. The adjudication of the council in
this bufinefs, when the papers had been
" redde," and the cafe confidered, was in
the nature of a compromife, for they did
not reftrain or limit either of the companies.
in their traffic, but ordered, that the merchants of the Staple, " intromitting the actys
medlings or faytis of the marchantys Adventurers," and in like manner the Adventurers
intromitting in the Staple, fhould be obe-
dient, in all fuch cafes, to the laws of the
refpective companies. At this decree, befides
the King's Majefty, and the bifhop of Lincoln, already named, there were prefent the
archbifhop of Canterbury (Warham, lord
Chan-

Chancellor) the Earl of Derby, mafter Row-
thal, Secretary, (afterwards bifhop of Durham,) Richard Guildford[p], knight, Mafter
Weft[q], LL. D. and others[r].

Of the court of Star Chamber the very
name has long been held in abhorrence: it
is not our prefent bufinefs to profcribe or de-
fend it. The hiftorians of the time with
which we are concerned, reprefent it as one
of the nobleft inftitutions of the kingdom,
nor will it be denied, that, in matters of civil policy, what is at one time found detri-
mental or dangerous, may in a different period have been expedient, or even neceffary.
A preeminent prerogative in the crown, exercifed through the council, might be requifite to curb the exorbitant and formidable
power of the barons; or, as in the inftance
before us to redrefs grievances not properly
cognizable in the courts of equity, or of law.
And yet fuch authority may be unneceffary,
if not unfafe, in a fyftem better poifed,
when civilization has meliorated the manners

[p] See above, p 31 note l
[q] I fuppofe Nicholas Weft, mentioned above, p 186 of
this fection
[r] See an Infpeximus of this decree of "Sterre Chambre"
T R ap. Knoll, 17 Dec fame year, Brit Muf Donation MS
4618 p 357—362

of

of the people, and juſtice, aided by the accumulated wiſdom of ages, is enabled to reach every violation of right.

The companies, whoſe diſputes were thus adjuſted, are the moſt ancient ſocieties of Engliſh merchants; but it is not generally agreed, which was the earlier of the two The Merchant Adventurers, who ſubſiſt now in the Hamburgh company, are ſaid to have been incorporated by Edward the firſt, in 1296; but the Staple appears to have been a company long before 51 Henry iii, 1268[s]. They traded principally in wool, the Adventurers in cloths, tin, and other commodities Each company had a coat of arms, and a common

[s] So I learn from a MS in the Library of Lincoln's Inn, Num 82 in which, about the middle of the vo'ume, are extracts from charters of the Merchants of the Staple, from the year 1268 to 3 Eliz See more of the rules and affairs of this company, chiefly temp H vii and H viii, in MS Parker cv. f 423 MS Dugd O f 266 b Rolls of Parl vol vi p 55 101 394 523 Journals of Lords, vol i p 8, 9 14, 15 Woods Annals, vol i p 467 Stowes Survey, ed Strype, 1720 B v p 256 and Weever's F Mon p 340—342 They were encouragers of the art of printing, Ames's Typogr. by Herbert, p. 314 The Mayor of the Staple was one of the gueſts at the ſumptuous inſtallation feaſt of Nevyl, Abp of York, 1464 Godwin, p 696 Richard York their Mayor was knighted at York, 1 H vii Cotton MS Claudius, C iii f 17

Q   ſeal;

ſeal; and both were veſted with the privilege
of electing a governour or mayor, in their
reſpective reſidences, either in England, or
in foreign partsᵗ. The Staple was in ex-
iſtence in 1640: when it became extinct I
have not learnt. They were a very wealthy
company, and have left monuments of their
liberality in many parts of the kingdom
Their motto was, " God be our Friendᵘ."

ᵗ Leave was given to the Merch Adventurers to elect a Governour where it ſhall pleaſe them to aſſemble within Calais
and its Marches, by writ of privy Seal, 21 H vii (1505) Brit
Muſ Donation MS 4618 p 435 " Yeven at Oxford Sept 28 "
If this proves, as I preſume it does, that his Majeſty was then
at Oxford, it is a royal viſit to the Univerſity unnoticed by
Wood   John Sheldon was Governour of the Mercn Advent in
1507 ibid p 485
ᵘ Howels Lcncinopolis, p 42   Sir Will Littlebury, lord
Mayor 1487, a Merch of the Staple, was a benefactor to the
preachers at Paul's croſs and the Spital ib 105   A hoſpital
at Okcham was founded by Dalby Merch of the Staple,
22 Ric ii   The arms of the company are over the weſt door
of Loughborough church (1790) Guillim blazons them, ne-
buly of 6, Arg and Az on a chief Gules a lion of England
ed 1724 P ii p 8   The coat of the Adventurers ſeems to
be borrowed from this   the field is the ſame, the chief quarterly, Or and Gules, 1 and 4 two red roſes, 2 and 3 a lion of
England ioid Walter Calcot, merchant of the Staple in the
reign of queen Elizabeth, who endowed a ſchool at Williamſcot
near Banbury, Oxfordſhire, exhibited, together with his own
arms (party per pale, Or and Gules, on a chief Argent 3 coots
proper, creſt on a wreath, a demi-griffon ſegreant Or, armed
and langued Gules) the field of the Staple arms rebuly, Ar-
                                                          gent

Smyth, in right of his fee, was Visitor of Oriel college, and in 1504 the society applied to him in that capacity The occasion was this: They are required by their statutes, as often as they become possessed of new estates to a certain amount, to increase proportionably the number of fellowships. They wished for a dispensation of this rule in a particular instance, and to be permitted to appropriate the manor of Shenington in Gloucestershire, which they had recently purchased, to the emolument of the Provost and Fellows as they then subsisted, without adding to the number[x]. The request appeared reasonable, and the visitor, whose power in that college, with the concurrence of the society, is competent to such regulations, ratified the ordinance in his mansion near the Temple, November 20, 1504[y].

---

gent and *Sable*, in the windows of " the lord's manor house ' at Williamscot, 1568, where they are carefully preserved by the present proprietor, my most esteemed Friend, John Loveday, LL D to whose extensive information and accurate taste these memoirs owe numberless important obligations

[x] Coll Oriel Registr Decani, p 64

[y] Reg Linc f ~8 b " Manerium de Schynnyngdon " Shenington is an insulated part of Gloucestershire, about five miles from Banbury Plot says, (Oxf ch vi § 85 p 175) these insulated parishes, in various parts of the kingdom, were reckoned in the county where the lords chief estates were

Norto

At this period, if not before, he had it in his thoughts to bestow some permanent mark of his affection on the University, where he had been educated, and of which he had been Chancellor. So I conclude from the circumstance of a purchase, which he made about this time, of an estate which lay in Oxford and its environs. It is called Basset's Fee, having probably belonged to the Bassets[z], Barons of Headington, a family of great note in the annals of ancient piety; who founded several monasteries, and were benefactors to more The estate is described as consisting of twenty acres of meadow, one hundred and eighteen shillings and nine pence in various quit rents, with lodging and board for one man, and the keep of one horse and one greyhound in Rewley Abbey[a].

North and south Tyndall were made parcel of the C of Northumberland by Act of Parl 11 H vi Rolls of Parl vol vi Compare Gent Mag 1793 p 297

[z] See Tanner's Not under Bruern and Burcester, Oxford-shire, C0acombe, Northamptonshire, Laund, Leicestershire, &c See also Dugd Bar 1 378—385 Wood's Colleges, p 4 note 10 Annals, 1 p 232 427 and Gent Mag 1798 p 765 2

[a] Centum et decem et octo Solidatos et novem Denariatos reddtus Et reddit vict et hospitii unius hominis, unius cant, et unius leporarii (i e canis leporarii Vide Gloss ad x Scriptores) Yate, p 64 The Bishop, in his will, calls the clear

It was furrendered to the bifhop, Edmund
Bury (a perfon often employed by him, who
in one of the documents is ftyled Edmund
Bury of Brightwell) Thomas Kay, clerk, and
John Buftard, February 3, 1504-5. In Michaelmas term following a fine and recovery
were levied for the premifes by the bifhop,
Charles Bothe, fo often named, Robert Brudenel and William Grevile, ferjeants at law,
Edward Tyrell efquire, Robert Toneys, Edmund Bury, and John Daland, againft Thomas Bulkeley of Eyton in the county of
Chefter, of whom the eftate had been purchafed for the fum of 150l This Thomas
Bulkeley of Eyton was probably the fon of
William Bulkeley of the fame place, Juftice
(or, as his epitaph[b] ftyles him, Deputy
Juftice) of Chefter and Northwales; whofe
daughter Catharine was married to Sir Ran-

clear annual value of this eftate 7l 6s 8d See App Num
xvi Mr Warton obferves, that Greyhounds were " a favourite fpecies of dogs in the middle ages," and that " in the
antient Pipe rolls payments are frequently made in greyhounds," of which he gives various inftances Hift Poet 1
363 note p They are prohibited in the Statutes of Magdalen
college Johnftons Kings Vifit Power afferted, 1688 p 337.

[b] In Davenham church, Chefhire " quondam locum tenens
Jufticiaru Ceftrie et Northwalie qui obiit—Maye 1, 1467 "
MS Harl 139. f 51

dle Brereton of Ipftones[c], knight, father of
Sir Rondulph Brereton, knight baronet[d],
Chamberlain of Chefter, who founded a Hofpital at Malpas in that county, where he lies
interred under a beautiful tomb erected in
his lifetime, fupporting the recumbent effigies
of himfelf and dame Helenour his wife.

[c] Chefh Ped of Ipftones

[d] So on the tomb, and on the elegantly carved lattice inclof-
ing the fouth chancel in which it ftands, in Malpas church —

 Hail, facred dome, where Townfon once was heard,
Eternal honours flourfh round thy head!
There fleeps his duft in peace, but if this page,
Protected by its fubject, live, " late times fhall know
I once was blefs'd in fuch a matchlefs friend!

SECT VIII.

Benefactor to Oriel College—to his native Parish
—to Lincoln College—Executor to Henry vii.
—engaged in a dispute with the Archbishop
of Canterbury about his prerogative—attends
Parliament—visits Oriel College

———

THE Historian of the English Worthies,
alleging Solomon's observation, that " a good
name is an ointment poured out," says bishop
Smyth " may be followed wherefoever he
went by the perfume of charity[a]." The remark is applicable no lefs to the ftages of his
life, than to the fcenes of his preferment ;
but, his beneficence ftill keeping pace with
his ability, the monuments of his piety, as
he advanced in years, are found to increafe
in number and magnitude. In this view
the year 1507 forms a kind of epoch in his
life. In the courfe of this year he founded

———

[a] Fuller's Worthies of Lancashire, p 119

a Fel-

a Fellowſhip in Oriel college, he eſtabliſhed
a School in his native pariſh; he prepared a
handſome benefaction for Lincoln college,
and projected the erection and endowment
of a new and permanent College of his own.

To Oriel college his firſt intention was to
give an eſtate in land[b], but money being at
that time more acceptable to the ſociety,
perhaps to aſſiſt them in defraying the expence of their recent purchaſe of Shenington[c], it was finally ſettled, that in conſi-
deration of the ſum of 300l given them by
the Biſhop, the College would obſerve the
following conditions: There ſhould be another Fellow, of the dioceſe of Lincoln, a bachelor of arts, who had determined with
credit[d], to be choſen within twelve months
of the date of this new ſtatute One of the
Fellows, a prieſt, ſhould annually receive
Four marks to pray for the Biſhop and his

[b] " Excellentiſſimo—Gulielm Linc Fpiſcopo Tuam in
nos ſingularem benivolentiam cum antehac in multis beneficiis
.tum ioc poſtremo et maximo,' that he deſigned to give them
' iuncum c. agros quo'dam, of which " Edm Bury tius fa-
mulus di .gentiſſimus had informea tnem Dat " xiii Kal
Apr " no year, but probably 1507 Coll Oriel Reg Decani,
p 68

[c] See above, p 227   [d] " Probabiliter "

parents,

parents, and for his predeceſſors and ſuc-
ceſſors, biſhops of Lincoln, in St. Mary's
church in Oxford · The ſociety, after his deceaſe, would keep his anniverſary; and at
public ſermons always mention him among
their principal benefactors Theſe ordinances,
dated in the college chapel, May 5, 1507,
and unanimouſly agreed to on the part of
the ſociety[e], were confirmed by the Biſhop
under his epiſcopal ſeal in the caſtle of Banbury, on the ſeventh of the ſame month[f].

It is memorable, that, at the firſt election
on this foundation, not only this new ſtatute,
but alſo a ſtanding rule of their original ſtatutes, was diſpenſed with. They are not allowed to have more than two Fellows, at
the ſame time, from the ſame dioceſe, and
there were then two who were natives of
the dioceſe of Lichfield; but notwithſtanding, by the leave of the Viſitor, and, as it
ſeems, in compliance with his wiſhes, Roger
Edgeworth B A " of the dioceſe of Lichfield," was pronounced eligible, and unani-

[e] Reg L nc f 169

[f] Ibid f 170 b The original, w th the ſeal appendant is
preſerved in the Archives of Oriel College ſee alſo MS Harl.
6953 p 73.

moully

moufly elected upon the new foundation,
Nov. 8, 1508; but with exprefs provifion,
that this deviation from the ftatutes fhould
not be made a precedent at future elections[s].
The perfon thus favoured, having been admitted actual Fellow, June 11, 1510[h], occurs
occafionally in the affairs of his college and
of the Univerfity[i], where he proceeded regularly in arts and divinity, and when he
quitted the Univerfity, being a diftinguifhed
preacher and a zealous papift, he became
amply dignified and preferred He was canon of Salifbury, of Wells, and of Briftol;
and likewife refidentiary and chancellor of
Wells, and vicar of St. Cuthbert's in that
city. He died in 1560, and was buried in
the cathedral at Wells, having, three years
before, publifhed a volume of " Sermons
very fruitfull and learned," containing, befides
other things, " an expofition on the firft

[s] Reg Oriel Decan p 79

[h] Ibid p 92 " ad initantiam dicti venerabilis Patris nunc
completum eft " Edgeworth is here faid to be " Cheftrenfis
diocef ' a proof of what has been remarked before, (p 143)
that this diocefe was called indifferently the diocefe of Chefter
and the diocefe of Lichfield

[i] He was auditor of fome of the public Chefts in 1513 &c
Reg G f 175 b 271 b 287 For his degrees fee Athen.
Oxon 1 Fafti, p 11 17 28 40.

Epiftle

Epiftle of Peter[k]." He was born, as we are informed, " at Holt caftle, within the Marches of Wales[l]," the feat of Sir William Stanley, brother to the earl of Derby, on the banks of the Dee, in the county of Denbigh, but within the diocefe of Chefter.

Smyth's benefactions to his native parifh come next in order. He had given 350l. to the monaftery of Laund in Leicefterfhire to affift them in procuring the appropriation of the rectory of Rofthorn in Chefhire. In confequence of this gift it is ftipulated, by a tripartite indenture, between the Bifhop and Chapter of Lincoln, the Prior and Convent of Laund, and the Mayor and Corporation of Chefter, that the faid Monaftery fhall pay

[k] Printed by Rob Caley, 1557 4to and 8vo Ames s Typogr by Herbert, p 831 It is in the Library of Baliol college There are anfwers alfo by Edgeworth, and other divines, to certain queftions concerning the facraments, in Burnet s Hift Ref vol 1 Collect of Rec on B iii Num xxi p 201 —244 3d ed and vol iii Coll p 68

[l] Athen Oxon 1 p 133 Tanner Biblioth The parliament rolls feem to defcribe Holt Caftle as being in Chefhire " The moiety of the manor and caftle of Holte in the county of Chefter Journ of Lords, vol 1 f vi b The town of Lione otherwife called the Holte is faid to belong to Sir W. Stanley, 1 H vii Rolls Parl vi 316. fee al o ibid 417

annu-

annually, to the Mayor and Corporation of
Chefter, the fum of 10l, which annuity the
Mayor and Corporation undertake to pay annually to the Mafter of the free School of
Farnworth in Lancafhire, for ever[m]. The
Schoolmafter, always to be nominated by the
Mayor and Corporation of Chefter, is to be a
clergyman, a Mafter or Bachelor of arts, or
at leaft a Mafter of grammar. Upon the
fuppreffion of monafteries, this ftipend, payable out of the revenues of the faid monaftery, was preferved by a decree of the
Court of Augmentation[n]; and continues to
be paid out of the tithes of Rofthorn before
mentioned, by the Dean and Chapter of
Chrift Church in Oxford, that appropriation
having been beftowed on the College, as
part of their endowment, by the Crown.

It does not appear that any diftinct building was erected at Farnworth for a fchool.
The church itfelf, or a part which Smyth
added to it, was probably defigned to anfwer
the purpofes both of infantile inftruction
and of religious worfhip This addition to the
church of Farnworth was a chapel or fouth

[m] Indent 20 Jul 22 H vii 1507 Yate 81
[n] 8 Feb 33 H viii (1541-2) Yate, ibid Archiv Drawer 4

aile,

ale, built by him for the sole use and accommodation of the township of Cuerdley. The name of the Founder is gratefully recorded on the walls, and his portrait, with an inscription underneath, and the initials of his name, coeval probably with the building itself, remained in the last century, till the arms of rebellion demolished these, among a thousand other, venerable remains of antiquity[o].

Another benefaction may properly here be noticed, which constant tradition ascribes to the same generous hand. There is a "double-style" path, leading from the village of Cuerdley to Farnworth church, which, it is said, bishop Smyth purchased for the inhabitants of Cuerdley, that they might repair to the house of God without fear of receiving infection from the plague, then raging in Farnworth, by passing, as they must other-

---

[o] Dodsworth, who visited this chapel " 20 May, 1635," says, " The south quyre here was builded from the ground by Will Smyth, Founder of Brazenose in Oxford, sometime Bp. of Lincoln, borne in Keuerdlegh In the East of which quyre, under his picture, are these words Orate pro anima Domini Will Smythe . ac pro animabus parentum suorum &c In several quarrells in the windowes ther be W S.' MS Dodsw 142 f 224 b See also vol 153 f 46 b

wife

wife have done, along the ftreet. Thofe
who report the ftory, enjoying ftill the benefit of this Via facra, are ignorant probably
of the truth of the fact, with which they
connect it.   But fince, as we have feen, the
plague did not only make its appearance in
England in bifhop Smyth's time, but likewife
peculiarly engaged his pious attention[P], thefe
collateral circumftances give a degree of probability to the tradition, and we may regard
this church-path and the chapel, to which it
leads, as concurring marks of affection in
Smyth toward Cuerdley, the feat and refidence of his anceftors.

His donations to Lincoln college confifted
of two eftates, one in Staffordfhire, the other
in Oxfordfhire.   The manor of Bufhbery, or
Aillefton, near Brewood, in Staffordfhire,
was fecured to the bifhop of Lincoln, together with his friend Sir Reginald Bray and
others, by a recovery enrolled in Chancery in
Michaelmas term, 1501, againft Humfry
Barbour, efquire, and Robert his fon and
heir, of whom, I fuppofe, the eftate had
been purchafed.   The manor of " Sengclere,
or Sencleres, in Chalgrave," Oxfordfhire, was

[P] See above, p 110

pur-

purchafed, December 21, 1506, of Edmund
Hampden, knight, who, I fufpect from the
coincidence of the name and place, was an
anceftor of Hampden, famous in the annals of
the grand Rebellion   Nor was this eailier
Hampden, though " guiltlefs of his country's
blood," altogether free from feditious practices; for about the year 1491, the Univerfity
of Oxford, of which he was then or lately
high Steward, had occafion to complain of
him as a diftuiber of the peace; nor was
tranquillity reftored, till his Majefty fummoned him before the privy Council, and
ftrictly commanded him, that he fhould
neither by himfelf nor his adherents affail or
moleft any member of the Univerfity[q].

---

[q] Reg F Epp 449—455 all relate to this bufinefs The
firft, from the chancellor, Bp Ruffell, is a very earneft exhortation to the Univerfity, fome of the academics having, as
it feems, at firft been in fault " For Godds fake perfuade all
our fcolers to remembyr the tyme, and the ftyll fyttyng of the
parliament houfe til the direccion of this mater be well per-
ceivyd —bidding them exhort the fcholars to behave fo " that
they may love and gete love of all our neybowres Feb 6
(1491-2) The laft letter, wherein his Majefty informs the
Univerfity of his order in the affair, begins with a fentiment
honourable to the feelings of this patron of literature " Quanto
fane magis elucefcet et clarebit virtute ac doctrina ifta noftra
academia, tanto fane nos illuftriores ditiorefque et feliciores
arbitrabimur Apr 5 1492

When

When thefe eftates were procured, and
their deftination determined, a licence of
mortmain was obtained by the college, em-
powering them to receive, and the bifhop to
beftow, the eftates, upon the fociety; for
which, as it paffed the great feal, the fum of
20l was paid into the hanaper, July 26,
1508[r]. Free fcope for his generofity being
thus opened, he configned the eftates over to
the college in perpetuity, by two feparate
deeds, bearing the fame date, October 24,
24 Henry vii. (1508) The inftruments are
both of them under the hand and feal of the
Bifhop, as well as of thofe, who were refpectively parties with him in the purchafe
and poffeffion of the two eftates[s]. Chalgrove
is joined with other eftates in the licence of

[r] Abftr of Evidences of Linc Coll penes Rectorem, p 5
To the late and prefent Rector (Dr Horner and Dr Tatham)
and to the Fellows of Lincoln college my beft thanks are due
for ready and repeated accefs to the Regfters and Archives of
their fociety

[s] Archives of Linc Coll "Chalgrove" and "Ellfton" i. e.
Aillefton The Bifhops feal affixed to Chalgrove, of a fmall
oblong form, in beautiful prefervation, is a W between three
rofes, in allufion to his arms The other, which is circular,
feems alfo to have borne the impreffion of a rofe, but it is
now crufhed and fcarcely diftinguifhable Chalgrove is alfo
figned by Hum Coningfby, Kings ferjeant, and Will Grevil,
ferjeant at law, both often employed by Smyth

mort-

mortmain; fo that the feparate value of it does not appear. Bufhbery is eftimated at fix pounds a year, and is defcribed as confifting of little lefs than two hundred acres of land of different forts. It is reputed the beft fingle eftate in the poffeffion of this college.

This ample benefaction, as far as appears, was perfectly gratuitous; clogged with no ftipulations or conditions on the part of the donor, but freely confided to the difcretion of the Society, for the general purpofes and benefit of the houfe. The arms of their benefactor, which were formerly in one of the windows of the chapel[t], do not now appear there; but they are exhibited twice in the arched roof of oak, feparately and impaling the fee of Lincoln. About fifty years ago, when hiftorical groups frequently formed the fubject of the Oxford Almanacks, bifhop Smyth and Edward Darby were introduced in a view of this college as the principal benefactors of the fociety[u], but as for the tale, which Wood relates from tradition, that

[t] Wood, Colleges, p 250

[u] See Oxf Alman. for 1743 Of Darby fee above, p 159

R   what

what the Bifhop " performed in Brafenofe
Hall was intended for this College, had the
then Rector and Fellows fully conceded to
his propofals[x]," it is, fo far as I can learn, totally deftitute of foundation; and at the fame
time inconfiftent with a circumftance remaining on record, which muft now, for
other reafons alfo, be mentioned.

Edmund Crofton, a native of Lancafhire,
and, through bifhop Smyth's kindnefs, prebendary of Bigglefwade and Rector of Winwick in Northamptonfhire, dying in Brafen
Nofe Hall (of which he had been Principal)
January 27, 1507-8, bequeathed the fum of
6l. 13s 4d. towards " the building of Bra-
fvnnofe in Oxford, if fuch works as the
bifhop of Lyncoln and Mafter Sotton intended there, went on during their life, or
within twelve years after[y]." This bequeft
fhews, that, inftead of the pretended project
of re-founding or enlarging Lincoln college,
Smyth's intention of founding a new college

[x] Wood, Colleges, p 2,9

[y] See his Will, dated 23 Jan 1507-8 Reg F f 59, 60
proved 4 June following, by the three executors named below,
or elfe 14 April, as it is ibid f 54   He was fucceeded,
20 Feb 1507-8, in the prebend of Bigglefwade, by Will
Smyth, M A MS Harl 6953 p 23

on a different fite was matter of public no-
toriety in Oxford, nine months at leaft
before his benefaction to that fociety took
place, and that, at this early period, it was
known as the joint defign of the bifhop of
Lincoln and Sir Richard Sutton

This firft benefactor to Brafen Nofe college, Edmund Crofton, appears to have been
one of bifhop Smyth's almoners, and being
apprehenfive that he had not, in that capacity, fully performed his duty[z], the firft
bequeft in his will is the fum of 4l. to his
" moft efpecyall good Lord of Lyncoln's
Grace," to be diftributed amongft his " almes
deeds," and he humbly intreats him to be
as kind to his foul, as he had been to his
body, and to be fupervifor of his will, and to
affift his executors in difcharging obligations
binding upon the teftator, and known to
his Lordfhip To Mr. Derby and Mr. Toneys (both friends of the Bifhop) he bequeathed legacies to be difpofed of for the
good of his foul, and left to Roland Meffenger the ufe of all his books, while he

---

[z] " Where that I haue bene neclıgent—ın not doyng my
Dutıe ın hıs almeffe Delaying [ı e almeffe dealyng] I gyve"
&c Will, ut fupra

fhould

fhould continue in Oxford, and after that to remain " in the liberay" in Brafen Nofe, if any fhould be made within twelve years; and if not, to go to his executors, Roland Meffenger, Mr. John Camby[a], and John Rogers[b]. He was buried, agreeably to his will, before St. Catharine's altar, in St Mary's church; where a handfome tomb was erected to his memory, the work of John Fufting[c], the fame architect who built the beautiful ftone pulpit there (long fince demolifhed,)

[a] John Camby was Regiftrar of the Archdeaconry of Oxford, which office was confirmed to him by Bp Smyth, 9 Feb 1506 and by the Chapter of Linc 27 March following. Act Capit Linc f 135, 136 He was joined with Edmund Bury in a conveyance of Baffet's fee to the Bifhop and others, 1 Sept 2 H. viii 1510 Yate, p 64 and was prefent at the delivery of it, 26 March, 1511 ibid p 65

[b] John Rogers " the yonger," as he is called, was probably the fon of John Rogers, who rented part of this eftate Yate, ibid and Rot. Burfl 7, 8 H viii Rogers and Camby had been bound for Crofton to " M John Kydwelle," which John Kedwelly, Principal of Edward Hall, 1502 Q f 116 was collated by Smyth to Preb Cent Solid 25 Jan 1508 being then LL B. MS Harl 6953 p 24 See alfo Q f 108 Athen Oxon i Fafti, p 16 Annals, i 658. Of Roland Meffenger we fhall often hear, as we proceed

[c] For a tombe made for Maftur Crofton xxii S iiii D all coftys reconnit—be fide hjs [Joh Fuftyng's] coftys and chargys—pulpit in St Marys-xx' Reg F f 66 b See Athen Ox i p 643 662

the

the benefaction of Edmund Audley, bifhop of Salifbury. Crofton's epitaph, ftill remaining on a plate of brafs, fhall be given in the notes, not certainly for the elegance of the Latinity, or correctnefs of the metre, (for a more confpicuous inftance of "committing fhort and long" will not eafily be found,) but becaufe it confirms fome parts of this account[d]

[d] Edmund Crofton M A was prefented by Ofeney to Buckenhull (Oxfordfhire) 25 Aug 1498 MS Harl 6953 p. 39. which he exchanged for the vicarage of Cudelyngton, on the prefentation of the fame convent, 22 Sept 1503 ibid p 46 Bp Smyth collated him to the Preb of Spaldwick in 1500 Willis, Cath iii p 232 appointed him (1502) and Edward Powell, mentioned above, p 118 to arbitrate a difpute between the Convent of St Fridefwide and Edmund Ayleard Reg Œ f 150—151 b gave him the Rectory of Winwick in Northamptonfhire, 21 July, 1505 MS Harl ib p 32 and the Prebend of Bgglefwade, 25 Mar 1506 Willis, ib p 146 He was Principal of Brafen Nofe Hall in 1501 Reg Œ f 101 and in 1503 ib f 47 See alfo ib 125 b On the plate affixed to his tomb (now over the door going to the organ gallery) he is reprefented praying to St Catharine, in this diftich

Auxiliare tuis famulum precibus Katerina
Vt mihi cum fuperis fit fine fine locus

Above, St Catharine herfelf, who prays alfo in verfe

Obfecro fumme deus veniam concede precanti
Edmundo crofton gloria fine carens

The epitaph is this

Hic lapis Edmundi crofton tegit offa fepulti
Olim qui viuus vir fuit eximius

lan-

From the Univerfity of Oxford we muft now attend Smyth to the court of his Sovereign An inftance has been mentioned, wherein he was employed as the difpenfer of royal bounty to Weftminfter abbey[e]. He was foon after included in another royal grant, which was not to take effect till after his Majefty's deceafe. This was an enfeoffment of the Dutchy of Lancafter, in truft, for the performance of his laft will. But as the Dutchy was part of the hereditary patrimony of the Crown, it was thought it could not be alienated, nor charged with any debts or demands, which fhould be valid againft a fucceeding monarch, without the concurrence of Parliament. The confent therefore

lancaftrenfis erat patria princeps et ceni
 Contubernioh providus atque fagax
procurator item refpublica pace quieuit
 poftque bikulfwadie prefuit ecclefie
poft chriftum natum labitur millefimus annis
 Et poft quingentos feptimus annus erat
Anteque calendas fextum februarius egit
 hunc ex hoc feculo cum rapuere fata
nec quicunque legis crofton memor efto precando
 vt fibi cum fuperis detur in arce locus

His arms, or rebus, a crofs piercing four Tuns, remains on the brafs, and was formerly in one of the windows of the Refectory of Brafen Nofe college A Wood, Hift and Ant 1 368

[e] See p 222

of the two Houfes was obtained, January 25,
19 H. vii. (1503-4,) as it had been to a fimilar grant before, February 20, 7 H. vii.
The prefent feoffees, befides the bifhop of
Lincoln, were Warham, archbifhop of Canterbury, Fox, bifhop of Winchefter, Sever,
bifhop of Durham, Audley, bifhop of Salifbury, Blithe, bifhop of Chefter, Geffrey Simeon, clerk, John Mordaunt, Humfry Co-
nyngfby[f] and John Kingfmele, ferjeants at
law The bifhop of Durham, Simeon, and
Mordaunt died before the King, the others
furvived, and are directed in his will to pay
the profits of the faid dutchy to his Majefty's
executors, in aid of other immenfe fums by
the fame inftrument committed to them, for
the fplendid purpofes therein mentioned.
Three of thefe feoffees, the bifhops of Winchefter, Salifbury and Lincoln, were alfo

---

[f] H Coningfby is one of the great lawyers often mentioned
in Smyths affairs See above, p 240 note s In 1510 he
was made Juftice of Com Pleas Dugd Chron Ser Smyth
granted him a licence to marry Alice Stavely, with banns twice
publifhed, in the chapel of Bygehull, Mar 29, 1499 Reg.
Linc f 116. b She was his fecond wife In his will, 1531,
(proved Nov 26, 1535,) he appointed a prieft in Aldenham,
Herts, to pray for him, and for Ifabel, Allice, and Jane, his
wives, deceafed. Collins s Peer v p 311 3d ed

named

named executors. The other executors were
the Countefs of Richmond, Bainbridge, archbifhop of York, Fitzjames, bifhop of London,
Fifher, bifhop of Rochefter; Thomas, earl
of Arundel, Thomas, earl of Surrey, Treafurer general, Sir Charles Somerfet, knight,
lord Herbert, chamberlain, Sir John Fineux,
knight, chief Juftice of the King's Bench, Sir
Robert Rede. knight. chief Juftice of the
common Pleas, Mr John Yong, Mafter of
the Rolls, Sir Thomas Lovell, knight, Treafurer of the houfehold, Mr. Thomas Routhal,
Secretary, Sir Richard Empfon, knight, Chancellor of the Dutchy of Lancafter, Sir John
Cutte, knight, undertreafurer general, and
Edmund Dudley, Efquire. To each of his
executors his Majefty bequeathed the fum of
one hundred pounds, to be paid when the
will fhould be fully performed[g] Thefe legacies therefore, moft probably, never were
received by any of the parties, for Henry viii,
as is well known, commenced his arbitrary
career by violating, in almoft every particular, his father's will, and, in defiance of

[g] See the Will, publifhed by Mr Aftle, Lond 1775 4to
The beginning is dated at Richmond, 31 Mar 1509, the conclufion at Canterbury, 10 April

the moft folemn injunctions, lavifhed, for
very different purpofes, the vaft treafures,
which he found in the royal coffers.

Henry vii died in his favourite palace of
Richmond, April 21, 1509 In his will he
had given directions concerning his funeral;
that his executors, in their difcretion, fhould
have fpecial refpect therein to the honour of
God, and the health of his foul, and fome
regard alfo to his dignity royal; yet avoiding
always " dampnable pompe and oteragious
fuperfluities." And the whole ceremony, in
the judgement of thofe times, was managed
in perfect conformity with thefe inftructions.
Solemn maffes were fung over the body, at
the palace of Richmond, nine fucceffive
days. After this it was conveyed in a chair,
drawn by feven great courfers covered with
black velvet, attended by a large train of
temporal lords, bifhops, officers of ftate, and
others, in grand proceffion, through the city
of London to St. Paul's, where the bifhop
of London, Fitzjames, received it at the weft
door; and when it was brought before the
high altar, performed a folemn dirge, affifted
by the abbat of St Alban's, and the abbat
of Reading On the morrow three folemn
maffes were fung, the firft, of our Lady, by
the

the excellent Dr. Colet, dean of the cathedral, the fecond, of the Trinity, by the bifhop of Lincoln; and the third, of requiem, by the bifhop of London   Then the bifhop of Rochefter, Fifher, " made a notable fermon." After dinner, before one of the clock, they proceeded to Weftminfter abbey, where the two archbifhops received the corpfe, and cenfed it   Solemn dirge was then performed, at which Nix, bifhop of Norwich, read the firft leffon, the bifhop of Lincoln the fecond, and Warham, archbifhop of Canterbury, the third

Next morning, May 10, before fix of the clock, the holy offices were refumed, and three maffes fung in due order, the third by the archbifhop of Canterbury, who was attended to the altar by eighteen bifhops and abbats in their facred veftments and mitres. The prelates then went into the choir, except the bifhop of Lincoln, who was deacon to his Grace, and the bifhop of Norwich, who was fubdeacon   Then the archbifhop, ftanding on the fecond ftep before the altar, the bifhops and abbats again giving their attendance, received the offerings made by the mourners, conducted feverally by two heralds in armour. The duke of Buckingham, chief mourner,

mourner, reprefenting the King's perfon, offered a teftament of gold, and then the
others, clergy and laity, in their order and
degree, the bifhops at the altar, the reft to
the archbifhop. When the offering was
ended, the bifhop of London " made a noble
fermon." Then the corpfe was laid in the
vault, with great reverence, by the fide of
his late confort, and in moft folemn manner
affoiled [abfolved] by the whole company of
bifhops and abbats, after which the archbifhop caft earth upon the corpfe. Staves of
office were broken, and the heralds proclaimed aloud the death of the Seventh, and
wifhed long life to the Eighth, King Henry.
This done, the mourners and others departed
to the palace, where a fumptuous entertainment was provided for them [b].

It is to the honour of Henry the feventh's
liberality, a virtue for which he cannot often
be commended, that he had begun in his
lifetime the noble hofpital of the Savoy, for
the relief of the diftreffed and indigent, a
fpecies of charity profitable, he obferves, and
then peculiarly neceffary. The date of the
foundation, as we learn from the infcription

[b] Add to Lel Coll London 1774 iii. 303—309

over

over the original gate, was 1505, and it appears from his Majesty's will, that it was constructed on a plan signed with his own hand[i], and endowed with lands and rents to the annual amount of five hundred marks, to furnish lodging and food to a hundred poor folks, and a certain number of priests and attendants For the completion of his design he had recently (24 H. vii) delivered ten thousand marks to the dean and chapter of St. Paul's, to be paid by them to the master of the building, as the work advanced; and if the sums, thus appropriated, should prove inadequate, the executors are ordered to supply the deficiency; as also to frame statutes and rules for the hospital, if such were not made by his Majesty in his life time[k].

What was left in this state of forwardness, situated under the very eye of the

---

[i] Henry vii was a great builder, at Richmond, at Woodstock, Warton's Sir T Pope, p 72 n (where Skelton s Nigramansir was plaid before him on Palme Sunday Hist Poet ii 360,) and at other places Fisher in his funeral sermon, mentioned above, p 250 celebrates this talent in his Majesty " His buyldinges mooste goodly and after the newest cast all of pleasure "

[k] H. viith's Will, p 15—19

prince, the prodigality of Henry did not fuffer to remain unfinifhed; and, of all the
charitable bequefts and inftitutions in his father's will, this is perhaps the only one, that
ever was carried into effect. By a patent,
dated at London, April 3, 2 Henry viii,
(1511) under the feal of the Dutchy of Lancafter, the Savoy being in that liberty, the
King gave the fite or ground fo called to his
father's executors, to found and eftablifh an
hofpital there, and by a fecond deed, Weftminfter, July 5, 4 Henry viii, [1512] he confirmed the former grant, and added diftinct
privileges The will of the founder mentions priefts or chaplains, as comprehended in
his plan, but the number was not fpecified,
nor, I prefume, the government of the hofpital fettled Thefe matters therefore being
adjufted by the executors, the King gave his
fanction to the foundation, by the name of
" The Hofpital of Henry vii, late King of
England, at the Savoy;" to confift of a Mafter and four Chaplains, to pray for the good
eftate of Himfelf and his confort Catharine,
and for the foul of the Founder, Henry vii,
Elizabeth his queen, and Arthur, late prince
of Wales[1].

---

[1] See the charter, Rymer, xiii p 333. Dugd Mon ii p 484

At

At the general furvey, 26 Henry viii, the
revenues of the Savoy were valued at 529l.
15s 7½d. according to Speed When a commiffion was iffued from the Crown, 5 Edward vi, to Sir Roger Cholmley, chief Baron
of the Exchequer, to vifit this hofpital, it
was found, that the number of fick and im-
potent refrefhed here, befides others nightly
lodged, according to the direction and intent
of the founder, amounted to eight thoufand
three hundred and thirty nine. It was diffolved in the laft year of Edward vi, at the
requeft of the city of London, and the furniture and moft of the lands given to the
hofpital of Bridewell, fo that, as our authors
remark, the charity was not deftroyed, but
what was in one place abufed was removed
to another, where it might be better employed. Queen Mary, in the fifth year of
her reign, reincorporated and endowed the
Savoy; upon which occafion the ladies of
the court and the maids of honour fupplied
it with beds, and other furniture, in very
ample manner. However it did not long
continue a hofpital for the poor, but there
were Mafters and Brethren of the Savoy
many years afterwards, and among them have
been feveral men eminent in their time[m].

ᵐ See Stowes Surv ed Strype, B i. 210. Newcourt, Rep
i. 696.

The Countefs of Richmond had recently (A. D. 1506[n]) founded Chrift's college in the Univerfity of Cambridge; to which an annuity of forty fhillings was granted, March 8, 1508-9, by Thomas Breton, rector of Navenby in Lincolnfhire, payable for ever out of the living; and the grant was confirmed by the bifhop of Lincoln the fame month[o]. In fanctioning this benefaction he acted

---

[1] 696 Fuller, Ch Hift B vi 355 viii 42 x 84 94 Pennants London, p 135—137 a view of it, p 172 253 Fuller was Lecturer at the Savoy It was named Savoy Place by Vetre earl of Savoy, the firft builder, brother to Boniface archbifhop of Canterbury, about 29 H iii (1244) Stowes Ann p 485

[n] Mr Baker, Pref to Fun Serm of Marg Countefs of Richm p xi

[o] Reg Linc f 129 b There was alfo a penfion from Navenby or Naanby (as it is now called) to the monaftery of Sion in Middlefex ibid f 72 But, fortunately for the living, thefe payments being fpecific fums of money, the rectory is at this time a valuable one, in the patronage of Chrift's college In 1383 Alan Stokes exchanged Navenby for Great Billing in Northamptonfhire with Philip Wen, to which they were feverally inftituted on the fame day, Oct 29, Stokes to Billing by prefentation from the Crown (as Wen alfo had been, Sept. 29, 1375) and Wen to Navenby, alfo by the Crown, "on account of the temporalties of the alien abbey of Seys' MS. Harl 6952 p 9 13 32 which feems to prove, that Navenby belonged to the abbey of St Martin de Seez in Normandy, a circumftance not noticed by the learned and accurate Hiftorian of the Alien Priories See his elegant work, vol 1 p 109, &c.

merely

merely in his official capacity as ordinary:
his authority was special and his powers ample, when that other monument of the munificence of the same illustrious Countess, St.
John's college, Cambridge, was to be erected.
The spot marked out for the new foundation
was the site of an ancient priory of the same
name. A papal bull therefore, as customary
in such cases, was procured for dissolving the
priory, and converting it into a college This
instrument, which was directed, 8 Cal. Jul.
1510, to the bishops of Lincoln and Norwich, authorized them, jointly or separately,
to execute the decree of his Holiness, " without asking leave of the Diocesan, or of any
other person whatsoever, and to coerce with
censures all who should contravene, and, if
there was occasion, to call in likewise the
aid of the secular arm [p]," —one instance,
among a thousand, of the controul usurped
by the sovereign Pontif, in those days, over

[p] Mr Baker's Hist of St John's College, MS Harl 7028
f 62, 63 and his Pref to Fun Serm of Countess of Richmond, p xxii where giving an account of this matter, he
says, " This Pope (Julius ii) was a son of thunder his bull
struck the old house at one blow, it dissolves as well as builds
by his sole pontifical authority, without consent either of the
King, or of the Bishop of Ely The expence of this bull was
1481 12s 4d ibid

the

the laity as well as the clergy of thefe realms. But we cite the refcript, not on account of the powers conferred, but as it affords, in the appointment of Smyth, an inftance of honourable preference or felection by thofe whofe approbation was then valued.

A difpute between the Vicar of Cheping Wycombe, and his parifhioners, which the parties referred to bifhop Smyth's arbitration, would hardly deferve to be mentioned here; though the decifion is a confpicuous proof of a trait in his character already pointed out, his exemplary care to enforce parochial refidence: but two circumftances on the face of the record may perhaps juftify this tranfient notice of it. The number of the parifhioners, it is faid, at that time, amounted to a thoufand, or rather more, an intimation, which may induce fome one who has opportunity, and is curious about a queftion lately much agitated, concerning the population of the kingdom, to compare this with the prefent population of the parifh, which probably would be found to have been doubled in the courfe of three centuries. Among the witneffes to the Bifhop's decree on this occafion, in his domeftic chapel in London, May 18, 1509, was " Thomas Vulcy," dean of Lincoln.

coln[q]. This man of future fame and folly, known yet only by his great talents, had been recently collated by Smyth to a prebend in his cathedral; and was foon after advanced by him to a better ftall, and held each of them fucceffively with the Deanery[r].

The prerogative of the archiepifcopal fee of Canterbury, efpecially in regard to that lucrative branch of it, the proving of wills, was the fource of frequent and tedious litigation between the primate and the bifhops of his province. At length, upon occafion of a warm difpute on the fubject, 1494, between Hill, bifhop of London, and archbifhop Morton, the rights of the primacy were fully eftablifhed, and ratified by four diftinct bulls from the Pope[s].

But though the general right was thus af-

[q] Reg Linc f. 131   The vicar at this time was Thomas Heywood, B of Decrees (i e. of canon law) who is ordered, on account of the extent of the parifh and number of inhabitants, to refide himfelf, and to have an affiftant, and, in cafe of ab fence, to provide two curates, " capellanos " See Chron Preciof p 132 134. 137 or, as Mr Warton underftands the word, "officiating clergymen " Kiddington, p 9

[r] Preb Welton Brinkhall, 20 Feb 1508-9 preb. Stow longa, 3 Mar. 1509–10. MS. Harl 6953 p 24.

[s] Dat. 1495. MS. Linc. Inn, 84. f. 92. b.

certained,

certained, the exact limits and extent of the
power were still undetermined. The matter
therefore was agitated again, when Warham
was archbishop, 1509, by Fox, bishop of Winchester; who being much in favour with the
new King, and together with great wealth
and influence, combining, the historian says,
an innate loftiness of spirit, could not pa-
tiently brook the archbishop's prerogative.
Previously to the commencement of any legal procefs the parties had an interview;
when the archbishop, having shewn his
claims to be founded in prescription of more
than three hundred years, added with some
warmth, that he would not suffer the rights
of the church of Canterbury to be infringed
by the pertinacity of the bishop of Winchester. This provoked Fox to make that
memorable reply, That if Canterbury had
the higher rack, Winchester had the deeper
manger. The conference therefore, instead
of closing, having widened the breach, the
bishop forewith entered his plea in the court
of Rome against the archbishop. Fitzjames
bishop of London, the bishop of Lincoln,
and his friend Hugh Oldham, bishop of
Exeter, joined with Fox in the common
caufe; of which they probably entertained a
better opinion, and entered into it with the

greater

greater zeal, becaufe the archbifhop himfelf had not only, when he was advocate in the court of Canterbury, taken part with Hill in the former difpute on this queftion, but had afterwards, as bifhop of London, acted in defiance of the fuppofed prerogative, and actually fent John Yong, LL. D. as his commiffary to Rome on the bufinefs[t] At this juncture he was tranflated to Canterbury, and then faw the matter with very different eyes, or elfe found the claim refted on better grounds than he had before fuppofed.

The ftate of the controverfy was briefly this. The archbifhop claimed, that, when a perfon died poffeffed of Bona Notabilia in feveral diocefes, the will fhould be proved before him; or if the party died inteftate, that the adminiftration fhould be taken out in his court. The bifhops infifted upon thefe limitations · Firft, that, under the denomination of fuch goods, fhould not be comprehended the inheritance of lands or rents, nor defperate debts: Secondly, that unlefs the goods amounted to the value of ten pounds, they fhould not be accounted Notabilia ·

---

[t] Wilkins Corcil iii p 655 657 where p 653 &c is the Summa litis, ex Reg Exon Oldham, f 44

Thirdly,

Thirdly, that the archbifhop fhould not appoint any perfon to appraife goods in the diocefe of his fuffragans, but that the oath of the executors or adminiftrators fhould be taken for the value of the goods : Laftly, that feveral peculiar jurifdictions fhould not be reputed as diftinct diocefes.

Such a plea as this, which promifed to be lucrative, the Pope readily received, and as readily iffued out a citation from his court againft the archbifhop   When this came to bifhop Fox's hands, he employed William Pawlet, then fteward of his lands, afterwards Marquis of Winchefter, and lord high Treafurer in three fucceffive reigns[a], to put it in execution.   Pawlet accordingly cited the archbifhop, whereupon the fuit was for fome time clofely followed by both parties, and as carefully delayed and drawn out by the court. The bifhops at length prevailed upon his Holinefs to refer the matter to the King's arbitration ; who looking upon it as a difparagement to himfelf and to the kingdom, that the prelates of his realm fhould have fuch contention at Rome, required them, in the

[a] Lloyd, who fays, " He got fpent and left more than any fubject fince the conqueft " State Worthies, vol 1 p 481

firft

firſt place, to ceaſe their ſuit there; and
then proceeded to determine the controverſy;
which he did in moſt points agreeably to
what the biſhops had deſired This award
was limited to three years; after which time
the parties, if they found themſelves ag-
grieved, might proſecute their right in law.
The archbiſhop humbly ſhewed his Majeſty,
that the prerogative of his ſee was confirmed
by long uſage and ancient records, and at
the ſame time repreſented divers inconveniences, which might follow from theſe innovations. At length however, for the ſake
of peace, he was content to recede from his
ſtrict right in the principal points, with ſome
regulations only to prevent the inconveniences that might otherwiſe enſue. And thus,
ſays the hiſtorian, the matter of the prerogative of the archbiſhops of Canterbury, which
had been ſo often and ſo warmly conteſted,
was, by the temperate and equal moderation
of Warham, finally ſettled and compoſed[x].

It is probable that the biſhop of Lincoln,
mild and pacific as he was, took a part in
this buſineſs, and ſeconded Fox, with the
greater alacrity, not only becauſe he was

---

[x] Parker Antiq Brit. in V. Warham

ſup-

supported by ancient precedents, in this material article of the revenues of his fee[y]; but
because he himself had already been engaged
in the controversy. One of the charges
against the Hospitalars, as we have seen[z], regarded the proving of wills; and, prior to
this, he had successfully defended his own
right of granting administration, in the case
of a person dying intestate, within his diocese, when a plea was preferred against him
in the Archbishop's court of audience[a]. He
was anxious therefore, that the occasion of
future litigations might be cut off, by an
exact and authoritative determination of the
rights of the respective parties.

Smyth was summoned to the first and
second parliament of Henry viii. The first[b],
January 21, 1509-10, was opened, as was

[y] In the probate of the will of William Ayhton, archd of
Bedford, dat 19 May, 1423, though he died possessed of Bona
notabilia in different dioceses, it is said, that administration, at
least for effects within the diocese of Lincoln, by ancient custom
peaceably enjoyed, was known to belong to the Bishop of that
fee Extr Reg. Flemyng, MS Harl 6952 p 138 Comp
also ib 170

[z] P 187

[a] Reg Linc f 67—70 Dat 1499

[b] Reg. Linc. f. 243 T R ap Westm 17 Oct and Journals.

then

then cuſtomary, by a ſhort ſpeech from the
chancellor Warham on a text of Scripture ,
and he choſe a theme never unſeaſonable,
but peculiarly appoſite at the commencement
of a new reign: "Fear God, honour the
King." During this parliament however I
do not find, that the Biſhop of Lincoln came
forward in any matters of public deliberation.
He was preſent in the ſecond parliament[c],
1512-13, when, among other weighty affairs,
a diſpute between the Companies of Merchants
already mentioned[d], the Staple and the Adventurers, was referred to the examination of
Sir John Fineux, knight, chief Juſtice of the
King's Bench[e], and Richard Elyot, King's
Serjeant at law[f], who, the enſuing year, was
conſtituted one of the Juſtices of the Common Pleas[g].

It was cuſtomary in this age for biſhops to
viſit ſuch colleges as were under their juriſdiction, as they do their dioceſes, from time
to time, when they deemed it proper or
convenient, although no ſpecial matter de-

[c] Journals of Lords, i p 11 15
[d] See p 223
[e] Dugd Chron Ser 11 H vii 1496
[f] Pat 22 H vii 9 Jul 1507 ib
[g] Ibid 5 H viii 1514 26 Apr

manded

manded their prefence. It has already been obferved[h], that Smyth vifited fome parts of his diocefe in 1510, and he gave notice on that occafion, that he intended to vifit Oriel college; and the fellows were accordingly fummoned to wait upon him on the day appointed, October the 8th[i], when if any particular bufinefs was to be tranfacted, beyond the common dictates of his regard for learning and for this fociety, it was fome inquiry or fome direction in confequence of an affair, which appears to have been pretty well determined and fettled before.

John Lewis, fellow of Oriel, was one of the moft incorrigible fons of riot, that perhaps ever difturbed the peace of any feminary of learning He had leave given him, April 2, 1508, to proceed to the degree of Mafter of Arts on certain conditions[k]; which he did not fulfil, but on the contrary he oppofed the Provoft in his office, and endeavoured to fubvert the good order and difcipline both of the college and of the uni-

---

[h] See above, p 131

[i] The Bifhop's mandate, dated Lidington, 24 Sept 1510 The certificate from the Provoft and Fellows, 28 Sept 1510 Coll Oriel, Reg Decan p 44

[k] 2 Apr 1508 Coll Oriel, Reg Decan p 81

verfity.

verfity. He was frequently cited and repre-
hended before the Provoft and Fellows; and
the Provoft was more than once empowered,
agreeably to the ftatutes, to pronounce his
expulfion. At laft, after two years of ineffectual endeavours to reclaim him, he was,
with the concurrence of the Vifitor, publicly
and abfolutely amoved[l]. Still however he
hovered about the univerfity, and ftill attempted to create difturbance in his late college; till, upon the formal requeft of the
fociety, he was inhibited by the Vice Chancellor from entering within the walls[m].

He now applied to the King and privy
Council, complaining that he had been griev-
oufly injured by the Provoft and Fellows of
Oriel. His Majefty, by his royal letters, directed to the bifhop of Lincoln, "Vifitor and
ordinary of the fame" College, "referred the
determination of the matter to his difcretion.
By whom," he fays, "upon his fpecial inqui-
fition for the fame in his Vifitation, we be
made certified, that the faid J. Lewis, for
great difobedience, and violation of the good

l 11 Jun 1510 Ibid p 91, 92
m The requeft is, 16 March (1511) A. f 150. The inhi-
bition in confequence, 5 April, 1511. ib. f 137. b.

ftatutes

ſtatutes by our noble progenitors eſtabliſhed, is condignly expulſed, and ſo is by the ſaid reverend Father declared." Whereupon his Majeſty commands the Vice Chancellor, to whom the letter is addreſſed, to ſee "ſtrayte correctyon miniſtered upon Lewis and his adherents[n]." After this we hear of charges of perjury and defamation brought againſt him[o], and he ſeems, in February 1512-13, to have eſcaped out of priſon[p]; but of his future fate or fortune nothing is known.

The viſitation here mentioned was, no

[n] "Yeuen vndre owr ſygnett at owr manour of Grenwych, the thyrd day of May," (1511) ¶ f 150 In the text I have reformed the orthography according to the preſent ſtandard, but not altered his Majeſty's words This and the other letter on the ſame page of the regiſter are not entered chronologically, for the dates before and after are "Sept 1511," and "1511" at the head of the page ſeems to be a different hand, but I take it to be the true date.

[o] Dec 10 et circ 1512 Ibid f 181 Perhaps a lampoon, "carmen famoſum," on the Provoſt, Dr Wylford, affixed to St Mary's, 26 July, 1514, (Ibid f 226 b) was written by Lewis, for he was poſſeſſed of ſome wicked wit See Reg. Oriel, as above, p 91.——I muſt not conclude this laſt note reſpecting Oriel college without expreſſing my thanks to the worthy Provoſt, Dr Eveleigh, and to the Gentlemen of the ſociety for facilitating and aſſiſting my reſearches in the records of their houſe

[p] ¶ f 187.

doubt,

doubt, that which, as we faid, was holden in
October, 1510; when, as it feems, the Vifitor re-examined and confirmed in perfon
the fentence of expulfion, which had been
previoufly pronounced with his approbation.
It is memorable, that the College, of which
the Bifhop of Lincoln is here recognifed as
Vifitor by a Prince fufficiently jealous of
his prerogatives, has fince claimed and obtained exemption from this epifcopal jurifdiction, and is now fubject to royal vifitation
alone.

One thing only remains to be noted with
regard to Smyth and Oriel college, that, in
grateful refpect to the memory of their Benefactor, his arms are exhibited on a handfome efcutcheon of ftone, over the paffage
which leads to the inner court.

SECT.

SECT. IX.

Foundation and Endowment of Brasen Nose College.

———

IN the impoverished state of the University of Oxford, at the close of the fifteenth century, in the penury of science and the brutality of manners which reigned there, we have seen how much the aid of wise and seasonable munificence was wanted to cherish and encourage those studies and attainments, which constitute the scholar and adorn the man We have also beheld, in the tenor of Smyth's life, his uniform attention to these great objects by endeavouring to promote the inseparable interests of religion and learning. But all this while he had in contemplation a greater work in the same important cause; to which, as in his life, so in our narrative, all the other parts are subordinate and

intro-

introductory. This was the founding of Brafen Nofe College; an undertaking, by which he raifed a noble monument to his own honour, and conferred a lafting emolument on his country.

We have no account at what time the Bifhop, with whom I conceive the defign to have originated, firft communicated his thoughts on the fubject to Sir Richard Sutton, and concerted with him the plan and method of confummating the work. All that is certain on this head has been already noted[a], that it was known in Oxford as their joint defign, as early as January, 1507-8; when the fite alfo of the building appears to have been chofen. The enfuing autumn, October 20, 1508, Mr. Sutton obtained of Univerfity college a leafe of Brafen Nofe Hall and little Univerfity Hall, with their gardens and appurtenances, for the term of ninety two years, at the annual rent of three pounds. It was ftipulated in the covenant, on behalf of the college, that Sutton fhould difcharge them of the annual payment of one fhilling, iffuing out of Brafen Nofe Hall

[a] See above, p 242.

to

to the church-wardens of St. Mary's parifh; and that there fhould be expended, in new building or repairing the faid tenement, the fum of forty pounds, within the fpace of a year. The college, on their part, engaged not only to renew the leafe at the expiration of the term, but likewife to releafe to Sutton all their right in the premifes for ever, as foon as he fhould convey to them lands of the clear yearly value of three pounds.

The grant, thus circumftanced, was made to " Richard Sutton, efquire, John Port, Rauf Legh, John Sutton thelder, John Sutton the yonger, Gentlemen; and to Mr. John Hafter, John Forneby, Roland Meffynger, and John Legh, clerks[b]." Sutton afterwards, June 1, 3 Henry viii, 1511, by a deed enrolled in Chancery, affigned the leafe to truftees for the performance of his will[c], and at laft, May 6, 15 Henry viii, 1523, conveyed the premifes, for the remainder of the term, to the Principal and Fellows of Brafen Nofe[d]. No eligible eftate was procured, to exchange for thefe premifes, till the

[b] Yate, p 83   [c] Ibid p 84   [d] Ibid.

termi-

termination of the firft leafe; when land, near Oxford, was bequeathed for that purpofe by Mr. William Leech; who appears to have been Fellow of the college : but his generofity, I prefume, was greater than his affluence, for I find a decree of the fociety, June, 1602, to pay to his widow, on account of this bequeft, the fum of one hundred marks[c]; which was probably the full value of land, intended as an equivalent for a rent charge, which did not exceed three pounds a year.

The premifes, thus conveyed, are defcribed as abutting upon School ftreet on the eaft, upon a hall and garden called Salifbury on the fouth, and to the north upon ftreets that go from School ftreet towards Lincoln college. This therefore was precifely the fite of the prefent college.

The following fummer Edward Mofeley granted a leafe of his ftone quarry in Headington fields, to bifhop Smyth, Richard Sutton, efquire, and Mr. Roland Meffenger, clerk, for their joint lives; and they were

[c] Yate, p. 84.

admitted

admitted tenants, by a copy of the court roll, fometime before the feaft of St. John Baptift, 1 Henry viii, 1509[f]. Whether the quarry was furnifhed with ftone already dug, and feafoned for ufe, we are not informed; nor have I been able to fatisfy myfelf as to the real date of the foundation of the college. There is an infcription in the fouth weft corner of the quadrangle, which I ufed to regard as recording, in its circumftantial date, the day and the year, when the venerable Founders in perfon laid the firft ftone of the future edifice; but upon confulting many intelligent perfons, it appears, by their different conftruction of the matter, that the true intent of it is extremely doubtful. The infcription itfelf I exhibit for the firft time accurately, leaving it to the reader to determine, whether in this, which we may fafely pronounce the firft fummer of building, the walls might have been raifed feven feet from the ground on the firft of June, fo that the date belongs to the individual ftone that bears it, or whether it is a duplicate of the foundation ftone:

[f] Yate, p. 111 Plot fays, I know not on what authority, that Brafen Nofe, as well as fome other colleges, which he names, was built with ftone dug near Wheatley, on the Worcefter road Oxfordfh ch iv § 27 p 77

𝔄° 𝔛𝔭𝔦ˢ 1509 𝔢𝔱 𝔚𝔢𝔤' 𝔥' 8' 𝔭𝔯𝔦𝔪𝔬

𝔑𝔬𝔦𝔢 𝔡𝔦𝔲𝔦𝔫𝔬 𝔩𝔦𝔫𝔠𝔬𝔩𝔫̄
𝔭ˈ𝔰𝔲𝔩 𝔮°: 𝔰𝔲𝔱𝔱̄𝔬. 𝔥̄𝔞𝔠 𝔭𝔬𝔰𝔲
𝔢𝔯' 𝔭𝔢𝔱𝔯𝔞̄ 𝔯𝔢𝔤' 𝔞𝔡 𝔦𝔭𝔦𝔲̄

𝔭𝔯𝔦𝔪𝔬 𝔡𝔦𝔢 𝔍𝔲𝔫𝔦𝔦   i e.

Anno Chriſti 1509 èt Regis Henrici viii primo
Nomine divino Lincoln præſul quoque Sutton
Hanc poſuere petram [h] regis ad imperium
primo die Junii

Such is the inſcription, of which one
thing is certain, that there is a ſignificance
and propriety in it, which may eſcape thoſe,
who are not appriſed, that it is over the door
which led to the original chapel of the college; whence alſo the ſtaircaſes begin to be

---

[g] This abbreviation, from the Greek, was ſo common, that
Berchanus in his moral or theological Dictionary (Nuremb
1476. Colon. 1477 &c) has the word Chriſtus under X, and
not, as might be expected, under C See alſo Gent Mag 1796
p 719. 746

[h] The cuſtomary expreſſion on theſe occaſions. On the firſt
ſtone of H. viith's chapel " Illuſtriſſimus Henricus vii—poſuit
hanc petram—xxiii die Jan A D mccccii et anno dicti
regis H vii decimo octavo" Stowe's Ann. p 484 Dart's
Weſtm Abbey, i. p 32. On the firſt ſtone of Chriſt Church,
Oxford, " Rev.—Thomas Wulcy—hanc petram poſuit—20 die
Mart A. D. 1525 " Prefixed to Wolſey's Statutes penes Rev
Decan. et Capit dicti Coll and in Wood's Colleges, p 421
note 40. both ex Reg Car. Boothe Heref Epiſc

num

numbered; tacitly fuggefting, what the door
of another academic chapel explicitly recom-
mends, " Primo quærite regnum Dei[1]."

The next grant was obtained from Oriel
college. That fociety, in confideration of an
annual rent of thirteen fhillings and four
pence, releafed to them by the convent of
St. Fridefwide at the inftance of the bifhop
of Lincoln, made a conveyance, February 20,
1509-10, to Mr. Sutton and others, parties
with him in the former purchafe, of their
meffuages called Salifbury and St. Mary Entry, with the gardens and appurtenances, for
ever[k]. No part, I apprehend, of the prefent
college, unlefs perhaps the kitchen, ftands
upon thefe premifes. Smyth's epitaph appears to be hiftorically accurate, in faying,
" he renewed," or rebuilt, " Brafen Nofe
Hall[l]," except that the new edifice probably

[1] Over the chapel of Exeter college

[k] " Salefury and " Seynt Marye Entre " Oriel, Dean's
Reg p 46 Yate, p 85, 86 —St Mary Entry was probably,
like Friar's Entry, an open paffage with a tenement over it
It was between Salifbury and little Edmund hall, and paid
20 fhillings a year to the church-wardens of St Mary's MS
Wood, 8514 52 p 264 And fee his Annals, vol 1 p 521
11 p 761

[l] " Aulaque fumptu hujus renovata eft Enea '

T 2   included

included the whole extent of that meffuage
and gardens, together with little Univerfity
Hall Salifbury Hall was taken down, and
the ground converted into a garden, which
is occupied by the prefent library and inner
court. To thefe two original purchafes five
other Halls, which ftood near, were afterwards added : little Edmund Hall, Haberdafher's Hall, Black Hall, Staple Hall, and
Glafs Hall. Of each of them, while the college is building, fome notice may be acceptable.

Brafen Nofe Hall, Salifbury, little St. Edmund, and Haberdafher's Hall, extended
from Lincoln college lane to the high ftreet
The three firft abutted to the eaft, as the
college does, on what was then called School
ftreet; which led by the weft end of St.
Mary's church to the prefent fchools. Haberdafher's Hall was fituate a little weftward,
facing the high ftreet. The prefent lodgings
of the Principal were, about the year 1770,
erected on the fpot. The other three Halls
ran parallel to thefe, on the eaft fide of
School ftreet, in what is now the area of the
Radclivian Library.

Brafen Nofe Hall, as the Oxford antiquary
has

has fhewn[m], may be traced as far back as the time of Henry iii, about the middle of the thirteenth century; and early in the fucceeding reign, 6 Edward the firft, 1278, it was known by the name of Brafen Nofe Hall; which peculiar name was indubitably owing, as the fame author obferves, to the circumftance of a nofe of brafs affixed to the gate[n]. It is prefumed however, this confpicuous appendage of the portal was not formed of the mixt metal, which the word now denotes, but the genuine produce of the mine: as is the nofe, or rather face, of a lion or leopard, ftill remaining at Stamford, which alfo gave name to the edifice it adorned[o]. And

[m] Wood, Annals, vol ii p 734 755

[n] " So called without doubt from fuch a fign which was in ancient time over its door, as other Halls alfo had, viz Hawk or Hieron Hall, Elephant, Swan, and Bull Hall." Annals, ii. p 6. ad ann 1514 Polydore Vergil, who was collated by Smyth to the Preb of Scamlefby, 13 Apr 1507 (MS Harl. 6953 p 22) fays, " Per id quoque tempus Gulielmus Smyth epifc Linc Margaritæ exemplo ductus, Oxonii eorum adolefcentium qui bonis difciplinis dediti fe in literis exercerent, collegium collocavit in aula, quam vulgo vocant Brafyn Nofe, hoc eft, æneum nafum, quod eo loci imago ærea facie admodum immani pro foribus extet " p 618.

[o] An elegant drawing of this brafen nofe at Stamford, the gift of that refpectable nobleman, Thomas late Lord Dacre, is preferved in the lodgings of the Principal of Brafen Nofe

hence,

hence, when Henry vııı debafed the coin, by an alloy of *copper*, it was a common remark or proverb, that " Teftons were gone to Oxford, to ftudy ın *Brafen* Nofe[p]."

Little Univerfity Hall, annexed to Brafen Nofe on the north, was of a much more ancient date, ıf, as fome have faid, it was the fecond of the three Halls founded by Alfred[q]. It is however uncertaın, whether ıt was ın honour of thıs ılluftrıous Prınce, the reftorer of Oxford and of learnıng, or whether ıt was out of complıment to the reıgnıng Sovereıgn, that the buıldıng here erected by Smyth was called, ın ıts chartered tıtle, " THE KING's HALL AND COLLEGE OF BRASEN NOSE[r]."

[p] Ray's Prov p 259. It has thıs meanıng ın our tranflatıon of the Bıble fee Deut vııı 9 Teftons or Tefters, fo called from a *Head* that was upon them, Bp Fleetwood fays, were coıned 34 H vııı —they were *brafs*, covered wıth fılver, and went for 12 D but 1 Edw vı were brought down to 9 D and then to 6 D wıich ftıll retaıns the name Chron Precıof p 41

[q] Wood s Annals, 1 p 34 36 11 p 756 &c It was at the N E corner of the prefent college

[r] The Latın tıtle, " Aula Regıa et Collegıum de Brafennofe, (fee the Coll Statutes, xxxıı p 93 and the ınfcrıptıon under the buft of Alfred, Wood's Colleges, p 371) favours the notıon of allu/ıon to Alfred But the other fuppofıtıon ıs countenanced by a receıpt of " Rowland Meffingere Burfar of the *Kıng s Coll ge* of Brafennofe," 15 Jan 4 H vııı Yate, p 65

and

A buft of Alfred, which is deemed one of the beft reprefentations of that great monarch, and another fuppofed of John Erigena, the firft reader in this hall, which are faid to have been found in digging the foundation of the college, are to be feen over the hall door; and have been more than once engraved[s].

Salifbury Hall, adjoining Brafen Nofe on the fouth, in the reign of Edward iv appears to have been dedicated to grammar and poetry; but the readers at that time feem to have been better known, one by his vene-

and by an endorfement of feifin " pro *Collegio Regali* de Brafen Nofe," 20 Jul 5 H viii ib 15. All that can be faid is, that in thefe days they were not accurate or uniform in denominating collegiate bodies, any more than they were attentive to the orthography of men's names The legend on the college feal is,

𝕾igillu. coie. colegii regalis de. brafin. nofe. in. oxonia.

It confifts of three Gothic niches or compartments, with a figure in each That in the centre was, I fear, intended to reprefent the Trinity, feated The perfonages on either fide, ftanding, each of them adorned with a mitre and a crofier, are probably St Hugh and St Chad, the fainted bifhops of Lincoln and Lichfield, to whom the college is dedicated. But if Mr. Anftis's rule (in Fiddes's Wolfey, Coll. Num 58 p 113) might certainly be depended on, thefe figures fhould not be bifhops, but abbats , for they carry their crofiers in their right hands Underneath is a fmall fhield with Smyth's arms

[s] See Spelman's L of Alfred, and Wife s Annal Ælfredi

rable

rable perſon, the other by his art or pro-
feſſion, than by their proper names. For the
grammarian, who was of Braſen Noſe, but
taught in Saliſbury ſchool, is ſtyled, " The
Maſter of grammar with the bald head';"
the other is ſtyled ſimply, "The Poet reading in Saliſbury ᵘ."

Haberdaſher's Hall, little Edmund Hall,
Glaſs Hall, and Black Hall, were granted to
the college, May 12, 1536, by the convent
of Oſeney, upon a renewable leaſe of ninety
ſix years. The firſt immediately became the
property of the college, by a releaſe to the
convent of lands lying near Oſeney ˣ; but the
other three were not veſted in the college in
fee till March 6, 1655, upon a ſimilar exchange and releaſe with Chriſt Churchʸ; to
which ſociety great part of the property of
Oſeney was given at the diſſolution ·

Glaſs Hall, ſeparated from St. Mary's
church yard by a narrow ſtreet leading into
Cat ſtreet, ſtood oppoſite to the original
lodgings of the Principal of Braſen Noſe Col-

ᵗ MS Wood, 8514 52 p 256. 258. 259 261.
ᵘ Ibid p 268.
ˣ Yate, 85
ʸ Ibid 89

lege ;

lege[z], and was converted into ſtables for his
uſe, which were removed in the preſent century to prepare the ſite for the Radclivian
Library.

Black Hall, as Wood ſays[a], was a ſpot
from the remoteſt days ſacred to the Muſes.
It was kept in repair and tenanted by members of Braſen Noſe, till it was demoliſhed
to make way for the Library juſt mentioned,
the north ſide of which occupies this ancient
ſite.

Staple Hall, between the two laſt mentioned, had belonged to the abbey of Eynſham as early as the reign of Edward the
firſt; and came into the hands of Lincoln
college, Wood ſays[b], at the general diſſolution. But this appears to be a miſtake;
for before that time they granted a leaſe of
it, May 26, 1527, for the term of one
hundred years, to Richard Lyſter, the King's

[z] See Wood's Annals, ii p 750 753 761 The ancient
lodgings of the Principal were adjoining the gateway on the
ſouth, whence, by doors in the party walls, he ſeems to have
had acceſs both to the common hall, and to every room in the
college In Lincoln college the Rector ſtill has a door from
his own apartments into the hall.

[a] Ibid p 733, 734   [b] Annals, ii. p 741, 742.

Attorney

Attorney general[c], afterwards lord chief Baron
of the Exchequer. Whether this was meant
for the convenience of Brafen Nofe, I do not
know, but if not, the chief Baron, I prefume, furrendered his leafe for their accommodation; as the Rector and Fellows of
Lincoln demifed the premifes to Brafen Nofe
for ever, November 2, 1556, at the annual
rent of twenty fhillings[d]. It feems to have
been taken down foon after it was leafed to
the Attorney general, for the two laft named
halls are defcribed, in 1530, as abutting on a
garden, where Staple Hall lately ftood[e]. It
was afterwards rebuilt, and appears to have
furnifhed commodious apartments for the
ftudents of Brafen Nofe, as an upper chamber here was let in 1596 for twenty, and a
lower for ten, fhillings[f], which were material
fums in thofe days.

There ftill remains a fmall fpace of ground,
which we have not covered in this peram-
bulation of the fite of the college. This was
a garden, which lay between little Edmund
Hall and Haberdafher's Hall, the eaftern wall
of it being oppofite to St. Mary's church

---

[c] Yate, p 90
[e] Ibid p 86

[d] Yate, ibid
[f] Ibid p 397

yard[g]. The prefent chapel, built in part
with the materials of the ancient chapel of
St. Mary college[h], where Erafmus ftudied,
feems to occupy the identical fpot[i] Lady
Catharine Field, abbefs, and the convent of
Godftow, granted it, December 22, 1481, to
John Caryfwall, in exchange for lands in
Garfington; and Antony Caryfwall, clerk,
fon and heir of the former, fold it to John
Port, efquire, July 4, 1516, for the fum of
eight pounds. Antony Fitzherbert, ferjeant
at law, and Thomas Port, Matthew Smyth,
and William Aleyn, clerks, were parties with
Port in the purchafe[k] As it is called in
1530 " a garden of Sir John Port, knight,

[g] Yate, p 90 86

[h] See a letter to lord Huntingdon on the fubject in MS
Carte, F F F p 112 in Bodl Libr by Gowin Knight, dat.
Merton Coll 1672 The new chapel was confecrated by
Blandford Bp of Oxford Nov 17, 1666, when Ralph Rawfon B D fellow of the college, a very learned and orthodox
divine, who had been ejected by the rebels in 1648, preached
on the very appofite text, " In all places where I record my
name, I will come unto thee, and I will blefs thee " Exod xx.
24 Yate, p 290 Of Rawfon, who was a native of Chefhire,
fee more in Walker's Suffer of Cler P ii p 101 Wood's
Ann ii p 596

[i] Wood however fays it is built where little Edmund Hall
ftood Colleges, p 373 The chapel and cloifters probably
occupy the fite both of the hall and garden in queftion

[k] Yate, p 91

Juftice

Juftice of the King's Bench[1]," he probably
purchafed it, not as agent for his friend Sir
Richard Sutton, but in his own right, and
made a prefent of it to the college.

It appears by this account, that the fpo
which our venerable Founders chofe for their
college, has been from the remoteft days of
the Univerfity, in an eminent fenfe, claffical
ground ; the very eye and centre of this our
Athens ! where fcience was cultivated, and
arts improved , where academic laurels, held
forth to view in the neighbouring fenate, in-
cited diligence and rewarded merit ; and religion, in her adjoining temple, regulated the
manners, and infpired the foul. Here Bacon
ftudied , and here—but I check the pleafing
vifion. The ground is ftill the fame ; and
may thofe who tread on it gather treafures
of ftill fuperior learning, guided as they are
by a purer faith !

There is another remark refpecting the
fite, which muft not be omitted Having,
as we have feen, been often and varioufly
built upon, it is elevated confiderably above
its ancient level. You defcended a ftep into

_____

[1] Yate, p 86.

the

the area of Black Hall[m], which we may fuppofe was not originally below the adjacent
ftreet. Deep fchool, commonly called Hell
fchool, a little north of the former, on the
fame fide of the ftreet, acquired its name
from the pecuharity of its fite, being deep in
the ground. Wood fuppofes, " the ftreet
reached up to the lower windows[n] " When
the college had occafion, in 1790, to fink
and repair an ancient drain, near the fouth
wall of the chapel, to the depth of fixteen
or feventeen feet, it was found upon examination, that the foundation of the chapel
was fix or feven feet deeper ftill; and it is
not likely, that the architect would think it
neceffary to dig many feet in the natural un-
difturbed gravel. This accumulation of earth,
from a variety of concurring caufes, may be
found, I believe, in a greater or lefs degree,
in all towns, which have been inhabited from
remote antiquity. In Bath, in Lincoln, and
in Chefter, remains of Roman temples, or

[m] This and fome other particulars, refpecting thefe ancient
Halls, were communicated to me, in 1791, by Mr James
Fletcher, the late very intelligent Bookfeller in the Turl, who
remembered the premifes well before Radcliffe's Library was
built Mr Fletcher died June 12, 1795, aged 88 See Gent
Mag 1798 p 533
[n] Annals, ii. p 744.

other

other edifices, have at different times been
difcovered under the prefent cities.   In London the workmen often meet with walls and
pillars, in their original pofition, beneath the
modern houfes; and when Sir Chriftopher
Wren built St Paul's, digging for a firm
foundation for the noble fuperftructure which
he had planned, he found, at different depths,
regular rows of graves, Saxon, Britifh, and
Roman, and below thefe a folid bed of pot-
ter's earth; which, as it had fupported the
former weighty fabric, he concluded might
reafonably be trufted again.   But having the
curiofity to fearch further ftill, after finking
about 40 feet, he came to fhells and fea
fand, and he fuppofed all above this to have
been raifed in a feries of ages, from a time
long before this ifland was known in hiftory,
but fubfequent to the flood[o].   The ground,
whereon Brafen Nofe ftands, has not perhaps
been raifed fo much as twenty feet; but
has partly accumulated, and partly been difturbed, to that depth, by former ftructures
in various ages.

The building of the college advanced,
though the exact mode and progrefs of the

---

[o] Wrens Parentalia, p 265, 266 285

work

work cannot be afcertained; further than
that it appears to have been conducted with
little or no interruption of the bufinefs of
education. This may be collected from feveral concurring circumstances.

Mr. John Fornby, fucceffor to Crofton already mentioned[p], cautioned for Brafen ?
Hall at the ufual time, September 9, 1509
which was for a twelvemonth to come and
fince he occurs as principal, June 27, 1510[r],
I fuppofe he was alfo principal in the intermediate year, when the foundation of the
college was laid. On the twenty fourth of
Auguft, 1510, he refigned, and Matthew
Smyth was admitted principal in the common form[s]. Next year Mr. Meffenger cautioned for the hall, in Mr. Smyth's name[t];

[p] P 242

[q] f 65 b. The day of cautioning was Craft B Mar.
Virg (i e 9 Sept) D f 49 Lib C Proc Boreal f 48 b.
The common form of " cautioning," i e giving fecurity to the
Univerfity for the payment of the dues accruing from the
members of a hall, was to depofit a book as a pledge Vide
ibid f 49 b 112

[r] f 112 b He gave a promiffory note, 25 Aug 1510,
to pay Thomas Shelton, brewer, 45S 4D ibid f 118 John
Rogers being " fuerty" for him of whom fee above, p. 244

[s] Ibid f 118   [t] f 149

and

and Smyth cautioned for it in his own name, on the ufual day, in 1512[u]. As yet therefore the hall exifted in fome fhape; there was fome edifice, old or new, the government of which was received at the hands of the Chancellor, or his deputy; not a corporate foundation, eftablifhed by royal charter, and difpofed of at the pleafure of the Founders. As the building of the college commenced in the fouth weft corner, and Brafen Nofe Hall ftood where the prefent tower is, it is not improbable, that the old building was fuffered to remain for the accommodation of ftudents, till new apartments were ready for their reception.

And it is certain, that there were ftudents at this time belonging to Brafen Nofe Hall; though the evidence of the fact happens to be no proof of their good behaviour. Fox, bifhop of Winchefter, had begun to build Corpus Chrifti college, and, whether it were owing to any invidious comparifons between the two rifing fabrics, or to what has often already been noted, the ferocious manners of the times; fo it was, that there was more than one affray, between certain members of

[u] Ibid f 169 b.

Brafen

Brafen Nofe hall and the workmen employed about the other college. An undergraduate of the hall, named Haftings, was
committed to prifon, at the fuit of a fervant
of the bifhop of Winchefter, in Auguft,
1512[x], and Fornby himfelf, the late principal, was bound in a recognifance, fome
time after, to keep the peace towards William Vertu and William Eft, freemafons,
and Humfry Coke, carpenter, mafters of the
works of the bifhop of Winchefter's new college near Merton[y].

All were not, I hope, infractors of the
peace. There was a laudable cuftom about
this period, which with fome modification
ftill fubfifts, of appointing fome of the fenior
and diftinguifhed members of the Univerfity
to preach on the great feftivals, and during
Lent   Mr. Smyth, bachelor of divinity, of
Brafen Nofe hall, was called out in this honourable way in Lent, 1508; and again, by
the very fame defcription, the firft Sunday in
Lent, 1512[z]. This however was not the
principal, Matthew Smyth, for he was at

---

[x] H f. 165   [y] H f. 232 Aug 1514.

[z] H f. 264. 264. b

U   this

this time only master of arts[a], and was not
ordained subdeacon till December 18, 1512[b].
The person intended I take to have been
Gerard Smyth, a Francifcan friar, who was
admitted to the degree of B D February 6,
1507-8[c], and occurs occafionally in thefe
times. But, whoever he was, his appointment to preach before the Univerfity furnifhes another proof, that the members of
Brafen Nofe were in refidence, and that it
was ftill fpoken of as a hall in 1512.

Manciples, the purveyors general of colleges and halls, were formerly men of fo
much confequence, that, to check their ambition, it was ordered by an exprefs ftatute,
That no manciple fhould be principal of a
hall[d]. Chaucer, in delineating the manners
of the times, defcribes his manciple of the
Temple as not only in his occupation a pattern to all caterers, but " paffing the wifdom
of a heap of learned men," and able to " fet

---

[a] 24 Feb (1513–14) M Matheus Smyth mag in artibus
fupplicat &c G f 217

[b] MS Harl 6953 p 64

[c] G f 51 b with f 39   He was the Afhwednefday
preacher in 1510–11 d f 264 b

[d] Lib C Procuratoris Boreal f 48 b the gift of Ric
Flemmyng Proc Bor A D 1407 f 9 b

the cap" of the whole legal fraternity[c].
However, if wife or witty, they were not
always a wealthy people ; as was the cafe of
the manciple of Brafen Nofe hall. Stephen
Standifh had feveral actions brought againft
him for debt, in the Vice Chancellor's court;
one of which was, June 10, 1513, for beer,
delivered, to his order, at Cowley[f]. But at
laft, September, 1514, "Mr Matthew Smyth,
Principal of the College or Hall of Brafen
Nofe," and Mr John Fornby, appearing in
his favour, matters were compromifed and
profecution ceafed[g] Either therefore the
members of Brafen Nofe withdrew to Cowley, about the beginning of 1513, becaufe
the hall was now taking down, or they retired from the Univerfity a while, as many
others did this year, on account of the
plague[h] However that matter might be,
this is the firft time that we meet with "the
College of Brafen Nofe" in thefe regifters,
and from the manner of introducing it, it
feems not yet to be the familiar defignation
of the new building.

[c] Canterb Tales, Prol 569
[f] ¶ f 194 See more about him, f 202. b 233 b f 241
241 b f 250 f 256 258
[g] Ibid f 236
[h] Woods Annals, ad ann 15.3 vol ii p 6

The

The Charter of foundation, granted to William Bishop of Lincoln and Richard Sutton Esquire, under the King's own hand, with authority of parliament, is dated January 15, 3 Henry viii', (1511-12.) But it would require time to prepare matters, under the powers of this patent, for the solemn investiture of the Principal and Fellows with their respective offices; and to give them possession of the new College, and delegate the whole to their care Accordingly we have seen, that on the ninth of September this year, Matthew Smyth cautioned for the Hall, in the common form[k] The earliest of the annual rolls of the college accounts, now

The original Charter, beautifully written and in perfect preservation, is in the college Archives, under the broad seal in green wax, attached by a cord of green and white silk The impression—Henry viii sitting in state, in his right hand the sceptre, in his left a globe surmounted with the cross Reverse—the king on horseback, in armour, on his left arm a shield, charged with the arms of England and France quarterly His right hand extended holds a drawn sword The legend, ' Henricus dei gracia Rex anglie francie dominus hibernie ' There is a copy of the charter in the Rolls Chapel, in Rymer, vol xi i p 320—322, and in Yate, p 1 Henrys broad seal, somewhat different, after he had assumed the titles of " Defender of the faith, and Head of the church," may be seen in Sandfords Genealog Hist p 427

[k] P 283

extant,

extant, is for the year commencing at Michaelmas, 7 Henry viii, (1515,) and ending at Michaelmas, 8 Henry viii, (1516,) when John Legh and Hugh Charnock were burfars. But various items, under this and fubfequent years, concur to prove, that the College, in its proper corporate capacity, tranfacted bufinefs in 5 Henry viii; and that for an entire year, terminating at Michaelmas; John Fornby and Roland Meffenger being burfars Thus then we travel back as far as September 29, 4 Henry viii, 1512 Before this date Edmund Bury, bifhop Smyth's agent, receives the rents of the eftates, purchafed for the endowment of the college. On the ninth of this month Matthew Smyth renewed his right to the Hall, and January 15, 4 Henry viii, (1512-13) Roland Meffenger figns an acquittance, as " Burfar of the King's College of Brafen Nofe[1] " So far all is clear and confiftent.

It is not certain however, that the fociety received their charter, and became a college, on the feaft of St. Michael. The rolls of accounts, of which the receipt of rents conftitutes a principal part, run from Mi-

---

[1] Yate, p 65

chaelmas

chaelmas to Michaelmas, agreeably to the
cuftom of fuch payments; though the annual audit, in conformity with the ftatutes,
was then, as it is now, holden in December.
Now as the payment of rents, in thefe times,
appears to have been chiefly annual, not
half-yearly, whenever feifin of lands was
given to the college, it would naturally intitle them to the rent of the current year;
fo that if they were thus poffeffed of property prior to Michaelmas, 5 Henry viii,
the account for that year would regularly
commence from the preceding Michaelmas,
4 Henry viii, 1512. The eftates of the diffolved Priory of Cold Norton were tranf-
ferred to the Principal and Scholars of the
King's Hall and College of Brafen Nofe by
an inftrument under bifhop Smyth's own
hand[m] and feal, dated May 8, 5 Henry viii,
(1513;) and on the fame day the college,
under their common feal, conftituted John
Fornby and Roland Meffenger their proxies
to receive feifin in their name, which Richard Wade, with proper powers from the bifhop, accordingly delivered to them on the
twentieth of July following[n].

[m] See a fac-fimile of it in the mifcellaneous plate.
[n] Yate, p 13—15

We

We muſt recur therefore, for the delivery
of the charter, to that portion of 4 Henry viii,
which is between Michaelmas and the fifteenth of January, on which day Meſſenger,
as already ſaid, appears in the capacity of
burſar, and within this period I know but
of two probable days for the purpoſe. One
of theſe is the feaſt of St. Hugh, November 17, by which the internal year of
the ſociety is regulated; on which day perhaps, in 1512, the College firſt roſe a permanent Corporation: though, on the whole,
I am inclined to fix the date a little earlier.
The feaſt of the Dedication of the Chapel°
appears to have been between St Giles's day,
September 1, and the feſtival of St. Luke,
October 18; and it is perfectly in the ſpirit
of the good Biſhop's character to ſuppoſe it
was his wiſh, that the manſion of divine
worſhip and the ſeminary of learning ſhould
have the ſame date and origin, and when

° See an entry in the Plate Book, p 5 under the year 1520,
" in feſto Dedicationis Capelle " By the Statutes (c xvii) it
is one of the leſſer feaſts, but having been long diſcontinued,
probably upon the erection of the preſent chapel, I have not
been ſo fortunate as to diſcover the exact day We may however aſſuredly correct A Wood, who ſays the original " Chapel" was " never conſecrated as I can yet find " Colleges,
p 373

he

he confecrated the one, he inftituted the other.

We have no proof, that the Bifhop was in Oxford more than three or four times, while the college was in building. He was entertained by Magdalen college in 1509[p], perhaps at the time when he laid the foundation of his college; and again the enfuing year, poffibly in October, when he vifited Oriel college, as already mentioned[q]. And he was alfo at Oxford April 24, 1511[r]. From the variety of tranfactions, in which Sir Richard Sutton was concerned, for expediting the bufinefs, it is highly probable, that he, a man of lefs occupation, viewed the rifing work more frequently, and was prefent, no doubt, when the venerable Prelate, in the name of both, conftituted the firft Principal, and gave him the royal Charter and the Statutes of the college, named the Fellows, and

[p] "Pro vino et ferculis dat Domino Lyncholn—iii S iiii D ' Comp Burff Coll Magd Lincoln is elfewhere fo written in this audit, and " Domino herffordenf' occurs, which no doubt means " my Lord of Hereford   In the fucceeding Computus (from Martinmafs 1 H viii to Martinmafs 2 H viii) " pro vino dat Epifc Lincoln—iii S iiii D "
[q] P 265
[r] Mr Fardell, ex Regift

ap-

appointed the Officers, with short but emphatic exhortation to care and fidelity; and not, certainly, without appropriate benediction and prayer, that, through His blessing, by whom alone human institutions live and flourish, the house which they had founded might ever remain the parent of literature and the nurse of religion!

The original Fellows were John Haster, John Fornby, Roland Messenger, and John Legh. These four, who were clergymen as early at least as 1508, appear in various transactions relative to the foundation of the college; and as their names are twice recited in the above order[s], I presume it was not by accident. I have placed Haster without positive proof among the Fellows, because it is highly probable, that he was the first Vice Principal. He was a benefactor to the library[t] The two next, as we have already

[s] In a grant from Oriel college, Dean's Reg p 46 Yate, p 85 and in a grant from University college, Yate, p 83 However in another grant the same year, 1508, Legh stands first Yate, p 97

[t] Some of his donations were an illumined copy of Burcharius's Dictionary (mentioned above, p 274 n g) 3 vol folio, fine dat Servius's Virgil, Ven 1487 A Latin Concordance by Joannes de Secubia, Baf 1496 and the works of the Subtle Doctor, Duns Scotus

seen

feen[u], were the firſt Burſars. Fornby was collated by the Founder to the rectory of Winwick in Northamptonſhire, September 10,
1510[x], and to the prebend of Thorngate in
the church of Lincoln, July 12, 1512[y].
Meſſenger, by favour of the ſame munificent
patron, ſucceeded Fornby in the living of
Winwick, December 20, 1512[z]; and was
collated to the prebend of St. Botolph's,
Lincoln, July 31, 1513[a]. John Legh was
rector of Gretford in Lincolnſhire, a living in
the gift of the Crown, in 1514[b], but whether
he obtained any preferment from Smyth I
have not diſcovered.

Beſides theſe four, the following perſons
alſo were nominated by the Founders, or
were on the foundation ſhortly afterwards :

5 Richard Shirwood, who proceeded M A.
July 3, 1514[c], and was junior burſar in 1518[d].

[u] P 293
[x] MS Harl 6953 p 34
[y] Ibid p 26   See and correct Willis, Cath ii 254.
[z] MS Harl 6953 p 34.
[a] Willis, Cath ii 150
[b] H f 232
[c] G f 237 b   He had the care of one of the Univerſity
Cheſts in 1515 ib f 272
[d] See Rott 7—10 Hen viii. William Shirwood, Rector of
Stanton

6. Richard Gunſton, B A. in 1511^e, M. A. 1515. He ſeems to have been fellow, perhaps burſar, 12 Henry viii^f, (1520.)

7. Simon Starkey, often employed in purchaſes by the college, and perhaps burſar, 13 Henry viii^g, (1521.)

8 Richard Ridge, who was junior burſar, 19 Henry viii, (1527;) but he often occurs before and after that time^h

9. Hugh Charnock was incorporated B A.

Stanton Harcourt, died about Mich 1497 MS Harl 6953 p 41 John Shirwood was incorporated M A and B D from Cambridge, 29 Oct. 1456, by George Nevyl, the Chancellor, afterwards Abp of York, ſon of Richard earl of Saliſbury, and brother to Richard the great Earl of Warwick Aa f 99 b Which J Shirwood was Archdeacon of Richmond in 1484. Rymer, xii p 220—223 252, 3 272. But what relations the ſaid W and J Shirwood were to Richard, I cannot tell.

^e G f. 124 142 b M A Apr 1515 ibid 248 251 inceptor, 2 Jul. 260 b He was auditor and guardian of ſome of the Univerſity Cheſts in 1515, 1516 ib 271 b 272 308.

^f Rot Burſſ

^g Rot Burſſ See Yate, p 74 94 &c There were Starkies of Olton, of Stretton, and of Wrenbury, in Cheſhire, but I ſee no Simon in the pedigrees Hugh Starkey of Olton, eſquire, (or knight, Suppl to Collins's Peer p 391) married Margaret d of Philip Egerton, eſq a great niece of Bp Smyth. See p 6 Simon Starkey was one of the executors of Sir John Port (ſon of Judge Port) 1560 and was living in 1572 Yate, p 165, 166 But whether this was Simon Starkey of Braſen Noſe is doubtful

^h See Yate, p 124 129 Rott 12 16 19—27 H viii.

from

from Cambridge, or fome other Univerfity, June 15, 1514[i]. He is mentioned in the roll, 16 Henry viii; having, apparently, been burfar before that time. Yate thinks he was burfar, 8 Henry viii, 1516[k] He was ftill fellow in 1535[l].

---

[i] G f 221 Inceptor in arts, 3 July that year ibid f 237 b. Cuftos criftæ Burnell, 1516 ibid f. 288 b Richard Charnock was ordained acolyte at Coventry, 20 Sept 1494 Reg Lichf f 180 fubdeacon, 13 June, 1495, upon a title from the priory of Byrkynhed, Chefh. and deacon, 19 Sept ibid f 185 And a perfon of both his names was Prior of Chrift Church, Midd about 1497 (Tanner, Not p xliii) and he or another Ric Charnock was head of St Mary college, when Erafmus ftudied there about this time   See Knight s L of Colet, p 32. and his L of Erafmus, p 20   All thefe Charnocks, I apprehend, were of Charnock, near Wigan, Lancafhire, where the family poffeffed a fair eftate till near the middle of the prefent century, when they became extinct James Charnock, elected Fellow of Brafen Nofe in 1559, infcribed an epitaph to his nephew Edw Chernock of Brafen Nofe, only fon and heir of Robert Chernock, efquire, of Chernock, Lanc who died Aug 5, 1581

" Quod patruo melius, currentibus ordine fatis,
       Trifte dares carmen, do tibi, chare nepos ' &c
See the whole on a brafs plate, with a portrait of a perfon in a gown, praying, a book on a defk before him, on a pillar near the north door in St. Mary s church, Oxford See other Charnocks, writers &c in Athen. Oxon ii 657 658 MS in Afhm Muf 7630

[k] Yate, p 415 See alfo Rott Burff 17 19—22 H viii
[l] Copy of Valuation 1535, in Firft Fruits Office, penes me.

10. Ralph Boſtock was admitted B. A. in January, 1513-14[m]. He was burſar 18 or 19 Henry viii, or both[n], and died 22 Henry viii, or before[o].

Other names occur of perſons who were fellows of the college within a few years of the time of the foundation; but it may be

[m] G f 215 b 217 b   [n] Rott
[o] His Executors are mentioned in Rot Burſl 22 H viii The Boſtocks were a large and reſpectable family (ſtyled in one of their pedigrees in the Brit Muſ " ampliſſima Boſtoko-rum familia') which flouriſhed many ages at Boſtock, at Churton, at Belgrene, and other parts of Cheſhire This Ralph Boſtock, fellow of Braſen Noſe, appears to have been the ſecond ſon of Robert Boſtock, who enfeoffed him, together with John Fornby, B D and others, 15 H viii, in certain eſtates and Saltworks at Middlewich, in Cheſhire, which occaſioned a ſuit at law, upon the deceaſe of the feoftee Ralph Boſtock, between the college and a nephew of both his names Yate, p 152 The college, in 1539, were poſſeſſed of eſtates in Middlewich of the annual value of 6l 9s in the tenure (or part of them) of John Boſtock and Ralph Boſtock of that town. Rot Burſſ 31 H viii But as this is the only memorial I nown of any property at Middlewich belonging to Braſen Noſe, perhaps the heir at law above mentioned, whoſe father's name was John, recovered it from the college My worthy friend the Rev Sir Charles Rich (created a Baronet June 21, 1791, having married Mary Frances daughter and heir of the late Sir Robert Rich, bart) is deſcended from the Boſtocks of Cheſhire by his father, the Rev John Boſtock, D D canon of Windſor, educated in Braſen Noſe college, for which he retained the moſt cordial affection to the day of his death, Feb. 18, 1786.

queſ-

queftioned whether the number actually appointed by the Founders exceeded four, or
fix at moft. Sir Richard Sutton, though
affociated with the bifhop of Lincoln in the
charter of foundation and previoufly known
by his intention of being joint-founder with
him, feems hitherto to have affifted only in
procuring the fite and in conducting the
building: but not yet to have contributed
any permanent benefaction for the fupport of
the houfe And, long after the deceafe of
both the founders, in the year 1535, when a
general valuation was returned to government of all ecclefiaftical property in the
kingdom, on which occafion the fociety feem
careful to fpecify all neceffary outgoings and
expences, it is very obfervable, that the
Principal and nine Fellows only are mentioned, without the leaft intimation that
they were bound to fuftain more[P] Twelve
were comprehended in the original plan,
but the houfe, as it feems, had not its full

[P] Copy of valuation, as above, " by virtue of a commiffion
under an act of Parl 26 H viii" meaning the act for paying
firft fruits and tenths to the King, 26 H viii c 3 and accordingly tne college paid, after the rate of the faid valuation,
a tenth part of their clear income, 1 l 2 s 1 d in 1536 See
Rot Burff 28 H vii. But I do not find any fuch payment in
fucceeding years

comple-

complement, till, in a feries of years, the eftates given or purchafed were fufficient for their maintenance ; for money in thofe days, in the cuftody of the fociety or in truft for them, was of little or no benefit till it was converted into land.

The eftates, with which Smyth endowed his college, were chiefly two ; Baffet's Fee, already mentioned[q], and the entire property of the fuppreffed Priory of Cold Norton.

This houfe of canons of the order of St. Auguftin was founded by William Fitz Alan, early in the reign of Henry ii, according to bifhop Tanner[r] A charter of Reginald, earl of Bolonia, and his countefs Ida, confirming former grants, is dated in 1201. It was dedicated to St. Mary, St John the Evangelift, and St Giles. The manors and eftates, given to it by various benefactors, were conveniently fituated in the adjacent parts of Oxfordfhire , excepting, what were not very diftant, certain meffuages at Thenford in Northamptonfhire, with a moiety of the rectory

[q] P 228   [r] Not Mon Oxfordfhire xx

Upon

Upon the death of John Wotton, the laft
prior, on the eve of Palm Sunday, 11 Henry vii, (1496,) for want of canons to elect
another, it was feized by the Crown, as an
efcheat.   Some years afterwards, February 21,
22 Henry vii, (1506-7,) Hugh Croft, efquire,
who perhaps was heir to fome of the ancient
benefactors, releafed to the King, for himfelf
and his heirs, all right and title to the priory.
An inqueft at Dorchefter, April 24, 1507,
and another at Northampton the laft day of
the fame month, found that the priory had
efcheated, as already faid, to the Crown[s];
and the fame year the King, with the authority of parliament, by writ of privy Seal
under his own hand, dated at Weftminfter,
July 6, and witneffed by Henry Prince of
Wales, the two Archbifhops, and others,
granted the faid diffolved monaftery to the
Dean and convent of St Stephen's, Weftminfter, " in free, pure, and perpetual alms[t]."
In fuch honourable terms runs the royal donation.   But what from Henry was " free,"
was not always gratuitous, for it appears by
two acquittances, one of them under his
Majefty's own hand, that he received for

---

[s] Yate, p 9   [t] Yate, p 10

his

his benefaction the fum of Seven hundred marks [u].

The priory however, though not altogether a free gift, was neverthelefs a profitable bargain, to the convent of St. Stephen's, for what they purchafed of the Crown for Seven hundred marks, they fold in a few years to the bifhop of Lincoln for Eleven hundred and fifty [x]. This fale, it feems, was agreed upon by the mediation of Fox, bifhop of Winchefter, and at the inftance of Robert Brudenel, William Grevil, and William Fairfax, Juftices of the Common Pleas, and Humphry Coningfby, Juftice of the King's Bench; for the termination of difputes, which had arifen, it is faid, between the parties, notwithftanding the grant by royal patent

The earl of Bolonia, above mentioned [y], procured a charter from king John for a fair once a year in his village of Cold Norton, which lafted three days, on the feaft of St. Simon and St. Jude and two days following [z]. Various ancient grants, remaining in

---

[u] Yate, p 11   [x] Ibid   [y] P 303.

[z] Anno 2 Johannis (A. D 1200) Dodfw 67 f 1. Bp Kennett, mentioning the circumftance, calls him Earl of Bo-

logne

the college archives, indicate Cold Norton
to have been a place of some size and consequence. There is one deed in particular,
apparently very old, but certainly not later
than the beginning of the fourteenth century, which describes land given to the priory as lying in "Stockwellstreet[a]." Whether
the decay of this considerable village were
owing to the extinction of the priory, or to
whatever cause, so it is, that the very name
and memory of it seem totally lost. The
name of the Priory alone subsists, preserved
from utter oblivion by a modern farm house
erected on the spot, itself now almost de-
serted, about a quarter of a mile east of Chapel House, parcel of the ancient possessions

logne and Dammartin, lord of the manors of Merton and Pi-
dington (Co Oxon) Par Antiq p 161

[a] Brasen Nose Archives, Cold Norton, C 2 Box, D 2
The donor, Richard Wine, charges it with a quit rent of 13 D
to the Knights Templars, who were suppressed by the Council
of Vienne (so it should be, not Vienna) A D 1312 Tanner's
Not Pref p xv "Luke of Oseney' (I suppose abbat) and
' Peter, clerk of the hospital," who acted as secretary on the
occasion, are two of the witnesses   The quit rent was afterwards paid to the Hospitalars, to whom the estates of the Templars were granted. See Rott 21—23 H viii, the first of
which says it was payable " de *tenement* vocat Baker's house,"
and the next " de *terr* vocat Baker's house," the house having
perhaps in the mean time been taken down.

of

of the priory. There was a Chapel here,
whence the prefent inn has its name, for the
neighbouring laity; and a Church at the
monaftery for the ufe of the Religious. When
the college of Brafen Nofe became poffeffed
of the priory, they provided a prieft, who
officiated in one or both of thefe facred edifices, and they received annually from the
Pix[b] there a variable fum of a dozen or
twenty fhillings, increafing uniformly till the
latter part of Henry the eighth's reign, when
it dwindled rapidly[c]. The bells were fold,
32 Henry viii, 1540, for ten pounds and
twenty pence halfpenny[d].

The Priory was very agreeably fituated on
the brow of an eminence, which projects into
a winding vale, or dell; along which a feeble
ftream, a branch of the river Glym, finds its
way, chiefly fed by a perennial fpring at the
priory. It formerly fupplied a mill for the
convenience of the neighbourhood[e], and ponds

---

[b] Henry vii ordered Pixes for keeping the facrament of the
altar to be made of filver gilt, value 4 L. each, for every parifh
church in the realm, not having one already See his Will,
p 38 It feems by what is here faid, that the Pix alfo contained the gifts of thofe who attended mafs

[c] Rott Comp Burff   [d] Plate Book, p 8

[e] Rott 23 24 H viii

for the use of the convent[f]. Not a wall, not a stone, of the ancient structure is now to be seen! Bones, which had reposed within the precincts of the church, or in the exterior cemetery, are sometimes dug up. A solitary yew and half-leveled mounds, which shew the extent of the premises, on the summit of the hill and the sides sloping to the sun, are the only indications of former splendor! Among the various charters and other original instruments, relating to this Priory, which are preserved in the archives of the college, I have only found one mutilated impression of the conventual seal; but as it has never been engraved or described, such as it is, it shall be given to the reader, and in the appendix an improved list of the priors[g].

[f] One of these, "unum stangnum—prope stangnum conventuale' was let to John Staunton, one of the canons, for a flagon of wine, "unam lagenam vini," to be paid every Christmas day 37 H vi (1459) Yate, p 20

[g] See the miscellaneous plate, and App. Num xv

SECT. X.

*Completion of the Building—Review of the Sta-
tutes—Death of the Founder—his Will and
Character.*

WE muft now return to the college;
which, though prepared for its inhabitants in
1512, was not yet completely finifhed and
furnifhed, as to fome parts and certain articles of lefs conftant and neceffary ufe.

The expence of leading the tower, 12l.
1s. 2d. was defrayed by inftalments, in three
fucceffive years, the firft not till 1517[a],
which feems to confirm a former conjecture[b],
that Brafen Nofe Hall, which ftood on that
fpot, was fuffered to remain, till the new
buildings were confiderably advanced. The
proportions of Gothic architecture, if there
were any independent of the eye, are not
known. But, in juftice to the original plan
of this tower, it muft be obferved, that it

---

[a] Rot. 9 H viii   [b] See above, p 288.

was very properly adapted to the building, which it was defigned to grace; till the addition of the Attic ftory, about the time of James the firft, I believe, deftroyed the fymmetry, and very fenfibly diminifhed the beauty of the whole. The plate annexed gives a view of the building, as it was before thefe alterations were made.

The chapel, where the prefent common room is[c], was fitted up for divine fervice, we may fuppofe, when it was folemnly dedicated to that purpofe[d]; and accordingly we find the neceffary expences of bread and wine and wax tapers, for the ufe of the chapel, form a material article in the annual accounts of the earlieft date extant.

The library was on the north fide of the quadrangle, oppofite to the chapel. It was glazed, and furnifhed with locks and other iron work in 1520; and the following year the books were chained, and what elfe feemed

[c] Some of the original Gothic windows are ftill difcernible on the fouth fide.

[d] See above, p. 295

[e] Pro vitro feris et aliis ferramentis circa librariam— vii L xS iD Rot. 12 Henry viii

necef-

COLLEGIVM ÆNEI NASI, 347

neceffary was done[f]. The arms, which were in fome of the windows[g], as well as many of thofe in the hall, have long fince difappeared.

Bifhop Smyth compofed a body of ftatutes for the regulation of the college, which he fpeaks of in his will, December 26, 1513, as having been, at that time, long promulgated[h]. He, no doubt, delivered one or more copies to the fociety at their firft inftitution; but none of thefe is at prefent known to exift. He was aware, as he fays, that other ftatutes, ufeful and convenient at leaft, if not abfolutely neceffary, might be added to thofe already compiled; and likewife that in thefe there might arife doubts, which would require explanation. He therefore gave full power to his executors, to retrench what was

[f] Rot 13 Henry viii pro cathenacione librorum &c xxxS viiD They were again chained on their removal into the new library after the Reftoration, nor were releafed from their confinement till about the year 1780, when the library was new modeled according to a plan of Mr Wyatt's, on which occafion the Rev Thomas Barker, D D Principal of the college, generoufly contributed 300L towards the completing of the work See Wood s Colleges, App p 275.

[g] Wood, Colleges, p 371

[h] " Per memetipfum jampridem edita " See his will, Append No xvi

fuper-

fuperfluous or inconvenient, to fupply de-
fects, to expound difficulties, and alfo to
frame whatever new ftatutes they fhould
judge to be conducive to the honour and advantage of the college. Accordingly a code
of ftatutes, figned and fealed by four of the
executors', a majority of the whole, was
given to the college, and is ftill preferved.
This was confequently the law of the fociety, but after a trial of fome years it was
found, that this fecond edition was ftill capable of correction and improvement. The
Principal therefore, in 12 Henry viii, as it
feems, waited upon the furviving Founder,
Sir Richard Sutton[k], at the monaftery of
Sion, of which he was Steward, to confer
with him on the fubject of a reform of the
college ftatutes. They were revifed with
care, many important alterations, in matter
as well as language, were made; feveral new
ftatutes were added, and the whole reduced
into a more commodious and fyftematic or-

' William Smyth, Henry Wilcocks, Gilbert Smyth, and
Robert Browne

k M[o] Principali pro expenf fuis equitandi—ad Syon pro
[ftatut]is Col[legii no[ftri re]formandis   Rot 12 H viii   As
tre roll is mutilated, it is not quite certain whether it is for
11 & 12 H viii or 12 & 13   In this and the following roll
there are payments for tranfcribing the ftatutes

                                                der,

der, and finally ratified by the feal of the
Founder, on the firft day of February, 13 H.
viii, 1521-2, in the name of the Father, and
of the Son, and of the Holy Spirit

By fome fatality or fome accident, now
unknown, it has happened, that this final
authentic volume, as well as bifhop Smyth's
firft draught, is loft, and there remains only
one ancient copy of it, with fome later tran-
fcripts. Under thefe circumftances it is impoffible to form an accurate comparifon between the firft fketch by the Bifhop and the
work finifhed by Sutton, though I fufpect
the executors did not very materially alter or
add to what Smyth had performed. Had
they done much, they would probably have
changed the feries of the chapters, which is
in fome parts obvioufly incongruous and unconnected, a circumftance which might naturally be expected, if diftinct regulations
were framed, as they occurred to the original
contriver, who did not live to methodife and
put the laft hand to his work But a great
mind, viewing at leifure the valuable but
fcattered materials, would bring together parts
that were fimilar, and give the whole as far
as fuch a body of laws will admit, the form
and connection of a fyftem.

It

It may be obferved in general of both copies of the ftatutes, that they are in many
parts copied from thofe of Magdalen college,
then recently founded, which latter are faid
to be taken in great meafure from Wykeham's ftatutes, and thofe again from prior
inftitutions. Thus each fucceffive founder
availed himfelf of the fame liberty, which
Cicero profeffed himfelf to ufe in philofophy;
and borrowed from thofe, who had preceded
him in the fame province, " as much as he
pleafed, and in what manner he pleafed[1],"
adapting to his own particular views what
experience had proved to be generally ufeful
And hence, with refpect at leaft to fuch
colleges as were eftablifhed before the Reformation, it will commonly be found, that
the more modern are the beft conftituted.
Such, in human operations, is the effect of
progreffive improvement, and what is juftly
ftyled the wifdom of ages

Of the alterations made by Sutton in the
ftatutes of Brafen Nofe the moft prominent
feature is lenity The mulcts are leffened,
leave of abfence is enlarged, and the fellow,
promoted to ecclefiaftical preferment, enjoys,

[1] De Off 1 1

during

during what is termed the year of grace, the powers as well as the emoluments of his fellowship; whereas, by the former statutes, he had the emoluments only, as is the case in some earlier colleges.

But in an undertaking like the present, it may seem requisite to give a succinct view of the plan and economy of the society itself, whose history we record. This therefore we shall attempt; and, tracing the outline of the institution, shall add chiefly such other traits, as are characteristic of the age, with some of the peculiar points of difference between the earlier and later statutes.

The preamble is in substance as follows:

In the name of the Holy and undivided Trinity, Father, Son, and Holy Spirit[m]. We William Smyth, bishop of Lincoln, and Richard Sutton, esquire, confiding in the aid of the supreme Creator, who knows directs and disposes the wills of all that trust in him, do out of the goods which in this life, not by our merits, but by the grace of His ful-

[m] The Virgin Mary, St Hugh and St Chad, and St Michael the archangel are added in the original, without the least scruple or alteration of phrase. " Pudet hæc opprobria!"

nefs,

nefs, we have received abundantly, by royal
authority and charter, found and eftablifh, in
the Univerfity of Oxford, a perpetual College
of fcholars, to ftudy philofophy and facred
theology, commonly called, **The King's
Haule and Colledge of Brafennofe in Oxford**[n], to the praife and honour of Almighty
God; for the furtherance of divine worfhip,
for the advancement of holy church, and for
the fupport and exaltation of the Chriftian
faith.

After this exordium they proceed to ordain, that their college fhall confift of a
Principal and twelve Fellows, all of them
born within the diocefe of Coventry and
Lichfield; with preference to the natives of
the counties of Lancafter and Chefter, and
efpecially to the natives of the parifh of
Prefcot in Lancafhire, and of Prefbury in
Chefhire[o].

In fixing upon the exact number of Twelve
fellows, it is probable the Founders had an
eye not only to their own ability of per-

---

[n] "The King's Hall and College of Brafinnofe of Oxford,"
firft copy, but in another part " Brafennofe "

[o] Stat cap 1

formance,

formance, but alfo to the number of our Lord's Apoftles. The numbers Twelve, Forty, and Seventy were regarded, in thefe ages, with a fond but harmlefs fuperftition, as peculiarly facred and aufpicious, on account of the hiftorical or prophetic ufe of them in holy Scripture Our Founders however manifefted no inviolable or foolifh predilection for their favourite number; but freely allow and earneftly intreat perfons of piety and generofity, not only to augment the revenues of their fellows, but likewife to add to the number. provided, neverthelefs, that Their ftatutes and every part of them remain fafe and unhurt[p].

There is a claufe in the firft ftatutes, which illuftrates this permiffion. It is there ordered, that, befide the aforefaid number of twelve, there fhall be two Fellows, mafters of arts or bachelors, natives of the diocefe of Sarum or Hereford, agreeably to the intent of a compofition between Edmund Audley, bifhop of Salifbury, and the College, for that purpofe : but fo that the faid compofition be not prejudicial to any of the ftatutes[q].

[p] Cap 1 p. 4

[q] Inferted after " poterunt," p 4 1 8. of the printed Statutes.

The

The benefaction, which is here spoken of in terms as if it was actually conferred, appears, whatever might be the reason, never to have taken effect. However, we see clearly, by the provision respecting it, in what manner additional fellowships, if any should be endowed, were meant to be ingrafted on the original stock. The particular place of a candidate's birth and other extrinsic circumstances, antecedent to election, are properly regarded as indifferent matters; wherein it is permitted, to each respective benefactor, to indulge without restraint his own views and partialities. But, by the act of election, all and every Fellow is incorporated into one body, and becomes subject to one and the same law.

One of the senior fellows is annually to be elected to the office of Vice Principal[r], and two others, Bursars, to whose care all the receipts and disbursements of the college are committed[s]. It is a judicious direction, that, whenever it may be necessary to erect new buildings on any of the college estates, or to undertake considerable repairs, the work shall begin in the month of March, and end be-

Cap. ix.   [s] Cap x

fore

fore the feaſt of St. Simon and St. Jude[t].
One of the very few reſtrictions, impoſed by
Sir Richard Sutton on former liberty and diſ-
cretion, was, that no eſtate belonging to the
college ſhould be let to the Principal, or to
any of the Fellows[u].

The veſtments and plate, and the regiſters
and other books, are injoined to be kept with
a ſcrupuloſity and care, the particulars of
which need not be recited; but one direction, now that the art of printing has long
ſuperſeded the common uſe of Manuſcripts,
is become a matter of ſome curioſity. It is
ordered, that in all books, belonging to the
library, the name of the donor, with that of
the college, ſhall be inſcribed on the ſecond
leaf, and in like manner that the volume itſelf ſhall be deſcribed in the catalogue by the
firſt word of the ſecond leaf[x] The firſt leaf
of a book is moſt liable to accidental injuries,
and to the corroding effect of time; but beſides this, the illuminations, ſo common in
manuſcripts, and often ſplendidly beautiful,
perpetually expoſed the firſt page, which was
moſt frequently thus adorned, to the depre-

[t] Cap xxxiv p 97.   [u] Cap xxxiii p 95
[x] Cap xxxii p 93

dation

dation of bold curiosity. The second leaf
therefore was, on all accounts, the safer
guardian of whatever was committed to it
But in compofing a catalogue the object was
to identify the volume, which could not be
done by exhibiting the mere title or firft
words of the work   But it will rarely happen, that two copyifts fhall fill their page
precifely with the fame number of words,
whence the initials of the fecond leaf of a
manufcript will mark that individual copy,
and no other. For this reafon the mode
here prefcribed was the common precaution
and cuftom of the times.

The only language tolerated for public
ufe, unlefs when ftrangers are prefent, is
Latin[y]; a regulation, of which, if rigoroufly
enforced, the utility may well be queftioned:
but the excellent Afcham[z] had not yet de-
monftrated the danger, left the fluency thus
acquired fhould be a vicious volubility of
words ill felected and worfe arranged. Perhaps, with proper attention, the modern
practice of making the learned language the

<hr>

[y] Print Stat p 66 with p 40 l 22   Nifi tempore gau-
diorum   Firft copy, fiat penult

[z] See his Works, publifhed by Bennet, 1761 4to p. 202.

vehicle

vehicle of public difputations participates the advantages of the two oppofite fchemes, without the inconveniences of either. Apt phrafeology will eafily be found for the difcuffion of a queftion previoufly known and confidered ; and a dexterity and command of words will grow familiar. But the effufions of the moment, as well on literary as friendly topics, it is perhaps fafeft to truft to that language, in which the ideas are prefented to the mind[a], and in which confequently they will be expreffed with greateft facility, fpirit, and effect

The admiffion of ftudents, fubject to the difcretion of the Principal and Vice Principal[b], is regulated by the fize and number of apartments[c], and although the edifice was not very ample, and confifted, as we have feen[d], only of a ground room and firft floor, yet, according to the habits of the age, and the order in the ftatutes conformable to thofe

[a] The ingenious author of the " Religion of Nature delineated, a work which cannot be uniformly commended, maintains that men always think in their native language Sect v p 123

[b] Cap viii.   [c] Cap xxx

[d] See p 310. and the plate annexed

Y   habits,

habits, a confiderable company might be received and lodged. For in each of the upper rooms, which by the firft ftatutes are referved for the Fellows, there were to be two large beds and one truckle bed.

Sir Richard Sutton, in revifing this chapter, affigned three inhabitants to the upper and four to the lower chambers[e], but he banifhed the truckle bed; from his ftatutes, I mean; for in his college it probably ftill maintained its ground, as it certainly did in other houfes. Shakefpear, painting, it is prefumed, the manners of his own times, makes the truckle bed part of the furniture of his facetious Knight[f]. and Hall, at a later period, fatirifing a " gentle fquire" and a domeftic tutor, reprefents it as the firft condition requifite in the latter,

> " That he fleep upon the truckle-bed,
> Whiles his young maifter lieth o'er his head[g]."

c Stat ъхъ

f Merry Wives of Windfor, Act iv Sc i

g Book ii Sat vi There was a high bed and truckle bed at Woodftock manor in 1649 Plot's Oxf ch viii § 41, 42 In Henry viiith's time (9 July, 1529) Sir Thomas Nevile, by letter, requefted John Hales, Baron of the Exchequer, to accept Mr Attorney General, Sir Chriftopher Hales, to be his bedfellow in his chamber in Grays Inn Dugd. Orig Jurid.

ъ 273

What

What number of ſtudents the college contained, when they were contented with this crowded mode of living, I have not diſcovered. Upon a muſter of names in the reign of Edward vi, it appeared, that there were ſeventy in Braſen Noſe[h], and the college was then, in point of numbers, the fourth in the univerſity, which rank it has generally maintained, and ſtill holds, though ſeveral colleges have been founded ſince that time.

The Founders expreſs a proper diſapprobation of ſumptuouſneſs at the tables of the clergy and of ſtudents[i], and, as far as regards their college, it will be thought in the preſent day, that they took effectual care to prevent all ſuch extravagance in their Fellows, when it is told, that they allow them no more than twelve pence for their weekly commons[k], two ſhillings at the three great

[h] MS Wood, 8514 52 p 208 ex G G f 68 The total number was 1015 Magdalen was the firſt, then Chriſt Church, New College, Braſen Noſe, &c

[i] Cap xvii

[k] It was the ſame at St Johns college, Cambridge, " only 12 D per week was allowed in commons to a Fellow, and only 7 D to a Scholer " Mr Baker, Pref. to Fun. Serm of Counteſs of Richm p xliv. The charter of this college was given in

the

festivals, and sixteen pence on thirteen lesser
feasts. There is no doubt however, that,
when the college was founded, this was fully
competent for what the statutes prescribe,
" moderamen dietæ;" and permission is given
to augment the allowance, when a quarter
of wheat shall fetch twelve shillings or more,
in the public market[1]

tne same year with that of Brasen Nose, " April 9, 1511 " ib
xxxi But the society did not commence a corporation till
July 29, 1516 ib xlix See above, p 121 In another " college in Cambridge [probably, Queens] founded about the
year 1450, the statutable allowance to each Fellow is 5 L per
ann to find him in diet, clothes, and all other necessaries "
Cnron Preciof p 143

[1] For the sake of throwing light on this and other passages,
which occur in these memoirs, I will here bring together a
few miscellaneous notices, which shew the price of various
commodities within the space of forty years before and after
the year 1500, a period for which bishop Fleetwood, in com-
piling his highly curious and valuable Chronicum Preciosum,
laments tnat nis materials were very barren and scanty A
horse, sanis oculis &c 13S 4D A D 1461 Reg Aaa, f 193
In 1495 a horse 33S Comp Coll Magd another 35S 4D,
ibid a few years afterwards about 18S ibid in 1533, 14S
Rot Coll Æn Naf 18S for 2 horses, 1534 ibid A cart
load of hay, 2S in 1545 ibid Hire of a horse 5 weeks,
11S 8D. 1503 Œ f 55 Three kine and three calves,
26S 8D 1510 J f 146 b where also, " 15 shepe with
tner roll, 12S a sowe with 6 pyggs 4S ' and " a nel off
Wolfrd, 3S 4D' Four chicken 4D 1511 Warton Hift.
Poet iii p 327 Four knots of whipcord, 4D 1496 Comp
Magd. A pair of boots, 3S 6D 1503 ibid Two pair of
gloves

It was the good bifhop's wifh, that in
drefs as well as diet his college fhould exhibit

gloves given to the Bp of Hereford (Mayow) 16D 1508 ib.
Gloves to the abbat of Notley, 8D 1497 Comp Coll Nov
Among the evidences of Cold Norton a referved rent of land
was one penny and " vnas novas chirothecas vnius denarii "
perhaps temp Edw iii Yate, p 33 Half a hide of white
leather for bawdryks, 8D ob A D 1492 MS Wood, 8514
p 265 pro 1 bawdryke ad campanam, 16D A D 1461 ib.
p 251 a bawdryck for the Paruis bell, 10D A D 1550. ib.
p 277 pro uno ly hyde corn pro ly bawdrykys, 16D making
them, 8D Comp Magd 1496 fee alfo 1502 le bawdryke
pro una campana A writer employed in 1464 at 3S 4D a
fheet Reg Aaa, f 233 A [malter] carpenter 6D a day
Magd Comp fæpe A cup or goblet called " ly Cardinalls
hatt" made by a London goldfmith at 3S 10D per ounce,
44S 9D ib A D 1501 Red wine in 1504 at 4L per dolium (i e a pipe or butt of 126 gallons Chron Preciof.
p 115) Claret, per dolium, 3L 13S 4D Somner's Canterb P ii App p 27 Malmfey 1½D per pint, temp H vii.
Howel's Londinop p 102 A perfon was difcommoned for
felling " antiquum et inveteratum vinum pro novo—lagenam
—pro 10D—unam quartam—pro 2D ob " Reg G f. 9 b
—a proof of what Bp Fleetwood obferves, that Lagena or Flagon (derived from it) holds a gallon Chron Preciof p 91.
101 In the fenior Proctors book of Statutes, marked C f 102.
102 b there is a curious table of the affize of bread, wine, and
beer, probably temp Edw iv in which Waftell bread, Coket
bread, Simnel and Trett bread are mentioned, words which I
do not underftand, further than that Simnel appears to have
been the fineft, Waftell next and Trett the coarfeft The fcale

* Bayley fays Bawdrick was a cord or thong for the clapper of a bell
Chaucer has it for the ftring of a bugle horn, Prol to C T verfe 110
" An horn he bare, the baudrick was of grene Ard Spencer for a belt.
See F Queen B i, vii St xxiv

a pattern of fobriety. He therefore injoined
all the members of the houfe to wear fuch
garments only as are proper for ecclefiaftics[m],
who fhould be " as lamps burning before the
people." Two forts of boots, the red and
the white, are totally prohibited; as are alfo
fhoes with long peaks[n], and mantles, and

of wheat by which the weight is regulated, runs from 12 D
the quarter to 12 S the quarter, which it was thought, I fuppofe, not likely, communibus annis, to exceed " Wygges and
Symnelles for Lent occur in 1464 Reg Aaa f 214 b Mr
Warton obferves that 6D the allowance for a fermon in 1441,
was " worth about 5S of our prefent money' Hift Poet ii
p 106 Bp Fleetwood ftates the common price of wheat from
1440 to 1460 at 6S 8D the quarter In the reign of H vii.
it feems generally to have been under that fum A remark of
the judicious Blackftone fhall conclude this long note " Bifhop
Fleetwood—has fully proved 40S in the reign of H vi to have
been equal to 12 L per annum in the reign of queen Anne,
and, as the value of money is very confiderably lowered fince
the Bifhop wrote, I think we may fairly conclude,—that what
was equivalent to 12 L in his days is equivalent to 20 at prefent' (1765) Comment B i Ch ii
    = This was reftricted by Sir R Sutton to the Principal and
Fellows, with a difcretionary claufe refpecting other members
Cap xvi
    n " Calciamentis roftratis' Mr Warton informs us, that
" in Eton college ftatutes, given in 1446, the fellows are forbidden to wear fotularia roftrata, as alfo caligæ, white, red, or
green Hift Poet add in vol ii on vol i p 428 Mr
Granger fays, " In the reign of Rich ii the peaks or tops of
fhoes and boots were worn of fuch enormous a length, that
they were tied to the knees, and that a law was made in the
                                                        fame

tippets°, and coftly furs called fables, or Martrons[p].

fame reign to limit them to two inches " vol i p 118 8vo.
ed See alfo Hamlet, Act v Sc 1 and the commentators
The cuftom however, but perhaps not in its full extravagance,
appears to have been of earlier date For in a chantry founded
at Winchefter in 1318, the members are ordered to go " in
meris caligis et fotularibus *non roftratis,* nifi forfitan *botis* uti
voluerunt " Warton, ibid This prohibition of peaks is omitted in Suttons ftatutes, the caprice of fafhion, more potent
than law, having in the mean time lopped off the demi-cref-
cent and introduced a fhoe or flipper adapted to the foot; as
appears by the portraits of Henry viii On the fubject and
form of ancient fhoes and boots fee alfo Dugd. Mon ii 720
739 White's Selborne, 370 Gent. Mag 1796 384. 456
1797 1086

° " Liripipio — vocato tippet " Stat " Their lerripippes
reach to their heels, all jagged " Peck, Defid Cur ii p 570.
ed 4to

[p] Sables are well known from the commentators on Shakef-
pears Hamlet, Act iii Sc 1 in illuftration of which this paffage of the Brafen Nofe ftatutes has been adduced See Gent.
Mag 1786 p 375 The fur of *Martrons* (for that is the true
reading, but not hitherto underftood) that is, Marterns or Martens, was lefs efteemed and is rarely mentioned Mr Warton
cites " an old poem written about 1436, entitled the *Englifh
Policie, exhorting all England to keepe the fea,'* where the writer,
fpeaking of Ireland, fays

—" *Martens* goode been her marchandie,
Hertes hides, and other of venerie,
Skinnes of otter, fquirrell and Irifh hare,
Of fheepe, lambe, and foxe is her chaftare "

Hift. Poet iii p 123 The Book of St. Alban's on Hawking,
Hunting

The bifhop of Lincoln is Vifitor of the college, and his decifions are final, and without appeal; unlefs he proceeds fo far as to depofe the Principal, in which cafe every legal mode of defence is permitted [q].

Such are the particulars moft material to be noticed in the epifcopal ftatutes; except that, in framing the abftract, we have not adhered to the original order, but for the fake of brevity have compreffed and combined parts in any meafure fitted to coalefce; which in the code itfelf have their proper fize, and feparate allotment.

When Sir Richard Sutton, with the approbation, if not with the aid, of the firft Principal, fet himfelf to revife this prior draught of ftatutes, he improved them by every mode in which improvement can be

Hanting &c by Juliana Barnes or Berners, printed at St Alban's in 1486, has this paffage

—" Wherefo ye comen in play [plain] or in place
Now fhal I tel you which ben beftes of chace
One of the a buck, another a doo,
The ffox, and the *marteryn*, and the wilde roo
And ye fhall, my dere fones, other beftes all,
Where fo ye hem finde, rafcall hem call "
                    Hift Poet ii p 171 n c,

[q] Cap xxxv

effected .

effected, by leaving out, by altering, and by adding.

The parts difcreetly cancelled are in general too minute for diftinct recital, neither could their propriety be accurately eftimated without a comparifon of what was expunged, and what was retained But there is one paffage, partly retrenched and in part altered, which is fomewhat curious. Both the Founders allow noblemen or others on the footing of what are now ftyled Gentlemen Commoners, to the number of fix ; provided they have a Tutor, Sir Richard Sutton fays, who fhall be anfwerable to the college for their expences[r], but the Bifhop places them under the care of " Creditors, commonly called Creanfers[s]." Where it may be noted, that the only Tutor recognized by the ftatutes is, according to the original import of the word, a Guardian, for the duties of a preceptor did not, in thofe days, conftitute an appropriate part of his office, as public lectures, in the fchools and in the college, were then the only mode of inftruction. The other term, Creanfers, affords an inftance, out of many

---

[r] Stat viii
[s] De extraneis non introducendis ad onus collegii.

which

which might be adduced, to shew how familiar the use of French words formerly was in England The word is also memorable for its peculiar acceptation on the continent. For it seems, our ancestors were so liberal in lending, or else their Gallic neighbours were so tardy in payment, that it was proverbially common with them to call their creditors " the English;" and " creansers" and " les Anglois' became synonymous terms[t]. Whether the memory of British forbearance is effaced, and the proverb grown obsolete, I have not learnt.

Under the head of alterations we meet with some judicious corrections of the statute respecting the election of fellows[u]; which, by simplifying the regulations, make them more easy to be understood, and consequently more likely to be observed. The Bishop, unwilling that any part of his bounty should be unfruitful or dormant, ordered all

---

[t] See Barrington on Anc Stat p 209 n q and Sir G Carew in Bircas Negot p 513 Camden his [Gallos] " Anglos hodie amicos non minus quam olim hostes innato odio ingrate prosequi, et toties in re pecuniaria fefellisse, ut creditores quos fraudare statuert l Anglos avere o vocitant " Annal ad ann 1590 p 568 ed Eliz 1639

[u] Cap vi

vacan-

vacancies to be filled up, as often as they happened, in the fpace of a few days; and he was one of the firft, who fet this example in the univerfity, for in general, in the earlier foundations, the elections are only annual[x]. To the principle thus laid the fecond Founder wifely adhered; but he extended the time of vacancy, which before was too much confined, allowing forty days, inftead of fifteen.

He alfo expunged a well-intended but vague precept refpecting the qualifications of candidates, and fubftituted a claufe lefs liable to evafion; in virtue whereof, as far as is poffible in human inftitutions, the ftatutes of the college, like the laws of the land, fpeak one and the fame language to all, and, in every inftance, it may truly be faid, that the fociety merely pronounce, the Founders elect.

But the capital improvement was an al-

---

[x] Perhaps Univerfity college, founded and refounded at different times, affords an exception Three Yorkfhire fellowfhips in Magdalen college, not given by Waynflete, though eftablifhed in his time, are alfo filled up in any part of the year as the vacancies happen

teration,

teration, flight in itfelf, as to the cuftody of
the common feal, and the functions of the
fociety in its corporate capacity. In the original ftatutes the defign clearly was, as in
many fimilar inftitutions, that the major
part of the fociety fhould be prefent at every
act of the body[y]. But reafon fuggefted, and
experience had in part fhewn, that the
weightieft affairs of the college, though its
numbers fhould be augmented, might fafely
be entrufted to the difcretion of feven of the
members; and therefore, as upon the firft
plan fewer than feven could not act, fo now
that fpecific number was rendered competent
to tranfact all bufinefs with effect, whatever
number of fellowfhips (two more having in
the mean time been eftablifhed) might afterwards be added to the original twelve.

The advantages of this regulation are
principally two: it fecures the refidence of

[y] Cap iv p 17 l 17 " Sex focii feniores" is fubftituted
for " omnes et finguli focii of the firft ftatutes , in which alfo
the deciding claufe (l 24 ib) ftands thus " et quod in et
fuper premiffis communiter per omnes convenientes, per majorem partem, vel per fex feniores cum confenfu &c And in
many other paffages, where the later edition has " the fix fe-
niors," (p 73 l 7 p 75 l 9 &c) the former had " the major part of the Fellows

a proper

a proper number of fellows to tranfact the affairs of the fociety, and to enforce difcipline, and it commits thofe affairs and that difcipline to perfons, who, in regard to prudence and experience, may be prefumed to be beft qualified for the truft. It is not in nature, that the ftudies and the morals of a confiderable feminary of young men fhould be directed with equal facility and effect by one or two individuals, as by a larger number acting in concert. They are an example and encouragement to each other, as well as to thofe under their care mutual advice affifts deliberation, confentient authority imparts ftrength; and they perform their refpective duties with an alacrity and fpirit, free from the folicitude of that painful reflection, the force of which every fuperintendant of numbers has experienced, " I am not able to bear all this people alone[z]."

Thefe advantages were forefeen and intended. Another, which was not perhaps in the contemplation of the Founders, has eventually fprung from the fame fource. In confequence of this inftitution, and, what has in part refulted from it, the fuperior

[z] Numb xi 14

emo-

emolument of the fenior fellowfhips, the junior part of the fociety generally quit their
refidence in college for a few years, foon
after they have proceeded to their fecond
degree; and fo relinquifh certain habits and
connections, at once innocent and captivat-
ing, but yet not a little obftructive of difcipline   It is faid that thofe, who have long
worn fetters, cannot walk well when firft
they are releafed; and though the ftrongeft
reftraints of difcipline are comparatively but
flender fhackles, yet it may naturally be expected, and is generally found, that when
thefe are taken off, as in great meafure is
the cafe when the ftudent commences mafter of arts, he will not inftantly frame his
conduct with the fame punctuality and cir-
cumfpection as before. At the fame time
the younger claffes, from which he is juft
advanced, court and carefs him more than
ever, for the credit and countenance of his
friendfhip; and, without intending harm, he
caufes or aggravates petty irregularities in his
juniors; and, while he multiplies faults, increafes alfo the difficulty of correcting them
It is happy therefore for all parties, if the
polity, of which he is a member, does not
invite but rather diffuade his refidence at this
period: and when he comes back, he returns
fully

fully convinced of what no fenfible perfon can live long without being convinced, that the unbounded familiarity of equals, whether it be in a college or a camp, is abfolutely incompatible with vigour of difcipline, and the falutary coercions of good order.

The additions are confiderable in number and importance, confifting of five new chapters, with the infertion of many other material claufes[a]. One of the new ftatutes gives the Principal leave to admit a clergyman poffeffed of preferment exceeding in value what is tenable by the ftatutes, provided he conforms himfelf to the rules of the houfe, and has his apartments in little Edmund Hall It is not improbable, that this ftatute originated in a wifh to accommodate fome particular perfon, and from that fingle cafe a general rule was formed. Whether Dr. Roger Dingley was the perfon intended to be thus favoured, is not certain; but he appears to have been one of the firft that availed himfelf of the privilege[b]. He had been fellow of All Souls' college, and proctor

---

[a] Chap xii xxii xxiv xxxvii. xxxviii with great part of viii and xxiii

[b] See Rot Burff 19 II viii

of the univerſity[c]; after which he was recommended, with William Griſe of Magdalen college, to cardinal Wolſey, for the
purpoſe of reviſing the academical ſtatutes[d].
He was alſo, as Wood ſays, chaplain to
Henry viii, and obtained two or more dignities in the church. Rector Parks[e], rector
Vernam[f] (that is, Vernon) and rector Caple[g]

[c] In 1518 Wood, Faſti in ann   He ſays he does not
" know whether he be the ſame with Roger Dingley of All
Souls mentioned in the Annals, an 1520," as one of the re-
viſers of the ſtatutes, but there ſeems no reaſon to queſtion it
The name is ſo uncommon, that I have met with it only once
beſides   In John Higgins s ed of the Mirrour of Magiſtrates,
1587, " Flooden Field, ſaid to have been penned " fiftie yeares
ago, is ſubſcribed " Francis Dingley,' the name of a poet
(Mr Warton ſays) who has not otherwiſe occurred   Hiſt
Poet iii 261

[d] Bodl Arch A 166 (Reg FF) Ep 129 f 69   They
are both ſtyled S T B but Dingley's college is not named,
whether becauſe he had now quitted All Souls and reſided in
little Edmund Hall, I cannot tell   The date is probably 1524,
the Cardinal s anſwer (Ep 130) being dated Aug 18 of that
year   Ep 131 again to the Cardinal, when Dingley and Griſe
were ſent to him   In the ſame vol f 32 b f 33 Roger
Dyngley is jun Proctor, Oct 13, 1518   He proceeded D D
June 11, 1526 Athen i F 42

[e] Rot Burſſ 28 H viii

[f] Ibid 32—38 H viii and i Edw vi   In 32 H viii he
lived in Black Hall   Vernon in vulgar pronunciation is Vernam at this day in Cheſh e

[g] Ibid 35 H vi .—i Edw vi

are

are others, who, by a liberal conſtruction of the ſame ſtatute, were ſoon afterwards permitted, together or ſucceſſively, to have apartments, and proſecuted their ſtudies in Braſen Noſe college.

The fifth additional ſtatute, which cloſes the volume, is a ſolemn ratification of all that precedes, with a prohibition of all ordinances repugnant to theſe, or to the true ſenſe of them. Beſides this it enacts, that " Roland Meſſynger ſhall not be Fellow of the college, nor have a room in it, nor ſtay there beyond a ſingle night." The reaſon of this harſh ſentence, known, we may preſume, at the time, has never ſince been diſcovered, nor even with probability conjectured. Perſonal pique or prejudice, which originating from ſlight cauſes often proceeds to very unwarrantable lengths, can hardly be ſuppoſed to have riſen to ſuch a height of malignity and injuſtice, as, by a ſingle act of arbitrary legiſlation, to eject a perſon from his freehold, if it had been forfeited by no crime : and yet we have not found any thing, which, even in appearance, trenches upon the moral honeſty, temper, or conduct of either of the parties.

Roland Meffynger (the fame perfon, I prefume,) of the diocefe of Carlifle, was ordained deacon upon a title from the priory of St Andrew's in Northampton, by bifhop Smyth's fuffragan, in Lent, 1496, at Buckden[h], and the following year he was ordained prieft, by the fame fuffragan, at Lincoln ; John Colet, afterwards the celebrated Dean of St. Paul's, being admitted to the fame order at the fame time[i]. Meffynger proceeded mafter of arts at Oxford, June 30, 1505[k]; three years after which he was the northern Proctor of the univerfity[l], being then Principal of little Univerfity Hall[m]. In 1511 he was Principal of Black Hall[n], and fhortly afterwards was prefented by the abbey of Godftow to the vicarage of High Wycombe[o]. In December following bifhop Smyth gave him the rectory of Winwick in Northamptonfhire[p]; and, in the fpace of a

---

[h] MS Harl 6953 p 64.

[i] Ibid

[k] G f 3

[l] Ibid f 59 b 74

[m] ꟼ f 65 b   MS Wood, 8514 p 162

[n] ꟼ. f. 149

[o] 12 Mar 1511–12   MS. Harl 6953 p 59 on the refignation of Heywood mentioned above, p 258 note q

[p] 20 Dec   Ibid p 34   Bridges' Northampt. 1 605

few

few months, collated him to a prebend in his cathedral[q]. This accumulation of prefer-ment, from various quarters, feems ftrongly to befpeak the worth of Meffynger, which is alfo implied in what has already been noted, and muft here be recollected, that he was repeatedly employed by both the Foun-ders in matters of truft, and nominated by them one of the firft Fellows. His ejection therefore, and that by an injunction perpe-tuated in the ftatutes, is the more extra-ordinary. It is poffible he might be removed on account of the vicarage of Wycombe, no benefice of that defcription being compatible with the ftatutes, and if this circumftance was at firft difpenfed with in his favour, it is only parallel to what the Bifhop, as we have feen[r], did at Oriel, in the cafe of the fellow-fhip which he founded there, deviating from his own rules in the firft inftance, to gratify private friendfhip, or to reward eminent merit. But the furviving Founder might feel it his duty to remove, before he died, whatever was in direct oppofition to the fta-tutes, and fo pronounced Meffynger non-

[q] St Botulphs 31 Jul 1513 MS Harl 6953 p 26 Williss Cath ii 150
[r] P 233

focius

focius, which he did with lefs reluctance, as knowing him poffeffed of very competent preferment: though, after all, it muft be confeffed, that the terms and manner of his difmiffion rather feem to indicate fomewhat of warmth and difpleafure. When he was, upon whatever caufe, ejected, cardinal Wolfey took him up, and employed him as one of the Comptrollers of his works, in building the magnificent college of Chrift Church[s]. Browne Willis thinks he died and was buried at Winwick, in 1546[t], where however, as I am informed[u], no memorial of him is to be found.

But we muft return to the Bifhop; whofe days, when he had compiled his ftatutes and delivered them to the college, were now

[s] A D 1525—1529 Wood, Colleges, p 425 Mr Warton obferves, " it was common to depute churchmen to this department from an idea of their fuperior prudence and probity " Hift Poet 1 306 n z where he gives many inftances

[t] Cathedr ut fupra Bridges however mentions no other rector till 1554

[u] By the Rev James Williamfon, B D the worthy Vicar of Winwick, author of a fenfible and ufeful volume of fermons, preached at the Bampton Lecture in 1793, as alfo of a clear and candid Defence of the Church of England from the charges of the Rev Jofeph Berington and the Rev John Milner, 1790.

haften-

haftening to their end. His age is not known; but a life of temperance and piety feems to have been crowned with a gentle diffolution[x]. He was at Lidington, December 15, 1513[y], and on the 23d of that month we find him at Buckden. This winter journey, as there was no travelling but on horfeback, fhews, that he laboured under no great infirmity or ficknefs, but he appears confcious of the approach of that period, which is the lot of mortality, and is preparing for its arrival by fettling all his worldly affairs.

Erafmus very juftly obferves, that the proceffions, and carrying about of images, and various other ceremonies of the church of Rome, had their origin in the correfponding cuftoms of paganifm[z]; to which they cer-

---

[x] His hand writing betrays no fymptoms of imbecillity, nor is fenfibly different from the very few other fpecimens, with which I have been able to compare it See the fac-fimile in the plate, copied from the conveyance of Cold Norton to the college, May 8, 1513 Sir Richard Sutton's hand, as appears by feveral inftances, altered more, and towards the laft he began to write, as Cicero elegantly expreffes it, " vacillantibus literis "

[y] Mr Fardell, from Reg Linc

[z] See the paffage in Jortins Erafmus, vol. ii p 197—199 from tom v Leyd ed c 1120 The fame fubject is profecuted at large in " The Conformity between modern and an-

cient

tainly bear a very ftriking refemblance. What
follows is an inftance of that kind, which, I
believe, has not been noted. The Romans,
on their death-bed, ufed to manumit a certain number of their flaves[a], who were hence
called Orcini[b]: and in perfect conformity
with this practice, whether apprized of it or
not, the Bifhop by diftinct inftruments, which
were confirmed by the chapter of Lincoln,
liberated Thomas Paul and Edward Wolley,
with their refpective iffue, from all fervice of
villenage, due to him and his fucceffors, or
the church of Lincoln[c]

cient Ceremonies, Lon l 1745, tranflated from the original
French, printed at Leyden, 1667 and in Conyers Middleton's
famous "Letter from Rome, fhewing an exact Conformity between Popery and Paganifm"

    [a] ———————— Illum
       Hefern capite induto fubiere quirites
                  Peri Sat iii 105

    [b] Saeton in Aug c 37
    [c] Buckden, 23 Dec 1513 Reg Linc f 54 b confirmed
by Chapter, 30 Dec 10 A fynod under Anfelm, A D 1102
ordered, that " none prefume hereafter to fell men like bruite
beafts" Fuller, Ch Hift B iii p 19 but he adds that "this
confitution found not general obedience," of which the following is one proof "Ego Thurftanus Difpenfator domini
Regis dedi ecclefiæ B M de Ofeneye Walterum filium Helie,
nativum meum, cum omni progenie fua, quæ de eo procedit,
et cum omnibus catellis fuis ubicunque fuerint fuper terram
meam, pro viginti fex folidis &c no date. Yate, p 49

Three

Three days after this, December 26, he made his will On the 29th he granted a leafe of the manor of Nettleham in Lincoln-fhire, given to the fee of Lincoln by Henry the firft[d], to Richard Smyth, who is ftyled his fervant[e], and was probably one of his kinfmen His nephew William Smyth, arch-deacon of Lincoln, was with him[f]. He ex-pired at Buckden, January 2, 1513-14[g]. The archdeacon by letter informed the chap-ter of the event, and the fame day, Janu-ary 4, they appointed a deputation to wait upon the archbifhop of Canterbury with a notification of the death, recommending to his Grace Simon Foderby alias Grene, pre-centor, the faid William Smyth, John Con-ftable, archdeacon of Northampton, and Ed-ward Darby, archdeacon of Stow, all of them perfons preferred by the late Bifhop, that one of the four might be conftituted official, during the vacancy of the fee[h]. Conftable was appointed[i].

---

[d] Dugd Mon iii 261.2

[e] Reg Linc f 55

[f] Ibid f 56

[g] Ibid it is Jan 5 Reg Warham, f 284

[h] Darby's preferments have already been mentioned, p 159, Of Archdeacon Smyth there will be occafion to fpeak again. Foderby alias Grene, D D fellow of Lincoln, and fometimes

Com-

The Bishop's will may be seen in the appendix[k]; but it seems necessary in this place to give a summary account of it.

First of all he commends his soul to Al-

Commissary of the University, was collated by Smyth to the Prebend of Welton Beckhall, 6 Nov 1509 MS Harl 6953 p 25. on the death of William Atkinson, D D (also collated by Smyth, 4 Apr 1503 ib p 20) who translated the famous book of the Imitation of Christ at the " commaundement of the full excellent Prynceffe Margate, Moder to Henry the vii, printed by W de Worde, 1502 Ames's Typogr ed Herbert, p 138 231 249 In 1510, March 28, Smyth collated Foderby to the Precentorship of Lncoln Willis, ii p 85 and gave him the Preberd of Empingham, Mar 28, 1512 MS. Harl ib p 25 and the Prebend of Bigglefwade, 2 Dec following ib p 26 He died Mar 27, 1536, and was buried in the Chanter's aile See his epitaph in Willis, p 36. and in Peck's Defid Cur p 297

' Jan 13 Reg Warham, f 284, 284 b This John Conftable, fourth fon of Sir Robert Conftable of Flamborough, Yorkfhire was collated by Smyth to the Treafurerfhip of Lincoln, July 14, 1508 MS Harl ut fupra, p 23 and to the Archdeaconry of Huntingdon, 1 Dec 1512 ib p 26 He was made Dean of Lincoln, 1514 and o d July 15, 1528 See Athen Ox i p 14 In the epifcopal Archives at Buckden, Paper Book, L L f 7 is a letter by Conftable to the " Archbifhop of Cantourburye," refpecting " procuracies with other cafuolle revenovs, which he had received for his Grace's ufe, remitting to his mercy " certeyn poor dekeyd places, that were not able to pay Dated March, probably 1520, upon the death of Bp Atwater.

[k] See No xvi

mighty

mighty God and to the Virgin Mary; and directs his body to be buried in the cathedral of Lincoln, at the west end of bishop Alnwick's grave, which however, whatever might be the reason, appears not to have been done. For the grave of bishop Alnwick was on the north side of the nave, near the third pillar from the west end, but Smyth was buried on the south side of the nave, at the west end of bishop Gynwell's grave, Judge Mounson afterwards occupying the space between Smyth's grave and the last pillar, near the west door[1].

In the next place he wills, that the Principal and Fellows of Brasen Nose College should pay annually to the Dean and Chapter of Lincoln the sum of twelve pounds; out of which the sum of six pounds thirteen shillings and four pence was to be paid annually to a priest to pray for his soul, and for his parents and benefactors, in the chapel of St. Sebastian, on the south side of the ca-

---

[1] See the plate in Dugd Mon III p 356 and in Willis's Survey of Cath vol II Dr Gordon, late Precentor of Lincoln, took " an ichnography of the Cathedral, pointing out exactly the situation of all the old grave stones,' before the church was new paved " By this it appears that Dugdale and Browne Willis are right.' Mr Fardell

thedral,

thedral, near the place chofen for his fepulture : the firft nomination of the faid chaplain or prieft by the teftator himfelf, then
by his executors, and after their deceafe by
the Dean and Chapter.

He alfo directs, that the mafter of the chorifters, with the boys, fhall chant certain refponfes, and fay certain prayers, daily, at the
weft end of his grave, with proftrations and
genuflections, after the manner ufed before
the crucifix in St Paul's in London. For
which the chorifters are to receive annually
fix fhillings and eight pence, and their teacher
twenty fhillings.

The remainder (five marks) was to be diftributed among the canons in refidence, and
other minifters of the church, obferving his
obit, every year, agreeably to the cuftom of
bifhop Ruffell's obit.

This payment to the Chapter of Lincoln,
but with fome addition[m], the reafon of which
does not appear, was regularly made by the
college towards the end of Henry the eighth's

[m] The fum paid was 13l 6s 8d   See the annual Comp
Burff 1543—1547

reign,

reign; but when chantries were fuppreffed in the firft year of his fucceffor[n], the college, by a fuit in the court of Exchequer and in the Dutchy of Lancafter, prayed to be difcharged of this rent, inafmuch as the lands from which it iffued, being vefted in the college, were not within the meaning of the ftatute of chantries. It was alfo fet forth, that the value of the eftates was very materially diminifhed by the diffolution of religious houfes, which paid a good part of the rent[o]. On thefe grounds their petition was granted, and the payment ceafed.

To the college of Brafen Nofe he bequeathes, for the ufe of the chapel, the books, chalices, and veftments of his domeftic chapel, of which an inventory is given in a fchedule[p] annexed to the will.

Of the furniture of the original chapel of Brafen Nofe college an inventory remains,

[n] 1 Edw vi c 14
[o] Yate, p 66 This was an evil of fome magnitude Payments and quit rents charged on particular eftates attached to the property, and were ftill recoverable, but rents payable out of the eftates *general* of an abbey, when the abbey was fuppreffed and the eftates divided, were commonly loft
[p] See App No xvii

which

which feems to have been made before the
year 1520[q]   If this is compared with the
aforefaid fchedule, the two lifts will be found
fo widely different, that it may be doubted
whether any, certainly very few, of the numerous articles bequeathed by the Bifhop,
are defcribed in the inventory of the college; nor is his name once mentioned as
the donor either of plate, or of veftments,
though other benefactors are carefully recorded.   There are alfo feveral volumes in
the college library, which were given by bifhop Smyth[r], but not a fragment has been
found of the fervice-books mentioned in the
fchedule.   In Sir William Dugdale's Mona-
fticon there is an inventory of jewels and veftments belonging to Lincoln cathedral, taken
in the year 1536, in which are many fuperb
veftments, " the gift of Lord William Smith,
Bifhop of Lincoln[s]. ' but thefe again differ
totally from thofe which he bequeathed to

[q] Plate Book, p 1 App No xviii
[r] Lanfranc et Berengarii de Sacram Euch difputatio &c
MS No 11 Augufini Opufcula MS No 12 Medical Tracts
by John Mefua, ed Ven 1495 Pfalterium b Brunonis (a com-
mentary on the Pfalms, by Bruno, a German bifhop of the
eleventh century) per Anthonium Roberger impreffum, 1497
Anfelmi Opufcula   And perhaps others, my fearch for thefe
curiofities not having been very careful or exact
    See App No xix

his

his college chapel When fortune forfook her favourite, cardinal Wolfey, one of the charges exhibited againft him was, that he " had the more part of the goods of Dr. Smyth, bifhop of Lincoln," and of other bifhops, whom he fucceeded, " contrary to their wills, and to law and juftice[t]" Hence it was, that the furniture of the pious Founder, if it ever quitted the epifcopal chapel, never reached its deftination in Brafen Nofe.

To the Hofpital of St John Baptift in Banbury he gives one hundred pounds, for the purpofe of conftructing new edifices and repairing the old; over and above the fum of fixty pounds, already beftowed by him on the faid hofpital.

This houfe is faid to have been founded as early as king John's time[u] It has been conjectured, that the fite of it was on the Northamptonfhire fide of the river Cherwell[x], but this is probably a miftake. The

---

[t] Fiddes L of Wolfey, Collect p 220 Herbert's L of Henry viii, p 299

[u] Not Mon Oxfordfh 1

[x] Not Mon ib n a " St Leonard's hofpital" here mentioned, and confounded with St John's, ftood, I fuppofe, where

ſtreet leading to Oxford is called St. John's
ſtreet, and a large building, now uſed as a
barn, lying eaſt and weſt, on the brow of
the hill, is ſtill called St. John's chapel.
From the identity of names thus preſerved
and appropriated, though the ſtructure in
queſtion has no marks which determine it to
be a religious edifice defecrated, there can
be little doubt, that St John's hoſpital, the
aſylum of leproſy and diſeaſe, ſtood on this
ſalubrious eminence, without the ancient
bars of the town The maſterſhip, which
has long been a finecure, is in the gift of the
biſhop of Lincoln.

To **Thomas Smyth** of Cheſter, merchant,
he bequeathes certain ſums, due to him upon
bonds in the cuſtody of the ſaid legatee,
and alſo four hundred marks, which Sir John
Warburton of Cheſhire, knight, will be re-
ſponſible for to the teſtator and his aſſigns,
agreeably to the tenor of indentures made
for that purpoſe, on account of the marriage
of Elizabeth Winnington, daughter and heir-
eſs of Richard Winnington, eſquire, if ſhe
ſhould attain to the age of twenty one.

the "Spical houſe is (as the name intimates) adjoining the
turnpike, in the county of Northampton.

Theſe

Thefe fums were to be diftributed, at the difcretion of the legatee, among the Bifhop's poor relations of both fexes.

It appears, that Elizabeth Winnington was married to Peter Warburton, eldeft fon of the faid Sir John Warburton, 2 Henry viii, three years before the date of Smyth's will[y]. The pecuniary obligation, a perquifite to the Bifhop for the marriage of the heirefs, his ward, was probably contracted on that occafion Richard Winnington, the grandfather[z] of this lady, married Jane, daughter of Gilbert Smyth of Cuerdley, one of the Bi-

[y] Chefh Ped of Winnington

[z] Or her father, according to Ped 3 which feems more probable, otherwife the Bifhop muft have lived to fee his great great niece married However marriages, efpecially with heiretfes, were often contracted very early The Countefs of Richmond, being much folicited in marriage, gave anfwer "determynately' when fhe " was not fully nine years old" Fifh Fun Serm p 8 And Elizabeth daughter of John Fitton of Gofworth, Chefhire, was married to Thomas Davenport of Henbury on the feaft of St Aldin, May 25, 8 H viii, being only nine years of age Chefh Ped of Fitton and Davenport This Jane Winnington, daughter of Gilbert Smyth, had to her fecond hufband Philip Egerton of Egerton, and from that match the Egertons of Olton, Chefhire, are defcended, who confequently are of kin to Bp Smyth Ped of Winnington and Ped of Egerton, as above, p 7 and Suppl to Collins's Peer p 391

fhop's

fhop's brothers; and it was partly, no doubt,
owing to this affinity between the houfes of
Winnington and Smyth, that the Bifhop was
appointed by his great nephew guardian to
his two infant daughters, for there was a
younger, named Catharine, who died without iffue, 22 Henry viii.   From this match
the Warburtons, baronets, of Arley in Chefhire, are defcended; who confequently, as
before noted[a], are of kin to the Founder of
Brafen Nofe   Jane Warburton, daughter of
Sir Peter Warburton by his wife above mentioned, married Sir Laurence Smyth[b], probably the eldeft branch of the Cuerdley family, and thus the connection of the houfes
was renewed.   With regard to the right, implied in the preceding contract, whereby the
guardian had not only the power of difpofing
of his ward in marriage, but alfo of demand-
ing a valuable confideration for his confent.
it continued in force till the Reftoration[c],
when, with many other circumftances of oppreffion in our ancient tenures, it was totally
abolifhed.

[a] P 6
[b] Married 1 to Sir Will Brereton of Brereton, Kn 2 to
Sir Laurence Smyth, Kn   Pedd. of Warburton and of Brereton
[c] 12 Car 11   Blackftone, 11 p 70 76, 77 ed 4to.

But

But to return, and finifh the will He
appoints William Smyth, archdeacon of Lincoln, Gilbert Smyth, archdeacon of Northampton, (two of his nephews,) Henry Wilcocks[d], LL. D Robert Toneys[e], LL. B. ca-

[d] Henry Wilcocks, LL D was Moderator of the civil law
School as Deputy for Warham Mafter of the Rolls, Aug 4,
1501 D f. 98 b He was prefented to Hafeley (Com Oxon)
by the Dean and canons of Windfor, Aug 12, 1504 MS
Harl 6953 p 47 and to the vicarage of Eynfham in the
fame county by the Convent of that place, Jan 7, 1505 ibid.
p 49 Smyth gave him the prebend Sexaginta Solidorum,
June 14, 1505 ib p 22 the preb of Dunham, 1507. Willis,
Cath ii p 179 preb of Welton Ryval, May 21, fame year
MS Harl ibid preb Lidington, 18 Dec following Act Cap
Linc f 1 b preb Cropredy, Aug 26, 1508 MS Harl ibid.
p 23. He was inftalled by proxy, Sept 7 Act Cap f 25
He occurs as the Bifhop's Chancellor in 1510 Reg Linc in
the ordinations, and Yate, p 64 and often as Vicar general
Reg Linc f 233, &c ordinations, 1508 One John Wilcocks " S T P in univerfitate Cantaronenfi," or " Tanta-
ronenfi," was incorporated at Oxford, Dec 7, 1508 Reg G
f 66 but what univerfity that is, I am as much to feek as
Wood was before me Ath Oxon. 1 F 14 Smyth collated
the faid John (having perhaps patronifed him in his ftudies
abroad) to the living of Cranford, Sept 28, 1510 MS Harl
ibid p 33

[e] Robert Toneys B of Decrees, who occurs as a notary at
Smyth's vifitation of his cathedral in 1501, was afterwards
collated by him to three fucceffive ftalls, to Welton Brinkhall,
Mar 24, 1501-2 MS Harl 6953 p 156 to Clifton, Aug
31, 1504 ibid p 21 to Langford manor, May 8, 1505 ibid
p 22 In 1507, Mar 26, the Bifhop appointed him his fcribe
(or fteward) of Lincoln, which was confirmed by the Chap-

non of Lincoln, Thomas Smyth of Chefter,
merchant, and Robert Browne[f] of Newark,
his executors; and leaves to them the re-
fidue of his goods, to be difpofed of by them
in works of piety and charity, for the welfare of his foul. The will was proved January 30, 1513-14, and, as is fuppofed, by
all the executors; but on the 10th of March,
1540-1, Gilbert Smyth, for no reafon that
now appears, renounced in form by his proxy
the office of executor[g].

His body wrapped in cerecloth, with a
ring on his right hand, was decently depofited in a ftone coffin[h], and interred, as al-

.

ter the next day. Act. Cap f 136 He was afterwards counfellor to cardinal Wolfey, and honoured with the correfpondence of Erafmus, to whom he was warmly recommended by
Sir Thomas More Erafmus fpeaks highly of his benevolence
and his learning . " Quæ res eruditiffimi viri Roberti Tonefii
tam non vulgarem benevolentiam conciliavit?" Knight's Erafm
p. 47 Willis by miftake calls him Tovies Cath ii p 168
259 &c The name is not common John Tonneys, an Auf-
tin friar of Norwich, Provincial of his order, is a writer mentioned by Bale, f 209 b and by Pits, p 676 He died in
London about 1490

   [f] Rob Browne of Newark is ftyled Receiver general to the
Bifhop in a transfer of Baffets fee, Sept 1, 1510 Yate, p 64

   [g] Prerog Off vol Fettyplace, 29

   [h] Willis, Cath ii p 59 It is noted as one of the lateft inftances

ready mentioned, in the nave of the cathedral[1], but on what day, and with what mournful folemnity, does not particularly appear. No tomb was erected over him, but a marble gravestone richly adorned with brass, of which we have an account in the words of Sir William Dugdale, who luckily saw and described it on the 10th of September, 1641, "but the instant," as lord Orford observes, "before it became piety to commit devastation[k]."

"In the middle of Lincoln minster, neere to the west dore, was a very large marble, and thereon the portraiture in brasse of a bishop, vested for the altar, in a rich cope, and mitred; his right hand holding up, as in benediction, and in his left a crosier. On this great plate of brasse (which almost covered the whole stone) were the figures of the twelve apostles (as it should seem) six on a side[l].—At each corner of the stone was

stances of the use of a stone coffin Gough's Sep Mo vol ii p lvi

[i] See p 345

[k] Anecd of Painting, vol i p 61 3d ed

[l] The epitaph, here introduced, will be given presently Peck has it, but inaccurately, Desid Cur ii p 305 and Wil-

an efcutcheon of armes in braffe graven. The firft was defaced: the fecond was a falter betwixt four flower de luces[m]: the third a cheveron betwixt three rofes: and the fourth the arms of the bifhoprick of Coventry and Lichfield. I fuppofe that the firft was the armes of the bifhoprick of Lincoln[n]." Dr. Stukeley, in his Itinerarium Curiofum, Table xvi, has a plate of this gravestone from an exact draught of it taken by Sir William Dugdale at the fame time.

Dr. Yate, a name never to be mentioned without gratitude by any member of Brafen Nofe college, had formed a defign to reftore this monument; but increafing infirmity, it is prefumed, delayed, and his death, which happened a few years afterwards[o], finally pre-

---

lis, Cath ii p 59 where what follows of bequefts to "Queen s and Allfoul s colleges is a total miftake

[m] A falter Ermine, between four fleurs de lis Or, is on Bp Longland's tomb, and is commonly fuppofed to have been his arms; but Mr Gough, obferving the fame among the badges of Bp Ruffell s chapel, thought them "falfely afcribed to Longland." Sep Mon ii p 324 It feems to have been a favourite coat with the bifhops of this fee, but who firft bore it and ftampt it with credit, I am yet to learn. Longland s arms are totally different in Wood's Colleges, p 195 324 and in Willis, Cath ii. p 16

[n] Inclofed in a letter, of which fee an extract, App No xx

[o] Thomas Yate, D D died April 22, 1681, in the 79th

vented, the execution of what he pioufly intended. It was referved therefore for another Principal, the Rev. Ralph Cawley[P], D. D. a perfon dear to all who knew him, to pay that tribute of refpect to the memory of Smyth, which his meritorious predeceffor

year of his age The book fo often cited by his name, an Abftract of the Evidences and Charters of the College, is a work of infinite labour, executed with moft exact fidelity and judgement He was born in Chefhire, was ejected by the rebels from his Headfhip in 1648, as he had been two years before from the rectory of Middleton Cheney, "which was the more to be lamented (fays the hiftorian) becaufe he had prepared ftone, timber, &c to build a parfonage houfe there, but his fucceffor [John Cave] with a meannefs of fpirit peculiar to the party, fold them, and contented himfelf with fitting up an old malt-houfe" Walker's Suffer of Clergy, P ii p 101 He was reftored to his preferments, when others were, in 1660, and by his univerfal merits, both as Head of the college and as a Benefactor to the fociety, juftly intitled himfelf to the character on his monument in the college cloifters: " Collegii pater et patronus, Et tertius tantum non Fundator " See the whole in Wood, Colleges, p 376 He gave to the fociety a meffuage called Willoughby Houfe, now Yate's court, in the parifh of St Clement Danes, London, and the advowfon of Middleton Cheney in Northamptonfhire

P Dr Cawley died, Aug 31, 1777, aged 57; and was buried in the antechapel of Brafen Nofe college He gave the eaft window in the chapel, painted by Pearfon with figures of our Saviour and the four Evangelifts, whole length, from defigns of Mortimer See Wood's Colleges, p 366 374, 375 App 275 And bequeathed his books to the fociety for the ufe of fucceeding Principals

medi-

meditated. The original graveftone, then remaining, but fince removed with others when the cathedral was new-paved, he caufed to be thus infcribed, agreeably to what Sir William Dugdale had fuggefted to Dr. Yate[a]:

"Ds. Ds W. Smyth, Epifcopus, ob Jan. 2do 1513^{tio},
Si plura velis, Lector, adi vicinum marmor "

The mural monument, to which this refers, of white marble, near the great weft door, has this infcription, with the Bifhop's arms above, impaling the fee of Lincoln:

Epifcopi quondam Lincolnienfis pientiffimi,

Primi Walliæ Præfidis,

Academiæ Oxon Cancellarii,

Necnon collegii Ænei Nafi ibidem Fundatoris primi et præcipui,

Quicquid infra cœlum fupereft juxta hic conditur.

Cujus quidem memoriam effigiem et infignia

Pofteris olim quantum potuit prodidit ænea lamina,

Tabulæ marmoreæ perquam eleganti et magnificæ affixa,

Hanc tamen laminam tabulamque facram,

Prope oftium occidentale primitus locatas,

Et in priftino pene ftatu anno 1641mo adhuc remanentes,

Cromwelli flagitiofus grex paulo poft rerum potiens diripuit,

Lucroque fuo avide et fcelerate appofuit.

[a] See App No xx

En

En tamen veteres ipfiffimafque infcriptiones
A Willielmo Dugdale Armigero (poftea Equite aurato)
Deque antiquariis præclare merito, feliciter affervatas ·
Et Dᵒ. Thomæ Yate S. T P.
Collegii Ænei Nafi Princ. anno 1668ᵛᵒ. demandatas.

Ad effigiei caput fe dedit hæc infcriptioʳ:
Sub marmore ifto tenet hic Tumulus offa
Venerabilis in Chrifto Patris et Domni Domini Willielmi
Smyth
quondamCoventrienfis et Lichfieldienfis etᵃdeinde Lincolnienfis Prefulis qui obiit fecundo die menfis Januarii Anno
Domini millefimo quingentefimo decimo tertio cujus animæ
propitietur Deus.   Qui pius et mifericors, et in die
tribulationis
mifericors peccata remittit.   Ecclefiaftici 2. 11.

Ad pedes vero hæc
Ceftrenfis Preful poft Lincolnienfis, amator
Cleri, nam multos cis mare tranfque aluit:
Quique utriufque fuit Præfectus Principis Aulæᵗ,
Fundavitque duas perpetuando Scolas.
Aulaque fumptu hujus renovata eft Enea   Crifte
Hic fitus eft, animæ parce benigne fuæ.

ʳ The profe epitaph was on the verge of the ftone, circumfcribed,
beginning at the head.   The firft line ended with "offa,' the fecond
with "Lincolnienfis," the third with "Januarii, ' and the fourth with
"Ecclefiaftici iiᵈᵒ " The verfe (11) is a modern addition, referring
to the Englifh apocrypha, in the Vulgate it is verfe 13.
    In Dugdale &c "ac "
ᵗ Prefident of the Council to prince Arthur and prince Henry

Ut tanta nunc iterum de Tanto Homine hic loci pateant
marmoream quam fpectas Tabulam proprio fumptu
fubftituendam curavit
Radulphus Cawley S. T P. præfati Collegii Princ.
A. D. 1775to.

It was a rare inftance of felicity and dif-
cernment in Smyth, that, among thofe whom
he patronifed and preferred, he numbered fo
many perfons who rofe to the higheft honours of their country in church and ftate.
Atwater bifhop of Lincoln, Mayow and
Boothe bifhops of Hereford, Fort bifhop of
Achonry in Ireland, Bainbridge[u] and Lee[x]
archbifhops of York, the former a Cardinal,
the latter famous for his controverfy with
Erafmus, and more juftly efteemed for granting a penfion to Afcham[y], Oldham bifhop of
Exeter, Ruthall[z] bifhop of Durham, fecre-

[u] Moft of thefe prelates have been mentioned above Chriftopher Bainbridge, Provoft of Queen's college, Oxford, was
collated by Smyth to the prebend of North Kelfey Feb 26,
1495-6 MS Harl 6954 p 154   See Willis, Cath 1 p 42
Athen Oxon 1 p 651

[x] Edward Lee, fellow of Magdalen college, Oxford, was
collated by Smyth to the prebend of Welton Beckhall, Oct 30,
1512 MS Harl 6953 p 26 See of him Athen. Oxon 1
p. 62 and Tanners Biblioth

[y] See Afcham s Epift ed Oxon, L 11 Ep xvii

[z] Prebendary of Leighton Bofard, Jan 19, 1504-5 MS
Harl. 6953 p 21 on the confecration of Oldham bifhop of
Exeter,

tary of ſtate, and lord privy Seal ; Sherborn
biſhop of Chicheſter, Warham archbiſhop of
Canterbury, lord Chancellor of England, and
Wolſey the idol and the terror of Europe ;
all theſe illuſtrious perſonages owed ſome
of their early preferment to the venerable
Founder of Braſen Noſe college : in general
they adorned the exalted ſtations, which they
afterwards filled, with their virtues and their
talents, though ſome few, as might be expected in ſo large a number, were not equal
to the elevation which in humbler life they
ſeemed to merit, and became by their miſ-
conduct the warning and ſcorn of poſterity.
But—durat opus vatum—the chief honour
of a patron ariſes from the authors whom he
encourages and rewards : nor is the praiſe of
the Biſhop of Lincoln, thinly as the age was
ſtrewed with learning, here deficient. Of the

Exeter, who was collated to this ſtall by Smyth in 1497 Willis, ii 205 and to the Deanery of St John's Cheſter, Feb 13,
1492-3 Reg Lichf f 157 See of him Athen Oxon i 657.
and of Ruthall, ib p 661 and Tanner s Biblioth Eraſmus
dedicated Lucian s Timon, and his Paraphraſe on Galatians to
Ruthall. See Knight s Eraſm. p 149—154 and Jortin s
Eraſm i 24 Ruthall and Oldham ſtudied both at Oxford and
at Cambridge Of Sherborn ſee above, p 27 There is a
view of Leythorn houſe, Suſſex, built by him, in Gent Mag.
1799 p 1097

prelates

prelates already named feveral were writers, and to thefe muft be added the names of others diftinguifhed more by their abilities than their rank. Bernard Andree of Touloufe, preceptor in grammar to prince Arthur, laureat and hiftoriographer to Henry vii and Henry viii, was collated by Smyth to St. Leonard's hofpital in Bedford[a], on the confecration of Fitzjames bifhop of Rochefter, the late mafter. Of Andree's poetical and hiftorical pieces fome not inelegant fpecimens are extant. I know not whether John Argentine M D. phyfician to prince Arthur and dean of the chapel royal, who was collated by Smyth to a prebend at Lichfield[b], wrote any thing now remaining, except his famous performance at Cambridge in the year 1470, when he challenged the whole body of regents in that Univerfity[c]. Dr. At-

---

[a] April 4, 1498 MS Harl 6953 p 61 See Tanner's Biblioth and Knight s L of Erafm p 26 118. Mr Warton (I know not why) calls him Andrew Bernard Hift Poet ii p 132 As fome atonement for the " wretched falfe quantity ' (if the reading is correct) quoted there p 133 n x fee an elegant hexaftich by Andree in Ames's Typogr ed Herb p 202.

[b] Preb of Dernford, Nov 12, 1494 Reg Lichf f 146

[c] Wood, Annals ii p 56 Tanner in Biblioth fays it is in tne library of Corpus Chrifti college, Oxford

kinfon and Dr. Hornby, both of Pembroke
hall, Cambridge, and Powel and Brinknell[d],
educated at Oxford, enjoyed preferment each
of them from the difcriminating generofity
of Smyth; and all of them gained applaufe
by their theological writings, chiefly in defence of popery againft Luther and his fol-
lowers. But the moft brilliant talents cannot give perpetuity to error. The ingenuity
and erudition, which would have adorned the
caufe of their antagonifts and have lived in
the immortality of truth, withered in the increafing effulgence of day; and their works,
framed of perifhable materials, experienced
the mortality of the caufe they defended.
Polydore Vergil, a learned Italian, a dignitary
of Lincoln through Smyth's kindnefs, wrote
in a good ftyle the firft regular hiftory which
we have of England, and was the author of
feveral other works, which were tranflated
and read with great avidity throughout Europe, when they firft appeared, and are ftill

---

[d] Thomas Brinknell S T P collated to the prebend of
Marfton St. Laurence, Jan 7, 1510-11 MS Harl 6953
p 25 and to the hofpital of St John's, Banbury, the fame
day ib p 54 on the death of John Stanbridge M A alfo collated by Smyth, Apr 22, 1501 ib 42 Brinknell was of Lincoln college His book againft Luther is commended in Reg
F F Ep 89 Willis calls him Brinkhall Cath ii 215

attended

attended with juft fame. I will clofe the
lift with Chriftopher Urfewyke, collated fucceffively by Smyth to two archdeaconries and
a prebend of Lincoln[e], who, if he wrote
nothing which is known to remain, was the
friend and patron of literature and of Erafmus, was eleven times an ambaffador at foreign courts; refufed the bifhopric of Norwich, refigned preferment as freely as others
feek it, and died in 1521, full of years and
of honour, in religious retirement at Hack-
ney.

Quick to difcover and ftudious to cherifh
the latent feeds of excellence, embellifhing
his ftately cathedral by his munificence, and
filling it with the train of virtue and fcience,
it is no wonder that Smyth was loved and
revered by his clergy; and that, wedded as
they were to ceremonies and tenacious of
their own dignity and privileges, we fee them

[e] Archd of Huntingdon, Mar 5, 1495-6 MS Harl
6934 p 155 prebendary of Milton ecclefia, June 14, 1501
ib 6953 p 20 archd of Oxford, Nov 15, 1504 ib p 21
See a view of his beautiful tomb in Knight's L of Erafm
p 78 his epitaph ib and in Jortin's Erafm 1 p 48 and Willis, 11 p 118 See more of him in Athen Oxon 1 p 12
641 652 Tanners Biblioth and Gent Mag 1796 p 275
468 2 and 1798 p 327 2

breaking

breaking through common forms and ancient
precedents in their defire to pay him uncommon honour Indeed the teftimony to
his attainments and worth was univerfal The
wifdom of Bray, the penetration of Henry vii,
and the piety of that mirror of her age, the
Countefs of Richmond, found an early friend
and counfellor in Smyth: they confided to
his integrity matters of high importance;
they placed him in ftations elevated and arduous; and their efteem and affection for
him ceafed only with their life

In the character of diocefan he appears
intitled to particular commendation. Plu-
ralities, the difgrace of the age, though in
fome degree excufable from the real paucity
of learned men, had no countenance from
his example. Refiding punctually in his province, and feldom long abfent, even when
the civil department which he filled, frequently demanded his prefence and attention, he was ftrict in enforcing parochial refidence, and in providing for the due celebration of divine offices. Careful alfo to in-
ftitute competent paftors, folicitous at once
to maintain the peace of the church and the
rights of his fee, watchful over the monafteries, jealous of papal encroachments, di-
ligent

ligent in his visitations, and dignified in his
censures, he stands eminently conspicuous
among the prelates of his own age, a model
not unworthy of the best times which have
ensued.

Of private habits and peculiar strokes of
character, discoverable in the free and undis-
guised correspondence of friends and in the
freer moments of social intercourse, the transf-
actions of public life and the materials of
general history seldom afford opportunity to
judge. Smyth is praised by his contemporaries for his wisdom in counsel, and dexterity in business, for the piety of his life,
and mildness of his manners, qualities, which
he found or transfused into the virtuous prince
Arthur. Of his epistolary correspondence we
have only one specimen which approaches to
the confidential frankness of a letter to a
friend; and in that, through the veil of its
antiquated language, we readily discern that
humanity, which is always valuable, and that
good sense, which is always the same.

But ideal perfection is an ideal monster,
and the account which we have of the great
Alfred has been deemed unnatural, because
history, in transmitting her finished portrait

of

of that renowned monarch, prefents us with a piece of faultlefs excellence. The character of Smyth is fo far natural, that it is not exempt from imperfection, the infeparable attribute of man. Trained from his infancy in the doctrines and forms of an intolerant religion, when he was conftituted a governour and guardian of the church, he perfecuted thofe, whom that church pronounced heretics: though even here he could hardly efcape the fplendid infirmity of being "overcome by his native goodnefs[f]," and of acting better than his principles would allow. For while he fentenced fome, who were convened before him, to prifon or the ftake, he difmiffed others without punifhment or cenfure, bidding them go home, and adorn pure religion by an anfwerable life.

His faults were few in number and tranfient in their effect, the vices of the age and of the church, rather than of the man. His virtues were various and folid, public and lafting Afcribing his rife and fuccefs in the world, not to perfonal defert, of which he does not boaft, not to high birth, to which he makes no pretenfions, but folely to the

[f] Cic de Off L 1 c 1

liberal

liberal hand of Providence, " THE LORD IS
MY EXALTATION[g]," he employed the affluence, which Heaven beftowed, in thofe
works of mercy, which Heaven loves.   His
bounty was fo difinterefted and large, that he
retained others befides the immediate members of his houfhold to difpenfe his favours;
and many had caufe to blefs his beneficence,
to whom his perfon was unknown   He ca-
reffed merit wherever he found it, extending
his patronage with equal alacrity to diftinguifhed individuals of either Univerfity.   His
love of letters was fo ardent, that he en-
couraged and enabled men of genius to cultivate the liberal arts in foreign feminaries, as
well as at home.   To the joint fervice of literature and religion, to hoary age and hope-
ful youth, his permanent munificence and
occafional donations were alike devoted: his
inftitutions, like the works of a great mafter,
live and flourifh; and grateful pofterity, in
juftice to his merit, affigns him an eminent
place among the benefactors of his country
and of mankind.

<hr />

[g] His motto   See p 92.

POSTSCRIPT.

POSTSCRIPT.

KINSMEN

of

BISHOP SMYTH.

SEVERAL of bifhop Smyth's kinfmen have been incidentally mentioned in the foregoing pages. A more diftinct account of them, which, in the courfe of the narrative, would have caufed too great a deviation from our main object, feems to be neceffary before we conclude our inquiries I will therefore, in this Poftfcript, bring together the moft material circumftances, which I have been able to collect, of the Bifhop's kinfmen living in his days and preferred by him, without apologizing for the repetition, if fome

few

few of the particulars happen to have occurred feparately before.

We begin with one who is beft known
and moft diftinguifhed: WILLIAM SMYTH
ARCHDEACON OF LINCOLN exprefsly calls
himfelf " the Coufin (that is, Nephew[a]) and
Heir of William Smyth late bifhop of Lincoln[b] " The pedigree drawn up by Penfon,
Lancafter herald in the time of James the
firft, makes him the eldeft fon of Richard
Smyth, the Bifhop's eldeft brother[c]. The
two accounts therefore illuftrate and confirm
each other. We have no certain account of
the archdeacon in the diocefe of Lichfield,
unlefs he is the William Smyth, who was
repeatedly Mafter of St John's hofpital in
Lichfield, while the Bifhop was rebuilding
and re-endowing that ancient foundation[d]

[a] " My *nephew* John Sutton—and my *cofen* his wife " Sir
Richard Sutton's will   Matthew Smyth conftitutes his " *ne
phew* Will Smyth' one of his executors, and he is ftyled " *ne-
pos* defuncti, and calls himfelf " *confanguineus* et hæres" of the
teftator Yate, p 162.

[b] Archiv Univerfit Oxon K 2 18 " confanguineus et
heres and he fubfcribes " per me Will Smyth archid Lincoln " dat Nov 27, 14 H viii (1522)

[c] App Ped 2

[d] See the lift of Mafters, App No iv.

Smyth

Smyth had been tranflated to Lincoln
fome time, and had conferred much of his
ample patronage upon others, before he promoted his own relations. When they were
of proper age, or when he thought good to
bring them forward, this his eldeft nephew
received the firft token of his favour He
collated him to the archdeaconry of Northampton, January 4, 1499-1500, at which
time he is ftyled LL B.[e] He was inftalled
by proxy on the firft of February following[f].
He was with the Bifhop at Lidington on the
26th of the faid month of January, a witnefs
to the deed whereby the rectory of Swinfhead
in Lincolnfhire was appropriated to Weftminfter abbey[g]. Shortly afterwards, it is
prefumed, with the Bifhop's advice he left
the kingdom, to polifh his ftyle and complete his ftudies in fome foreign univerfity.
For in 1501, at the memorable vifitation of
the cathedral, it was alleged in behalf of the
archdeacon of Northampton, that he had the
Bifhop's leave of abfence, and was profecut-
ing his ftudies in parts beyond the fea[h]. He

[e] MS Harl 6953 p 19
[f] Ib 6954 p 155
[g] Reg Linc f 19—36
[h] See above, p 118

returned

returned from abroad in 1505 or before, if, as I apprehend, he was the William Smyth, who, on the 24th of June in that year, was installed in the prebend of Clifton[i], in which he was succeeded, about 1506 or 1507, by John Fotehead[k]. In 1506 he resigned the archdeaconry of Northampton[l], and was installed archdeacon of Lincoln and prebendary of Lowth on the 21st of August in that year[m]. In the ensuing year he appears as proxy for his friends and fellow dignitaries, Edward Darby and Henry Wilcocks; who were installed, the former prebendary of Ketton and archdeacon of Stow[n], the latter successively prebendary of Lidington and Cropredy[o], in the person of the archdeacon of Lincoln. He now vacated Lowth, in which he was succeeded by John Cutler treasurer of Lincoln, and was collated to the prebend of Sutton cum Buckingham, which Willis

---

Willis, Cath ii 168

[k] Ib Willis calls him Forehead, but see MS Harl. 6953 p 25

[l] Willis, Cath ii 112

[m] Act Capit Linc f 119 b

[n] Preb Keton, 18 Dec 1507 Act Capit f 1 b Archd Stow, 12 Feb ib f 5

[o] Preb Lidington, 18 Dec 1507 ib f 1 b Preb de Cropery, 7 o pt 1508 ib f 23

says,

says, " was the best endowed in the whole cathedral, and would (if now in being) have the largest corps of any prebend in England, for it consists of the great tythes and impropriation of King's Sutton, Co. Northampton, with its members or antient chapelries, viz. the county town of Buckingham, with Horley and Hornton, two parishes (as they are now called) Co Oxon," and the right of presenting to the said four churches. It was valued in 1534, after all deductions, at 110l 3s 6d[p] He is styled at this time, February 18, 1507-8, Doctor of Laws[q], to which degree I suppose he had been admitted abroad.

The Chapter of Lincoln possessed the or-

---

[p] Willis, Cath ii 245

[q] " Utriusque juris Doctor (i e of civil and canon law) MS Harl 6953 p 23 and Reg Linc i 243. b He is therefore, apparently, not the William Smyth " decretorum Doctor in alia universitate ' who was incorporated at Oxford, June 28, 1506, and excused residence, because he was " commissary of the Bishop of Lincoln " Reg G f 21 But then the same Harl MS p 84 calls the said W Smyth prebendary of Kings Sutton simply " Decretorum Doctor" (i e Dr of canon law only) which is " confusion worse confounded One " Mr William Smyth" was admitted ad eundem at Cambridge in 1504 from Ferrara, but his degree is not mentioned Reg Univ Contab Gamma, f 23 b

dinary

dinary jurifdiction of fome of the parochial churches within the city of Lincoln, which they commonly vifited by the Præpofitus. Towards the end of the year 1507 they appointed the archdeacon of Lincoln and Richard Rofton, the Præpofitus of the year, to vifit two of thefe parifhes, St. Mary Magdalen and St. Margaret's within the Clofe[r]; and the following autumn, when they had audited their accounts, they elected the Archdeacon Præpofitus for the year enfuing[s]. Humphry Smyth, collated to the prebend of Bigglefwade, was inducted by his proxy the archdeacon of Lincoln, January 23, 1508-9[t], and as he was afterwards promoted fucceffively to the prebend of Marfton St Laurence and Welton Beckhall[u], it is likely he

[r] Act Capit f 9 Richard Rofton Decr Doct had been Commiffary general to Smyth, when he was bifhop of Lichfield Reg Lich f 159 b He is fometimes called Roifton alias Smyh He was inftalled in the prebend Centum Solidorum by proxy, July 13, 1499 MS Harl 6954 p 156 and perfonally, March 21, 1501–2 ibid and collated to Carleton cum Tnurlby, March 28, 1502 ib 6953 p 19

[s] Act Capit f 25

[t] Ib f 43 But there feems to be fome miftake, for MS Harl 6953 v 24 and Willis, p 146 fay Matthew Smyth was collated to Bigglefwade, Jan 16, 1508, on the death of William Smyth, and he, Matthew, quitted it for Banbury, Dec 2, 1512 Willis, io and MS Harl ib 26

[u] Preb Marfton, Dec 31, 1509 MS. Harl 6953 p 25
Welton

was of the Bishop's kindred, though he does not occur in any of the genealogies.

He was now commonly associated with the Bishop in his transactions. Basset's fee, part of the intended endowment of Brasen Nose, was conveyed to him and others[x]; and the conveyance of Chalgrove to Lincoln college bears his hand and seal[y], a small elegant cipher with the initials of his name; the same with which he sealed the statutes of Brasen Nose college, and the surrender of certain estates in Marlow and the neighbourhood to Sir Edmund Bray in 1522[z], both which are also distinguished by his signature.

In the first year of Henry viii a convo-

Welton Beckhall, June 26, 1512 ib 26 which he resigned on or before October 30, when he was succeeded by Lee afterwards Archbishop of York ib.

[x] Yate, p 64

[y] See above, p 240

[z] Univ Arch K. 2 18 The cipher is formed like that in the miscellaneous plate (which is one reason why I caused it to be engraved) but without the crosier. This episcopal cipher, on a small lozenge of glass, I picked up at Royston in Hertfordshire, whither it had perhaps wandered from some parochial church or episcopal palace, where it was an intended memorial of bishop Smyth

cation

cation was fummoned to be holden in St.
Paul's cathedral on the 26th of January,
1509-10, on which occafion Henry Wilcocks, the Bifhop's vicar general, and the
archdeacon of Lincoln were unanimoufly
chofen to attend as proxies and reprefen-
tatives for the clergy of the diocefe, to receive for their expences a halfpenny out of
every mark that fhould be raifed as a tax by
the clergy, and, if the convocation fhould
continue to fit after Eafter, three farthings
for every enfuing term while they fhould be
affembled[a]. There are no acts or regifters of
this convocation remaining and it has even
been doubted whether the convocation did
meet at this time, but it fhould feem from
his Majefty's writ of fummons to the Bifhop
of Lincoln, and from the confequent proceedings of the clergy, as here mentioned,
all which are recorded at large in the epifcopal regifter. that the doubt is ground-
lefs In 1510 he prefented a perfon named
Richard Smith to the vicarage of Buckingham[b], who was perhaps his coufin german[c];
but Richard Smyth occurs fo often and with-

---

[a] Reg Linc f 243—244 b MS Harl 6953 p 75
[b] Willis s Hift of Buckingham, p 8
[c] Iration of Gilbert Smith, the Bifhops brother Ped 2

out

out any certain marks of identity, that it is difficult to discover even a probable way through the labyrinth of names. On the said Smyth's death, whoever he was, the archdeacon gave the vicarage to Thomas Caufe or Cawce, November 14, 1511, who has been mentioned in the preceding memoirs[d] as steward of the Bishop of Lincoln's houshold, prebendary of Lincoln, and rector of Hinton about ten miles from Buckingham, and on the death of Caufe, he prefented George Heyworth[e], who furvived his patron.

His ample preferment, though I do not find that he held any living with his dignities, enabled him after fome years to purchafe a confiderable estate in Lincolnfhire, the manor of Sutton, with lands in Skegnefs, Winthorp, and Burgh, on the eaftern coaft of the county[f] The eftate was fold for the fum of 360l by John Newdigate ferjeant at law, of Lincoln's Inn, of which honourable fociety for his learning and merits he was repeatedly chofen Reader and Governour, and had the honour to be King's

[d] P 206   [e] Willis, ut fupra

[f] Wils p 73 dat 29 Jan 8 H viii (1516-17)

ferjeant

ferjeant in 1521[g]. He married Amphilicia daughter of John Nevill of Sutton, who, being heir to her father, was a party with her hufband in the fale of the eftate, and in fuffering a recovery to fecure the right of the purchafer. John Newdigate died Auguft 16, 1528, leaving iffue, by his faid wife Amphilicia, a fon of his own name, from whom in direct line is defcended Sir Roger Newdigate, baronet, a man of genuine worth, found learning, and claffical tafte, who ferved with high honour and integrity in five parliaments for the Univerfity of Oxford[h], and who is now enjoying ftudious retirement and diffufing charity at Arbury in Warwickfhire.

In one of the conveyances of thefe eftates, before they were finally transferred and fet-

---

[g] Dugd Orig Jurid p 250 252 258 326 Chron Ser 1511 1521 In one of the deeds relating to thefe eftates he is called John Newdigate of Honfield, Middlefex, Gentleman Yate, p 72 The Baronetage of 1741, vol iv p 621 fays he was bred in Gray s Inn, miftaking him, I fuppofe, or Richard Newdigate ferjeant at law in 1660, whole arms were in Gray s Inn Dugd ib p 303

[h] A Wood, Hift and Ant by Gutch, Fafti, p 200, 201 See alfo Anna's, ii p 808 810 948 and add to and correct the Index

tled

tled upon Brafen Nofe college, the Archdeacon engaged to warrant them againft
John [Iflip] abbat of Weftminfter and his
fucceffors', but what right that wealthy convent had or pretended to have to the property is not known There was another
claimant, whofe ingrefs was not fo eafily prevented. The fea, which commonly under-
mines and gains upon a bold and rocky
coaft, and retreats from the more effectual
rampart of fand, rufhed at laft over the bar-
riers which had been raifed on this level
fhore, and recovered his ancient poffeffion ;
fo that, after great expence and labour in
cleanfing dikes and repairing mounds[k], that
part of the eftate, which lay in Skegnefs, has
for two centuries or more been known only
by the defcription of " Terra aqua fub-
merfa."

Thefe Lincolnfhire eftates, though the
moft confiderable, were not the firft benefaction of the Archdeacon to Brafen Nofe
college. He gave in 1524 the fum of 6l.
13s 4d, and perhaps was an annual con-

ˡ Yate, p 74

ᵏ See the Rott Burff 55—58 H. viii.

tributor

tributor to that amount as long as he lived[l]; but it is certain, that he was the donor of plate, which was fold in 1541 (agreeably to his directions, it is prefumed,) for the fum of 14l. to be lent annually to the junior Burfar at the commencement of his office, on condition of being repaid by him at the general audit[m].

In 1525 the Archdeacon, in right of his prebend, prefented William Banefter to the vicarage of King's Sutton in Northamptonfhire[n], and three years afterwards, June 13, 1528, he prefented John Bennet to the vicarage of Earl's Barton in the fame county, by virtue of a grant from the abbey of De la Pre[o], near Northampton, of which houfe, it is believed, his coufin Emma Smyth was at this time abbefs[p]   This was one of the laft acts of his life, for nine days afterwards, according to Willis, both his ftalls, vacant by his death, were conferred on Richard Pates,

[l] Rot Burff 16 H viii —19 H viii   It is not clear whether it was an annual donation, or the fame fpecific fum annually audited

[m] Plate Book p 8

[n] May 20 Bridges' Northampt i p 179

[o] Ibid ii p 139

[p] See App Ped 2

who

who in 1555 became bishop of Worcester[q].
Willis thinks archdeacon Smyth " was buried
at Bucks," though the gravestone, which he
assigns him, was before his time " robbed of
its brasses." He gave a superb cope of green
cloth of gold, adorned with the Salutation of
the virgin Mary, to Lincoln cathedral, which
remained there in 1557[r]

Another archdeacon of both his names
next claims our attention, WILLIAM SMYTH
LL B ARCHDEACON OF STOW, eldest son
of Gilbert Smyth, one of the Bishop's brothers[s]. Of him but little is known, for we
lose him almost as soon as he is admitted to
our acquaintance. He was installed archdeacon of Stow, November 24, 1506[t], and
on the 20th of April, 1508, the chapter,
with the approbation of the Bishop, decreed
that a person or persons might administer to
the goods and chattels of William Smyth
late archdeacon of Stow and canon residen-
tiary deceased[u], whence it should seem that

[q] Cath ii p 103 247
[r] Dugd Mon iii p 285 2 297
[s] App Ped 2
[t] In utroque jure Bac Act Capit Linc 1501—1507 f.
127 b Mss Harl 6974
[u] Act Capit 150; i ii b

he

he died inteſtate. In the mean time, December 14, 1507, Edward Darby was collated to the archdeaconry of Stow and to the prebend of Ketton, both void by the death of William Smyth[x]. Darby was inſtalled in the ſaid prebend on the 18th of December[y], and in the archdeaconry on the 12th of February following[z]; William Smyth archdeacon of Lincoln being his proxy both times. In truth the cathedral was at this time ſo peopled with perſons of the name of William Smyth, whether kinſmen of the Biſhop or not, that it is almoſt impoſſible to eſcape miſtakes in arranging them; though it is not very difficult to correct ſome miſtakes, into which others have fallen. It appears by the chapter records, that William Smyth was inſtalled in the prebend of Bigglefwade, February 12, 1507-8, by his proxy Mr. Roſton[a]; and that William Smyth M A. was perſonally inſtalled in the ſaid prebend of Bigglefwade, September 26, 1508[b] A double inſtalment, firſt by proxy and then in

---

[x] MS Harl 6953 p 22.

[y] Act Capit 1507 f. 1. b

[z] Ibid f 4 b

[a] Act Capit 1507 f. 4. b.

[b] Ibid f 25

perſon,

perfon, was not unufual[c], this therefore, as far as yet appears, might be one and the fame perfon; but who he was I prefume not to guefs, further than it was not the archdeacon of Stow, for he, as we have feen, died before the 14th of December, 1507; and confequently, if, as is nearly certain, the faid archdeacon was alfo prebendary of Ketton, it is not true, as Willis ftates[d], that the prebendary of Ketton exchanged it for Bigglefwade, fince he vacated it by death.

Let us now attend to other authority. William Smith M. A. was collated to Bigglefwade February 20, 1507-8, void by the death of Edmund Crofton (not Edward Crofton, as Willis has it[e]) on condition of paying Stephen Berworth, late prebendary thereof, an annual penfion of 24l[f]. This collation was eight days after one William Smyth had been inftalled in this prebend, and is not inconfiftent with the former account, if the perfon now collated (whether the fame, or another of both his names) was

[c] See p 376 note r and fee another inftance in Willis, ii 94.
[d] Cath ii 192
[e] Cath ii 146
[f] MS Harl, 6953 p 23

per-

perfonally inftalled, September 26, in preferment which he did not long enjoy. For
on the 16th of January, 1508-9, Matthew
Smyth was collated to this fame prebend of
Bigglefwade, then void by the death of Mr.
William Smyth[g] We have therefore, at one
and the fame time, two if not three dignitaries of Lincoln named William Smyth,
befides the archdeacon of Lincoln mentioned
above, namely the archdeacon of Stow, canon refidentiary and prebendary of Ketton,
who died before December 14, 1507; another, who was prebendary of Bigglefwade a
few days in February, 1507-8, and another
ftill (or the fame collated again) who died
before the middle of January following, in
pofieffion of this prebend, and alfo, as it is
probable, of the prebend of Ryton in Lichfield cathedral, to which Richard Wyot was
admitted, February 10, 1508-9, on the death
of William Smyth, whom bifhop Smyth had
collated to the ftall in February, 1493-4[h]

---

g MS Harl 695, p 24

h Reg Iichf f 140 b penult Ieb He was admitted by
his proxy John Dalance, the fame I prefume who occurs occafionally in bifhop Smyths affairs who, in the conveyance of
Cnalgrove to Lincoln college, and of Coldno ton to Bra e
Nofe college, fubfcribes himfelf " John Dalon '

to which he was admitted on the 30th of
April, 1494[i].

GILBERT SMYTH ARCHDEACON OF
NORTHAMPTON was the younger brother of
the forenamed William archdeacon of Stow[k]
He was collated, June 28, 1498, to the prebend of Gretton in Lincoln cathedral, on
the refignation of James Whitftons, upon
condition of paying an annual penfion of 20
marks to William Skelton late prebendary[l].
He was ordained fubdeacon, March 23,
1503-4, deacon on the 6th of April, and
prieft on the firft of June enfuing[m]. He was
inftalled archdeacon of Northampton, Auguft 26, 1506[n], and about two years afterwards was collated to the prebend of Leighton manor, quitting his former prebend for
it[o] We have mentioned above that he was
one of the Bifhop's executors, and in that
capacity put his hand and feal to the Statutes of Brafen Nofe, though at length,

[i] Willis, Cath 1 459 He calls it Ruiton.

[k] App Ped 2.

[l] MS Hail 6953 p 18 correct the names in Willis, vol 11.
p 187

[m] MS Harl ib p 64.

[n] Willis, Cath 11 p 112

[o] Ib p 209

---

[i] Willis, Cath 1 459   He calls it Ruiton
[k] App Ped. 2
[l] MS Harl 6953 p 18 correct the names in Willis, vol 11.
p 187
[m] MS Harl ib p 54
[n] Willis, Cath 11 p 112
[o] Ib p 209

March

March 10, 1540-1, for no reason that has
been discovered, he renounced his executo-
rial office. The corps of his prebend consisted of demesne lands in Leighton Bromswold in the county of Huntingdon, which,
as Willis informs us, contained in themselves
a manor, and Smyth, imitating the piety of
the good Bishop, his kinsman and patron,
obtained permission from the Crown, 19 Henry viii, to found a chantry in the church of
St Mary at Leighton Bromswold[p], and he
also, as Leland says, ' made a Free-School
there[q] " The income of the prebend was
considerable (rated in the general valuation
at 57l. 15s 2d) and there being a good
house upon the estate, built by Smyth's pre-
decessor, it was " coveted by courtiers[r]," and
Smyth was prevailed upon to alienate it,
February 25, 1548, to Sir Robert Tirwhitt,
and it has continued a lay fee ever since
He was the last archdeacon of Northampton
while it remained a member of the church
of Lincoln, and became, by the foundation
charter of Peterborough, dated September
4, 1541, the first in that new bishopric. He

[p] Priv Sigill H viii inter MSS Rawlinson
[q] In Willis vol ii 209
[r] Willis, ib p 208

resigned

refigned the archdeaconry in 1548[s], about eight months before he alienated the prebend, but when he died, or where he was buried, I cannot afcertain

It is natural to fuppofe thefe three archdeacons, men competent to receive prefciment in no long time after the Bifhop had it to beftow, were all of them fons of his elder rather than of his younger brothers. It was for this reafon, that, in the beginning of thefe memoirs, I ventured to follow Penfon in calling the Bifhop the Fourth, rather than, as Lee and others more generally call him, the Second fon of his father[t]. We have contemporary and certain proof[u], that the pedigree entered by Lee in his vifitation of Oxfordfhire, notwithftanding it was figned by one of the family, is yet inaccurate in making a layman with a numerous progeny the oldeft fon of the Bifhop's oldeft brother (and confequently heir to the Bifhop) inftead of an ecclefiaftic without iffue, as Penfon truly reprefents the matter But on thefe obfcure and dubious points, where probability

[s] Willis, ibid p 514
[t] See App Pedd 1, 2.
[u] See p 372

is all that can now be expected, " abundet
quifque fuo fenfu "

MATTHEW SMYTH, the firft Principal of
Brafen Nofe college, is intitled to a place
here by his perfonal merits and probable kin
to the Founder, though none of the pedigrees of the family, which I have feen, acknowledge him, nor have I been able, from
any other quarter, fully to authenticate the
fact   He was born in Lancafhire[x], and educated in Oriel college, where he commenced
B A in 1505[y], and was chofen fellow of the
college the enfuing year[z]. When he was admitted to the degree of M A. I have not
learnt, but he frequently occurs as a regent
Mafter, entrufted with the care of fome of
the public chefts, and on other occafions, in
1709 ard the following years[a]. He was
afterwards Bachelor of divinity, but, as it
feems, not till the year 1545[b]. On the

[x] H   Fodef Lichf MS   Woods Colleges, p 364
[y] He petitioned for his degree June 21, being then only of
three years ftanding, and the requeft was granted on certain
conditions Reg G f 2
[z] H i Lchf and MS Wood, 28 f 66 b
[a] Reg G f 82 83 65 b 86 b 96 105 b 136 169 b
217
[b] MS Wood, 8514 p 203

24th

24th of Auguft, 1510, he became Principal
of Brafen Nofe Hall, ftill retaining his fellowfhip in Oriel college ; which, as it appears[c], he had not refigned on the 16th of
March, 1511-12. He had, before this time,
affifted in the conveyance of certain eftates
for the ufe of the Bifhop of Lincoln, part of
the intended endowment of his college, of
which, as we have already faid, he was
conftituted the firft Principal in autumn
1512, and his vigilance and activity in that
important fituation befpeak him not unworthy of the truft, which the pious Founder
repofed in him. But to particularize the
tranfactions, in which he was concerned,
would be to detail the affairs of the fociety
at large for the fpace of almoft forty years ·
I fhall therefore content myfelf with briefly
mentioning the preferment which he enjoyed,
through the munificence of the Founder,
and the benefactions which he beftowed,
proofs of his own congenial merit.

Matthew Smyth was collated to the prebend called Centum Solidorum in Lincoln
cathedral, October 2, 1508[d], vacant by the

[c] Reg T f 150
[d] MS Harl 6953 p 24

death

death of the former prebendary. On the
16th of January, 1508-9, he quitted this for
Bigglefwade, on the death of William Smyth,
as mentioned above[f], and was fucceeded in
his former ftall by John Kidwelly LL B.
the 25th of the fame month[g] On the 2d
of December, 1512, he was collated to the
prebend of Banbury, on the death of James
Whitftons[h], and was ordained fubdeacon the
18th of the fame month, and prieft the
12th of March following[i] His patron dying
within twelve months from this time, he
probably obtained no other preferment In
his will, dated December 11, 1547, he conftituted Mr. Robert Morwent (the fecond
Prefident of Corpus Chrifti college, a man
of great eminence in his time) and his nephew Mr. William Smyth, Parfon of Barton
in the Clay, his executors, bequeathing a
tenement and lands in Sutton, in the parifh
of Prefcot, Lancafhire, to his nephew Baldwin Smyth and his heirs, on condition that
they fhould pay 20s yearly to the Ufher of

---

[f] P 285

[g] MS Harl ut fupra Kidwelly has been mentioned above,
p 244 ut ſeq b Wills by miſtake calls him Philip Cach in
p 166 2 2

[h] MS Harl ut fupra, p 25

[i] Id p 64

Farn-

Farnworth fchool. His other lands in Sutton he gives to Brafen Nofe college to pay
20s. a year to a Scholar born in the chapelry
of Farnworth, or elfe in the parifh of Pief-
cot, or near to it[k]. Wood fays he died February 6, 1547-8, and was buried in St.
Mary's church, Oxon, without any memorial[l] In the accounts of the church wardens of that parifh, for the year 1549, is a
receipt " for Mr Matthew Smith's grave
3s 4d[m]." On the 20th of June, 1548, the
executors above named appeared before Walter Wryght LL D. archdeacon of Oxford,
Principal of Durham college, then Vice
Chancellor of the Univerfity, and formally
renounced the executorfhip, whereupon the
faid judge, at their earneft requeft, pronounced the deceafed to have died inteftate,
and committed the adminiftration of his er-
fects to his afore faid nephew, William Smyth
B. D An indenture was afterwards made,
September 20, 1557, between the faid William Smyth and John Hawarden, Principal
of Brafen Nofe college, granting to the fociety the tenement in Sutton, on condition

[k] Yate, p 162, 163
[l] Colleges, p 364
[m] MS Wood, 8514 p 275

that

that they kept an obit for Matthew Smyth
on the 6th of February, the anniverſary of
his death[n]. The place of his birth, the
ſituation of his eſtates, and the tenor of his
bequeſts concur to prove him to have been a
branch of the Cuerdley family   If his nephews, William and Baldwin Smyth, were
the two brothers ſo named, ſons of Robert
Smyth, as ſtated in two of the pedigrees[o],
he muſt have been a brother of the Biſhop
of Lincoln, who has eſcaped the reſearches
of the heralds and genealogiſts, but in that
caſe it does not appear how William, the
eldeſt ſon, but not of the eldeſt brother,
could be, as he ſtyles himſelf, heir to his de-
ceaſed uncle[r], unleſs it were by virtue of
the will, to which he refuſed to adminiſter.
Baldwin Smyth, a name that rarely occurs
elſewhere, was an aſſiſtant to the manciple
of Braſen Noſe and alſo groom of the college, in the year 1544, and afterwards[q], but
we can hardly ſuppoſe a perſon occupying
either or both thoſe humble ſtations to have

---

[r] Yate, ut ſupra

[o] App Pedd 2, 3

[p] See above, p 372 note a

[q] Vide Rott Burſi 1544—1547   There is a Baldwin
Smyth ſon of Richard in Ped 1

been

been a nephew of the Principal; though it is not inconfiftent with the unaffuming manners of the age. It was not degrading in archbifhop Warham to have a nephew, who was alfo his godfon, William Warham, knight, in the train of his domeftics[r], when, as we have feen[s], the pride of nobility gladly ftooped to wait upon him, and, long before the title of efquire was ufurped by every upftart, a perfon of that rank was one of the academic bedels[t].

Of the other kinfmen of the Founder, and of thofe who matched with the family, we have nothing material to add to the flight notices, which the pedigrees furnifh, except with regard to John Collinridge only, who is faid to have married Margery Smyth[u], a great niece of the Bifhop of Lincoln. He frequently appears in the college accounts,

[r] Athen Oxon 1 p 669

[s] P 215

[t] Rob Wryght, Armiger, utriufque juris generofus bedellus Reg Aaa, f 236 b 237 267 A D 1466 See alfo above, p 124

[u] App Ped 1 See and correct A Wood, Colleges, p 353. n 2ª who calls her Margaret and her hufband Collins A perfon named Colyngryge (and it is not a common name) occurs in 1503, as an inhabitant or ftudent of Oxford Reg Ⅽ. f 56.

but

but whether as a leffee of lands belonging to
the college, or as a benefactor to the fociety,
or both, it is not eafy to determine[x]   He
makes an annual payment to the college, of
variable amount, from the year 1530 till the
time of his deceafe, after which his widow
Margery Collinridge continues the payment[y];
which is once faid to be for lands in her
tenure, and in another audit fhe is in arrears
for lands in Skegnefs and Sutton[z].   Perhaps
therefore her hufband held from his deceafed
kinfman, the Archdeacon of Lincoln, part of
the Lincolnfhire eftates, which the Archdeacon had conveyed and fettled on Brafen
Nofe college, and paid on that account a vo-

---

[x] De pecun recep' de Jon Colyngryg de Lincoln Gent ut
de fornt in L vii S vi D Rot 2 H viii Payments from
land occur under the defcription of "forinfeca," when the
eftates, I prefume, did not yet form a part of the general rent-
roll, but this payment from John Colyngryge is always defcribed as nou   and the fum, though commonly 7 L varies
from 4 L 7 S 6 D as above, to 7 L 18 S 8 D yet he is never
faid to be in arrears, which feems to indicate a free donation,
rather than a legal debt See the following Rott till 32 H viii

[y] Ib 33 H viii In Rot 35 H viii is this item "Pro
terr in Co Linc modo in tenura Margerie Colyngryg viduc,
vii L" but in the fame audit the lands in Sutton, Skegnes,
Wynthrop, and Borow in Com Linc form a feparate article,
and are rated at xxvi L iiii S vi D

[z] Rot 38 H viii

luntary

luntary acknowledgment, rather than a fixed
rent, during his life, after which it was at
the abfolute difpofal of the fociety, and was
put on the fame footing as their other eftates.
But this is conjecture only. John Collinridge, gentleman, was principal Verger and
Conftable of the cathedral of Lincoln, but
whether he obtained eithe of thofe offices
(if they are diftinct offices) from the hands
of bifhop Smyth, I have not learnt. His
epitaph is here given from **Peck**: " Hic jacet
Johannes Colyngryge generofus, principalis
virgarius ac conftabularius iftius ecclefie cathedralis; qui obiit vicefimo tertio die menfis Novembris, anno Domini M°. ccccc°.
XLII° anno regni regis Henrici octavi tricefi-
fimo fecundo. Cujus anime propitietur Deus,
Amen[a]."

The reader, it is hoped, will pardon the
addition of a fingle name, connected with
the Founder by friendfhip only, not by affinity, Brian Higden, a man eminent in his
time and a generous benefactor to the college of Brafen Nofe. We firft meet with
him while Smyth was Chancellor of the Univerfity, in the year 1502, when he was a

[a] Defia Cur L. viii p 310

bachelor

bachelor of civil law, and appears occafionally
as proctor in the Vice Chancellor's court[b]. In
June, 1505, he petitioned for leave to commence Doctor in his faculty[c], which being
granted, he proceeded accordingly, but, as it
feems, not before May 28, 1506[d]   At this
time he was Principal of Broadgate Hall[e],
on the fite of which Pembroke college
ftands.   He was ordained fubdeacon in Ofeney abbey, March 8, 1504-5, on a title from
that monaftery[f], by which alfo in the enfuing fummer, June 15, 1505, he was prefented to the rectory of Buckenhull, Oxfordfhire[g]   In 1508 he was appointed one of
the Judges or confervators of the peace of
the Univerfity[h].   He had now conciliated
the efteem, and began to enjoy the patronage, of the Bifhop of Lincoln   He collated him to the prebend of Welton Ryval[i],

[b] For Ofeney abbey, Mar 30, 1502 and Mar 19, 1505 6
Reg Œ f 125 b f 234 b for a Londoner ib f 232
[c] Reg G f 1 b June 21
[d] Ib f 18   See of him alfo, f 22 b—24
[e] Reg Œ f 225
[f] MS Harl 6953 p 64.
[g] Ib p 48
[h] Reg G f 59 b
[i] MS Harl 6953 p 24 inftalled, Sept 5 Act Capit
Linc f 23

Auguft

Auguft 29, 1508; to the living of Kirkby
near Repingale (in Lincolnfhire) July 3,
1511[k], and to the Subdeanery of Lincoln,
on the 12th of November following[l]. He
had afterwards the prebend of Clifton[m], and
in 1523 he exchanged the Subdeanery for
the prebend of Ailefbury, with John Talbot[n], referving to himfelf, according to a
common but not very laudable cuftom of
thofe times, a penfion of 12l. out of his
former dignity[o]. In June, 1516, he was collated to the prebend of Ulfkelf at York[p],
and in the fame month was admitted Dean
of that cathedral[q], of both which dignities
he died poffeffed June 5, 1539, and was
buried in York cathedral. He gave in his
lifetime and with his own hands the fum of
100l. to Matthew Smyth Principal of Brafen Nofe college, and afterwards conveyed
to him the further fum of 10l. by the
hands of a friend; but died before affurances

[k] MS Harl 6953 p 29

[l] Ib p 25

[m] Willis, ii p 168 MS Harl ib p 89

[n] Willis, ii p 98 134

[o] MS Harl 6953 p 90 Talbot alfo, upon his refignation
in 1535, referved a fecond penfion of 40s ib p 95

[p] Willis, i p 172

[q] Ib p 69

were

were made and the conditions of his benefaction diſtinctly ſpecified.   It was therefore
covenanted by a tripartite indenture, September 10, 3 Edward vi, 1549, between the
executors of the ſaid " right honourable
Bryan Higden Lord Dean of York," Owen
Oglethorp Preſident of Magdalen college,
and John Hawarden then Principal of Braſen
Noſe college, that the ſociety of Braſen Noſe
ſhould accept and maintain one additional
Fellow, to be choſen alternately out of the
counties of York and Lincoln[r].   Power of
entry and diſtreſs, if the conditions are not
fulfilled, is reſerved to the Preſident and Fellows of Magdalen college, from which circumſtance, and from the coincidence of
names, it is probable the benefactor Brian
Higden was a kinſman, perhaps brother, to
his contemporary John Higden, Preſident of
Magdalen college and a great benefactor to
that ſociety[s].   But this is certain, that in
this worthy Dean of York, now " departed,"

[r] Yate, p 164

[s] See Woods Colleges, p 314, 315   He was the firſt
Dean of Chriſt Church ib 422 428   He was preſented,
Sept 27, 1510, by the Convent of Croyland to the vicarage of
Sutterton MS Harl 6953 p 29 and by the Convent of
Reading to the rectory of Hanborow, Oxfordſhire, July 2,
1518 ib p 83

as

as his epitaph expreſſes it, " to the mercy of
Almighty God[t]," we have another inſtance,
added to many which have occurred before,
wherein the munificence of biſhop Smyth
profited the college long after his deceaſe;
his ſurviving friends, in gratitude to his memory and veneration of his worth, cheriſhing
the ſociety, which he piouſly founded for the
advancement of literature and ſupport of religion

---

[t] See Willis, 1 p 69 One Mr Hygden reſided in Braſen
Noſe college in the years 1539—1541, as appears by the Rott
Burſl but whether he was a kinſman of the Dean of York, I
cannot ſay

THE

LIFE

OF

SIR RICHARD SUTTON.

queror, who held the Earldom of Chefter as
freely by his fword, as the King himfelf held
England by his crown, or from Hugh Kevelioc[b] in the following century, is a little uncertain. It was on account of this office,
granted by one of thefe diftinguifhed earls,
that the Suttons of Sutton bore three bugle
horns for their arms; which is regarded by
good judges as the original coat of this
branch of the Suttons, though fome of
them, at a late period[c], exhibited in the firft
quarter a lion rampant. What in heraldry is
called a coat of affection, taken out of refpect to fome great houfe of the fame name,
was formerly not unufual; and it is fuppofed

Coll Armor 1 D 14 f 245 "Adam—held—by the charter
of Hugh Earl of Chefter in the name of a *Fofterfhip*" MS
Harl 1505 a blunder, I prefume, for Forefterfhip

[b] ' Adam—holdeth—by the charter of Hugh Kevelioche
Earl of Cnefter, in the name of the Foreftfhip of Macclesfield
in Com Cheft" MS Harl 218- In the Chefhire pedigree of
Davenport of Davenport it is faid, " Richard Davenport (fon
of Thomas, who lived temp Hen 11) to whom the Earl of
Cnefter gave the Forefterfhip of the foreft of Macclesfield '
This grant however might not be by Kevelioc, who lived in
the reign of Henry 11, out by his fon, the famous Randal
Blundeville, earl of Chefter

[c] A D 1580 as mentioned in note a p 405 fee alfo
MS Harl 1457 f 124 and notes fubjoined to the pedigree,
App No xxi

the

the Chefhire Suttons quartered the lion with
their paternal coat in compliment to Sutton
lord Dudley, whofe bearing it was, a family
no way related to them but by name[d].   On
the tower of Macclesfield church there are
numerous efcutcheons of arms, the memorials, it is prefumed, of benefactors to the
building: among thefe, on the weft fide, are
the bugle horns for Sutton, without any
quarterings.

In the penury of our private annals, during
the lapfe of fome centuries from the Norman invafion, feveral circumftances are related refpecting the houfe of Sutton.   Ralph
de Sutton had a grant from Edward the firft,

---

[d] J C Brooke, Somerfet Herald   Others however fay, a
lion rampant, queve furche Vert, in a field Or, was the common badge of the houfe of Sutton, confidering the Suttons
lords Dudley, barons of Malpas, and the Suttons of Sutton as
one and the fame family   Of this perhaps it may be fome
confirmation to obferve, that " Johannes de Sutton, dominus
de Malpas," prefented to one moiety of the rectory of Malpas
in 1389 Reg Lichf vi f 54 as did " Johannes de Sutton de
Duddeley, miles," in 1391 ib f 56 and " Johannes Sutton,
miles, dominus de Dudley," in 1404 ib Reg vii f 91 b
And I am informed, from MS Harl 2065, f 28 that Johannes de Sutton chevalier, held a moiety of the whole barony
del Malpas, 8 H iv (1406) and that John was his fon and
heir   Compare what follows here.

within the foreſt of Delamere[c]   Ivon de
Sutton was Bailiff of the foreſt of Maccleſ-
field in the thirty fourth year of the ſame
puiſſant prince[f]   John de Sutton ſenior held
the manor of Sutton with its appendages in
Diſtelegh, within the foreſt of Macclesfield,
from Catharine queen of England, in capite,
by knight's ſervice ; and John de Sutton was
his next heir, 6 Richard ii,[g] (1382) William Sutton, who died in 1428, in the reign
of Henry vi, is ſtyled Valet of the Crown to
our Lord the King[h].   John de Sutton and
Richard Sutton, in the ſame reign, held the
office of itinerant Bailiff in the county of
Cheſter, by patent from the Crown, for their
joint lives[i], and at the ſame time Richard
Sutton was Præpoſitus or Provoſt of Mac-
cleſfield[k]

[c] In Sutton infra foreſt de la Mara 13 Edw the firſt MS
Harl 2074 f 203 11 Edw ii John Sutton mil fil Ric Sut-
ton mil ib f 205 Johanni fil Johannis fil Ric ue Sutton et
Iſabellæ ux ejus filiæ Johannis de Chorleton ib f 206

[f] Baly foreſt de Macclesfield MS Harl 2040 Benedict
de Sutton et Bertha uxor, in a fine, 8 Edw ii ibid

[g] MS Harl 2065 f 54 12 Edw iv Johannes Sutton te-
nuit &c Johannes eſt filius et heres ib f 132 36 Edw iii
Johannes de Sutton (de Macclesfield) &c Johannes fil Ric de
Sutton eſt ejus heres propinquior ib f 28

[h] MS Harl 2040 Weever, Fun Mon 605

[i] 22 H vi 38 H vi MS Harl 2040

[k] 29 H vi MS Harl ib He is alſo called " Rich Sutton,
Cach-

In 1467 William Sutton was one of the Proctors of the Univerſity of Oxford[l], and the enſuing year we find him Principal of Braſen Noſe hall[m]. He afterwards became D D frequently bore the office of Commiſſary or Vice Chancellor[n]; and quitting Oxford, as we ſuppoſe, about the time when St Mary's church was building, the Univerſity, ſoliciting the aid of their friends for carrying on the work, addreſſed two letters

Cachpole, 38 H vi " ib which, no doubt, means Bailiff, and is a proof of what Cowell in Johnſon ſays, that Catchpoll was in ancient times uſed without reproach, for ſuch as we now call ſerjeants of the mace, or any other that uſes to arreſt men upon any cauſe —The particulars contained in the above paragraph, together with ſeveral pedigrees of the family of Sutton, were communicated to me, April 28, 1800, with the genuine liberality of a friend to antiquarian reſearches, by William Latham, eſquire, of Nottingham Place, London, who, from the late Dr Gower's papers, and from his own large collections, will in a ſhort time, it is anxiouſly hoped, gratify the public with that great deſideratum, a juſt Hiſtory of the County Palatine of Cheſter

[l] Reg Aaa, f 253 b 255 and A Wood, Faſti, ad ann 1467 who conceives him to have been of Univerſity college See alſo his Annals, vol 1 p 627

[m] Reg Aaa, f 257 269

[n] Wood, Faſti, 1480—1484 Magiſter W Sutton was arbitrator in a diſpute, A D 1450 Reg Aa, f 43 b but this was probably a different perſon

to him, among others, on that occasion[o]. The Divinity school was completed a few years before, while he resided in Oxford, and it was probably in compliment to him, that the Sutton arms, as they were now borne by the Suttons of Chefhire, three crofs crofslets quartered with the bugle horns, were exhibited in the rich ceiling of that beautiful room[p]. If this conjecture is well founded, it is natural to conclude, that Sir Richard Sutton, to whom we muft now confine our inquiries, would feel a predilection for Brafen Nofe hall, the fite of his intended college, on account of this his kinfman, who, in his own early days, was for many years the refpected Head of the houfe.

Richard Sutton, born, it is believed, at the family feat of Sutton in the parifh of Prefbury, was the younger fon of Sir William Sutton, knight, who was Mafter of Burton Lazar's in Leicefterfhire in 1456[q], which he had quitted, by death or refig-

---

[o] Reg F Ep 427 about the year 1490 Ep 456 about 1493

[p] Wood's Annals, ii p 783. They are over the pulpit.

[q] Not Mon Principals of Rel Houfes

nation,

nation, before March 22, 6 Henry vii,
(1490-1) when George Sutton, of the fame
family probably, occurs as Mafter[r] of this
well-endowed hofpital, a lay foundation, one
of the military orders, the chief of all the
Lazar houfes in England, but dependent on
the great houfe of St. Lazarus at Jerufalem.

The time of his birth is uncertain, and
of his education we have no account He
was a Barrifter, of the Inner Temple, probably in confiderable repute and practice
Of his growing affluence there is this ground
of prefumption, becaufe in the year 1490 he
bought certain eftates in Leicefterfhire; and
continued, from that period, to make occafional purchafes, in different parts of the
kingdom, as long as he lived Of his juft
and increafing reputation it may be deemed
a fufficient proof, that one of the moft cautious and prudent of monarchs, Henry vii,
felected him to be a member of his moft

---

[r] Yate, p 98 There is a memorable abfolution granted by
this George Sutton and the fraternity of Burton, " ordinis mi-
litie," remitting all the fins of Thomas de Winnington and
Elena his wife, except fuch whereupon the apoftolical fee muft
be confulted Dat 1491 MS Harl 2077 p 41 Compare
this with what was alleged againft another military order, the
Hofpitalars, as ftated above, p 186

honour-

honourable privy Council. The firft time
that we fee him in this important character
is February 3, 1497-8; when Sir Richard
Pole, knight, alfo fat in council, the fame
who was now, or foon afterwards, one of
the Prince's council[s] Sutton attended the
court during feveral enfuing years, when
councils were holden at Greenwich, at Richmond, and other places[t], but of the refult of
thefe confultations no documents have been
feen, which furnifh information interefting
at prefent to the ftatefman or biographer.

In 1505 he was one of the Governours of
the Inner Temple[u], an annual office, to
which he had frequently the honour of being
chofen, and once, 1520, in conjunction with
his friend Sir John Port

In the year 1514 he was joined with

[s] See above p 58 63

[t] See Dockets of Court of Requefts, 13 H vii—21 H vii
1497—1505 p 17 27 28 29 40 He is ftyled " Sutton
jurifperitus,' ' Ricardus Sutton, " Ricardus Sutton armiger,'
and it is certain that the Founder is intended, fince in conveyances of eftates he is called, by others and by himfelf, " Ricardus Sutton de Confilio domini Regis   Yate, p 105

[u] Dugd Orig Jurid p 172 He was Governour for the
laft time, 14 H viii, 1522

others

others in a deed of fettlement, which re-
quires to be mentioned, as it throws fome
light upon the hiftory of the family. William Cholmeley of Norton in Hales in the
county of Salop, gentleman, made a grant
and feoffment of all his eftates in Worcefterfhire, Shropfhire, Gloucefterfhire, and elfewhere, and of all his goods and chattels, to
Richard Sutton, efquire, John Pefall of Check-
ley, John Sutton of Sutton, and Roger Legh
of Ridge, gentlemen; bearing date, September 13, 6 Henry viii, the intent of which
enfeoffment was declared to be, that the
feoffees and their heirs fhould ftand poffeffed
of the premifes for the ufe of the faid William Cholmeley and Margery his wife, during
their joint lives, and after their deceafe, for
the ufe of Thomafin their daughter and
John Sutton her hufband and their heirs for
ever[x]. It is remarkable, that Richard Sut-

---

[x] Chartæ antiquæ penes Joh Darke, armigerum, 1799,
No 1, with the feal appendant and livery of ' poffeffion" en-
dorfed It appears by No 2, 3, dat 22 H viii (1530) that
John Sutton, gent was then living and poffeffed of thefe
eftates, and that Thomafin his wife was deceafed A pedigree
of Sutton in the Brit Mufeum, MS Hafted, 5529 t 64 fays
John Sutton, who married the heirefs of Cholmley, died 28 H
viii and that Richard Sutton his fon, lord of Sutton, died before his father

ton, grandfon of the faid Thomafin, giving
in his pedigree at the Chefhire vifitation in
1580[y], and quartering the arms of Cholmondeley in confequence of this match, mentions neither the name of this his paternal
grandmother, nor her father's name, nor
have thefe obfcure points ever been made
out, till the original deed, here quoted, with
many others highly curious and of more ancient date, were kindly entrufted to me, for
the purpofe of thefe inquiries, by John Darke,
efquire, of Bredon, Worcefterfhire, the worthy proprietor of the eftates conveyed in the
faid feoffment; which eftates one of his anceftors, John Darke of Alfton in Worcefterfhire, purchafed in 1545 of Richard Sutton
of Sutton, efquire[z], grandfon of the faid John
Sutton and Thomafin his wife.

The date of the marriage between John
Sutton and Thomafin Cholmeley has not

[y] See the Pedigree, App No xxi

[z] Chartæ, ut fupra, No 5 dat Apr 21, 37 H viii   The
eftates, as appears by No 6, were finally releafed to Darke,
Sept 20, 5 Edw vi (1551) Both thefe inftruments bear the
feal and fignature of Richard Sutton, whofe hand-writing
(whether by accident or ftudied imitation) ftrongly refembles
that of his diftinguifhed kinfman, Founder of Brafen Nofe
college

been

been difcovered. It was probably not long
anterior to the date of the feoffment made
for their benefit, at which time Sir Richard
Sutton, firft named in the truft, was Steward
of the monaftery of Sion[a], near Brentford, in
Middlefex. He occurs in this office in the
year 1513, he had chambers in the monaftery, and often refided there during the remainder of his life. Anne Smyth, a great
niece of the Bifhop of Lincoln, was about
this time a nun of Sion[b]. It was a houfe
of Brigittines, the only one of that order in
England, which differed from all other inftitutions in requiring a certain number of men
in every convent, though in different apartments from the women. Sion houfe, which
was very amply endowed, is memorable in
the literary hiftory of thofe days Here was
a large library, well furnifhed with books;
of which the catalogue, written in a beautiful hand, ftill remains[c]. That famous divine Thomas Gafcoign, fometime Chancellor of the Univerfity of Oxford, tranflated
the Life of St Brigit for the ufe of the nuns

[a] Yate, p 103

[b] App No 1 Ped 2

[c] Inter MSS Parker in Coll C C Cantab num cxli
catal Nafmith

of

of Sion; and in his will he bequeathed to the monaftery "Scripture Verities," a work of his own, and many other books[d]. Henry viii gave them his "Affertion of the feven Sacraments againft Luther[e]" Simon Wynter, a brother of the houfe, wrote and gave them feveral things; particularly a piece called "Regina Celi," or "a Notable Treatife in praife of the Virgin Mary[f]." Richard Whytford, the friend of Fox, of More, and Erafmus, retiring from the world, became a monk of this houfe, where he tranflated many books, and wrote others, one of which was "A dayly exercyfe and experience of deathe," at the requeft of dame Elizabeth Giles, abbefs of Sion[g]. He commonly fubfcribed himfelf, "The wretche of Syon, Rycharde Whytforde"

---

[d] See his Will in Reg Aaa, f 166 and fee Tanner, Biblioth v Gafcoigne

[e] This ftood on fhelf "O 23" MS Parker, ut fupra The fhelves extended as far as "V 20'

[f] Ib d This S mon Wynter (if I have not by miftake made an author of one whofe humbler office was that of a tranfcriber only) is a writer, who has efcaped the refearches of Pits, Bale, and Tanner

[g] Tanner, Biblioth v Whytford Ames calls the abbefs "Elizabeth Gybs ' Typogr p 400 See more of Whytford, io 168—170 &c

Sir Richard Sutton gave certain eftates, purchafed in the neighbourhood, to the monaftery of Sion, and a legacy of 20l. to the lady abbefs, but it does not appear, that he was a benefactor to the library. He contributed however not a little to the celebrity of the houfe, by a fplendid work publifhed at his expence, and called, in honour of this monaftery, " The Orcharde of Syon." Having not been fo fortunate as to obtain a fight of this very rare book, of which there was a fine copy in the Earl of Oxford's library[h], I will lay before the reader an account of it, which I owe to the kindnefs of the late Mr Warton.

" Under the title is a wood-cut of S Catharine of Sienna, at a defk, in the habit of her monaftic order, crowned with thorns and a glory, an heart in her left hand, and both hands wounded and bleeding Above, God the Father, with a triple crown, in the clouds, from whence rays proceed to the breaft of the faint, where they terminate in a

[h] See the Catal vol iii p 124 No 1557 It had paffed through very few hands The firft was Lady Llizabeth Strykland a nun of Sion, Sir Richard Asfheton, Sir Henry Sacheverell &c

focus: in the rays is a dove flying towards
her. Over this cut is a ribband, with, "Ecce
Ancilla Domini," in red. The title, in red,
is at top, viz. " Here begynneth the Or-
charde of Syon | in the whiche is conteyned
the reuelacyons of feynt Katheryne of Sene |
with ghoftly fruytes and precyous plantes
for the helthe of mannes foule." At the
back of this title-page, is another print in
wood of S. Catharine, crowned as before,
fitting and holding an heart in her right
hand, a book open on her knees, the devil
fprawling on his back at her feet, and twelve
nuns ftanding around her, fix on either fide.
There are two Prologues ; and the Table of
Contents is followed by a third Prologue:
after which is another cut of S Catharine at
her devotion, and before her the perfonifi-
cation of Obedience and Difobedience. Nine
leaves are taken up in what is hitherto defcribed. Then in fignature a, 1, " Heie begynneth the booke of dyuyne doctryne
That is to faye of goddes techynge   Gyuen
by the perfone of God the fader | to the in-
telleccyon of yᵉ gloryous vyrgyn feynt Ka-
theryn of Seene | of the ordre of faynt Do-
mynyck. whiche was wryte as fhe endyted i
her modar tonge | whan fhe was in cō-
templayco and rapt of fpyryte | fhe herynge
                                     actualy

actualy. And ī yᵉ fame tyme | fhe told be-
fore many what our lorde god fpake ī her."
This in red ink, and over the print in the
title-page, but without the ribband. The
work is diftributed into feven parts, each of
which has five chapters, and thefe are feverally marked with running titles. The
title of each part is printed in red, with an
elegant wood-cut prefixed¹ It is concluded
with a petition of S. Catharine, which ends
thus · " That I maye feythfully renne with
perfeccyō ī this deedly way with very obe-
dyence and with the lyghte of holy feythe |
with the whiche lyghte me feemeth thou
haft made me now lately ghoftly drunke | ."
Then follows, " Lenuoye of Dane James
the tranflator," which ends thus : " Euery

¹ " The leaves are not numbered By fignatures it contains B 4, in the fecond alphabet, in fixes, but it is to be obferved, that the firft alphabet has three characters after Z.'
Amess Typogr Antiq by Herbert, p 159 I know not whether Mr Warton, who thought he could procure me the fight
of this curious volume, furnifhed Mr Herbert with the defcription of it, or whether what he gave me, in his own hand,
as here printed, was in part copied from Herbert, but the general agreement between the two accounts is too minute to
have been accidental Mr Warton, at this time, knew who
the " Richard Sutton" was, of which Mr Herbert was ignorant, and therefore queried whether it might be Richard father of Thomas Sutton, Founder of the Charter Houfe

good

good thynge the more it be communycate
and difparfed abrode | the more fruyt and pro-
fyt cometh thereof | —— This confyderynge
a ryghte worfhypfull and devoute gentylman
mayfter Rycharde Sutton efquyer | ftewarde
of the holy monaftery of Syon | fyndynge
this ghoftly trefure thefe dyologes and reue-
lacyons of the newe feraphycall fpoufe of
cryfte feynt Katheryne of Sene | in a corner
by it felfe | wyllynge of his greate charyte it
fholde come to lyghte | that many relygyous
and deuoute foules myght be releued and
have cōforte therby | he hathe caufed at his
great cofte | this booke to be prynted | truft-
ynge that moche fruyte fhall come therof |
to all ȳ fhal rede or here of it defyrynge
none other thīge therefore but onely yᵉ re-
ward of god and theyr deuoute prayers | for
the helthe of his foule   And thus endeth
this booke | Imprynted——The yere of our
lord ᴍ. ccccc. & xix and the xxviii daye of
Septēberᵏ " On the laft leaf is a cut of S.
Catharine as on the back of the title-page
In folio. Prynted by Wynkyn de Worde.

ᵏ Herbert adds, " The form of printing the conclufions of
tne feveral parts is very remarkable for the time, " though not
unfrequent at the latter part of the century." This peculiarity
confifts in lines of different lengths, fo as to refemble a crofs
&c of which he gives a fpecimen

In

In point of ornament and other refpects, it is the moft fuperb and curious fpecimen of ancient Englifh typography that I remember: and muft have been a work of very confiderable expence. I take the Tranflator Done (that is Don or Dominus) James, to be the fame who tranflated into Englifh rhymes a French poem called *Le Chateau de Labour*[1]."

S. Catharine of Sienna died April 26, 1380, and fourfcore years afterwards, 1461, when none of her contemporaries were living to detect forgeries, the church of Rome, with their ufual prudence in fuch cafes, canonized her[m] upon which fhe became a very popular faint in nunneries. For one thing fhe is juftly celebrated, the purity of her language, which is reckoned the ftandard of the Senneze. Another circumftance alfo contributed to her repute in Italy fhe was inftrumental in bringing back the pope from

---

[1] Whether this is a miftake I do not know, but " The caftell of Labour wherein is Rycheffe, Vertue, and Honour," printed by W de Worde, 1506, was tranflated by Alex. Barklay, monk of Ely, who alfo tranflated the famous Ship of Fools See Ames, ut fupra, p 145 293 253 797. Tanner, Biblioth v Barklay, Alexander Athen Oxon 1 p 86

[m] See the bull at large in Cherubinus's Bullarium, vol 1. 290—292

Avignon. Sir Alexander Barklay tranflated
her life out of Latin into Englifh, which is
perhaps what was printed by Wynkyn de
Worde, called, "The lyff of that gloryous
vyrgyn and Martyr Saynt Katheryn off fene
with the reuelacions of Saynt Elyfabeth the
kynges doughter of Hungarye[n]." In the library at Sion there was a life of S. Brigit,
the foundrefs of their order, but I do not
find that they had (unlefs it were in private
hands) any life of S Catharine, nor a copy
of this Orchard of Sion, which was to fpread
their fame in the world.

I know not who firft fet the example of
denominating a work, not from the fubject
of which it treats, but from fome favourite
fpot, where it was compofed or publifhed.
The inftances, which occur, are chiefly on
religious topics, and the defign is ingenious.
The garden or the grove prefents to the
mind a pleafing image, we open the volume
recommended by fuch a name with a portion of the tranquillity and delight, which
the fcenes themfelves naturally infpire. we
read for recreation, and are imperceptibly

[n] Ames's Typogr p 207 Printed alfo before by Caxton,
ib 84

charmed

charmed into wifdom, or foothed into piety.
The Orchaid of Sion, while fuch lore as it
contains was in vogue, appears to have been
fo much frequented and worn by the devout,
that fcarcely a fragment of it is to be found,
and what in times more enlightened is valued as a curiofity only, is feldom reprinted.
But the Golden Grove of Jeremy Taylor,
the production of a better age and of true
genius, has gone through numberlefs editions,
and will ftill be the refort of religious retirement, while pure devotion and the Englifh language continue to have charms.

This monaftery of Sion was fuppreffed at
the general diffolution by Henry viii, reftored
by Mary, and finally diffolved by queen Elizabeth   The nuns on that occafion tranf-
ported themfelves, firft to Zurickfea, in Zea-
land, then to Mechlin, in Brabant, thence
to Roan, in Normandy, and at laft fettled
at Lifbon. "They took away with them,"
not only what treafure they could carry, but
likewife, as we are informed, "the keys of
Sion houfe and the iron crofs from the top
of the church, *by way of keeping up their claim
to this their ancient poffeffion* Thefe they conveyed with them in all their changes of ha-

bitation,

bitation, and *still retain* at their prefent houfe
of Sion in Lifbon°."

The part which Sir Richard Sutton bore
from the firft in the foundation of Brafen
Nofe College, has fufficiently appeared in
the account of that bufinefs in the memoirs
of bifhop Smyth   The fociety were not yet
invefted with their charter, when he had the
fatisfaction of being employed in purchafing
the firft permanent benefaction beftowed on
the new feminary. This was the manor of
Pinchepolles in Faringdon, Berks, with lands
in Weftbrook and Farnham in that county,
which he bought of William Fermor, July
12, 1512, for the fum of one hundred
pounds. Part of the property at Faringdon
confifted now or lately of a horfe mill[p]   An

° "Account of Engl Convents eftabl fhed abroad, fubjoined
to Coghlans Directory for 1797 p 31 by "J M   I fuppofe Mr John Milner of Winchefter, the converter of the
champion of Italian miracles and reviving lilies   See Gent
Mag 1796 p 853 1076

[p] See a leafe, dat 23 Sept 2 H viii (1486) by Edmund
Bury of Winrufh (the former proprietor) who married " *Jane*
daughter and heir of Pinchepolles, who in a fine, 3 H viii,
is called " *Jeharra* uxor ejus, a proof (if wanted) that Johanna and Jane are the fame name   Yate, p 115, 116

elegant

elegant Greek epigram in the time of Augustus, when mills of a different conftruction were a new invention, congratulates the damfels who ufed to grind the corn, that now they might enjoy repofe, regardlefs of chanticleer proclaiming the dawn, for henceforth the water-nymphs would perform their tafk for them[q] But in fmall as in greater matters the genuine fruits of liberty are gathered flowly. In England fifteen centuries or more elapfed, before thefe watery deities, if they releafed human drudges fooner, refcued the generous horfe from the toil of the mill, and in fome parts of Scotland to this day the quern is retained, and worked, as formerly, by two women fitting face to face[r].

When Sir Richard Sutton bought thefe eftates in Berkfhire, he fignified that the purchafe was for the ufe of Elizabeth Morley of Weftminfter, widow. Accordingly Mrs. Morley, having in conjunction with

---

[q] Anthol Cephalæ, 653 The epigram defcribes an overfhot mill, with a double pair of ftones

[r] See Pennant's Tour in Scotland, vol 1 p 281 286 and the Plate there Compare St Matt xxiv 41 St Luke, xvii 35 See alfo on the fubject of mills, Bp Lowth on Ifai xlvii 2 Gent Mag 1797 p 829 Brit Crit vol iv p 313 xi p 532

Wil-

William and Richard Fermor demifed the
eftates to the college, Auguft 20, 1515, declared the purpofes of her benefaction, by an
indenture tripartite, between herfelf, William
Porter, Warden of New College, and Matthew Smyth, Principal of Brafen Nofe:
which purpofes were, That the Principal
fhould nominate one of the fellows of his
college, a prieft, who fhould celebrate mafs
for her in the college chapel, and likewife
preach once a year, himfelf or by deputy, in
St. Margaret's church, Weftminfter, praying
there exprefsly for her foul: and That an
obit or commemoration fhould be kept for
her after her deceafe, on the 26th of January, at which the Warden of New College is to be requefted to attend, and he is
to receive for his attendance eight-pence and
a dinner[s].

This firft benefactrefs to the college, Elizabeth Morley, was the widow of Robert
Morley, citizen and draper of London, who
died about the end of Henry the feventh's
reign   He probably was a native of Yorkfhire, as his father and mother were buried
at Guifborn in that county.   Dying without

[s] Yate, p 113. dat Nov 27, 1515

iffue,

iffue, his legacies, pious and charitable, were
very numerous   To his wife Elizabeth,
whom he conftituted " foole Executrice" of
his will, he gave the term of years which he
had in the " wyne taverne in the which he
dwelt called the bell in the kings ftrete at
Weftminfter," together with another tenement "within the fanctuary of Weftminfter,"
both of them held by leafe under the abbey.
He bequeathed to his " fervant and coufyn
Johane Sutton x maiks fterling when fhe ys
married," to be kept for her till then in
fome " fure mannys hands " To " Robert
Leyfonby his fervant and kinnefchilde[t] x^{li}."
To " xx maydens in Cleveland, of his kin or
alye," or, in defect of fuch, to others, " xx
nobles, that is to fay vi and viii to each,"
towards their marriage . Legacies to all his
men fervants and women feivants , and " to
the company crafte and myftery of drapers
of which he was a broder in their clothing
x^{li} fterling, or a cupp" of equal value, on
condition that they provide " a lowe maffe
of requiem," at St Michiel's Cornhill for
" xxxii yeres" to come , the officiating prieft

---

t Probably his nephew, as he leaves " to myn awnte Margaret Lafonbe xl^s ferl To another " kinnefchilde Thomas
How xx^s " " To my broder John Dunftall x^{li} fterl "

" to

" to remember him by name amongſt the
broder and ſuſtern in the bederoll " To William Bate, ſon of William Bate, " citezen
and paynter ſtayner, toward his fynde to
ſcole at Oxeford xxˢ " To " Hugh Denys
gentilman (one of the overſeers of his will)
my grete hope [hoop] of golde with a tur-
queys therin, weying iiiʰ fyne golde to my
miſtreſſe his wife my wrythen ring of golde
that I am wont to were upon my formaſt
fynger."

He died poſſeſſed of certain eſtates in the
pariſhes of Mehethe[u] and Melborne in Cam-
bridgeſhire, which he left in truſt for his
wife to keep an obit for him during her life,
at St. Margaret's, Weſtminſter, where he
lived, and in the " choer" of which church
he ordered his body to be buried ; entailing
the ſaid eſtates, after her deceaſe, 1. on his
brother Chriſtopher Morley, and the iſſue of
his body: 2 on the aforeſaid " Robert Lay-
ſonby ſon of Thomas Lyſonbe of Marton in
Cleveland," and his iſſue: 3. on Hugh Denys above named, and his iſſue · and in default of lawful iſſue by them, to be ſold and
diſtributed in deeds of charity.

[u] Probably a miſtake for Melrethe

The

The will, which is dated October 10, 1505, was proved by the executrix, May 27, 1508[x]. She feems to have furvived till 1524, for her anniverfary was firft kept by the college in 1524-5[y]. As her hufband left a legacy to his coufin Johanna Sutton, and as Sir Richard Sutton appears as the agent and friend of the family, it is probable that one of the Chefhire Suttons, unnoticed in the pedigree, had married a Morley

But the eftates, which Sir Richard Sutton himfelf gave to Brafen Nofe college, muft be briefly fpecified

One of thefe was the manor of Burgh, or Borowe, or Erdeborowe, in the parifh of Someiby, in the county of Leicefter, which he purchafed, March 22, 1490-1, of Thomas Waftenes, who gave a bond for performance of covenants to George Sutton mafter of Burton Lazarus, and received from him half of the purchafe money[z] fo that probably this George Sutton was a kinfman of Sir Richard's, though the degree of relationfhip

---

[x] Prerog Off vol Adeane, xxxvi (fol penult)

[y] Rot Burff

[z] Yate, p 98

does

does not appear.   Other estates, in the same
parish and neighbourhood, were afterwards,
1499, purchased of Thomas Chesilden of So-
merby [a]: all which estates and others in Mid-
dlesex were granted by Sir Richard Sutton,
July 15, 1508, when he was preparing to
build the college, to John Legh, knight, Richard Sneade, John Port, John Sutton senior, John Sutton junior, Roland Messenger,
and others, in trust, for his own use, and for
the performance of his last will [b].   He put
his nephew, the said " John Sutton thyon-
ger," in possession, in the presence of " Mr
Thomas Norton, knight, Master of Burton,
Sir Richard Alkeborowe parson of Borowe,
Sir John Coper," and ten other young gentlemen, " being scholars at Borowe, with
the parson there [c]," which may be noted as
an early instance of a private academy or
school in a clergyman's house, prior perhaps
to the institution of any grammar school in
the county, except one at Loughborough,
which was founded in 1494 [d].

Of the estates above mentioned in Mid-
dlesex the principal part was a messuage

[a] Ycc, p 97   [b] Ibid
[c] Id 98.   [d] Inscription on the school
                                        called

called the White Hart, in the parish of St.
Mary in the Strand[e], which, together with
certain lands at St. Ives in Cornwall, was
sold, December 4, 1505, to Richard Sutton
by William Harris, who made a conveyance
of the whole to him and John Sutton of
Sutton and his son Richard Sutton[f], who appears, by the pedigree, to have been Sir Richard's great nephew[g] These premises in
the Strand were sold by the college, in the
time of Charles ii, 1673, to Sir Christopher
Wren and others, Commissioners for enlarging the streets after the fire of London, for
the sum of 1700l, with which an estate
was purchased at Burwardescot or Burscot in

[e] Yate, p 92

[f] Yate, p 105

[g] Unless, as may seem more likely, the John Sutton here
mentioned is John Sutton senior, Sir Richard's brother, in
which case this Richard son of John will be Sir Richard's nephew, a younger son of his brother John, for among the trustees of Macclesfield school, under the will of Sir John Percival
the founder, dated Jan 25, 1502–3, are "John Sutton of Sutton the elder, and John his *eldest* son, which implies that he
had other sons, though the pedigree gives him one only See
Sir J Percival's Will, in the custody of Mr Peter Wright,
Town Clerk of Macclesfield and Steward of the school, by
whom, through a common friend, I have been favoured with
minutes of the said will and of other ancient deeds in his possession

Oxford-

Oxfordſhire[h], which has recently been exchanged, under authority of an act of parliament, with Edward Loveden Loveden, eſquire, for other lands at Stanford in the vale of White Horſe. Of the eſtates in Cornwall, which do not ſeem to have come into the poſſeſſion of the college, I know nothing memorable ; unleſs it be this, that ſoon after the purchaſe, when the title was queſtioned by one Thomas Penny, his claim was diſproved on this ground, becauſe " it is not poſſibill a man to ride from St Ives to London in three dayes[i]," an allegation, which in theſe days of improved roads, or of ſuperior horſemanſhip, would perhaps hardly be admitted

A more conſiderable eſtate was the manor of Cropredy, in the county of Oxford, and certain lands there, of which he purchaſed the reverſion, November 26, 1512, for 230 marks, of Edward Grevyle, eſquire, of Milcote in Warwickſhire ; and by a ſubſequent agreement with Richard Shetford, who had ſold to Grevyle, and was tenant for life, he came into actual poſſeſſion of the eſtate[k]

[h] Yate, p. 106 309   [i] Ibid p 105.
[k] Ibid p 92

This

This might feem fufficient, but the routine of conveyancing, with a multiplicity of deeds and in various fhapes, continued nine years longer, in the courfe of which Grevyle and Sutton were both of them knighted[l] It fhould here be obferved, that the manor of Cropredy was granted by queen Elizabeth, by patent, May 8, 1560, to Thomas Lee of Clatercote, efquire, and Bartholomew Brokefby, under this defcription, as " lately parcel of the eftates of John Duke of Northumberland[m]." If there were two manors here, the college of Brafen Nofe, in confequence of a purchafe made of the late Sir William Botheby, or of his heirs, in the year 1789, is now in poffeffion of them both.

The laft eftate neceffary here to be mentioned was fituate in North Ockington or Wokyndon, otherwife called " Wokyndone feptem fontium," in the county of Effex. Sir Richard Sutton purchafed this, June 16, 1513, for the fum of 40l of his kinfman George Sutton, gentleman, who had himfelt purchafed it ten years before of Thomas Pafmer[n]. There are deeds in the college ar-

[l] Yate, p 94

[m] Ibid p 95

[n] Ibid p 103. with 92

chives

chives relative to this eftate as early as 1316.
in the reign of Edward the fecond.

All thefe eftates, in value nearly equal to
thofe given by bifhop Smyth, Sir Richard
Sutton granted to the college of Brafen Nofe
by leafe, July 18, 11 Henry viii, (1519,)
and on the 29th of November following, by
a conveyance under his own hand and feal
he releafed them to the Society for ever,
engaging, for himfelf and his heirs, to warrant the title againft John [Iflip] abbat of
Weftminfter, and his fucceffors[o]. A fimilar
inftance of fpecial infurance againft the abbat
of Weftminfter has occurred before[p]. The
common form anciently was to warrant an
eftate againft the Jews. This alteration in
the mode and terms of conveyancing feems
to countenance a fufpicion, that the frater-
nities of monks, particularly of this affluent
convent in the metropolis of the kingdom,
were as formidable in this age to proprietors
of land, as the Jews had been formerly, but
there was now upon the throne a monarch,
who, according to the prediction already
cited[o], annulled the claims of the abbat of

<hr />

[o] Yate, p 93

[q] P 77 n

[p] See p 381.

Abing-

Abingdon and the abbat of Weftminfter, and all their iffue for ever.

On the fame day that thefe eftates were demifed by leafe to the college, namely July 18, 1519, an agreement was entered into by indenture between Sutton and the college, to the following effect: Firft it was covenanted, that the fociety fhould keep an anniverfary for ever for William Smyth late bifhop of Lincoln, and for Mr. Sutton, on the days of their refpective deceafe; when certain fums fhould be diftributed among thofe prefent, being priefts. It was further covenanted, that every perfon, on his admiffion to a fellowfhip, fhould take an oath to obferve all the ftatutes, made or to be made by Sutton, for the good governance of the college. It was likewife ftipulated, that the college fhould pay annually to three priefts five marks apiece, who fhould officiate as chaplains to the college, the faid priefts to be nominated by Sutton and his heirs of the manor of Sutton, which priefts, if not previoufly on the foundation, fhould, upon a vacancy, if eligible, be admitted fellows[r]

---

[r] Yate, p. 111

This

This compofition was immediately and
punctually fulfilled, in regard to the anniverfary of bifhop Smyth[s], nor was that more
material article. refpecting the chaplains, deferred, for payment was made to the chaplains of Mr. Richard Sutton, 13 Henry viii[t],
(1521,) but who they were, is not known.
In 1535 they were Thomas Typpyng and
Thomas Hawarden, fellows of the college,
and Thomas Allen[u], B. A. who was afterwards chofen fellow. Thefe chaplains, one
or more, continued to be nominated by the
heirs of Sutton, agreeably to the purport of
the original compofition, till the middle of
the prefent century. But in confequence of
the great and increafing diminution of the
value of money, the ftipend, originally competent, having become totally inadequate to
the maintenance even of a fingle chaplain,
divine fervice is now performed by the fellows, each in their turn, a plan in many refpects preferable to the former method.

This was a fruitful year of Sutton's life in
works and defigns of beneficence. Befides

---

[s] Rot Burff 12 H viii 1520.
[t] Rot. iftius anni
[u] Extr of Record in Firft Fruits Office, penes me

trans-

transferring his eftates, as now mentioned, to the college, and framing the compofition, to which we have referred, it will be recollected, that in this fame year, 1519, he provided for that expenfive and fuperb publication, the Orchard of Sion. Of the indenture, made at this period between him and the college, one of the conditions, as already noted, refpected ftatutes, framed or to be framed by him, for the regulation of the fociety; and, in virtue of that agreement, he now undertook to revife the exifting ftatutes, calling to his aid, as it feems, the Principal of the college, who, on the fure ground of experience, could inform him what was deficient or redundant, what might be altered and what retained with advantage. Of the merits of the revifal we have already fpoken diftinctly, and need not repeat what has been faid[x] When the work was completed, he affixed his feal to the authentic copy (though now loft) on the firft day of February, 13 Henry viii, (1521-2)

His benefactions however and his care for the fociety did not here terminate. In the enfuing year, May 14, 1522, he purchafed

---

[x] See above, p 312 &c

an eftate in Garfington and Cowley, in Oxfordfhire, of William Coton of Oxford, clerk,
for the fum of 461[y]. The eftate, which was
then or lately the property of Antony Carif-
wall, parfon of Hanworth, Middlefex, was
granted, in the reign of Edward the firft, by
Nicholaus de la Gn̄a to Philip Mimekan, in
reward of his fervice as Forefter of Sothere
or Sothore[z], the fame, it is prefumed, which
has long been called Shotover. Sir Richard
Sutton put the college in poffeffion of it by
leafe and releafe, 13 and 14 July, the fame
year. He afterwards made the college a prefent of 5l for building a wall, which is acknowledged in the audit roll for the year
1524, having probably been given in that
year.

One of the pureft gratifications, which can
be enjoyed by a great and generous mind,
is to behold an inftitution of beneficence,

[y] Yate, p 109

[z] Ibid and the original in the Archives, C 2   The war-
ranting claufe is a fpecimen of the Latinity and cuftom of the
times   " Ego et heredes mei—contra omnes homines mares et
feminas tam Judeos quam Chriftianos—warentizabimus ' The
quit rent referved, payable at Chriftmas, was " vnum clauum
gazophili, but what that means I have not learnt   Is it a
knot of filk ?

planned

planned with deliberation and executed with care, fix itself firmly in the world, attracting the notice and conciliating the favour of the wife and good, that it may more abundantly answer the important purposes, for which it was established. The Bishop of Lincoln, surviving the foundation of his college little more than a year, could only accompany the infant seminary with his dying prayers and good wishes, but Sir Richard Sutton, who lived ten years or more after the decease of his venerable brother Founder, had the satisfaction to see the society daily rising in consideration and repute, enriched with many occasional donations and permanent benefactions.

What authority Antony Wood had for saying, that Oldham, bishop of Exeter, had an intention to join with bishop Smyth in founding Brasen Nose college[a], he has not informed us, but since the arms of this distinguished patron of literature, the friend of Smyth and of his friends, the executor of Bray, the supervisor of the will of the second earl of Derby[b], were displayed in the win-

---

[a] Colleges, p 393

[b] Hist of House of Stanley, p 44

dows

dows of the original library of Brafen Nofe college[c], there can be no doubt but he contributed to finish or to furnish the room; though his principal benefactions were beftowed on the contemporary foundation of Corpus Chrifti college, and, through that fociety, on his native county of Lancafter; where he founded, at Manchefter, a grammar School, which has always ranked high among the claffical feminaries of the kingdom, and never flourifhed more than at prefent, under the fuperintending vigilance and ability of Charles Lawfon, M A fometime fellow of Corpus Chrifti college. Over the gateway of that college the arms of Sir Richard Sutton are ftill vifible, in the cornice of the room in which the firft Prefident, the learned John Claymond, lived, himfelf an eminent benefactor to Brafen Nofe college, thefe great contemporaries, with meritorious liberality of mind, mutually aiding and encouraging each other in the caufe in which they were refpectively engaged, the advancement of literature and of Oxford.

Other arms, formerly in the refectory of Brafen Nofe college[d], which the affairs and

[c] Wood, Colleges, p 371   [d] Ibid p 368

connec-

\

connections of Smyth and of Sutton help us
to account for, are thofe of Bury (intended
probably for Edmund Bury, the conftant
agent of bifhop Smyth) Brudenell, Grevile
and Fermor. Sir Robert Brudenell, chief
Juftice of the Common Pleas 1521[e], an anceftor of the Earl of Cardigan, was one of
the learned ferjeants at law employed by
Smyth in the reign of Henry vii His country refidence was at Dean in Northamptonfhire, near Smyth's favourite palace of Lidington. His firft wife was Margaret, daughter and cohen of Thomas Entwifell of Stanton Wyvill in Leicefterfhire[f], whence the
arms of Entwifell were impaled with Brudenell in the Brafen Nofe window.

William Grevile, Serjeant at law, 1505,
Juftice of the Common Pleas, 1510, gave his
affiftance, jointly with Sir Robert Brudenell
and others, in terminating certain difputes
refpecting Cold Norton, and in expediting
the fale and conveyance of the eftate to bifhop Smyth[g]. But it is not certain whether
the Grevile arms in Brafen Nofe were a me-

[e] Dugd Chron Ser and Orig Jurid p 127
[f] Collins's Peer 3d ed vol iii p 384
[g] See above, p 305

morial

morial of this learned Judge, or of his contemporary and kinfman, Edward Grevile, of
Milcote in Warwickfhire, of whom Sir
Richard Sutton purchafed the manor of Cropredy; who received the honour of knighthood, October 13, 1513, for his brilliant behaviour at the fiege of Tournay and the
battle of Spurs This gallant anceftor of the
prefent Earl of Warwick married Anne
daughter of John Denton, efquire, of Ambrofeden[h] in Oxfordfhire, of which family,
it is prefumed, was Thomas Denton, who
joined with Grevile in levying a fine for the
eftates at Cropredy, 20 Henry vii[i]. (1505)

William Fermor, clerk of the crown in
the King's Bench in the reign of Henry vii
and Henry viii, fold certain eftates at Faringdon, Berks, as already mentioned[k], to Sir
Richard Sutton, agent for Mrs Morley. He

---

[h] Collins s Peer vol iv p 665 John Denton, efquire,
prefented to the vicarige of Ambrofeden in 1547 Kennet s
Paroch Ant p 695

[i] Yate, p 92 and in another deed, Apr 12, 1524 iv
p 94 Grevile is ftyled Efquire, Nov 26, 4 H viii (1512)
and Knight, term Hil 5 H viii (1513-14) ib p 92 The
arms of Thomas Denton were in the Hall of the Middle Temple Orig Jur d p 229

[k] See p 424

after-

afterwards, 24 Henry viii, fold other eftates at Shelfwell in Oxfordfhire to John Claymond, which conftituted part of Claymond's benefaction to Brafen Nofe college[l]. His younger brother, Richard Fermor, merchant of the Staple[m], who raifed a noble fortune and was the common progenitor of the Earls of Pomfret and the Fermors of Tufmore in the county of Oxford, was a party with William in various deeds both on this and on the former occafion. On account of thefe tranfactions and this intercourfe with the Founders of Brafen Nofe, the Fermors, the Greviles, the Brudenells, and Buries gave their refpective arms, accompanied probably with pecuniary gratuities, to embellifh the common hall of the new college

Others at the fame time, without " the pomp of heraldry," were known by their beneficence. Sir John Blount, knight, gave to the fociety 6l. 13s 4d in the year 1516; and confiderable fums at feveral other times,

---

[l] Yate, p 147

[m] Yate, p 146 and fee Collins s Peer vol iii p 496 They were the fons of Thomas Ricardes alias Fermour by his fecond wife Emmotte widow of Henry Waynman Richard Wenman (the fame name) is a party with them in a fine, 3 H viii. Yate, p 116

as well as a legacy by his laft will, about the
year 1524ⁿ. Sir John Hufey, knight, who
feems to have been a friend of Sir Reginald
Bray°, alfo beftowed certain free gifts on the
college, in the time of the fecond Founder,
and after his deceafeᴾ.

Thefe were tranfient donations Others
were of a permanent nature , of which Mrs.
Morley's, already mentioned, was the firft.
The chaplain on her foundation has a payment in the audit of 1517. In the following year the college received another bene-

---

ⁿ Rot Burff 8 & 17 H viii Plate Book, f 5, 6 The
whole amount feems to have been 461 13s 4D I have
not afcertained who the perfon was Thomas Blount was
knighted by H vii at the battle of Stoke Cotton MS
Cleud as, C iii i 13 and Thomas Blount (but not ftyled a
knight) died in Feb 1515-16 directing his body to be buried
at the Temple Church Prerog Off Holder, viii

° The office of Senefhal and Receiver of Grantl am and
Stanford i Lincolnfhire was granted to Reginald Bray
and Joan Hufey by Patent, 16 Jan 11 H vii (1495-6)
Rolls Chapel

ᴾ Rot Burff 9 13, 16 H 11 The amount appears to be
25L 6s 3D In the Plate Book, p 5 we have " In manibus Jon Hufey Militis (no fum) " In manibus magiftri
Tho Blunt militis, xx " which looks like a debt payable on
demand , but on comparing the feveral entries and varying
fums, I take it that fome of the payments at leaft were volun-
tary and gratuious

faction.

faction. John Cox, of Kyrtleton, Oxfordshire, wool-merchant, gave a messuage called
the Red Lyon in Cheping Wycombe[q], and
120L. in money to purchase lands to provide
two priests, being Fellows, one of them an
Oxfordshire or South country man; to make
annually, each of them, a sermon at Kyrtleton, and to pray for the Founder. This
composition was settled in the same manner
as Mrs Morley's, by a tripartite indenture
between Cox, himself, and William Porter,
Warden of New College, and the Principal
and Fellows of Brasen Nose[r], who, if the
statutes were then literally fulfilled, must apparently have consented to an impossibility,

[q] It was sold, 2 Aug 4 H viii, to John Cox and Juliana
his wife by John Yorg clerk, LL D master of the Rolls;
who, two years before, purchased it, possibly for Cox, of John
Ravenynge and Katherine his wife Edmund Bury (probably
bishop Smyths agent) was a party with Cox in the purchase.
The rent of this Inn, 20 Ed iv was 8L 6S 8D Yate,
p 119, 120 The college let it for 4L and yet seem to have
been obliged to distrain for the rent Rott 14 H viii 16 H
viii In 1535 it was rated at 3L only Extr of valuation
in F rst Fruits Office It were a curious but perhaps fruitless
speculation to inquire to what local or general circumstances
this rapid decrease in the value of an inn was owing, amidst
the general rise of other property I think I have seen evidence that property of the same description elsewhere experienced a similar diminution in value

[r] Yate p 118 22 Jul 10 H viii, 1518

in engaging to find a native of Oxfordſhire
or of ſome ſouthern county in their own
body, whereas they were all required to be
natives of the dioceſe of Lichfield and Coventry. Whatever expedient was found for
this difficulty, whether the letter of the ſtatutes, or the letter of the compoſition, gave
way, the two chaplains make their appearance, though not by name, in the annual
audit from the ſecond year after the date of
the benefaction⁵, in which year alſo Cox's
anniverſary was kept, ſo that he did not
long ſurvive the ratification of his indenture.

John Port was a party with Sutton in the
grant of Saliſbury hall, and in the original
leaſe of Braſen Noſe hall   He appears alſo
frequently in other tranſactions relating to
the foundation of the college, but it is not
always certain when he acts for himſelf, and
when he is only the agent of the college or
the Founders   He was the ſon of Henry
Port of Cheſter, and grandſon of Henry a

---

⁵ Rot 12 H iii 1520 Pro indenturis Joh Cokks Rot
11 H viii In 155, "Mr Jacobus was one of Cox's Chaplains, though no perſor of that Chriſtian or ſurname appears in
the liſt of Fellows Mr John Leche, a Cheſhire man, then
Vice Principal was the other Extr from Firſt Fruits' Office,
ut ſupra

merchant in that city, who were, one or
both of them, occafionally Mayor and Sheriff
of Chefter[t] He was of the inner Temple,
one of the Readers there[u], Treafurer and
Governour[x] of that honourable fociety. In
1515 he was conftituted Solicitor general to
the King, created Serjeant at law, 1521[y],
knighted and made one of the Juftices of
the King's Bench in or before the year 1527[z];
and died before 1540[a]. He married Jane
daughter and heirefs of John Fitzherbert of
Etwal in Derbyfhire[b], whence the arms of

[t] Vale Royal, B 1 p 80 &c B 11 187, 188

[u] Dugd. Orig p 163 poftea Attorn Reg general But in
the Series, 6 H viii, he calls him Solicitor general. Perhaps
he had fucceffively both thofe offices

[x] Ibid p 170 172

[y] Dugd Orig p 114—117

[z] The Series Chron fays Juft K B Jan 26 1533 but the
Brafen Nofe audit roll ftyles him " Joh Port Miles, Juftic domini Regis' in 19 H viii (1527)

[a] Nuper Juftic domini Regis de Banco Comp Bur
32 H viii (1540)

[b] Pedigree of Port, Vifit of Staffordfhire, 1583, in Queen's
Coll Oxford, MS Williamfon, H 10 f 152 Randle Holme
fays, Mr Juftice Port married Dorothy d of Sir Antony Fitzherbert Pedigree of Afhton, 1660, in Archiv of Brafen Nofe,
Drawer, 29 Antony Fitzherbert, ferjeant at law, is joined
with Sir J Port in a purchafe, 8 H viii Yate, p 91 and
again, 16 H viii, the faid A Fitzherbert being then Judge of
the Common Pleas ib 94 John Port (fon of the faid Judge
Port)

Fitzherbert were impaled with thofe of Port at Brafen Nofe. He gave to the college a fuit of veftments and a cope of black and red damafk for the ufe of the chapel[c]. He alfo gave the fociety a garden lying on the fouth fide of the college[d], and afterwards conveyed to them a more ample benefaction. John Williamfon, Rector of St. George's in Canterbury, had agreed, 12 Henry viii, to con-

Port) who was knighted at the coronation of Edw vi (Cotton MS Claudius, C iii f 166) gave an annuity of 3 L a year to Brafen Nofe, in confideration of the pious intent of his great uncle William Fitzherbert D D canon refidentiary of Southwell (whofe lands he inherited) who meant in his life time to beftow a benefaction on the college, and alfo in confideration of his father's regard for the fociety. Feb 9, 1554-5 Yate, p 125 In lieu of this rent charge of 3 L payable out of the manor of the diffolved monaftery of Dale in Derbyfhire, Henry the third earl of Huntingdon, whofe brother Sir George Haftings (afterwards earl of Huntingdon) married Dorothy daughter and coheir of Sir J Port, gave to the fociety of Brafen Nofe the houfe and fite of St Mary college, the beloved retreat of Erafmus when he ftudied at Oxford Yate, p 126 the date, 22 Eliz (1580) The faid Sir J Port by his will, 1560, bequeathed 200 L to endow a Lecture in Philofophy and another in Humanity in Brafen Nofe college ib p 165 He founded a fchool at Repton in Derbyfhire MS Carte, F F f 44 and Topographer, vol ii p 278—281 See alfo ibid. p 224—228

[c] See App No xviii

[d] See above, p 282

tribute

tribute the fum of 200l for the endowment of two fellowfhips in the college of
Brafen Nofe, but he died before the bufinefs
was fully arranged and completed. It was
therefore covenanted by an indenture, bearing date July 3, 14 Henry viii, (1522) between the college, John Port ferjeant at
law, and John Hales efquire, one of Williamfon's executors, that with the faid fum
of 200l paid by Hales, lands fhould be
purchafed of the annual value of 9l for the
maintenance of two fcholars or fellows, born
in the city or in the county palatine of
Chefter, of the name, coufenage, or lineage
of John Williamfon, or John Port, and
power was referved to keep the places void,
till fome one anfwering the terms of the
compofition defired to be admitted[e] No
eligible purchafe being immediately found,
Sir John Port, to give the more fpeedy effect
to the benefaction, granted a rent charge of
the fpecified amount of 9l. iffuing out of
the manor of Mofeley hall in Lancafhire, and
other eftates of his in that county[f], in confequence of which arrangement, John Port (an
undergraduate, as it feems) occurs in 1524

[e] Yate, p 121   [f] Ib p 122

as " one of Mr Williamson's scholars;" and
the following year (John) Peke B A was
the other[g].

In this state of prosperity, chiefly through
the kindness of his own friends and those of
bishop Smyth, Sutton had the satisfaction to
behold the rising seminary, when he received from his Sovereign the honour of
knighthood We have not learnt where,
nor the exact time when, this honour was
conferred. He is styled simply Richard Sutton Esquire in May, 14 Henry viii[h], (1522)
and he was a Knight before the end of the
fifteenth year of the reign of that monarch
He was probably knighted privately, and not,
as was more usual, at some public festivity,
and so the fact seems to have escaped the
notice of those, who have made it their business to collect and record the creations of
the reign

---

[g] Solut pro lectura Joh Port unius scolarium Joh Williamson benefactoris hujus collegii pro dicto anno, iii S iiii D
Rot Burss 16 H viii Solut pro communis M Princ et
septem Sociorum pro uno anno, x i L xvii S viii D ob Pro
communis domini Peke et Joh Port scholarium Joh Williamson—iii L ii S vi D ib 17 H viii

[h] Yate, p 109

He

He made his will, and fubfcribed it with his " fjke hande," March 16, 15 Henry viii. (1523-4) His malady, if then dangerous, abated, as he was able to tranfact bufinefs feveral months afterwards[i]. An obituary mafs however was performed by the college for his foul before the year ended, but the day of the folemnity is not recorded[k] His will was proved, November 7, 1524. An annual commemoration of him is obferved by the fociety on the Sunday after Michaelmas, which is probably about the time when he departed this life. He betrays no anxiety about the place of fepulture, but only that, wherever it fhould " fortune him to deceafe," he might be buried there, " afore the image of our Lady," in whofe " meke praier" and " protection" he appears to repofe great confidence. It has been conjectured that he was buried at Macclesfield, becaufe he directs his obit to be kept there yearly, but the graveftone, which he orders, would there have had a fair chance of efcap-

---

[i] Yate, p 95

[k] Pro anniverfar domini W Smyth—fundatoris iftius Collegii—viS xi D —pro exequiis et miff Ric. Sutton Militis unius fundatorum iftius Coll —xxvS vD. ob Rot Burfl 16 H viii

ing

ing depredation, and of being known and
remembered　If he was buried, as is more
likely, in the monaftery at Sion, (a favourite
place of interment[1], while pofthumous piety
and prayers for the dead were in fafhion) all
memorials there were foon fwept away by
the　horned flood," which Henry viii poured
in upon them

His bequefts are almoft all of them religious and charitable　He gives 20 fhillings
to the Mafter of the Temple for forgotten
offerings, and iii^s iiii^d to every prieft there
to pray for him, and v^h to be diftributed to
the poor at his funeral.　He orders a chantry
to be endowed, at Sutton or at Macclesfield,
with a ftipend of iiii^h viii^s iiii^d for a prieft,
to be nominated by his heirs, to pray for him
and his kindred, and for the fouls of Edward iv, queen Elizabeth his wife[m], Elizabeth

[1] Ralph Haftings, knight, of Wanftead, Effex, bequeathed
his body to be buried in the church of S Brigit at Sion, Sept
17, 1495 Ped of Earls of Huntingdon, MS Wood, I 3
(8165) f 51 Thomas the fecond earl of Derby was alfo buried
at Sion, agreeably to his will, in 1521 Hift of II of Stanley, p 43 and Coll nss Peerage
[m] Daughter of Richard Widville the firft earl Rivers, widow
of Sir John Grey, father of Thomas Grey, lord Groby, created
marquis of Dorfet, 1175 Bolton's Extinct Peers, 1769 p 96
240

dutchefs

dutchefs of Suffolk[n], my Lord Rivers[o], my Lord Richard, my Lord Thomas late marquis of Dorfet[p], Nicolas Talbot[q], and Chriftopher Hyde[r]

[n] Elizabeth wife of John de la Pole, duke of Suffolk, was fifter to Edward IV The duke was Steward of the univerfity of Oxford, 1472, and died in 1491 Wood's Fafti, ed Gutch, p 182 and Bolton's Extinct Peers, p 277

[o] There feems to have been no " lord Rivers' living in 1524 Richard Widville, the third and laft earl Rivers of this family, died unmarried in 1491 Bolton, ib 240 Antony earl Rivers was beheaded in 1483 by Richard III, at Pomfret as was alfo Richard lord Grey, brother to the firft marquis of Dorfet ib Was he " my lord Richard" here intended? In Macclesfield church is a chapel called " Lord Rivers's chapel ,' but whether it belonged to this family, or to the Savages, earls Rivers, I do not know

[p] The firft marquis of this family, who died in 1494 His fon Thomas, marquis of Dorfet, lived till 1530 Bolton, ut fupra, p 96

[q] There is a letter of attorney by Nicolas Talbot, Gent Sept 15, 1 Ric III (1483) to give feifin of the manor of Harleford to Rich Jefley Arch Univ Oxf K 2 6 and he is mentioned in Jefley's conveyance of the eftate to Anne Countefs of Warwick, John Mordaunt &c Nov 6 5 H VI (1489) ibid K 2 8 This manor of Harleford or Harleyford (of which we have heard above, p 204) is now the property of Sir William Clayton, bart who holds an eftate in the neighbourhood, but not the manor itfelf, by leafe under the Univerfity of Oxford

[r] Thomas Hyde of Norbury, in Macclesfield hundred, is one of the truftees of Macclesfield fchool in 1502-3 See above, p 431 n g But I fee no Chriftopher in the pedigree Peter de la Hyde B A of Brafen Nofe, died in 1528 MS Wood, 8514 p 187 Edward Hyde of Chefhire " arm fil nat max ætat 17 " entered at Brafen Nofe in 1618 The

Chefh

Charity and devotion are not always exempt from caprice, otherwife curiofity might be tempted to afk, why fome of thefe names were ftrung on the bead-roll, and why others were not added   Did the teftator forget the court of Henry vii, in which he had been a privy Counfellor ? Or did he, as is more likely, not cordially love the reigning prince, the fon of that Henry, and therefore forbore to mention one, left the exclufion of the other fhould be more pointed ?

He appoints an obit, or " yere's mynde," to be kept for him, and alfo for his father and mother, at Macclesfield, and that certain gratuities be diftributed to the " Mafter of the Gramar fcole⁵," and others, for then

Chefh Ped males Edward fon and heir of Robert Hyde of Norbury two years old in 1615   The Hydes of Wiltfhire, of which family the earl of Clarendon was, defcended from the Hydes of Chefhire, and bore the fame arms

⁵ Sir John Percival, who founded this fchool, as already mentioned, p 451 n g was born at Macclesfield, lord mayor of London in 1498, made a knight in the fie'd by Henry vii, a worthy benefactor to the parifh of St Mary Wolnoth, London, where he and dame Thomafin his wife were buried   She alfo founded a free fchool at St Mary Wike, Devon, where fhe was born   Stowes Surv by Strype, B i p 28 262 ii 161 v 126 Savage, archbifhop of York, is regarded as co-founder of the fchool at Macclesfield. Deeds, ut fupra, in the hands

attendance at thofe times. He bequeathes
to his " nephew John Sutton's wife oon of
his gownes" To Clements Inn xxˢ. To
Roger Leghᵗ of Peckham he remits viiiʰ lent
him when he was firſt married, and alfo
bequeathes to him " a gowne and xxˢ." He
wills that " xlˢ be fpent abowte the making

of Mr Peter Wright By the fame deeds it appears, that, in
the 9th of Elizabeth, Richard Sutton of Sutton, efquire, with
other governours appointed by Edward vi, April 25, 1552,
difpofed of the old mefluage on the fchool bank, where the
original fchool was, having removed the fchool to its prefent
fituation in a different part of the town

ᵗ Roger Legh of Ridge (fon of Roger Legh, efquire, of the
fame place, who lived ann 1448) married Elizabeth daughter
of Sutton of Sutton (fifter, it is prefumed, to Sir R Sutton)
Their fon, Roger Legh of Ridge, efquire, married Mary
daughter and heir (or one of the heirs MS Harl 139 f 35
b by Laurence Boftock 1574) of William Sparke of Glen-
ham in Suffolk and of Surrey Chefh Ped The hufband of
the Surrey heirefs is probably the Roger Legh of Peckham in
Surrey his father, as we fha'll fee prefently, was one of Sir R
Sutton's executors Roger Legh the elder of the Ridge and
Roger his eldeft fon are two of the truftees of Macclesfield
fchool in 1502-3 ubi fupra Roger Legh of Ridge is a feoffee with Richard and John Sutton in William Cholmeley's
deed of fettlement, A D 1514 See above, p 413 The
Leghs of Ridge near Macclesfield fprung from a younger fon
of Peter Legh of Lyme, who bore the banner and took the earl
of Tankervil'e prifoner in the ever memorable battle of Crefly
Thomas Legh, mayor of Macclesfield in 1761, fold Ridge hall
to William Norton M D who left it to his fifter Mis Prin-
g'e, the prefent proprietor, 1799

G g 4   the

the high wayes abowte Saint Giles in the ffelde."

To " my Lady Abbeffe of the monaftery of Syon xx^h to pray for him " And that certa n houfes lately purchafed in " Braynforth" (Brentford) " fhall go towards the fynding of an honeft preeft to pray for his foule," and " to teche all thofe women that intend to be piofeffed and admytted unto the Houfe of Syon, and my Lady Abbeffe yf it pleafe her to gn,e the faid preft mete and drink and logging, and the faid preft to fay grafe dailey and to geve attendance upon the Steward of the faid Houfe of Syon at dinner and fupper and to do diune ferMce afore him."

To Thomas Sutton and his heirs male his ' Berehoufe" at the end of Brentford bridge. To William Sutton his (Thomas's) brother, v^h " To George Sutton his brother being in the newe College^u in Oxford xl^s towards his

---

u " Mafter Porter Wardeyn of the new Coll ge occurs in Reg C. f 222 ad ann 1505 but I have not heard of any George Sutton of tnat fociety in or near the year 1524 There was " M George Sutton" of Brafen Nofe who lived in Black Hall, 29 Henry vin (1537) Rot Burff

fynding."

fyndıng " " To the faid Thomas Sutton his
hool yeres wages aforchande unto the tyme
he may gett him a newe mafter within the
fame yere '

To his " nephew John Sutton of Sutton
and his heirs" all the profits of his lands in
Chefhıre, Shropfhıre, and Derbyfhıre, provided he truly " performe this his laft wille,"
and " do not fell any part of them, but
kepe a good houfeholde, and kepe his chıl-
dren to fcole, and help to fett love and cha-
rıtıe amongft his neighbours·" and likewife
the profits of all his lands " in Tottenhall
Court" after the deceafe of his " cofyn
George Sutton," and all his other lands in
Mıddlefex, except what were bequeathed to
the " Lady Abbes of Syon, and except the
fflod mede," which he gives to his " cofyn
George Sutton of the Queene's houfe for the
terme of his life." To " Rıchard Sutton
yoman of the chambre with the Queen's
grace" certain lands in " Iftilworth," of the
yearly value of v^h and more.

To " my Lady of Dartford[x] x marcs,"
to " my Lady of Dennye[y] xl[s]," to pray for

[x] In Kent, a houfe of Auftın Nuns
[y] Erafmus wrote a long letter to the Nuns of the order of
St

him. To his coufin Ellyn Copelande v marcs
to pray for him   To his nephew John Sutton of Sutton his " beddyng and houfeholde
ftuffe—in the Sion and in the Temple and
at St Giles," and his " crymfyn vellvet
doublett and oon of his beft gownes," and
to " my cofen his wife an other gowne," to
pray for his foul, appointing his faid nephew
refiduary legatee   The executors are John
(Young) bifhop of Callipolis[z], mafter of St
Thomas of Acres in London, his nephew
John Sutton of Sutton, his coufin Richard
Snede[a], John Port ferjeant at law, Richard

St Francis at Denny near Cambridge   Knight's Erafm App
No xviii p xlvi—lviii   Towards the conclufion he fays,
" Nominatim autem Greis fororibus ex me falutem dicatis "
Does this imply, that fome of the Grey family were at that
time nuns at Denny   Erafmus had been tutor to Thomas
Grey, fon of the marquis of Dorfet ibid p 18 and the mar-
quis was high in Sutton s efteem, as we have juft feen, p 453
Knight fays (L of Erafm p 292) thefe nuns of Denny to
the laft preferved a good character for their order and difci-
pline

[z] John Young titular bifhop of Callipolis in Thrace was
Warden of New College, much in favour with cardinal Wolfey, employed at different times in revifing the univerfity ftatutes See Wood's Annals, i p 666 ii 2. 3 15 18 Athen
Oxon i 663 He died in 1526 I do not find the mafterfhip
of St Thomas of Acres elfewhere reckoned among his preferments See of that houfe Not Mon London, No 48 Newcourt, &c Erafmus mentions it in his Peregrin Rel ergo

[a] Richard Snede or Sneyd was Lent Reader in the inner
Temple,

Lyſter[b], and Roger Legh of Ridge; and he
" wills that the ſaid John Poorte have v
marcs for his labor, Richard Lyſter v marcs,

Temple, 2 H viii Orig Jurid p 163 Recorder of Cheſter,
10 H viii, 1518, and continued in that office till 1535 Sir
P Leyceſters Antiq p 187 He was truſtee with Roger Legh
of Ridge for Sir R Suttons Leiceſterſhire eſtates in 1508
Yate, p 97 and for the ſite of Braſen Noſe college, 3 H viii
(1511) ib p 83 Executor to the ſecond earl of Derby, 13
H viii Hiſt of H of Stanley, p 43 William Sneyd, draper, (probably his father) was Sheriff of Cheſter in 1473, and
1503, mayor, 1478, 1516, 1531 Vale Royal, B i p 77, &c
B ii 187 William Sneyd, eſquire, mayor, 1543 William
Sneyd, knight, mayor, 1567 ib From the Recorder, couſin
(i e I ſuppoſe, nephew) to Sir R Sutton are deſcended the
Sneyds of Bradwell in Derbyſhire and of Keel in Staffordſhire,
or, as the author of Vale Royal ſpeaks of them, B ii p 77,
" the noble race of Sneyds, of great worſhip and account, and
of ampler revenues in Staffordſhire, which I the rather note,
becauſe they have great poſſeſſions in this county, and this
country and eſpecially this city of Cheſter boaſteth, that hence
they had their original " Compare Sir P Leyceſter, ut ſupra
  [b] Richard Lyſter was Lent Reader of the middle Temple,
7 & 13 H viii Orig Jurid p 215, 216 Solicitor general,
July 8, 13 H viii Chron Ser Attorney general before May
26, 19 H viii as we have ſeen above, p 281 Chief Baron of
the Exchequer, May 12, 1530 Knight, chief Juſtice of the
Kings Bench, Nov 9, 1546 Chron Ser His arms were in
Serjeants Inn Orig Jurid p 329 There is a head of lady
Lyſter, wife of Sir Richard, from a drawing by Hans Holbein,
in Imitations of original Drawings by him, publiſhed by J
Chamberlaine, Keeper of the King's Drawings Brit Crit
vol v p 266 John Lyſter is a party with Sutton in his Leiceſterſhire purchaſes, 6 H vii Yate, p 98

and

and Richard Snede v marcs." He " ordeyns"
the " said Lady Abbas of Syon, and Maister
John ffewterer[c] general Confeffor of the said
monaftery and Marfter Alexander Bell his
gooftly fader overfeers of this his laft Will
and Teftament, mooft humbly befeeching
them to foigive him that he has offended
theym in woide woike or thought, and of
their Charitie that it may pleafe theym to
pray for him with all the hole convent, as
he trufts he fhall pray for them in hevyn[d]."

The will was proved in St Paul's cathedral, November 7, 1524, by two of the executors, John Sutton and Roger Legh.

c In 1522 the college had 200 L in the hands of Mr John
fewterei Confeffor of he monaftery of Syon, concerning wh ch
there is this memorandum "prediata fum cc" in manibus
mag Joh fewterer expofita eft pro terris emptis a M Jon
porte' Plate Book, p 5 It was, I fuppofe, Mr Williamfon s
benefaction (the fum being the fame) which was fettled by
indenture with the college this fame year, 1522, but if fo, the
purchafe nere fpoken of, did not take effect See above, p 449
In "The Myrrour or Glaffe of Chriftes Paffion,' printed by
Redman, London, 1534, folio, the preface is dedicated "To
the honourable lord Hufey —From Syon the vi day of December 1533 your dayly oratour Johan Iewterer' Ames
Typogr p 391 Of Alexander Bell no other notice has been
found

d App No xxii

No military exploits have been traced in the life of Sir Richard Sutton. He chofe to be painted in armour, not for the fame reafon which induced the Romans to have their ftatues in the habiliments and garb of a foldier, becaufe they were ambitious of martial glory[c], but as it was a permanent drefs, and a compliment, as the open-faced knight's helmet fhews, to the ordei of knighthood, with which he had recently been invefted. The fcanty materials of his life do not fuggeft hints for a complete character, but in the general air and features of his poitrait we fee an epitome of the man. There is nothing in his looks of the defiance of the warrior or pride of the combatant, armed for the field or equipt for the tournament: his countenance breathes the fweetnefs of benevolence, his afpect is clothed with the ferenity of peace Among the Worthies of his country he has long been enrolled, but I have not learnt who it was that compofed the verfes, in the peifon of Biafen Nofe college, wherein he is complimented on finifhing what another began "The Mufes," on that occafion, it is faid, "feemed neither to fmile noi fiown, but kept their wonted

---

[c] Cic de Off i xvi i

countenance[f]." In truth he deferved a better encomiaft. But real worth does not require the aid of poetry to embellifh and fet it off to advantage. It is content with plain profe, in which they who " paint it trueft praife it beft." With a reputation eftablifhed on the folid foundation of fkill in the ftudy and integrity in the practice of the law, Sutton was called to be a privy Counfellor by Henry the feventh ; in whofe court, it has been remarked, favours came " unexpected, undefired[g]," the rewards of merit, not the price of importunity , and he frequently affifted the deliberations of a prince, who patronifed commerce and the arts of peace Many ample fortunes were raifed in that court, and many more at the fame time, as the preceding pages often incidentally evince, by the profeffion of the law Immenfe wealth, whether in the court or at the bar, Sir Richard Sutton feems neither to have coveted nor acquired. He obtained honourable affluence by honourable means , and what he acquired he devoted to the moft valuable purpofes of human life, to the honour and

Fullers Worthies, Chefh p 82

g Wottons Remains, p 369 Compare Bp Fifher's oration before Henry vii in Lel Itin vol ii p 100

advance-

advancement of religion and learning "The nobleft works and foundations," fays lord Bacon, " have proceeded from childlefs men, which have fought to exprefs the images of their minds, where thofe of their bodies have failed[h]." Unmarried himfelf, and not anxious to aggrandife his family, which had long ranked among the beft in a county juftly proud of its ancient Gentry, Sir Richard Sutton beftowed handfome benefactions and kind remembrances among his kinfmen, but he wedded the public, and made pofterity his heir An active coadjutor from the firft to the Bifhop of Lincoln in laying the foundation of Brafen Nofe college, he completed the building, revifed the laws, and doubled the revenues of the growing feminary, leaving it a perpetual monument of the confolidated wifdom and joint munificence of Smyth and of Sutton.

[h] Eflay vii

APPEN-

APPENDIX:

ORIGINAL EVIDENCES, LETTERS, AND PAPERS NEVER BEFORE PRINTED.

PEDIGREE I.

Extracted from Lee's Vifitation of Oxfordfhire, 1574,
in G. 3. fol. 31 b. in Coll. Armor. by J. C. Brooke,
Somerfet Herald, Jan. 6, 1790.

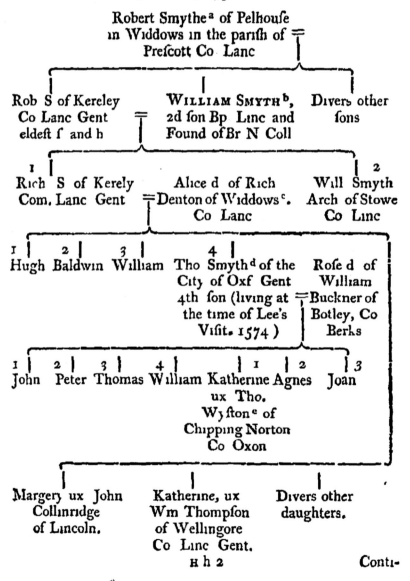

Robert Smythe^a of Pelhoufe
in Widdows in the parifh of
Prefcott Co Lanc

Rob S of Kereley
Co Lanc Gent
eldeft f and h

WILLIAM SMYTH^b,
2d fon Bp Linc and
Found of Br N Coll

Divers other
fons

1 Rich S of Kerely
Com. Lanc Gent

Alice d of Rich
Denton of Widdows^c.
Co Lanc

2 Will Smyth
Arch of Stowe
Co Linc

1 Hugh 2 Baldwin 3 William

4 Tho Smyth^d of the
City of Oxf Gent
4th fon (living at
the time of Lee's
Vifit. 1574)

Rofe d of
William
Buckner of
Botley, Co
Berks

1 John 2 Peter 3 Thomas 4 William

1 Katherine
ux Tho.
Wyfton^e of
Chipping Norton
Co Oxon

2 Agnes 3 Joan

Margery ux John
Collinridge
of Lincoln.

Katherine, ux
Wm Thompfon
of Wellingore
Co Linc Gent.

Divers other
daughters.

H h 2

Conti-

Continuation of the foregoing from a Pedigree with the arms beautifully blazoned, in the poffeffion of the Rev. James Long Hutton of Buckingham, brother to Mary Long Hutton laft named in it. Communicated Feb. 27, 1800.

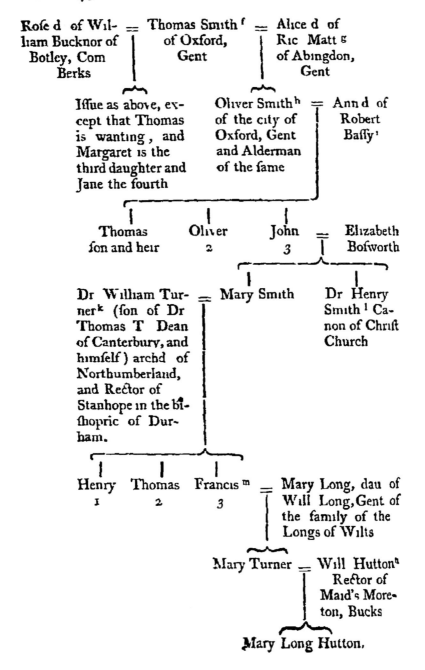

Mary Long Hutton.

From Miſcellaneous Pedigrees by William

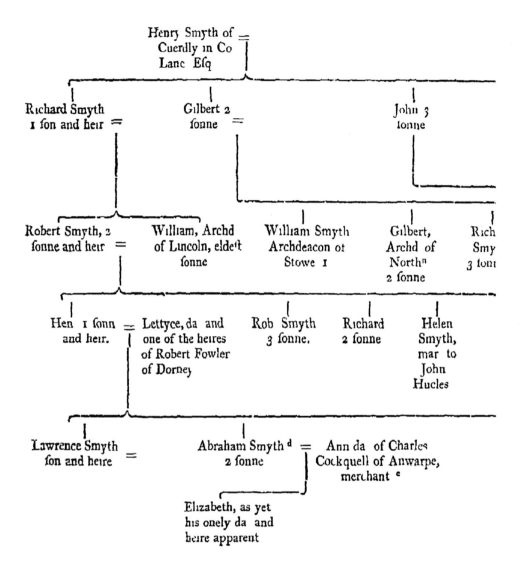

Henry Smyth of
Cuerdly in Co
Lanc Eſq

Richard Smyth
1 ſon and heir =

Gilbert 2
ſonne =

John 3
ſonne

Robert Smyth, 2
ſonne and heir =

William, Archd
of Lincoln, eldeſt
ſonne

William Smyth
Archdeacon of
Stowe 1

Gilbert,
Archd of
Northn
2 ſonne

Rich
Smy
3 ſonn

Hen 1 ſonn
and heir. =

Lettyce, da and
one of the heires
of Robert Fowler
of Dorney

Rob Smyth
3 ſonne.

Richard
2 ſonne

Helen
Smyth,
mar to
John
Hucles

Lawrence Smyth
ſon and heire =

Abraham Smyth d =
2 ſonne

Ann da of Charles
Cockquell of Anwarpe,
merchant e

Elizabeth, as yet
his onely da and
heire apparent

a MS Tanner, 236, is " Collect by Will Penſon Lanc. Herald," be
James the firſt
b Greenfield, a houſe of Ciſtertian nuns in Lincolnſhire
c I ſuppoſe De la Pre abbey, near Northampton, a houſe of Cluniac r
d " Vert on a cheveron betw 3 mullets Or, an egle diſpl B uppon
cock proper."
e " Ar 3 trefoils Vert, on a chief G a lyon paſſant crowned Or, upo
ing a trefoil Vert.

GREE II

Penfon,[a] Brit. Muf. MS. Harl. 1110 f 69 b.

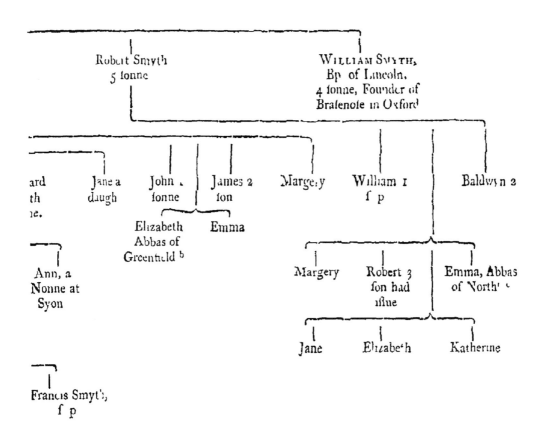

ard
th
ie.

Jane a
daugh

John
fonne

James 2
fon

Margery

William 1
f p

Baldwyn 2

Robert Smyth
5 fonne

WILLIAM SMYTH,
Bp of Lincoln,
4 fonne, Founder of
Brafenofe in Oxford

Elizabeth
Abbas of
Greenfild [b]

Emma

Ann, a
Nonne at
Syon

Margery

Robert 3
fon had
iffue

Emma, Abbas
of North [c]

Jane

Elizabeth

Katherine

Francis Smyth,
f p

ing, I fuppofe, the fame perfon. He was Lancafter Herald in the reign of

tuns, which Tanner claffes under Northampton, No 3
his Helme on a Torce Or, Vert, a roote of a tree leaueles, thereon a fefant

n his helme on a torce Ar, G, a demy lyon ramp coupe, crowned Or, hold-

The Pedigree of John Smith of Cuerdley in tl

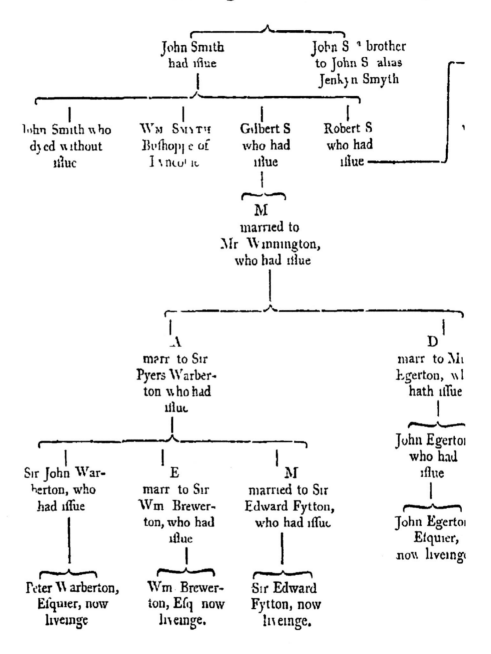

John Smith
had iſſue

John S ª brother
to John S alias
Jenkyn Smyth

John Smith who
dyed without
iſſue

Wᴍ Sᴍʏᴛʜ
Buſhoppe of
Lyncolne

Gilbert S
who had
iſſue

Robert S
who had
iſſue

M
married to
Mr Winnington,
who had iſſue

A
marr to Sir
Pyers Warber-
ton who had
iſſue

D
marr to Mr
Egerton, wl
hath iſſue

Sir John War-
berton, who
had iſſue

E
marr to Sir
Wm Brewer-
ton, who had
iſſue

M
married to Sir
Edward Fytton,
who had iſſue

John Egertoi
who had
iſſue

Peter Warberton,
Eſquier, now
liveinge

Wm Brewer-
ton, Eſq now
liveinge.

Sir Edward
Fytton, now
liveinge.

John Egertoi
Eſquier,
now liveinge

ª " Of this John Smith are deſcended Sir Thomas
mas Smyth Eſquier, ſonne and hayre of the ſaid Sir L:
for the truth of this pedigree, but it is not without ex
brother named John   Athen Oxon, 1 p 83 John D
6 Edw vi Chart. Antiq John Darke eſquire of Bred
Malpas, Cheſhire, vol 1

PEDIGREE III,

ιe Archives of Brafen Nofe College, Drawer 29.

ιe County of Lanc Father to Wm. Smith, fometyme Bufhoppe of Lyncolne.

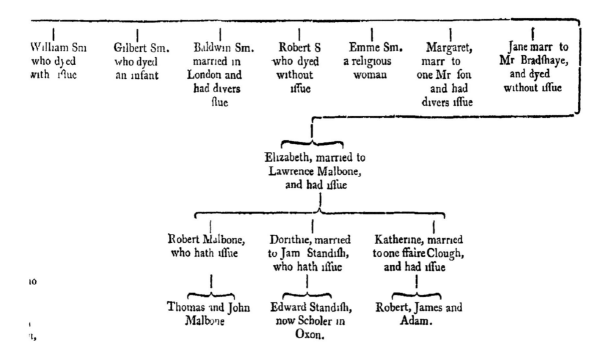

William Sm
who dyed
with iſſue

Gilbert Sm.
who dyed
an infant

Baldwin Sm.
married in
London and
had divers
ſſue

Robert S
who dyed
without
iſſue

Emme Sm.
a religious
woman

Margaret,
marr to
one Mr ſon
and had
divers iſſue

Jane marr to
Mr Bradſhaye,
and dyed
without iſſue

Elizabeth, married to
Lawrence Malbone,
and had iſſue

Robert Malbone,
who hath iſſue

Dorithie, married
to Jam Standiſh,
who hath iſſue

Katherine, married
to one ffaire Clough,
and had iſſue

Thomas and John
Malbone

Edward Standiſh,
now Scholer in
Oxon.

Robert, James and
Adam.

ιo

ι,

ι,

Smith of Chefter, Knt Sir Lawrence Smith, Knt fonne and hayre of the faid Sir Tho and Tho-
ιwrence and Edward Smith, fometyme Scholers in Brafen Nofe ”—I will not undertake to anfwer
ample for two brothers to have the fame name The famous antiquary, John Leland, had an elder
ιarke of Alfton, Worcefterſhire, had two fons of the name of John, parties in a bond, June 10,
ιn, No 7 Richard Stockton had two children named John buried, Nov 28, 1564. Par Reg of

NOTES ON PEDIGREE I.

ᵃ " Robert Smith of Pelehoufe—Gent' Pedigree in poffeffion of Rev J L Hutton, ut infra, and compare p. 8. above

ᵇ W Smith, Bp of Lincoln bore for arms, A a cheveron S between 3 Rofes G feeded Or, bearded V and the fame coat, when arms were eftablifhed to Brafen Nofe college, Oxford, of which he was one of the Founders, became a part thereof When Richard Lee Portcullis Purfuivant made a vifitation of the county of Oxford 1574, as marfhal and deputy to Robert Cooke efq Clarenceux king of arms, he vifited Brafen Nofe college, and regiftered the atchievement thereof, viz A fhield charged with a pale Or, thereon an efcutcheon with the arms of the fee of Lincoln, furmounted with a bifhop s mitre B garnifhed Or, on the dexter fide of the pale the arms of bifhop Smith, as defcribed above, on the finifter the arms of Sutton the other Founder, viz quarterly of 4, firft and fourth A a cheveron between 3 bugle horns ftringed S for Sutton, fecond and third, A a cheveron between 3 croffes patonce for Samfbury Under the arms is written, "Thefe be th auncient arms belonging and appertayning unto the Kings Hall and College of Brafen Nofe in the Univerfitie of Oxford, founded by William Smythe Bufhopp of Lincoln and Richard Sutton Efquire by the name of Principall and Fellowes of the faide Kings Hall and College within the Univerfitie Which armes I Portcullis do ratifie confirme and recorde in this my Vifitation made of the faide Univerfitie, A° 1574 At which tyme was . Harrys Principall of the faide Hall " Vide H 6 f 12 in Coll Armor which is of the writing of the faid Rich Lee J C Brooke

ᶜ " Widdons," in Mr. Hutton's pedigree, which is undoubtedly the true reading Correct A Wood, Colleges, p 353 and thefe memoirs, p 1 and p 8 n r

ᵈ In the entry of the pedigree by this Thomas Smyth 1574, the arms given are the fame as the Bifhop's, with a Martlet for difference. by which is this note " This armes was chaunged by Master Clarenceux and he now beareth A a fece dauncey between 3 Rofes G but this ys the right Cotte of Smythe Byfhope of Lyncolne, provyd by all parts of the College of Brafnofe in Oxford which he founded in 1513 " J. C Brooke

ᵉ " Miffon," in Mr Hutton's pedigree, which again (or Myfton, a difference in fpelling only) is the true reading. On examining the Regifters of Chipping Norton (Sept 5, 1799) no fuch name as Wyfton could be found, but in 1620, March 4, Elizabeth Myfton d of John Myfton was baptized; and in 1622, John Myfton s of John Myfton   In 1568 Allen Black married Joane Miffon   In 1611, May 23, died Rofe Miffone, in 1614, March 5, John Miffon, 1620, May 27, Anne Myfton d of John Myfton, 1622, Oct 9, John Myfton s of John Mifton   Whether the family is now extinct, as I was in queft of a different name, I did not inquire.

ᶠ The family arms with this pedigree are Argent, a fefs dancette between 3 rofes Gules. The Bifhop's arms, as ufual, the cheveron and rofes   Arms of Denton, Argent, 2 bars Gules, in chief 2 cinquefoils Sable.

ᵍ Arms of Matt, Barry of 6, Argent and Gules, in a chief Azure a lion paffant Or. Several of this family Mayors of Abingdon, intermarriages with Fettiplace, and with Lydall of Reading, fifter to Sir John Lydall

ʰ Wood fays, a party of the rebels at South Hinkfey in 1645 were continually playing on a party of the Oxford garrifon in Mr Oliver Smyth's houfe (held by him of Univerfity college) ftanding without the South port, but for the moft part repelled with lofs Annals, ii p 475 It is prefumed this was one of thefe Olivers, moft probably the fon.

Baffy, Barry of 6, Argent and Sable

ᵏ Turner, Or, a lion rampant between 3 croffes moline Gules, two in chief, one in bafe

ˡ Henry Smith of Chrift Church, D D June 17, 1674, a compounder; in February 1675 inftalled canon of Chrift Church, on the tranflation of Henry Compton from the fee of Oxon

Oxon to that of London   Athen Oxon ii F 196 Treaſurer
when great Tom was caſt in 1680   Colleges, p 452 n Willis, Cath ii p 408   He d ed and was buried in the cathedral
here without any memorial, Oct 21, 1702. and was ſucceeded
by Gaſtrell, afterwards biſhop of Cheſter ib 462

    m Francis Turner M A and Mary his wife are buried at
Finmere, Bucks, where, in the chancel, is a monument erected
to their memories by W Hutton LL B Rector of Maids Morton   Correct the epitaph thus   " By his Mother he was deſcended from [a brother of] William Smith Biſhop of Lincoln "

    n Hutton, Argent, on a feſs Sable, 3 bucks heads caboſhed.

PEDIGREE IV.

Copied from Chefhire Collections by Laurence de Boftok, about the year 1574. MS. Harl 139. f 51. b fee alfo f. 41. b The fame pedigree occurs alfo in MS. Harl. 2094 f 48 A. b.

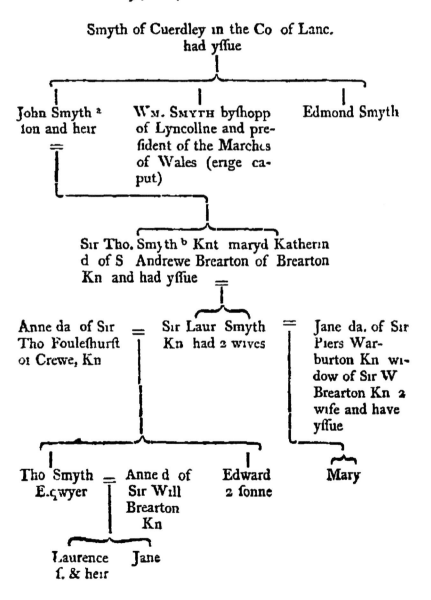

Smyth of Cuerdley in the Co of Lanc. had yffue

John Smyth 2 fon and heir

Wm. Smyth byfhopp of Lyncolline and prefident of the Marchis of Wales (erige caput)

Edmond Smyth

Sir Tho. Smyth b Knt maryd Katherin d of S Andrewe Brearton of Brearton Kn and had yffue

Anne da of Sir Tho Foulefhurft of Crewe, Kn

Sir Laur Smyth Kn had 2 wives

Jane da. of Sir Piers Warburton Kn widow of Sir W Brearton Kn 2 wife and have yffue

Tho Smyth Efcwyer

Anne d of Sir Will Brearton Kn

Edward 2 fonne

Mary

Laurence f. & heir

Jane

ᵃ In the Coll. of Arms, C 10 145, the Smiths of Hough in Cheshire, and the Smiths of Newcastle and Hanley in Stafford-shire, are deduced from two brothers, Edmund and John; the Cheshire family from " Edmund Smith of Chester," the eldest brother, the Staffordshire branch from John the second son The Bishop is placed above, but in what relation he stood to the brothers is not said

ᵇ Sir Thomas Smith of Chester Kn ob 1st July, 30 Hen. viii Pcd in Coll Armor The Cheshire pedigree of Smith begins with this Sir Thomas Smith, who is styled " Sir Tho-" mas Smith of Hough in Cheshire " And both these pedigrees, agreeing (except as excepted) with that here given and with each other, have more names than this pedigree by Bostock contains, and continue the descent two generations lower; where at last they differ, the pedigree in the Coll of Arms ending with " Hugh Smith ætatis 2 ann 1620, and Mary his sister " ux Geo Cotton of Cumbermere Esq Co Cestr " But the Chesh Pedigree has only " Thomas, infans 1610."

NUM. II.

Humaniffimo atque prudentiffimo viro ma-
giftro Willielmo Smyth Clerico Hampeii
meritiffimo Cancellarius vniuerfitatis Oxoni-
enfis vniuerfufque cetus Magiftrorum Regentium in eadem falutem plurimam dicunt.
Cogitantibus frequenter nobis de nonnullis
periculis que iamdiu perpeffi fumus, prop-
terea quod noftra priuilegia confirmationis
robore caruerant, tandem vifum eft ad Oxo-
nienfis reipublice amantiffimos viros pro eorundem priuilegiorum confirmatione effe fu-
giendum, ad teque inprimis, tum quod noftre
reipublice amantiffimus femper extitifti, tum
quod nos hac in caufa tua auctoritate plurimum juvare potes. Si igitur noftram ex-
pectationem, quam de te femper habuimus,
in confirmandis noftris priuilegiis non fallis,
rem nobis noftreque reipublice longe omnium
gratiffimam atque optatiffimam proculdubio
facies. Non poteft hac in caufa tua dili-
gentia tuumque confirmandi ftudium non
gratiffimum nobis probari. Qui fi accepto
regio fcripto tete ad noftrorum negotiorum
celerem expeditionem receperis, rem tantam

in

in noſtram rempublicam ipſum te contuliſſe
exiſtimabimus, quantam vix alius quiſquam
multos iam annos dederit. Vale.

Reg. F. f 159, b. Ep. 369.

NUM III.

Deans of the Collegiate Chapel of St. Stephen,
Weſtminſter.

1 THOMAS CROSS, the firſt Dean, Aug.
20, 1348. Pat. 22 Edw iii. p. 2. He died
before Jan 21, 1349. Newcourt Rep. 1.
p 746.

2 BAYNES, (no date) Regiſt Capellæ S.
Steph. Cotton MS. Fauſtina, B. viii. f 51.

3. THOMAS DE KEYNES, Nov. 26, 1355.
Pat. 29 Edw. iii Newcourt, ut ſupra

4. THOMAS ROUS, King's Chaplain, had
this Deanery given him by his Majeſty,
June 20, 1367. Newcourt. The Cotton
MS.

MS. (ubi fupra) has " Rowfe," but without date.

5. WILLIAM DE SLEFORD, May 17, 1369. Pat. 43 Edw. III. Newcourt. He was ftill Dean, 7 Ric ii. (1383) Fauftina, f. 4.

6. NICOLAS SLAKE, July 10, 1410, 11 Henry iv. Fauftina, f. 2. b. f. 3. Bledlowe, Bucks, was appropriated to St Stephen's and the living made a vicarage, Dec 8, 1413, Slake being then Dean. MS. Hail. 6952. p. 119.

7. JOHN PRENTYS, 1415 Willis, in Tanner. 1425 Fauftina, f. 1 f. 2. b. Feb 20, 6 Henry vi (1427-8) ib f 5 April 2, 10 Henry vi. (1432) ib f. 8. b.

8 WILLIAM WALESBY, about 1440. Willis, ut fupra

9. ROBERT KYRKHAM, Fauftina, f. 51 el. 1456. Willis. Mafter of the Rolls. Newcourt, i. p. 121.

10. JOHN ALCOCK, 1461. Tanner Biblioth Nov. 12, 1471. Fauftina, f. 29. 30. 33 Mafter of the Rolls, fucceffively bifhop of Rochefter, Worcefter, and Ely ; prefident of Wales (as noted above, p. 65) Founder of Jefus college, Cambridge ; Comptroller of the royal buildings to Henry vii. Warton's Hift. Poet i. p. 307. n. There is a letter from

from the Univerfity of Oxford to him refpecting the building of St. Mary's church,
about 1490. Reg. F Ep. 424. where Ep.
345 or 346 alfo is to him.   He was a man
of great learning for the times, Keeper of
the great Seal, 1473, lord Chancellor (being
ftill bifhop of Worcefter) in 1485[a], when
he opened the firft parliament of H vii.
(Nov 17) with a fpeech on Pfal. xlv. 4.
" Intende profpere, procede et regna " He
augurs the return of the golden age, quoting
Ovid's Metamorphofis : " ut deletis tribus
feculis aureum potiremus feculum " Rolls
of Parl vol. vi. p 267.   See of him Gent.
Mag 1799. p. 558. and his Life by Mr.
Cole quoted, ib p 656.

Ruffell, bifhop of Lincoln, among his other
preferments, is made Dean of St. Stephen's,
in Mr. Gough's Sepulchral Monuments, vol.
ii. p. 325. but the learned and ingenuous
Author of that fplendid work informs me,
that Richardfon's note in Godwin, on which
this was grounded, belongs to Alcock and
not to Ruffell, and he refers, for this correction, to Bentham's Ely, p. 181

11. PETER COURTNEY, June 10, 13 Ed-

---

[a] Dugdale (Ser Chron) has him not till fome months afterwards, Pat March 6, 1 H. vii. (1485-6)

ward

ward it. (1473) Fauftina, f. 33. f 34 b. el. 1472. Willis. There is a Patent for the Dean of St Stephen's, 15 Edw. iv " de certis prioratibus alienigenis ac aliis maneriis." Tower Records, Extr Pat p 386. Patent appointing Peter Courtney, Dean of St. Stephen's and privy Counfellor, Guardian of Henry Lovell, fon and heir of William Lovell, late lord Morley, and Alienora his wife, late lady Lovell. 17 Edw. iv. ib p 398. There is a letter to Courtney when bifhop of Winchefter, 3 kal. Dec. 1489, from the univerfity of Oxford. Reg. F. Ep. 381. Compare Ep. 383. Epiftle 345 or 346 is alfo to him.

12 HENRY SHARPE, November 24, 1478, 18 Edw. iv. Fauftina, f. 34. b. and July 28, 1480 ib f. 37. b   Henry Sharpe " juris utriufque B Oxon. LL. D ftudii Patavini" was incorporated at Oxford in 1450. Reg Aa. f. 48 b.

13 WILLIAM SMYTH, March 30, 1491. how long he had then been Dean is not known.   See above, p. 32. 42.

14. EDMUND MARTYN, 1496. Willis. An indenture between him and the canons on one part, and Henry Aynefworth and Hugh Oldom, clerks, executors of John Browne late canon, on the other part, conftituting

ftituting an obit for Browne, is dated Auguft 10, 1498. Fauftina, f. 42. f. 43. b.

15. THOMAS HOBBES occurs, July 6,
22 Henry vii (1507) when Cold Norton was
granted to St. Stephen's by the Crown.
Yate, p. 10. Ibid p. 26, is a leafe by him,
Nov. 12, 23 H. vii. to John abbat of Bruerne. To the original is affixed the conventual feal of Bruerne, a little mutilated, which
has never been engraved. The impreffion is
a graceful figure of the Virgin Mary (to whom
the abbey was dedicated) with the holy Infant in her arms. Beneath, a man, half
length, with a fpear or (perhaps) a crofier.
Thomas Hobbes was Northern Proctor of the
Univerfity, 1491. Wood, Fafti, p. 66. Warden of All Souls, 1494. Dean of Windfor.
1507, where he died and was buried in
1510. Colleges, p. 268.

16 JOHN FORSTER occurs, March 14,
1509, in the appointment of an obit for
archbifhop Warham. Fauftina, f 43 b.
He was canon of St. Paul's, collated by bifhop Smyth to the archdeaconry of Huntingdon, July 10, 1502, on the confecration of
Warham bifhop of London MS Harl. 6953.
p 20. In Reg F. Ep. 435. is to Mr. J.
Forfter archdeacon and refidentiary of St.
Paul's, but the date is probably about 1490,
before

before he was archdeacon of Huntingdon.
Willis fays he died anno 1512. Cath. ii
107.

17. THOMAS WOLSEY, Nov. 10, 4 Henry
viii (1512) in an Infpeximus of acquittances
by H. vii. for Cold Norton[b]. Brafen Nofe
Archives, Drawer 3. The bull of provifion
to Lincoln from pope Leo is addreffed " Thomæ Ulcei Decano Cap. S[u]. Stephani" &c.
8 Id. Feb. 1513-14 Rymer, xiii. p. 390

18. RICHARD SAMPSON, king's chaplain, a friend and correfpondent of Erafmus.
Knight's L. of Erafm p. 43, 44. 156 n.
He vacated the Deanery of Windfor, being
made bifhop of Chichefter, before Dec. 17,
1536. Donat. MS. Brit. Muf. 4622. p. 639.
He wrote in vindication of the King's fupremacy; was tranflated to Lichfield, 1543,
and fworn of the privy Council. Knight, ib.
Prefident of Wales, 35 H. viii—2 Edw vi.
MS. More, 390 f. 115   He died at Eccle-

b " Ad infianciam Thome Wol decani " fic , the engroffer
of the inftrument being doubtful, I fuppofe, of the orthography
of the name   In the Magd Comp Burff it is moft commonly
" Wulcy . as in Comp 1510, when one of his Majefty s pur-
fuivants brought letters from Mr Wulcy But " Wulfey' ib
1508; and likewife in Reg ſ f 31 when John Surle B A
imprifoned " ad inftanciam M[r] Wulfey, for an affault, was
releafed, on promife of good behaviour, March 7, 1499-1500

fhal,

fhal, Sept. 25, 1554, and was buried there.
Willis, Cath. 1. 392 where fee his epitaph.

19. JOHN CHAMBRE, in 1516, as ap-
pears by a letter addreffed " Prudentiffimis
et perdoctis viris Doctori Vefey, R Sacelli
Decano, et Doctori Chambre Capelle S".
Steph Weftm Decano " Reg. F F Bodl.
Arch A 166 f 24 b   He was M A of
Oxford, incorporated M D. from Padua.
Athen. Oxon 1 135 660. 684 F ib 50.
Pennant's London, p 228. Warden of Merton college, 1525 Wood's Colleges, p 8.
Smyth collated him to the prebend of Leighton Bofard, June 25, 1509 MS Harl 6953.
p. 24 Willis, Cath 11. p 205   He was
alfo archd of Bedford, June 11, 1524 Willis, ib p 124. Phyfician to Henry viii, when
the College of Phyficians was incorporated,
14 & 15 H viii. c 5.   He built adjoining
St. Stephen's chapel a cloifter of curious
workmanfhip to the value of 11000 marks
Topham's St Stephen's, p 6 Wood's Colleges, ut fupra.   He was the laft Dean of
St. Stephen's (fee above, p 33) and was
buried in the chapel there in 1549 Willis
and Wood, but Willis, p 205 fays he died
in 1545 which I fuppofe is a miftake

NUM. IV

Masters of St. John's Hospital, Lichfield.

1. WILLIAM DE WITCHENORE   On his resignation,

2. WILLIAM DE REPINGDON [Repton, Derbyshire] presbyter, one of the Brethren of St. John's, was presented by the brotherhood to the Mastership or Keepership, 4 kal. Apr. 1323   Admitted by the Bishop 3 kal. Apr protesting this not to injure the right of the bishops to present. Reg Episc Lichf. ii. (B) f 137.

3. Frater RIC DEL HUIL, capellanus[a], collated to the Priorship, 8 kal. Jun. 1330. on the nomination of the fraternity, upon Repingdon's resignation ib f 147

Henry de Weford, capellanus, presented by the Prior and Brothers of St John's to

---

[a] We re e rad "Capellanus' for a curate or officiating clergymen, above, p 258 n   It sometimes means Cantarista, a chantry priest, who officiates in a " capella" of that sort Pref Del Cur I vi No xxi p 229   It occurs perpetually in these institutions, but it is difficult in such instances to ascertain its meaning

the

William Bisshop of Lincoln

the chantry of John de la Bourne in capella B Marie juxta forum civitatis Lichf per Joh. de la Bourne capellanum noviter ordinatam; instituted 11 kal. Mar. 1332. ibid f. 153. b.

Simon de Swell, capellanus, instituted to said chantry on like presentation on the death of Weford, 18 kal Aug 1338. ibid f 162 b. (Weford died on Monday, the feast of St Peter and St Paul)

4. WILLIAM DE COMPTON was Prior of St. John's in 1351.

5 RICHARD DE WOTTON, collated, June 14 1388. Reg vi f. 33. b

6. THOMAS SEDGLEY occurs as Prior, 2 Henry vi.

7. HUGH LACHE, on whose resignation

8. THOMAS MASON was collated, February 12, 1454. Reg xi. f. 14 He exchanged with

9. THOMAS EGGECOMBE, Rector of Lamehith [Lambeth] who was thereupon collated, June 9, 1461. Reg xii. f. 41. He resigned by his proxy John Eggecombe, October 1, 1474 and the same day

10. THOMAS MILLEY, the Bishop's Registrar, was collated, on condition of paying a pension of ten marks per annum to the said Eggecombe. Reg xii f 49

11. WIL-

11. WILLIAM SMYTH; whose inftitution has not been found, but

12. Bifhop Smyth collated SAMPSON ALEYNE, bachelor of Decrees, June 3, 1494, on the refignation of William Smyth. Reg Smyth, f 145. b

13 WILLIAM SMYTH, collated September 21, 1494, on the death of Aleyne. ib f 146

14 HUGH OLDHAM, January 30, 1494-5, on Smyth's refignation. Oldham often occurs in preceding memoirs. See particularly, P 33—37 360

15 ROBERT FROST, April 20, 1498, on Oldnam's refignation. Reg. xiii f. 210. Bifhop Smyth collated him to the archdeaconry of Stow, May 20, 1497 MS Harl. 6953. p 18 He was prebendary of Gaia Major, Lichfield, June 25, 1497 Willis, 1 445. which he quitted for Prees, March 30, 1500 ib 455. He was alfo prebendary of York and rector of Thornhill in that county, and was buried there in a chapel erected by him See his epitaph, ib. ii p 129 He fucceeded Morton (afterwards archbifhop of Canterbury) in the archdeaconry of Winchefter, which he refigned, and was fucceeded by John Froft in 1502. Athen Oxon. 1. F. 33 The faid John Froft B D probably brother

to

to Robert, was collated by Smyth to the vicarage of Wibunbury, Chefhire, Auguft 18, 1494 Reg Lichf f 158. and to a canonry of St. Chad's, Salop, January 14, 1494-5 ib. 155 b.

16 RICHARD EGERTON, capellanus, 30 March, 1507, on the refignation of Froft. Reg xiii, xiiii f 26 He was prebendary of Daffet in Lichfield, January 2, 1486. Willis, 1. p. 438. which he quitted for Weeford, December 7, 1488 ib 471. and that for Whittington, October 5, 1506 and died in 1537, being Rector of Endfield, and canon of Lichfield ib. 474

17. GEORGE LEE, LL. B. collated by his brother Roland Lee, bifhop of Lichfield, March 23, 1536, on the death of Egerton He was prebendary of Bifhopfhill, Lichfield, May 7, 1537. Willis 1 p. 426 prebendary of Wellington, Dec. 21, 1538 ib 473 and quitted it for the Treafurerfhip, March 7, 1541, which he is fuppofed to have held till 1571. ib 411. He was alfo dean of St. Chad's, Salop, and the bifhop his brother died in his houfe there, Jan 24, 1542, and was buried in that collegiate church. ib. 391.

18. WILLIAM SALE, October 3, 1560, on the refignation of George Leigh, prefented by William Afpley, the next prefen-

tation having been granted by Richard Sampson bishop of Lichfield to the said Aspley
and others, August 19, 4 Edward VI. Reg.
xv P 2 f 2. b. alias f 30. b.

10. January 30, 1631. a master was admitted Reg xvi. f 86 b but the next leaf
is wanting, and the name does not appear.
Probably JOHN MACHON For

20 September 7, 1671, John Machon by
his proxy Henry Archbold[a], knight, resigned
the prebend of Wellington and the Mastership of St. John's, and was succeeded in
both by THOMAS MACHON, M. A on the
eleventh of the same month. Reg xvii.
P. 2 f 1 Willis says, John Machon, M A.
vicar of Hartburne, Co Durham, was admitted to Wellington, September 9, 1631,
and resigned both his preferments to Thomas
Machon in 1671. Cath. 1 473.

21 FRANCIS ASHENHURST, M A. March
4, 1673, on the death of Thomas Machon.
Reg. xvii P 2 f. 7. He had the prebend
of Oloughton Præcentoris, April 19, 1684.
Willis, 1 170 which he quitted for Wellington, June 18, 1689 ib 473 and in the
same year became archdeacon of Derby, ib.
422. and prebendary of Langford ecclesia in

---

[a] Henry Archbold was Registrar in 1662 Reg xvii f 17

Lin-

Lincoln. ib ii 198   He died in 1704, and was buried at King's Swinford, Staffordshire, of which he was Rector ibid

22 THOMAS GOODWIN, D. D. December 14, 1704, on the death of Ashenhurst. Reg xix p. 49. whom he succeeded the same day as archdeacon of Derby. Willis styles him B. D. May 27, 1704, when he was collated prebendary of Bishophill Cath. 1 p. 427. which he quitted for Wellington, December 29, 1704, also on the death of Ashenhurst ib. 473 and that for Collwich, July 17, 1713. ib. 473. He died in 1719; and was buried at Launton, Oxfordshire, where he was Rector. ib. 422.

23. EDWARD MAYNARD, D.D. fellow of Magdalen college, Oxford, collated July 22, 1719 Bishop's Subscr book   He was installed Precentor of Lichfield, November 15, 1700. Willis, 1. 426. He gave 697l. towards the New Buildings at Magdalen college   Wood's Colleges, p. 322. n 65.   He was Rector of Bodington in Northampton-shire, author of a volume of sermons, and published an edition of Dugdale's St. Paul's. See Gent. Mag. 1793 p. 515.   He put up a stone tablet over the door of the hospital (see the plate, p. 86) bearing, under the arms of the Founder impaling the see of

I i 4 Lich-

Lichfield, enſigned with a mitre, the following inſcription,

HOSP. S^{ti} JOHANNIS BAPT.
Quod venerab vir olim hujus ſedis Epiſc.
D^{us} GVLIELMVS SMITH
Pro Magiſtro et tredecim Pauperibus
Anno MCCCCLXXXV, extruxit
Idem Coll Ænean Ox munificentiſſimus Fundator.
In cujus memoriam hanc Tab poſuit
EDV MAYNARD Hoſp Mag^r
A D 1720

24 EDMUND BATEMAN, D. D. canon of
Lichfield, collated June 23, 1740, on the
death of Maynard. Bp. Smalbrook's Subſcr.
book He was Rector of Sevenoaks in Kent;
and was buried in the chapel of the hoſpital.

25. SNEYD DAVIES, D D collated July
2, 1751, on the death of Bateman Reg.
Fred. Cornwallis. He was educated at Eton,
and fellow of King's college, Cambridge,
canon of Lichfield, archdeacon of Derby and
rector of Kingſland in Herefordſhire, of which
he was patron. He is ſaid to have been
a man of moſt amiable character. his numerous poems, printed and manuſcript, " bear
ample teſtimony to his uncommon genius
and erudition " He wrote ſeveral of the
anonymous imitations of Horace in Dun-
combe's edition, 1767, and at the end of
vol.

vol. iv. is given the character of the ancient Romans from " an excellent poem" (I believe never publifhed) by him, ftyled, " The Progrefs of Science " He has many poems, alfo anonymous, in Dodfley's Collection. See vol. v. p. 95—106. vi p 138—147. 265. 284 Mr. Nichols's Collection is enriched with others by the fame hand. See vol vi. p 114—142. 151. 352. vii. p. 312 viii. p 307. Mr. Pennant has preferved fome animated lines by Dr Davies on Caractacus, which he fays were delivcred almoft extempore at one of the annual meetings, held on Caer Caradoc fome years ago by gentlemen from different parts, to celebrate the name of that renowned Britifh chieftain in profe or verfe. Tour in Wales, vol ii. p. 422.

26 THEOPHILUS BUCKERIDGE, M. A. rector of Mawtby in Norfolk, collated February 22, 1769 Reg Egerton. He is the prefent Mafter (A D. 1800.) and to his kindnefs, though perfonally unknown I am indebted for this lift of the Mafters of St. John's, and for the view of the Hofpital, p 86, generoufly contributed for the embellifhment of the volume fince that part was committed to the prefs.

NUM. V.

Irom Act Capit Line 1501 1507 f 1

Right worfhipfull Bretherne I recommend
me ynto you So it is that Maifter Mordaunt a fpeciall louer and frend of myne
hath recouered by a Ceffauit action[a] londs
and tenements ayenft Herry Rudyng Maifter
of the hofpitall of Saint Johns in Bedford
and by reafon of the fame Recouere the
fame John hath entered and therof is feafid
into whos poffeffion the fame Herry hath
releffid And for fo much as the fame Herry
hath other londs and tenements of the fame
John in recompence, therfore both I vnder
my Seale and alfo the Maior and Comminalte
of Bedford patrons of the fame hofpitall vnder their Sealls haue confermyd theftate of
the fame John in the fame londs accordyng
to the note herin inclofid Wherfore in as
harty wife as I can hartely prai you that ye
conferme the eftate of the fame John Mordaunt according to the dede which he fends

[a] above, p 100

vnto

\nto you, And I fhall do youre defires as gret
a plefure thus londs recoueied is vnder the
value of xviiiS by yere   And this confir-
macion is only to be made for the fuerty of
the faid Maifter Mordaunt and for no profit
of hym for he depart with as much londs.
and therfore of any thyng to be paid for the
ffee of the Chaptour feall other then for the
ffee of the Clerk of the Chaptour both I and
he will defire you to pardon hym therof.
And ye fhall haue of hym a louyng and affured ffrend in all your caufis to his power.
Jhefu preferue you ffro londone the xxth
day of March.

The faid Herry is very agid and fikely and
therfore I pray you it may haue the foner
and more fpedy expedicion

   Your lovyng brother W. Lincoln.

To my Right worfhipfull bretherne, the
Deane and Chaptour of lincoln be this Deli-
iiered

          NUM.

NUM VI.

Colendiffimo in Chrifto patri ac domino domino Wilhelmo Dei gracia Lincolnienfi epifcopo Cancellarius natus vniuerfitatis Oxonie vniuerfufque Regentium cetus in eadem fefe commendatiffimos faciunt. Dormiente cum patribus fuis fanctiffimo in Chrifto patre ac domino domino Johanne Dei gracia Cardinali et Cantuarienfi archiepifcopo, ex cuius obitu noftri Cancellariatus dignitatem ad tempus vacare contigit, dolebat vehementer, fanctiffime preful, mater noftra vniuerfitas Oxonie de tanti filii (quem acerrimum fuum omnino defenforem habuit) tam mortifera erracione Que de fue vetufte tranquillitatis felicifque perfeuerantie ex dicto iam cafu amiffione plurimum pertimefcens, nos indies lacrimis excitare hortarique in cum item eligendum non defiit, qui fe ab omnibus iniuriis ac moleftacionibus non fecus impofterum ac antea tueri valeat et defendere Quo fiebat vt prefufa Spiritus fancti ea in re pro obtinenda gracia, communi omnium oracione, ac celebrata deinde in noftre congregacionis domo folenni electione tua integer-

rima

rima paternitas ab omnibus (celesti² tamen
vti creditur spiramine quam humano judicio)
dignissima putaretur Quod vtique fecimus
memoratissimi nonmodo beneficiorum ves-
trorum que in nos quotidianis vicibus exercere non desinitis, sed ob precipuam illam
singularemque prudentiam plurimasque virtutes alias quibus vestram dignitatem orna-
tam esse satis ipsi cognouimus Huius rei
optatum exitum vt mater nostra predicta
plenius intellexit, quasi de graui somno excita
letissimoque vultu vndique perfusa, ad vestram celsitudinem has literas celerime mitti
fecit. Quibus materna prece instantius de-
precatur, vt, cum vestram amplitudinem in
hac nostra achademia alumnum olim sibi
progenuerit, etiam impresentiarum precipuam
patronam acerrimamque sui propugnatricem
grates consequatur Et cum nichill charius
aut preciosius quod tante vestre prestantie
elargiatur habeat inuentum, oblata munus-
cula (licet exigua) leto animo excipiatis sub-
nixius implorat. Habetis enim ex publicis
nostri senatus suffragis illam nostri Cancellariatus sedem illud tribunall confcendendi
potestatem, a quo maiores vestri non medio-
crem gloriam antea reportarunt. Ad quam

· · tam celesti, uti creditur

rem

rem letius fufcipiendam veftram dignitatem omnes vna inuitamus Semperque cum maxima felicitate profperetur dominacio veftra

Dat. Oxon. in noftre congregacionis domo menfis Nouembris die quinto Reg F f. 182 Ep 495

NUM VII.

Cupienti mihi hos multos dies, celeberrime cetus, literis veftris amore et gratia et[1] erga me refertiffimis refponforiam tranfmittere epiftolam, per inceffantes in tutandis innocentium caufis occupationes, perque deliberationem, in re maxime tam ardua, maturam, neceffario habitam, haud hercule licuit Ocii tamen paululum iam iam nactus, ne merito ingratitudinis vitio incufer, vos,

[1] Delendum f

hifce

hifce literis, noftri hac in re inftituti cer-
tiores efficere decreui quorum humanitatem
in me meofque vehementer amplector, ac li-
beralitatem maximi quidem facio Quippe me,
inter Anglie colendos antiftites indigniffimum,
ad veftre clariffime achademie rempublicam
agendam fovendamque, vnanimi, ut ad me
fcribitis, affenfu in patronum delegitis Qua
in re, licet eo Cancellariatus honore me longe
digniorem ac preftantiorem fungi deceat, pe-
titionibus veftris humaniffimis haud ibo in-
fitias verum regio precepto haud paucorum-
que clariffimorum virorum confilio actus, veftris morem gero defidens Et quoniam in
calce literarum veftrarum me ad id muneris
dignitatifve excipiendum, ut veftris utar verbis, fubnixus imploratis, accipio equidem,
ingentes veftre et humanitati et liberalitati
agens gratias, maiores fi quando dabitur fa-
cultas relaturus Enitterque, Deo duce, id
mea pro virili ibi efficere, quod noftre celeberrime matri achademie precis honoris ac
vtutis acce̅ſſioni futurum fit Itaque vos,
literatiffimi viri, vehementer hortor, obfecro
vt id una mecum curetis Haud velim hercule quenquam veftrum proprii tantum ftu-
dere commodis et honoribus, fed publicam
curare vtilitatem. Siquidem ciuitas vna-
queque dum priuate confulit vtilitati, quid
patrie

patrie conducat nihil penfi habet Vos igitur, viri fummatiffimi, nouitiorum tiruncu-
lorumque animos ad ftudendum virtutefque
exercendas re, verbis, ac operibus veftris iftic
augeatis quefo. Preterea venerabili viro ma-
giftro W. Attwater facre legis interpreti, cui
per viros fide dignos tum ob merita tumque
ob induftriam fuam plurimum apud nos com-
mendato vices noftras hac in re commifimus,
literas commifforias eidem pro bono publico
iftic noftra in abfentia regendo tutando fo-
uendoque tranfmittentes, et[b] non minus ac
nobis in fingulis quibuflibet rebus fuum fpec-
tantibus ad officium, adminiculo fitis velim.
Valete. Ibid f. 182 b Ep 496

---

[b] Aut delendum, aut " ei" legendum videtur

NUM.

NUM. VIII.

Ad dominum Cancellarium.

Si nos ulla fortune noftre felicitas oblectare vnquam poffet, magnifice prefull, quod precipuos viros (et eofdem maximos) huic noftro gignafio gubernatores olim pretulimus, qui et rempublicam noftram femper bene prudenter geffere, et eam pro viribus fatis atque fatis auxerunt; quam hodie gloriam noftram pluiis faciemus? quam felicitatem noftram admirabimur? eum te nobis preceptorem et magnificum patronum nacti, qui non fecus quam qui optime geffit, hanc noftram rempublicam gubernare poteft nec aliter quam qui opulentiffime auxit, addere quidem illi copiofe poteft. et illius priuilegiis cum libertatibus maxima virtute adeffe Speramus haud dubie, magnifice preful, te nobis et private patrie noftre natum effe ut profis; et nos item tue dignitati genitos effe. vt tam celebrem Anglie vniuerfitatem per nos in tuam fufcepiffe tutulam [1 tutelam] gratuleris. que fi antea vel virtute vel bonis artibus florebat (florebat autem vberius) nunc

к k tantas

tantas virtutes cum vſuris exercere confidit,
eum iam digniſſimum antiſtitem preſidem
ſibi conſecuta qui omni virtute numeroſus
bonas literas amplectitur et valde amat.
Tene igitur felix collatam tibi achademiam,
humaniſſime preſul et poſt datum ei iuſiurandum, quod ſemper tuis patribus hanc dignitatem aſcenſuris adminiſtratum eſt (ſic enim
leges noſtre inſtituerunt) vtere, rege, ama.
fieri quippe non poteſt, ut tuo in nos egregio
amori non vehementer reſpondeamus.   Hor-
tamur te maxime tandem, optime preſul, vt
hoc iuſiurandum tua gratia exhibeat magiſtro
Joanni Reede[c], sereniſſimi Principis capellano, et magiſtro Joanni Dunham, ſacre the-
ologie bachularus   Ibid Ep. 497.

---

[c] See above, p 157   Since thoſe pages were printed, the
Rev Dr Gauntlett, Warden of New College, having, at my
requeſt, ſearched the ancient Records of that ſociety, has,
among other memoranda of theſe times, obliged me with the
following reſpecting Reed   "Pro i refectione dat Mro Rede
capellano domini Principis, 2 S 10 D." Comp Burſſ 1497
The Prince was at Oxford twice about this time, as noted,
p 161   Reed occurs as Preceptor to his Highneſs ("digniſſimi
Principis Arthuri Informator") in an inſtrument dated "5 Jun
6 H vii 1491,' when the Prince was not yet five years old
Reg prim Coll Nov f 8 vel (antiq num) f 3

NUM.

NUM. IX

By the Prince

Trufty and right welbelouyd we grete youe wele And be credibli enformed- that the iome of gentleman Bedell of diuinite within the vniuerfite theie is now voide and yn youre difpofitione by the dethe of Henry Mochegood late occupyyng the iame whos foule god pardone | we hauyng tendre re- fpecte to the good dyfpofitione that oure fullwelbelouyd feruant John Stanley is off. and alfo confideryng his true feruice vnto vs heretofore doone | for the whyche and other his merits we haue hyme in ouie entire fa- uour and wolde be gladde of his furtherance and prouityone | Defyre youe therfore in oure affectuoufe wyfc to graunt youre good wyllys and myndys for oure fayd feruant to be electe and admitted to the fayd Rome afore any other | afcertenyng youe we haue inftanced our Ryght trufty and entierli wel- belouyd Counfaillour the byfchypp of Lin- coln piefident of oure Counfail and chaun- celier of the faid vniuerfite to graunt his good

wylle

wylle therunto and fo hath he done | ayenft
the whyche we trufte ye wyll nott gretely
be | the rather att the contemplatione of
thies oure lettres | wherby ye fhall not ooneli
be prouided of a fadde and fubftancyall ho-
nefte perfone to occupye that rome | butt
allfo do a thing of great plefure vnto vs
whyche we fchall not forgete butt fo re-
membre hereafter in any youre purfuts to be
vnto vs made as ye fchall thincke youre to-
wardneffe in this behalfe well employed |
yeuen vnder our Signett att the maner of
Beaudeley the xiith day of this Augufte |
ibid. Ep. 507

N U M X.

Obferuandiffimo Lincolnienfis fedis epifcopo meretiffimoque ftudentium Oxoniis pre-
fidi regentium contio immortales falutes.
Etfi nobis, pientiffime prefull, nichil vnquam
certius extiterit quam quod immenfa quadam

et

et incredibili benevolencia rem noftram publicam ampleƈteris, tamen non inanes nec
fruftra tue litere dilate funt Siquidem co-
piofiffime et apertiffime indices fuerant quod
nichilo premittis [f. pretermittis] noftris con-
fulere tenuitatibus quod nobis vel glorie vel
vtilitati putes. Sane facis [quod] ad opti-
mum quenquam prefeƈtum attinet; quo vno
faƈto tete pretura digniffimum oftendis Quare cum a fanƈtiffima paternitate tua nil [nl.]
videatur effe perfuafum quod noftre rei publice non effet ampliffimo futurum commodo,
curabimus pro mediocritate noftrarum viri-
um, ut piudentiffimis tuis confiliis hereamus.
Nichil enim faciemus precipitofi nec quic-
quam erit eleƈtionis tua veneratione inconf-
fulta. Aggreffus es enim in nos ita fempei
pius et manfuetus, ut cui potius obfeque-
remur habemus neminem. Reliquum eft ut
rogemus benignitatem tuam ut quemadmodum fifi fumus ita pro ampliffima et ingenu-
iffima mente tua perpetuo nos (ut facis) et
foueas et tuearis et defendas. Nofque bona
fide pollicemur tibi fi noftra aut induftria aut
opeia tue dignitati poffit effe vfui, poteris
eam peculiari quodam iure tuo et mancipare
tibi et dedicare. valeafque, fanƈtiffime noftei
prefes, in domino ex oxonienfi ludo xvº kal.
feptembres Ibid f. 184. Ep 502.

K k 3   NUM.

NUM. XI.

By the Kinges moder

Trufty and welbelouyd we grete youe wele. And vnderftonde the Rowme of gentilman bedell in Diuinite within youre vniuerfite | is now voide by deceaffe of youre late office [fic] in the fame wherunto ye in breue tyme intende to electe foome honeft and hable perfone we fpecially tenderinge thonnoure and thincreafe of lernynge in Diuinite and be credybly enformed by the righth reuerent father in god the byffchopp of Rocheftre and certaine other which be verray louers of the faid faculte that one Rychard Wottone is a right hable and conuenient perfone for the faid office. Defire therfore and pray youe fo to owe youre good fauores vnto hyme as rather for oure fake he may be proferryd to the faid Rome. wherby ye fchall not oonely do a thinge for the grete honowre and weale of youre faid vniuerfite. but alfo vnto vs full Singuler plefure Yeuen vnder Signet at the manor of Buckdoone the xxiii day of Augufte | Ib Ep. 509

NUM

N U M. XII.

By the Quene

Trufty and welbelouyd We grete you
wele | And where we be enformed that the
rome of gentylman bedyll for diuinitee by
the deceffe of Henry Mochegood is now
voyde and yn youre gyfte and dyfpofitione |
We tendring the weale and preferement of
oure welbelouyd John Greton feruant vnto
oure trufty and right welbelouyd Maifter
Rychard Mayou oone of my Lordys Coun-
faillours and Aulmongner | Defyre and pray
youe that at the contemplation of thies oure
lettres | ye wyll haue hyme to the fayd
Rowme of Bedelle before any other ad-
mitted | As oure verray truft is yn youe |
Wherby ye fhal deferue oure efpecial thancks.
yeuene vnder oure fignet at my Lordys Manor of Rychemount the xxviiith day of Sep-
tembre.   Ibid. Ep 506

NUM. XIII.

Reuerendiffimo in Chrifto patri ac domino domino W Dei gratia Lincolnienfis fedis maximo antiftiti, et vniverfitatis Oxon Cancellario digniffimo &c. Nemo ex omnibus tam fecunda unquam natus eft fortuna magnifice pieful qui non et tempori interdum et homini cedendum effe exiftimet Quantus enim Romanus olim fenatus fuit cui cum magno impetu et animorum varietate nonnulli pro tempore non aduerfabantur? teftis Cicero eft, quem nec tempus interdum vincere cum omni qua preditus eft eloquentia et fumma prudentia ferebat. teftis Pompeius, qui quum inuictiffimus idemque humaniffimus haberetur nonnunquam fui uoti iacturam perpeffus eft Conteftatur et Cefar ille magnus qui tametfi bello virtute ingenioque Romanos imperatores longe antecelluit (ut cafus interdum ferebat) vix fibi vel fuis coniunctiffimis frugi fuit Cuius rei iam noftris oculis exemplar ipfi perfpicimus qui dum magno robore niteremur ut tuis votis (id quod prefto fieri decernebamus) refponderemus magno fuffragiorum numero, cui

nec

nec pares eramus, a ſpe ab inſtituto ab opi-
nione depulſi fumus. Nec mirum illud quum
ſereniſſima princeps et domina nobis gratio-
ſiſſima, et maxime de nobis benemerita domina regis mater omnes obteſtaretur, ut Ri-
cardum preconem preficerent. Que tante
tamque preclare rogationes fuere, quibus non
parere nefas omnes ferme, quibus intereſſe
erat exiſtimabant Quare te ſatis atque ſatis
rogamus piiſſime antiſtes ut quemadmodum
cepiſti in Oxonienſem ſenatum optimus idem
ſingularis patronus eſſe ſic in tempora bene-
uolentiſſimus ei proficiſcere. pollicemur enim
dignitati tue, et tametſi hec tempora tuis
votis non faueant, omni cura quicquid alias
fieri iubebis bonis omnibus approbantibus per-
ficiemus. Ibid. Ep. 512

NUM.

NUM. XIV

Epistola ad Rev in Christo patrem Wil-
lelmum Smyth, Dei gratia Linc. Episc de
vita et actibus Roberti Grosthede.

Lincolnienfis apex præful falveto Wilelme,
  Clara facerdotum gemma, lucerna gregis
Eft tua vita decens, tibi fit jocunda[a] fenectus,
  Jugis profperitas, continuata falus
Te Deus elegit vas nobile, vas in honorem,
  Vas fpeciale fibi, vas generale fuis
Jam precor, O præful, quem cœlica fama venuftat,
  Sufcipe quod fcribo Bardenienfis ego
Nullus ad authorem refpectus fiat, honore
  Thematis hoc lector experiatur opus
Sum monachus Pater afpira metro, quia penna
  A te correcta fcandala nulla timet
Thema facrum feftinat opus, non author, honeftas
  Materiæ celebris materiata juvat
Dive vale decus ecclefiæ difpone precanti
  Portum naufragium tolle, faveto rati

Per magiftrum Richardum de monafterio
Bardenienfi monachum, anno Dom. MDIII.
Angl. Sacra, vol. II. p. 325.

[a] This muft not be added to the miftakes of father Richard
the word is, I believe, univerfally " jocundus" in MSS of the
claffics.

NUM.

NUM. XV.

Priors of Cold Norton.

In the year 1236 the vigilant bishop Grosthead, visiting the monasteries of his diocese, deposed, among others, the Prior of Cold Norton[a], name unknown, and substituted in his stead

1. W DE WILTON, a canon of Dunstaple. Annal. Dunst. vol. 1. p. 230. Browne Willis calls him Walter de Wilton, el. 1235. Mitied Abbies, Add. p 333

2. SIMON, 1264. Yate, p 45. Willis has Simon de Fallesham, a canon of the house, Prior, 8 Id. Dec. 1268. Mitred Abbies, vol. 11 p. 174.

3 ADAM DE WOODFORD, admitted 1283. Willis. Richard, abbat of Oseney, grants half a hide of land in great " Rollenderith" to Adam prior of Cold Norton. no date. Yate, p 50

4. PETER DE WADDINGTON, 1284. Willis.

---

[a] Pegge's L of Grossetesse, p 48

5. WIL-

5 WALTER, refigned in 1292 Willis. Walter prior of " Northon" is witnefs to a deed, fine dat. Yate, p 29.

6. ROBERT DE RAVENSBY, canon of Ef-feby [Canons Afhby, in Northamptonfhire] promoted hither by the bifhop of Lincoln, with confent of the convent, 1292. Willis

7. WILLIAM DE TEWL [i. e Tew] ca-non, elected " non. Oct. 1297." refigned in 1321. Willis.

8. JOHN DE WORTON admitted cal. Mar. 1321. dying about 1330, a Conge d'elire was granted by the patron of this priory, and the monks chofe

9. JOHN DE THENFORD, on the 8th of the calends of May, 1330. Willis.

10. WILLIAM DE STOGENORTON [read, Hogefnorton, Hoggefnorton, Hokenorton &c. according to the variations in fpelling.] de-prived in 1343. Willis.

11. WILLIAM DE TEUKESBURY, 17 cal. Oct. 1343. Willis. William Lynham abbat of Bruern and the convent granted to Will. de Tewkefbury prior of Coldnorton " 18 acras terræ cum femine rufcorum[b] feminat."

<hr />

[b] To this unknown article of rural economy (for it is not, I prefume, Virgil's " horric.or *rufco*,' Ecl vii 42 Georg ii 413 which is faid to be *boly*) may be added another equally obfolete Alexander de Aundevile grants to the prior &c
" quan-

in exchange for land of the priory in Pynke-well, on the vigil of St James, 31 Edw. iii. (1357.) Yate, p 25.

12. ROBERT occurs 1356 [q? see above] and 1361. Willis, in Tanner. Ricardus de Abberbury [Addesbury] Chivaler granted to "Robert by divine permiffion prior of Cold-norton" &c. four acres of land in Stepelafton and the advowfon of the church, 36 Edw. iii (1362.) And Thomas de Abberbury, lord of Stepelafton, granted the fame at the fame time, the convent engaging to find four ca-

"quandam porberiam in bofco meo de Wichewood ad porcos fuos proprios Ita tamen quod nihil fumetur de bofco meo ad faciendam prædictam porberiam Yate, p 43 Porcheria (with great variety of fpelling Porcary in Cowel) was a fwine's fty or hut, where, when the hogs run in the woods and forefts for pannage, the fwineherds fecured the drove at night, "ut ab incurfibus lupo m tuti fint' Du Frefne, v Porchoria, Ken-nett's Paroch Antiq p 259 and Glofl As for wolves, when they were completely exterminated out of England, I cannot at prefent fay In a grant to the monaftery of Joreval in Yorkfhire, l Conan duke of Britanny and earl of Richmond, is this claufe, "Precipio quod habeant maftivos ad lupos coer-cendos de pafturis fuis" the date about A D 1156 Dodfw MS 63 f 52 b and there is an order by Edw the firft for deftroying wolves, A D 1281 Rymer, 1 P 2 p 192 Balde-winus de Parles and Juliana his wife gave to the priory 15 acres of land in Rollendria (i e Rollwright) "cum paftura 200 ovium et 6 boum et 2 vaccarum et 20 porcorum" Yate, p 51. which feems to have been confirmed by a royal charter 22 Edw. iii fee Not Mon

nons

nons to pray for the foul of Thomas Abberbury, clerk. Yate, p. 56. The living was
appropriated to the convent, May 25, 1377.
ib. 57. Robert occurs alfo, 39 & 40 Edw.
iii. ib. p. 40 45.

13. THOMAS BRADLEGH, 1399. Willis,
ibid. A "Fullingmulle" (at Stanlake) granted
to him, 20 Apr. 1 Henry iv. (1400) Yate,
p. 46.

14. WILLIAM DEDINGTON, 1405. 1429.
Willis, ibid. William Dadynton, 20 Apr.
6 Henry iv (1405) Yate, p. 46. William,
8 Henry vi (1429) ib ρ 45.

15 RICHARD, 1462 Willis, ibid. Prior
Richard and the convent let their moiety of
Thenford to John Page rector of the other
moiety for four marks, 19 Henry vi (1440)
Yate p. 60 They had been in poffeffion of
the moiety a century or more ib. p. 59.

16. JOHN HUGELEY, in the time of John
Chedworth, bifhop of Lincoln, inter 1452—
1471 Willis, Mtr Abb I fuppofe a miftake in the name, for John *Hafeley* occurs,
May 1, 1452. Yate, p 23. and again the
fame year in an agreement with Euftachius
Barnard rector of Thenford ib. p. 60. and
in a leafe to John Staunton canon of the
houfe, July 8, 37 Henry vi. (1459) ib.
p. 20

17.

17. JOHN STAUNTON, 1474 16 Edw. IV. Willis. He and the convent granted a leafe of Stepclafton, with the manfe of the rectory, for 13l per ann. 16 Edw. IV. (1476) Yate, p. 57. A rent charge in Over and Nether Chalford[c] was given to John Staunton prior of Coldnorton and the convent by Richard Chock, one of the Juftices of the common Pleas, and Thomas Cornyfh, clerk. Yate, p. 36 no date. Richard Choke is Chief Juftice of C. Pleas, 1462. Sir Richard Choke Kn. J. C. Pl. 1471, 1472. and 1484. Dugd. Chron. Ser. Thomas Cornifh, fuffragan bifhop of Tyne, was Provoft of Oriel in 1493, and died 1513. Wood's Colleges, p. 127.

18. JOHN WOTTON the laft prior. Willis. He died on the faturday before Palm funday, 11 Henry VII (1495,) and, for want of canons to elect, the priory efcheated to the Crown. Yate, p. 9. See above, p. 304.

<hr />

[c] i e Salford, Com Oxon

NUM. XVI.

Teftamentum Will. Smyth, Lincoln Epifcopi

In Dei nomine, Amen Vicefimo fexto die menfis Decembris, Anno Domini millefimo quingentefimo decimo tertio. Ego Wilhelmus Smyth miferatione divina Lincoln. Epifcopus, compos mentis et fanæ memoriæ exiftens condo [et ordino[a]] teftamentum meum in hunc modum. Imprimis commendo animam meam Deo omnipotenti ac[b] præcelfæ Dei genetrici. gloriofæ Virgini Mariæ, corpufque meum fepeliendum in ecclefia cathedrali beatæ Mariæ Lincoln. ad finem occidentalem fepulchri bonæ memoriæ Domini Wilhelmi Alnewicke quondam Lincoln. epifcopi. Item volo quod Principalis et fcolares Aulæ Regiæ et Collegii de Brafen Nofe in Oxon. et eorum ibidem fucceffores pro tempore exiftentes, qui (præter et ultra fumptus

***

[a] D in vet exemplari ex Reg Fettyplace 26, in Off Prærog defcript et in Com Cift inter Archiv Coll Æn Naf repofit

[b] Et ibid

con-

conftructionis et ædificationis ipfius Collegii ac alia beneficia et dona eis et dicto collegio a me collata, et in pofterum, Deo dante, conferenda) habent et tenent ex donatione et conceffione meis terras in eorum proprios ufus perpetuo poffidendas vocat. Baffet's Fee in Comitatu Oxon. quas nuper perquifivi de Thoma Bulkley de Eyton ad valorem annuum feptem librarum fex folidorum et octo denariorum ultra reprifas. ac[c] etiam terras et tenementa quæ perquifivi de Thoma Manby[d] de Stow parke in Comitatu Lincoln. quæ ad valorem annuum quinque librarum trefdecim folidorum et quatuor denariorum fe extendunt folvant feu folvi faciant annuatim perpetuis futuris temporibus Decano et capitulo ecclefiæ cathedralis Lincoln prædict. duodecim libras bonæ monetæ

[D ib d]

[d] Of this eftate no other notice occurs The college feem to have been poffeffed of the Rectory of Wheathampftead (Herts) and of the Chapel of Harpeden The rectory was rented by Hugh Crifhall, who was commonly in arreals, 9 L 10 S Rot 8 H viii—14 H viii the chapel by Chriftopher Fawkener, clerk, who was conftantly in arrears, 11 L 13 S 4D Rot 5 H viii—19 H viii No fuch name as Harpeden occurs in the Villare, except one near Henley, Oxon, which belongs to All Souls college It is not known how the fociety of Brafen Nofe attained, nor when they loft or alienated, thefe impropriatios

L l

ad

ad duos anni terminos. videlicet ad festa
sancti Michaelis archangeli in mense Septem-
bris et Annuntiationis beatæ Mariæ Virginis
per æquales portiones   De quibus quidem
duodecim libris annuis volo et ordino quod
sex libræ tresdecim solidi et quatuor denarii
annuatim solvantur per præfatos Decanum et
capitulum pro tempore existent. uni Pres-
bytero in capella beati Sebastiani martyris ex
australi parte ecclesiæ cathedralis prædictæ
juxta locum sepulturæ meæ præelectum no-
torie existent. pro anima mea parentum et
benefactorum meorum imperpetuum cele-
braturo ad prædictos duos anni terminos
Quem quidem presbyterum per memet ip-
sum durante vita mea naturali præfici volo,
et post obitum meum cum ipsius locum vacare contigerit per magistros Will Smyth
archidiaconum Lincoln. Gilbertum Smyth archidiaconum Northampton. Henricum Wilcockes legum doctorem, Robertum Toneyes
in legibus bacchalaureum, Thomam Smyth
de Cestria mercatorem, et Robertum Browne
de Newark, vel majorem partem eorundem,
Decano et capitulo ecclesiæ cathedralis Lincoln. præsentabitur instituendus et admit-
tendus.   Omnibus vero prænominatis ab hac
luce subtractis, Decanus et capitulum ecclesiæ
prædictæ hujusmodi capellaniam vel cantariam

riam conferent, et capellanum idoneum in eadem   Dictum vero capellanum in præfata capella celebrantem in habitu chorali decenti juxta morem aliorum prefbyteiorum cantaristarum ecclefiæ [cathedralis^e] prædictæ chorum fequi et divinis officiis intereffe volo. Item volo et oidino, quod inftructor puerorum choriftarum ecclefiæ cathedralis prædictæ in cantu fingulis diebus poft completorium finitum ad caput occidentale fepulchri mei prædicti cum choriftis decantet antiphonam, Sancte Deus, Sancte fortis, Sancte et immortalis, mifeieie nobis   Nunc Chrifte te petimus, miferere quæfumus qui venifti redimere perditos Noli damnare redemptos cum verficulo, Adoramus te Chrifte &c et refponf. Quia per crucem, ac ratione^f Gloriofa mors et paffio tua perducat nos ad gaudia vitæ. Amen. cum genuflectionibus inclinationibus et proftrationibus juxta modum in ecclefia cathedrali S^{ti}. Pauli London. coram imagine crucifixi ad hoftium boreale ibidem ufitatum et fieri confuetum. ac cum pfalmo De profundis per ipfos choriftas dicendo et precibus confuetis. viz. Kyrie^g ely-

^e D ubi fupra
^f † ac oratione
^h "Kurie Chrifte Kurie Pater" Vetus exemplar, ubi fupra

L l 2   efon,

efon. Chrifte elyefon, Pater nofter, Ave Maria, Et ne nos [inducas[h]] Requiem æternam &c cum oratione. Deus qui inter Apoftolicos facerdotes &c   Item volo quod dictus prefbyter pro anima mea, ut præfertur, celebrans, cum uno faltem vicario chorali eccleiiæ cathedralis prædictæ et inftructore choriftarum ibidem una cum ipfis choriftis qualibet fexta feria fingulis ebdomadis coram imagine crucifixi in parte auftrali dictæ ecclefiæ exiftent. miffam de nomine Jefu vel de quinque vulneribus decantent cum nota, dict. viz prefbytero miffam ipfam celebran   fi ad hoc difpofitus fuerit, alioquin per alium ipfam celebrari faciendo, reliquis cantum miffæ (in hiis quæ ad chorum pertinent) profequentibus. Et volo quod hujufmodi informator puerorum præmiffa faciens et diligenter obfervans viginti folidos, ipfi vero choriftæ fexdecim folidos et quatuor denarios et vicarius hujufmodi choralis fex folidos et octo denarios, de prædictis duodecim libris fingulis annis percipient et habebant   Item volo et ordino quod de prædictis duodecim libris quinque marcæ bonæ monetæ fingulis annis imperpetuum pro obitu meo in præfata ecclefia cathedrali annuatim fervando inter canonicos refidentes

[r] D ibd

ac

ac præfentes ac alios miniftros ecclefia cathedralis prædictæ diftribuantur fecundum modum et formam in obfervatione obitus bonæ
memoriæ domini Johannis Ruffell nuper Lincoln epifcopi prædeceffonis mei in ipfa ecclef
cathedr. ordinata[1]. Item do et lego Aulæ
Regiæ et Collegii de Brafen Nofe prædict.
Principali et fcholaribus ejufdem et fuis ibidem fucceffonibus ad ufum capellæ ejufdem
collegii et ad deferviendum Deo in divinis
officiis ibidem, libros, calices, veftimenta, et
alia ornamenta ad capellam meam perti-
nentia, quæ in quadam fcedula five codicillo
præfenti teftamento meo inferius annexat.
duxi fingillatim fpecificanda et exprimenda.
Et quia præter et ultra ftatuta et ordinationes
pro confervatione et manutentione dicti collegii per memetipfum jampridem edita et ordinata quædam alia ftatuta ipfi collegio et
degentibus in eodem neceffaria feu faltem
utilia et opportuna adhuc reftant edenda, po-
terintque fortaffis ex ipfis jam editis ftatutis
aliqua emergere dubia declaratione feu inter-
pretatione explananda . [idcirco[k]] dilectis mihi
in Chrifto magiftris Will Smyth archidiacono Lincoln. Gilberto Smyth archidiacono

[1] In ipfam ecclefiam cathedralem ordinata ubi fupra
[k] D ubi fupra

Northampt.

Northampt. Henrico Wilcockes legum doctori Roberto Toneys in legibus baccalaureo,
Thomæ Smyth de Ceſtria mercatori, et Roberto Browne de Newark, ſtatuta quæcunque
putaverint ad honorem et commodum ipſius
collegii principaliſque et ſcholarium ejuſdem
pertinere de novo edenda et promulganda
quotiens opus fuerit. ipſiſque quoque ſtatutis
jam editis et in poſterum edendis addendi[1]
detrahendi eademque ſupplendi interpretandi
declarandi, aut ſi res ita exigit[m] prout eis aut
eorum majori parti viſum fuerit etiam mu-
tandi quamdiu ſuperſtites extiterint, aut eorum aliquis ſuperſtes extiterit plenam et in-
tegram do et concedo facultatem, poteſtate
hujuſmodi interpretandi declarandi et ſupplendi poſteaquam ab hac luce migraverint
ſucceſſoribus noſtris epiſcopis Lincoln. pro
tempore exiſtentibus in perpetuum reſervata.
Item lego domui ſive Hoſpitali Sti. Johannis
Baptiſtæ de Banbury centum libras ad ædi-
ficia in dicto Hoſpitali conſtruenda et antiqua
ibidem reficienda præter et ultra ſexaginta
libras quas eidem Hoſpitali contuli, et magiſtro ibidem nunc exiſtenti liberari feci.
Item lego et committo diſpoſitioni et volun-

[1] Addendi et detr ibid
[m] Exigerit ibid

tati

tati Thomæ Smyth de Ceſtria mercatoris omnes et ſingulas pecuniarum ſummas per quoſdam debitores meos mihi debitas quorum ſcripta obligatoria penes eundem Thomam et in ejus cuſtodia remanent una cum quadringentis marcis quas Johannes Warburton de Com. Ceſtriæ Miles per quædam ſcripta obligatoria et quaſdam indenturas deſuper confictas mihi et aſſignatis meis ſolvere tenebitur ratione maritagii Elizabethæ Wynnington filiæ et hæredis Ricardi Wynnington armigeri filii[n] domini Johannis Warberton ſi dicta Elizabetha vixerit donec ad ætatem legitimam pervenerit inter conſanguineos meos et conſanguineas meas pauperes juxta diſcretionis[o] ſuæ arbitrium dividend. et diſtribuend Reſiduum vero omnium bonorum meorum ſuperius non legatorum do et lego ordinationi et diſpoſitioni magiſtrorum Will Smyth archidiac Lincoln Gilberti Smyth archidiac. Northampt. Henrici Wilcockes legum doctoris Roberti Toneys in legibus baccalaurei eccleſ cathedr Lincoln canonicorum, nec non Thomæ Smyth de Ceſtria mercatoris et Roberti Browne de Newark, quos nomino

---

[n] Legendum videtur " et filii," vel " cum filio "

[o] " Suæ diſcretionis," vetus illud exemplar

ordino [facio*p*] et conftituo hujus teftamenti et ultimæ voluntatis meæ executores ut ipfi [ea*q*] difponant pro falute animæ meæ prout eis melius vifum*r* fuerit expedire. Præfentibus tunc ibidem Philippo Morgan*s* in medicinis et Olivero Coren*t* S T. doctoribus ecclef cathedi. B Mariæ Lincoln canonicis

---

p D ubi fupr

q D bid

r Melius viium on, verfo ordire, ' melius expedire

s Philip Morgan M D is collated by bifhop Smyth to the living of Whethamfted, May 5, 1509, on the death of John Smyth MS Harl 6953 p 6 having refigned Wafhgburn, to which Auguftin Fpifc Lidenfis (who often acted as fuffragan for Smyth See above, p 46 n) was inftituted, May 11, 1509, on the prefentation of Margaret Countefs of Richmond Vis Harl ib p 2) Smith collated Morgan to the prebend of Buckden, June 26, 1512 ib p 25 Willis, 11 i 155

t Oliver Coren, D D was collated by Smyth to the prebend of S Botolph, Lincoln, Sept 8, 1510 Ms Harl 6953 p 27 to Scamlib July 12, 1513 ii 26 and to North Kelfey Oct 20 1513 and (by the fucceeding bifhop) to Buckden inftalled Dec 23, 1514 Willis, Caen ii 155 of which he died poffeffed in 1542 MSS Harl ut fupra, p 100 He prefented Hugh Coren to the vicarage of Buckden, Nov 20, 1514. ib p 84 who was probably the Hugh Carwin or Coren (the fame name) who was archbifhop of Dublin in 1555, which by his own defire, he exchanged for Oxford in 1567, and died and was buried at Swinbrook Oxon, in 1568 He was of Brafen Nofe college (fee Yate, p 143) the fecond bifhop that iffued from the fe feminary There is a letter by him

et Jacobo Wolbeof[u] generofo cum multis aliis ad hoc fpecialiter requifitis.—Probat. penult. die Januar. A D 1513-14.

––––––––––

N U M. XVII.

Chapel ftuff geven and bequethed to the College of Brafon Nofe in Oxenforde[a].

Imprimis, A Dorfe and Redorfe of Crymfyn Velvet, with Flowres of Golde, in length,

him to archbifhop Parker, thanking his grace for remitting his option of the firft living in his diocefe of Oxford, Nov 26, 1567 MS Parker, cxiv p 511 a pedigree of Curwen, MS Dodfworth, 181, f 27 and, in other volumes of that induftrious collector, frequent notices of the family, from which Camden was maternally defcended

[u] The copy in the Archives has " Walbefle, a name which has not elfewhere occurred under either of its forms

[a] Sic Reg Fettyplace, ut fupra See Will s, Cath ii p 59 Yate, p 77

two

two yards three quarters, in depth one yarde
and one quarter. Item, a Dorfe and Redorfe of panyd[b] Velvett, fad tawny and marble colour, in length two yards, in depyth
one yard and one quarter   Item, two Dorfes
and Redorfes of panyd Velvet, fad tawny and
light tawny, in length two yards and three
quarters, in depyth one yard one quarter
Item, two paire of Curteyns for aulters ends,
of red Tartaryn.   Item, a paire of Curteyns
of grene Tartaryn.   Item, two cloths of
Diaper, in length the peice three ells, in
bredth one ell.   Item, two cloths of Diaper,
in length the peice three ells, in bredth one
ell.   Item, a playn cloth, in length two ells
one quarter, in brede one yerde   Item,
another plain cloth, in length three ells, in
brede one yerde   Item, two couife playn
cloths, in length the peice three ells   Item,
a Coffen for a Corporas, of Bords covered
with black Velvet, and thereon an image of
Crift made with Golde, Silke, and Perles,
and within that Corporas cafe of clothe of
Golde.   Item, another Coffyn like the fame,

---

[b] Striped or edged Warton, L of Sir T Pope, 2d ed
p 339 where he produces from an old romance this appofite
paffage " And with a mantell fche me clad It was of pur-
pur fayre and fyne And the *parc* of riche ermine'

with

with images of Mary and Gabriel, and a cafe for a Corporas in the fame black Velvett. Item, a caas, with a Corporas, the one fide Velvett powdred with Gold, and the other fide Ruffet Damafk. Item, a Corporas caas, the one fide clothe of Golde, and the other fide black Velvett. Item, a fuete of veftments of crymfyn Velvett, with three Copes of the fame, powdred with Flowres of Golde, lined with grene Bokeram. Item, a fuete of veftments of cloth of Tiffue, with aparel for the fame, lined with blew Bokeram Item, a Cope of crymfyn Velvet upon Velvet Item, a fuete of veftments of tynfel filk Item, two Copes of the fame Item, a veftment of Velvet, fad tawny, the Orfrays[c] of light tawny Item, a veftment of blewe Damafke the Orfrays of grene Damafke, powdred with Flowres of Golde, lyned with grene Bokeram Item, a maffe book, fecundo folio, Chorus Item, a maffe booke imprinted, fecundo folio, Ad te levavi Item, Antiphonar' fecundo folio, Sacerdos Item, a Antiphonar, fecundo folio, Jufticiam Item, a Anti-

---

[c] An embrodered edging From *Aurifrafium*, corrupted from *Aurifrifium*, properly perhaps *Auriphrigium* Fr *Orfray* Warton, ib p 349 n Compare that and the preceding Number with this and the two following Numbers of this Appendix

phonar,

phonar, fecundo folio, Dicne   Item, a Antiphonar, in fecundo folio, Nari   Item, a Antiphonar, with a Legend, in folio[d], Per omnia.   Item, a Grayle[e], fecundo folio, Tot   Item, a Grayle, fecundo folio, Sim.   Item, a Proceffional, fecundo folio, Juftum   Item, a Proceffional, fecundo folio, Excita   Item, a paire of Organs[f], late bought at London.

[d] 1 ' fecundo folio, vel ' in fecundo folio

[e] The Grail or *Gradual* contained all that was fung by the choir at high mafs Warton, ib p 338 n. " The *grayle* is not fayd " Feftival, p 33

[f] " Pro reparatione Organorum" is an entry in the Comp Burff 1524 and 1544 but it does not appear who was the donor of them, or when they were purchafed On the fubject of organs and other mufical inftruments in ancient ufe, fee much curious information in Wartons L of Sir I Pope, p 343—345 his Hift Poet 1 p 61 429 ii 225 n x 339 n and in Differt ii prefixed to that admirable work

NUM. XVIII

Ex Libro Jocalium Coll Æn Naf penes Cuftodem
Jocalium

Inuentarium Jocalium et alorum ornamen-
torum Capelle et Aule

In primis a croffe of filver and gylt

Item a fote for the fame of filuer and gilt

It iii chales of filver and gilt with foure pat-
tennes

It a cenfar of filver and gilt

It. ii Ciuettys of filver and gilt

It ii Cruettys of filvei

It ii Candleftickys of filver parcell gylt

It a paxe[a] of filvei and gilt

It a littill paxe of filver and gilt

It a fhippe[b] of filver

---

[a] Mr Mede obferves, that *the kifs of peace* was cuftomary in
the ancient church at the celebration of the Euchariſt, "in
ftead of which at length was brought in that foolifh ceremony,
ftill ufed among the Romanifts, for the prieft to fend a little
gilded or painted table, with a crucifix or fome faint's picture
thereon, to be kiffed of every one in the church before they receive the holy bread , which they call *the kiffing of the Pax* "
p 96

[b] " A fhipp of puter to putt in frankenfence ' Warton, ut
fupra, p 345 and ib 346 n he fays it was a fpecies of Cen-
fer;

It. a pixe[c] of filver and gilt

It. a ftanding cuppe with a cover of filver and gilt

It. an oder Cuppe with a cover of filver and gylt ex dono dni. Herford Epi[d].

It. a Corporas cafe with the Image of the refurrection of our Lorde fett with peerle and a fmall croffe of filver and gilt and in the handells the fame Image and ii Images of the knightjs of the fepulcre fett with peerle on [one] having a fmall axe and the other a fwerde of filver and gilt

It a Corporas cafe with the Image of the falutation of our Ladi and an angell fett with peerle and a fmall feptre of filver and gilt

It. ii corporas cafjs and ii coverings for the chaljs

It iii corporas cafys of redde faten of bruges

It viii corporas[e]

It hole reparell of the prieft decon and fub-

fer and refers to Dugl Mon iii 276 311 294 ibid Eccl Coll 84

[c] See above, p 307 n

[d] This item is interlined with frefher ink It was probably given by Boothe bifhop of Hereford, as already noted, p 115 n

[e] A different hand, originally vii

decon

decon[f] of clothe of tiffue and grownde
werke of redde velvett

It hole reparell of the prieft decon and fubdecon of redde tynfhill faten.

It. hole reparell of on prieft of white damafke

It hole reparell for on prieft of tawney velvett and yolowe

It hole reparell for ii priefts of redde filke

It ii coopys of fangwyne filke with flowrys
of yolowe filke[g]

It hole reparell for one prieft of dorneye

It. iiii hangyngs for ii awters of tawny and
yolowe velvett

Item on awter clothe of diaper x other awter
clothys

It three towellys[h]

It. a holl fute of veftments for the prieft decon and fubdecon and a coope of blacke
damafke and redde gyveyn by S. John
Porte knyght and iuftice of kyngs Pench

It a holl reparell of on prieft of white fay
and redd gyveyn by Mr John Hardyng[i]

[f] " Decon and fubdecon' croffed out

[g] This and the two preceding articles croffed out

[h] Thus far in the fame hand, except where noted otherwife

[i] John Hawarden (Mr Hardyng, as Wood calls him, MS
8514 p 208) was at this time fellow and afterwards Principal

It hole apparel for a preſt of the grownd of blewe and croſſe of redd ſaten and an Image of ſaint John Baptiſt

It hole apparel for a preſt whos grownd ys whit damaſke ſilk, the croſſe of ſatten of bridges[k] havyng the Image of god and oure ladye

It ii corporas caſes, with ii corporaſſes, one of blacke and red velvet, the other of diverſe colors and a blacke[l]

It a cope of red velvet with Images of [ſic]

It. an other cope whos grownd ys red ſylk and the borders blewe velvet

It. a cope of yelow ſylk with borders of cloth of gold and images

It ii veſtments gyven by Mr Rauff Alen Ju. of Warrngton aˆ 1560 [So far on p. 1.]

cipal of Braſen Noſe college The name is the ſame, but I do not know that he is the perſon intended

k i e bruges, as above We have 'ſatten of Bridges in Wartons L of Pope p 349

In the margin oppoſite the three preceding articles is this mem 'ex ſono doctor Cliſton ſundecani eccleſie Eboraenſis Dr William Clitton was ſubchauer of York, 1522 Willis, Cath i 182 ſubdean, 1529, and died in 1548 ib i 89 He gave to Braſen Noſe college in 1538 certain lands at Aſcot Doyley, Com Oxon, at Kingholme in Gloucesterſhire &c for the maintenance of one fellow, to be choſen from the counties of York and Lincoln alternately

It.

It an Aulter cloth of Diaper. ex dono Mⁿ. Ogle^m.

It for a preft decon and fubdecon of blue faten and a coope of the fame color [ib. p. 2.]

^m Humphry Ogle, I L B was collated by bifhop Smyths friend, Boothe bifhop of Hereford, to the prebend of Yne in that catnedral, March 1, 1520 Willis, Cath 1 607 to Moreton magna, Jan 24, 1522 ib p 584 and to the archdeaconry of Salop, Jan 28, 1523 which he refigned in 1536 ib p 555. He is called H Ogle of Salford, Com Oxon He gave 100 L o Brafen Nofe college, with which were purchafed lands in Hanbridge, adjoining the city of Chefter, for the fupport of two fcholars, born in the parifh of Prefcot, Lancafhire, or, in defect of fuch, from the diocefe of Chefter oi Lichfield He items to have received out of the eftates an annuity of 5 L during his life See Comp Burft 1540—1547

NUM. XIX

Veſtments given by biſhop Smyth to the Ca-
thedral at Lincoln

A Cheſable of cloth of Tiſhew, with two
Tunacles, and three Copes of the ſame ſuit,
with coſtly Orphreys of Gold, and Images of
needle-work, and 3 Albes[a] with the apparel of the ſame, of the gift of Lord William Smith, biſhop of Lincoln   Dugd. Mon.
iii p. 280.

It 7 Copes of red cloth of Gold of one
ſuit with red Roſes[b] and Oſtriges feathers, of
the gift of the ſaid Lord William Smith
Biſhop with his arms in the Morſes[c]

---

[a] See above, p 117 n

[b] In alluſion to his arms   whence alſo the head or volute
of his croſier is diſtinguiſhed by a roſe See the engraving At
Iddington, in the room adjoining the ancient hall, (ſee above,
p 92) is a biſhop in a rochet and mitre, kneeling, not more
unlike the portrait of Smyth than portraits of the ſame perſon
by different hands at different parts of life often are to each
other   but the head of the croſier, at preſent miſplaced in the
window, does not exhibit the appropriate badge of the roſe

[c] i e Claſps, morſus fibulæ   Du Freſne in v. See alſo
Aïnſworth.   Morſus

It.

It. 18 Copes of red Tinfel Sattin with Orphreys of Gold and Images of one fuit, with arms in the Morfes, of the gift of the faid Lord William Bifhop of Lincoln. ib.

Remaining, 18 May, 1553. Four Copes of red cloth of Gold of one fuit, with Rofes and Oftridges feathers. with the arms of Bi-fhop Smith in their Morfes. ib. p. 289.

In 1557. 14 Copes of red Tinfel, with orphreys of gold, with arms of Bifhop Smith in their Morfes. Ex dono ejufdem epifcopi ib. 295

10 Copes of red cloth of Gold of one fuit with red rofes the gift of William Smith Bifhop of Lincoln, with his arms in their morfes. ib.

NUM.

N U M. XX.

Extr from Brafen Nofe Archives, lower room

For my very worthy and much honoured Friend Dr Yates, Principall of Brafen Nofe Colledge in Oxford.

Honoured S^r

When I returned the paper you fent me, with my defire of what I thought fitteft to be copied, the Booke (wherein my draughts of the Figures of thofe monuments in Lincoln Minfter and other churches were) was not come up to London, but now that it is, I have fent you here inclofed an account of your Founder's monument there, approving very much of your grateful purpofe in reftering thereof, but forafmuch as it may be a temptation to thofe, who to benefit themfelves in a fmall matter care not what mifchief they do (as they that deftroyed this fair monument of that worthy Bifhop) I think it were beft to cut his name upon the ftone (which yet remains there) in fair large

letters

NUM. XXI.

PEDIGREE OF SUTTON.

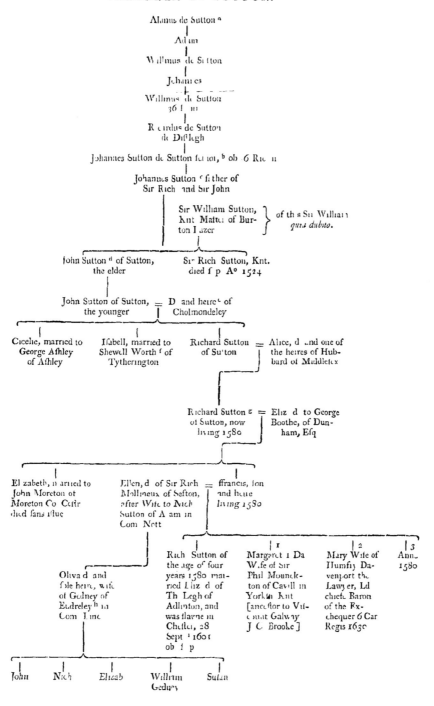

Alanus de Sutton a

Adam

Willimus de Sutton

Johannes

Willimus de Sutton
36 I m

Ricardus de Sutton
de Diflegh

Johannes Sutton de Sutton for ioi, b ob 6 Ric m

Johannes Sutton c father of
Sir Rich and Sir John

Sir William Sutton,
Knt Matter of Bur-
ton Lazer } of this Sir William
quis dubito.

John Sutton d of Sutton,
the elder

Sir Rich Sutton, Knt.
died f p A° 1524

John Sutton of Sutton, = D and heire of
the younger   Cholmondeley

Cicelie, married to
George Afhley
of Afhley

Ifabell, married to
Shewell Worth f of
Tytherington

Richard Sutton = Alice, d and one of
of Sutton   the heires of Hubbard of Middlefex

Richard Sutton g = Eliz d to George
of Sutton, now   Boothe, of Dun-
living 1580   ham, Efq

Elizabeth, married to
John Moreton of
Moreton Co Ceftr
died fans iffue

Ellen, d of Sir Rich = ffrancis, fon
Mollineux of Sefton,   and heire
after Wife to Nich   living 1580
Sutton of A am in
Com Nott

Oliva d and
fole heire, wife
of Gulney of
Eudreley h in
Com Linc

Rich Sutton of
the age of four
years 1580 mar-
ried Liz d of
Th Legh of
Adlinton, and
was flayne in
Cheftel, 28
Sept i 1601
ob f p

Margaret i Da
Wife of Sir
Phil Mounck-
ton of Cavill in
Yorkm Knt
[anceftor to Vif-
count Galway
J C Brooke]

Mary Wife of
Humfry Da-
venport the
Lawyer, Ld
chiefe Baron
of the Ex-
chequer 6 Car
Regis 1630

Anne
1580

John   Nich   Elizab   William   Sufan
Gedney

letters filled with white cement, and no more but his title and day of his death, and upon the next pillai to place a fair memorial of him, exprefling the time and by whom his tomb ftone was fo defaced by the taking away of the braffe, and to cut this epitaph (which I here fend you a copy of) thereon.

I did intreat that when you fent me the copies of what I defired concerning Cold Norton, &c—I pray you let me have them within ten days, in regard I fhall be preparing for my journey into the country about that time So I reft

yr. very much obliged fervt.

Willm. Dugdale.

London fr Mr Afhmole's Chamber in ye. Middle Temple Lane. 2°. Junii 1668.

NOTES ON THE SUTTON PEDIGREE

[2] This entire pedigree is copied from the Cheshire Pedigrees, with two or three slight corrections in the latter part from the Heralds Office Which pedigree in the Heralds Office (1 D 14 f 245) begins with Sir William Sutton Kn Master of Burton Lazarus (lord of Sutton and Master of Burton Lazars, MS Harl 2040 f 200 and 5529 f 64) and makes him father of John Sutton and Sir Richard This was entered at Glover's visitation in 1580 by Richard Sutton, and signed by himself The arms entered with it are quarterly of 4 First, Or a lion rampant, queue furche, for Sutton 2d Argent, a cheveron between 3 bugle horns stringed Sable, also for Sutton 3d Gules, 2 helmets in chief Argent, a Garbe in base Or, for Cholmondeley 4 Sable an estoil between 2 flanches ermine for Hubbard [which are the arms of Hobart earl of Buckinghamshire] Crest, out of a ducal coronet Or, a demilion rampant queue furche And it must be noted that all the pedigrees concur with this in giving the lion in the first quarter, which Mr Latham therefore considers as " the true arms of Sutton, and the bugle horns as their coat of augmentation only, in consequence of their foresterchip of Macclesfield, which cannot be properly borne, but as a quartering, for it is mentioned (he informs me) in all the quarterings of the arms of Sutton as appertaining to the forest of Macclesfield, in the same manner as those of Delamere forest were always quartered by the Kingsleys, who were foresters there " The reader will see and probably correct what (being myself no herald) I had previously advanced on the authority of Mr Brooke, p 406 With regard to the crosses often quartered in the Sutton arms, they are patonce over the gateway of Brasen Nose college, and were so in the hall window Woods Colleges, p 568 and this we have seen called the true bearing for Sams-

bury,

bury, p 469 note b one of the Suttons having (it is fuppofed) married one of the coheirs of Sir William de Samfbury Kn But they are more frequently crofs croflets, and are faid to be for Southworth who married a Samfbury of Samfbury, Lancafhire, and had with her the Samfbury eftate and affumed the family arms See MS Harl 1505 2040 f 200 where alfo the Worfley arms are quartered with Sutton in confequence of fome match with that family The crofs croflet fitchy in Sir R Sutton's furcoat (fee the plate) muft be a miftake of the painter, as that was the bearing of Davenport

ᵇ MS Harl 2040 f 200 The Chefhire pedigree has "junior," a manifeft blunder

ᶜ MS Harl 2040, which has all the higher defcents of the family and ends with Richard Sutton who married "Alice Hubbart," alfo makes this John Sutton the "father of Sir Richard and Sir John" The Chefhire pedigree (as here copied) is doubtful in this point MS Harl 1505 2113 f 66 f 80 2187 f 104 5529 f 64 all concur with the pedigree in the Heralds Office in making Sir William Sutton, Mafter of Burton Lazarus, the father of John and Sir Richard Sutton this therefore I have adopted in the Life If I might hazard a conjecture, it fhould be this, that this John Sutton was not brother (as commonly ftated) but father of Sir William, fince it is not likely, though certainly poffible, that John Sutton fenior, who died " 6 Richard 11," that is in 1383, fhould have a grandfon, as Sir R is ftated to be, who lived till the year 1524 But I find no evidence to fupport the conjecture, unlefs it be this, that the Harl MS 2113 f 66 and f 80 has two Johns immediate predeceffors to William, but then the firft of them is 16 Edw 11 (1322) and the other 46 Edw 111 (1372) which carries us back a little, inftead of bringing us lower down

ᵈ The Chefh Ped and feveral others make him a Knight, but I conceive it is a miftake

ᵉ Thomafin d of William Cholmeley and Margery his Wife Chart Antiq J Darke Armig No 1, 2, 3 See above, p. 413 and correct the only known pedigree where fhe is

named, MS Harl 2113 which calls her Elizabeth d and h
" Ranulphi de Cnolmondeley junior filius Ricaidi Cholmund-
ley armiger

f These names being uncommon are seldom given correctly
in the pedigrees Titherington and Sutton are both in the parish of Presbury ' Joan Worth of Tetrynton and John his
eldest son" are two of the original trustees of Macclesfield school
in 1502 See above, p 431 n The Chesh Ped of the family gives the said John Worth two sons, John the first son
sans issue, and Sewall married to Isabell daughter of Sutton of
Sutton In Presbury Church were these arms, Arg a cross
ragule couped Sable, for Worth, impaling, quarterly of 4,
first and fourth, the lion (as usual) for Sutton, 2 and 3 quarterly, first and fourth, the cheveron and bugle horns (as usual,)
second and third, a cheveron between 3 crosses moline, for
Sewall Worth of Tedderington gent and Isabell his wife,
daughter of John Sutton of Sutton esquire MS Harl 2151
f 28 See and correct ib 2040 f 200 f 209

g This Richard Sutton gave a window to Gawsworth church
(MS Harl 2151 f 97) and Northwich church (ib 139
1 12) in his own country, and to Witton chapel (ib 2151
f 96 b) in Lancashire In these several windows his arms
were exhibited with this inscription, " Orate pro bono statu
Ricardi Sutton et Elizabeth uxoris ejus qui istam fenestram
fieri fecerunt, an° 1547 ' The date of these benefactions is
memorable, it is the first year of Edward vi, the donor per-
naps feeling his pious affections warmed and expanded on the
accession of a Prince of benign virtue and excellent parts, under
hose auspices he hoped for more equitable government and
purer religion The "Orate' is no disproof of the surmise, as
the donor was living at that time, and lived many years afterwards Some other Richard Sutton (as it seems) was buried
at Gawsworth, for in the head of the chancell are two figures
in coats armour with this inscription under them " Orate pro
bono statu Ricardi Sutton et   uxoris ejus On the man s
surcoat, quarterly of four, the bugle horns and the cross cros-
lets At the man s back two sons On the woman s mantle,

Arg

Arg a chief Gules, an annulet for difference Behind her back two daughters MS Harl 2151 f 97

ʰ MS Harl 2187 f 104 has " Enderby, which I believe s right, as no such place as Eudreley can be found The same pedigree has Munkton " de Enwell in Com Ebor' inftead of " Cavill ,' and there, I believe, it is to be corrected by this

ⁱ MS Harl ib has it " 20 Sept 1601 and No 5529. f 64 " flaine iffuelefs," without date How the event happened I have not difcovered

I will clofe thefe notes with fome curious lines refpecting the family and arms of Sutton, which I owe, as I do alfo the principal part of thefe notes, to the very obliging communication of William Latham efquire , premifing only, from the fame Gentleman, a reference to Edmondfon s Baronag Genealog vol iv where, p 342 in the arms of Ward, vifcount Dudley and Ward, who married an heirefs of the Suttons, the 2d quartering is Or, a lion rampant double tailed Vert, " a full proof of their defcent from the Suttons of Sutton

Copied from MS Harl 886 f 39 b

Sutton beyreth or a lyon rampande vert
fourchie le quew, lingued and armed gules
a noble armes is this to us advert
that fyll ill are in Herehaults lyrned rules

Worthie for he a Royall lyon ys
his doble tayle a dobled ferte doth fhewe
his bloodie pawes with further profe of this
his corage hawte fettes clearlie to the view.

Ryche for he ys fuperior to golde
Fayre for his colere ys the pleafant greene
auncie it for he difplayed in battells ould
a terrore to his enemies ofte hathe beene
And att all tymes fewe englifhe fubjectes fhylde
myght of moe gentyllmen be borne in fylde

Three

Tnree annuletts Or inferted[a] is his creft
on helme in torfe Argent and Azure fett
With mantell gules ydobled Argent dreft
his worde Fraudem fuge abhore deceite

The lynked Rynges, betoken conftant faythe
Powznes[b] and trewthe, tne wreathe doth wynde in one,
Tne mantell corage fearfe on councell ftayeth
Tne worde declares, a hate to fraude alone

In divers houfes Sutton bears this cote
His worde and crefte to haddon[c] proper ys
to come of one theis armes doth them all note
tnere creftes there divers faues for poure doth mvs[d]
In worthieft lyne, in worfhipe to defende
Ytfelfe all thefe, that of ytfelfe defcende

[a] I beleve that is the word "The true meaning, as well as the heraldic term, is perifhed W I
[b] Might, puiffance
[c] 'Sutton or Haddon, Derbefhire" MS
[d] Mifcere, mix or mingle

NUM. XXII.

Sir R. Sutton's Will.

Extracted from the Registry of the Prerogative Court of Canterbury, 27 Bodfield, 25 Probat in ecclesia cath D. Pauli, London, Nov 7, 1524.

In dei nomine Amen   Quia media vita in morte fumus et omnes morimur et quasi aqua in terram dilabimur que non revertetur 3 reg. 4.   Ideo falvator noster volens nos omnes paratos invenire nos ortatur et eftote parati quia qua hora non putatis filius hominis veniet Luce 3ᵃ. Sed quia mortis tempus incertum eft, nefcit homo finem fuum . | . ecci 9º. Et vt inquid ftultum eft in tali ftatu vivere quo quis non audet mori. Ideo &c. I Richard Sutton Knyght of Hole mynde by the help and grace of the moft glorified Trinitie The xvith day of Marche in the 15th yere of the Reigne of Kyng Henry the viiith ordeyn and make my laft Will and Teftament Firft I bequeath my Soul unto the bleffed Trinitie thorough the meke praier of the moft pure and mekeft Virgyn the
                                                Mother

Mother of Jeſu criſt my body to be buried
afore the Image of our Lady there as it ſhall
fortune me to deceaſe with this Antem of
our Lady upon my grave ſtone Sub tuam
protectionem confidimus ubi infirmi acceperunt virtutem et propter hoc tibi pſallimus
dei genetrix virgo   Item I bequeath to the
Marſter of the Temple for my tythes and offerings forgoten and not paide and alſo to pray
for me 20ˢ. yf it happen me to deceſe there
Item I bequeth to every prieſt of the Temple bycauſe they ſhall ſay every knyght dynge during the month and maſs of requiem
on the morowe with note 111ˢ. 1111ᵈ. yf it
happen me to deceſſe there   Item I will
that at the day of my burying be dealed to
pour men vˡ every man a penny   Item I
will that a virtuous prieſt be round at Sutton or at Macclesfeld with the profits of
ſuche landes as I have purchaſed in Cheſhire
to pray for my Soule my father and moder
and all my progenye ſoules and for the ſoules
of King Edward the fourth quene Elizabeth
his wife Elizabeth ducheſs of Suffolk my
Lord Ryvers my Lord Richard my Lord
Thomas late Marquis Dorſet Nicolas Talbot
Chriſtofer Hyde and for all the ſoules that
God and I would have prayed for   Item I
will that the ſaid prieſt ſhall every weeke for

ever

ever on munday wednefdaye and frydaye
faye dirige with placebo for my Soule and
the Soules aforefaid and faye Maffe weekeley
on munday of the Annunciation of our
bleffed Lady on wednefday of the fyve
wounds of our Lord Jefu on fryday of Jefu
and fo for ever and all other dayes he fhall
fay maffe of the daye except a reafonable
caufe lett the fame and I will that my cofyn
John Sutton and his heires have power to
putt in the faid pieft unto the faid Chauntrie
and he be of myfgydynge to putt him owt
and putt in another provided that my faid
Cofyn or his Heires putt in a vertuous pieft
unto the fervice within IIII. weks or ells I
will that the Bifhop of Chefter for the tyme
being doo putt in a vertuous preft into the
faid fervice to doo as is atorefaid provided
that it be not prejudiciall unto my faid Ne-
vewe nor to his Heirs for the putting in of
the faid preft into the faid fervice but alonly
for that time as detawte fhall be in him or
them Item I will that the faid preeft have
yearly IIIIli VIIIs IIIId for his wages and
that he have landes appoynted unto him for
the fame Item I bequeth to my Nephew
John Sutton's wite oon of my gownes Item
I bequeth to Clements Inn xxs Item I bequeth and forgive Roger Legh of Peckham
VIIIli

viii that I lent him when he was firft
maried and alfo I bequeth unto him a gowne
and xx. Item I will that my obite be
kept yearly at Macclesfeld forever at fuch
tyme of the yere as it fhall pleas God to call
me owt of this worlde and that Dirige and
Maffe be kept there and that every preeft
therat being prefent fhall have v^d and the
fcole mafter of the Gramar fcole viii^d hartely praying him that all the children of the
Gramar fcole may be there to fay dirige for
my foule and the foules that God and I
woulde have prayed for   And I will that the
faid children fhall have yerely ii^s if they doo
as is aforefaid   And in likewife I will that
my fader and mothers obite be kept yerely
both at oon tyme and the preeft fcole mafter
and chyldren doing as is aforefaid have at
dirige and maffe of every yeares mynde of
my faid fader and moder and me as is above
rehearfed at my yeres mynde   And I will
that xx of the iffues and profits of my lands
in Chefhire go every yere to the performance
of every of the faid ii obits in Chefhire and
that remaineth of the faid xx^s I will hit be
dealed amongft poor folks at the faid obite
Item I will and pray my cofyn John Sutton
and my feoffees of my lands in Chefhire to
perfourme my will aforefaid and yf all my
                                feoffees

feoffees dye except thre then I will that
thefe III that overlyve make a new fcoff-
ment to ten perfones of my lovers and frends
to the intent aforefaid   And fo from tyme
to tyme as ofte as nede fhall require for ever
Item I will that xL^s be fpent abowte the
making the high wayes abowte Saint Giles
in the ffelde   Item I will that my Lady Abbeffe of the Monaftery of Syon have xx^l to
pray for me as I intend their weall moft
lowley befecching theym of their great charitie to do the fame to my poor foule and to
forgive me   Item I the faid Richard will
that all fuche perfons and their heires that
ftand and be poffeffed and feized of my
houfes and tenements in Braynforth which I
late purchafed of Jane Wolmer widdowe
and of a hofe that I have on the north fide
of the Kyngs highe waye there fhall ftande
be poffeffed and feafed thereof to thufe of
me the faid Richard and myn henes and to
perfourme my laft wille to the intent that
with the profits of the fame as farre as they
will extende they fhall go towaids the fynding of an honeft preeft to pray for my foule
and all the foules that God and I would
have praid for   And that the faid preeft
fhall have all the profits of the fame towards
his wages to teche all thofe women that intend

tend to be profeffed and admytted unto the
Houfe of Syon and my Lady Abbeffe yf it
pleafe her to give the faid preft mete and
drink and logging and the faid Preft to fay
grafe dailey and to geve attendance upon the
Steward of the faid Houfe of Syon at Dinner and Supper and to do divine fervice afore
him   Alfo I will that my fayde feoffees fhall
ftande and be feized of the premiffes in
Braynforth ende to the intent aforefaid unto
fuche time my faid Lady Abbeffe or her fucceffors may optain and gett of the Kings
grace his heirs or fucceffors licence of the
mortyfying of the premiffes to the faid Abbeffe and her fucceffors and alfo licence of
the Lords mediat and immediat and after
fuch licence by theym obteyned and had of
the premiffes then my faid Feoffees fhall
ftande and be feafed of the premiffes to thufe
of my faid Lady Abbeffe and her fucceffors
for ever and that my Feoffees fhall make a
fufficient eftate and feofment to my faid
Lady Abbeffe and her fucceffois of the premiffes for ever to the intent aforefaid fo that
the fayde licence be obteyned and gotten
within the fpace of twenty yeres next after
my decefe   Item I will and bequeth to Thomas Sutton my Berchoufe at Braynforth
brigge end to him and to his heires male of
his

his body provided always that the fayde
Thomas doo well kepe the Reparacions of
the fame and pay the chief rent thereof and
referved and excepted unto me and unto
myn Heires the Thached Houfe on the Weft
fide of the Berehoufe Item I bequeth to
William Sutton his Brother v^h Item I bequeth to George Sutton his Brother being in
the newe College in Oxford XL^s towards his
fynding Item I bequeth to the faid Thomas
Sutton his hool yeres wages aforehande unto
the tyme he may gett him a newe Mafter
within the fame yere Item I will that my
nephew John Sutton of Sutton and his heires
have all the profits of my lands in Chefhire
Shropfhire and Darbyfhire immediately after
my decefe fo that they truely and yerely
performe this my laft wille And fo that he
nor his heires do not fell any part of them
but kepe a good houfcholde and kepe his
children to fcole and help to fett love and
charitie amongft his neighbours Item I will
that my fayde Nephew have the profits of
all my lands in Tottenhall Court after the
decefe of my Cofyn George Sutton and all
my other Landes and Hereditaments in Mid-
dilfex except the Lands and Hereditaments
afore bequeathed to my Lady Abbes of Syon
and except the fflod mede whiche I give and

bequeth

bequeth to my Cofyn George Sutton of the queene's houfe for terme of his life and except other landes bequethed   Item I will that Richard Sutton Yoman of the Chambre with the queen's grace fhalhave all thofe Landes the which Lawrence Ledam holdeth to ferme in lftilworth whiche be yearley v^li and more   Item I will that my Lady of Dartford have x marcs to pray for my Soule and thofe Soules that God and I would have praide for   And alfo I will that my Lady of Dennye have XL^s to do likewife   I will that my Coufin Ellyn Copelande have v marcs to pray for me   Item I bequeth to my nephew John Sutton of Sutton my Beddyng and my Houfeholde Stuffe that I have in the Sion and in the Temple and at St. Giles   And I will that he have my Crymfyn vellvet doublett and oon of my beft gownes and my Cofen his Wife an other gowne for to pray for my Soule and for thofe Soules that God and I would have prayed for   Item I will my Funerall and my debts paid which is noon to my Knowledge that the Money that remaineth fhall goo to my Cofin John Sutton of Sutton   Item to the executing of this my laft Will and Teftament in the premiffes I ordain and make the Reverende fader in God John Bifhop of Calepole and Mafter of

St.

St Thomas of Acres in London my Nephew John Sutton of Sutton my Cousin
Richard Snede John Porte Serjeaunt at the
Law and Richard Lyftir and Roger Legh of
Rygge myn Executors lowly befeeching them
to doo for me and my Soule as they would
be doon for and charitable to fee my will
executed Wherefore I will that the faid
John Poorte have v marcs for his labor
Richard Lyfter v marcs and Richard Snede
v marcs and that all my faid Executors charitably do for my Soule Item I ordeyn and
make my faid Lady Abbas of Syon and
Maifter John ffewterer general Confeffor of
the faid Monaftery and Marfter Alexander
Bell my gooftly fader overfeers of this my
prefent laft Will and Teftament mooft humbly befeeching them to forgive me that I
have offended theym in worde worke or
thought and of their Charitie that it may
pleafe theym to pray for me with all the
hole convent as I truft I fhall pray for them
in hevyn I the faid Richard revoke all other
former wills except this prefent Wille and
In witnefs of the premiffes I have fubfcribed
this with my fyke hande by me S R Sutton
Knyght.

ADDITIONS AND CORRECTIONS.

P. 4. The family of the Smyths of Old-hough terminated in feveral brothers, who all died without iffue, about thirty or forty years ago. One of them, Norman Smyth, was chofen Fellow of Brafen Nofe college, Dec. 5, 1724, prefented by the fociety to the rectory of Cottingham in Northampton-fhire, Feb. 22, 1745, where he died in 1768 At the " old Hough," a farm which the Smyths held by a leafe for lives under the Crewes, I am informed there are two or three hundred volumes of books which be-longed to them, and " a portrait of a clergy-man in full drefs, in tolerable prefervation, three quarters length, reputed to be one of the Smyths, Ætat. fuæ 33. A. D 1663."

P 13 n. a. There was, I find, a James Stanley, who was prebendary of Driffield in York cathedral, November 11, 1460. Wil-liss Cath 1 p 131. and though Willis is wrong there in making him Bifhop of Ely, 1506 yet he might be the Archdeacon of
Chefter,

Chefter, 1478, who died in 1486 (ib. 413.)
which will correct one part of this note,
and perhaps he was the Rector of Warrington in 1476, which will render the correction of Knight's conjecture doubtful, so
that, after all, this bishop of Ely, son of the
first earl of Derby, might be the young nobleman alluded to by Erafmus There is
similar inconfiftency and confusion refpecting
James Stanley in Newcourt's Repertory, 1.
160. 428

P 26. l 11—13. This is a miftake. "The
Billa de Provifo [mentioned here in the note]
is to be found in the Rolls of Parliament,
vol. vi. p. 517. The original I have feen · it
confifts of an engroffment on a feparate piece
of parchment, ftitched between two fkins of
the parchment which contains the Act of
Subfidy of the 12 Henry vii, and it is figned
by the King in his own hand-writing.—Its
purpofe was not to confirm the privileges of
the Univerfity of Oxford, but to exempt the
Univerfities of Oxford and Cambridge, and
the Colleges of Eton and Winchefter, from
being charged with the aid and fubfidy
granted at that time to the King" Extract
of a Letter, Feb 6th. 1800, from the Right
honourable Henry Addington, whofe claffical

accom-

accomplishments in Brasen Nose college, remembered with pleasure by his contemporaries, were an early prelude to that dignity of deportment, solidity of judgement, and
splendor of talents, which an august Senate
daily witnesses and admiring nations applaud.

P. 47 and note t. I find this point of ordaining on a week day was so rigorously enforced by the church of Rome, that a cardinal Legate from pope Innocent the third,
in 1189, " kept a convocation of the clergy
[of Scotland] at Perth, in which all the
priests were deposed who were found to have
taken orders upon Sunday " Spotswood's
Hist. of Scotl 3d. ed 1668 p 41. There
is no surer mark of superstition than a zealous adherence to trifles and inattention to
matters of real moment. It well became the
church, which injoins the worship of images
and assumes the power of dispensing with
the laws of God, to punish severely the performance of a sacred act upon a sacred day.

P 54 There is a " view of the inner part
of old Somerset house" in Gent. Mag. 1798
p. 9.

P. 114 n. Browne Willis (Cath. 1 p. 410)
calls

calls Charles Bothe nephew to John Bothe, who refigned the treafurerfhip of Lichfield in his favour, which John having been prebendary of York as early as 1459, was not, I prefume, the Rector of Thornton, who was ordained in 1495. The faid John Bothe, treafurer, is there made nephew " Wilhelmi Epifcopi Dunelmenfis;" but I fuppofe there is a miftake in the name, for *Laurence* Bothe, afterwards tranflated to York, was bifhop of Durham when the monument there mentioned appears to have been erected, about 1467, but *William* Bothe, tranflated from Lichfield to York in 1452, who died about 1464, does not appear ever to have been bifhop of Durham.

P. 152. l 2 read " Liveries of knives."

P 163. It was hoped the annual accounts of New College might throw fome light on thefe vifits of prince Arthur in 1496, and 1501, but unfortunately the audit roll for one of thofe years (1496) is miffing, and the other furnifhes little to our purpofe. It appears, that in the year which ended at Michaelmas 1497, the Bifhop of Lincoln received a prefent of gloves and was treated with wine by that fociety; and on the 20th

of September, 1501, a gratuity was given to
a fervant of his Majefty's Almoner [Dr. May-
ow] bringing venifon to the college, which,
as the Prince of Wales was in Oxford on the
25th of that month, if not before, was probably fent on account of that royal vifit.
In the fame year (January 12, 1500-1) a
perfon named " Ffloyd," of the Prince's
houfhold, was entertained at New College.

P. 195. l 13. read " Harewdon," or, as it
is now ufually written, " Harrowden."

P 324 n l 6 read " Chronicon "

In Fleetwood's Elenchus Annalium, under
the word " Kallender," is the following item,
relating probably to fome matter of law, in
which, from the date, bifhop Smyth appears
to have been one of the parties; but I have
not been able to trace the circumftance in
the year books, nor to obtain any explanation
of it: " Euefques de Lincoln et Counte de
Kent 14 H vii. 29. a."

I have

I have feen a memorandum by Dr Yate, which fays, that Sir Richard Sutton bought an eftate of John Molley, Dec 4, 21 Henry VII (1505) and that the deeds are in the college Archives, in Drawer S But they have not been found, nor has any other notice of the purchafe occurred.

INDEX.

INDEX.

I N D E X.

INDEX

Melton,

Oldsworth

Preceptorie,

Welt,

THE END

Publifhed by the fame Author,

1. Eight Sermons, preached before the Univerfity of Oxford, in 1785, at the Lecture founded by the Rev. John Bampton.

2 Short Defence of the Church of England, addreffed to the Inhabitants of Middleton Cheney, Northamptonfhire

3 Poftfcript to the fame

4 Anfwer to a Letter from Francis Eyre of Warkworth, Efq

5. The Will of God the Ground and Principle of Civil as well as Religious Obedience; a Sermon preached before the Univerfity of Oxford, Oct 25, 1789 being the Anniverfary of his Majefty s happy Acceffion to the Throne

6 A Sermon, preached before the Univerfity of Oxford, on Friday, April 19, 1793 being the Day appointed for a General Faft

7 A Sermon at the Triennial Vifitation of the Right Rev Father in God, Spencer, Lord Bifhop of Peterborough, on Saturday, June 6, 1798

Lightning Source UK Ltd.
Milton Keynes UK
11 April 2011

170708UK00005B/104/P